# Saudi Arabia
## a country study

Federal Research Division
Library of Congress
Edited by
Helen Chapin Metz
Research Completed
December 1992

On the cover: The *shahada* or Muslim confession of faith:
"There is no god but God (Allah), and Muhammad is his
Prophet."

Fifth Edition, First Printing, 1993.

## Library of Congress Cataloging-in-Publication Data

Saudi Arabia : a country study / Federal Research Division, Library
of Congress ; edited by Helen Chapin Metz. — 5th ed.
    p.  cm. — (Area handbook series, ISSN 1057-5294) (DA
pam ; 550-51)
    "Supersedes the 1984 edition of Saudi Arabia: a country study,
edited by Richard F. Nyrop." T.p. verso.
    "Research completed December 1992."
    Includes bibliographical references (pp. 303–324) and index.
    ISBN 0-8444-0791-7
    1. Saudi Arabia.  I. Metz, Helen Chapin, 1928-  . II. Library
of Congress. Federal Research Division.  III. Area handbook for
Saudi Arabia. IV. Series. V. Series: DA pam ; 550-51.
DS204.S3115    1993                       93-28506
953.8—dc20                                       CIP

Headquarters, Department of the Army
DA Pam 550-51

# Foreword

This volume is one in a continuing series of books prepared by the Federal Research Division of the Library of Congress under the Country Studies/Area Handbook Program sponsored by the Department of the Army. The last page of this book lists the other published studies.

Most books in the series deal with a particular foreign country, describing and analyzing its political, economic, social, and national security systems and institutions, and examining the interrelationships of those systems and the ways they are shaped by cultural factors. Each study is written by a multidisciplinary team of social scientists. The authors seek to provide a basic understanding of the observed society, striving for a dynamic rather than a static portrayal. Particular attention is devoted to the people who make up the society, their origins, dominant beliefs and values, their common interests and the issues on which they are divided, the nature and extent of their involvement with national institutions, and their attitudes toward each other and toward their social system and political order.

The books represent the analysis of the authors and should not be construed as an expression of an official United States government position, policy, or decision. The authors have sought to adhere to accepted standards of scholarly objectivity. Corrections, additions, and suggestions for changes from readers will be welcomed for use in future editions.

Louis R. Mortimer
Chief
Federal Research Division
Library of Congress
Washington, D.C. 20540

# Acknowledgments

The authors wish to acknowledge the contributions of the writers of the 1984 edition of *Saudi Arabia: A Country Study,* edited by Richard F. Nyrop. Their work provided general background for the present volume.

The authors are grateful to individuals in various government agencies and private institutions who gave of their time, research materials, and expertise in the production of this book. These individuals include Ralph K. Benesch, who oversees the Country Studies—Area Handbook program for the Department of the Army. The authors also wish to thank members of the Federal Research Division staff who contributed directly to the preparation of the manuscript. These people include Sandra W. Meditz, who reviewed all drafts and served as liaison with the sponsoring agency; Marilyn Majeska, who supervised editing and managed book production; Andrea Merrill, who reviewed tables and figures; and Barbara Edgerton and Izella Watson, who performed word processing.

Also involved in preparing the text were Peter Tietjen, who edited chapters; Catherine Schwartzstein, who performed the prepublication editorial review; and Joan C. Cook, who compiled the index. Malinda B. Neale of the Library of Congress Composing Unit prepared the camera-ready copy under the supervision of Peggy Pixley.

Graphics were prepared by David P. Cabitto, and Timothy L. Merrill prepared map drafts. David P. Cabitto and the firm of Greenhorne and O'Mara prepared the final maps. Special thanks are owed to Farah Ahannavard, who prepared the illustrations on the title page of each chapter, and David P. Cabitto, who did the cover art from original calligraphy by Aftab Ahmad.

Finally, the authors acknowledge the generosity of the Saudi Arabian Information Office, the Armed Forces Office of the Royal Saudi Arabian Embassy in Washington, and the Saudi Arabian Oil Company (Saudi Aramco), who allowed their photographs to be used in this study.

# Contents

**Chapter 5. National Security** .................... 229
*Jean R. Tartter*

## List of Figures

# Preface

This edition of *Saudi Arabia: A Country Study* replaces the previous edition published in 1984. Like its predecessor, the present book attempts to treat in a compact and objective manner the dominant historical, social, economic, political, and national security aspects of contemporary Saudi Arabia. Sources of information included scholarly books, journals, and monographs; official reports and documents of governments and international organizations; and foreign and domestic newspapers and periodicals. Relatively up-to-date economic data were available from several sources, but the sources were not always in agreement. Most demographic data should be viewed as estimates.

Chapter bibliographies appear at the end of the book; brief comments on some of the more valuable sources for further reading appear at the conclusion of each chapter. Measurements are given in the metric system; a conversion table is provided to assist those who are unfamiliar with the metric system (see table 1, Appendix). The Glossary provides brief definitions of terms that may be unfamiliar to the general reader.

The transliteration of Arabic words and phrases posed a particular problem. For many of the words—such as Muhammad, Muslim, Quran, and shaykh—the authors followed a modified version of the system adopted by the United States Board on Geographic Names and the Permanent Committee on Geographic Names for British Official Use, known as the BGN/PCGN system; the modification entails the omission of all diacritical markings and hyphens. In numerous instances, however, the names of persons or places are so well known by another spelling that to have used the BGN/PCGN system may have created confusion. For example, the reader will find Mecca rather than Makkah and Medina rather than Al Madinah. In addition, although the government of Saudi Arabia officially rejects the use of the term *Persian Gulf* and refers to that body of water as the Arabian Gulf, the authors followed the practice of the United States Board on Geographic Names by using *Persian Gulf* or *gulf*.

Saudi Arabia uses the lunar Islamic calendar, in which the first year was that of the Prophet's migration to Medina in A.D. 622. The year has 354 days in twelve lunar months, a month being the time between two new moons, approximately twenty-nine and one-half days. Months alternately consist of twenty-nine and thirty days; to adjust for a slight overlap, an additional day is added eleven times during normal years. Months thus have no fixed relation to the seasons but make a complete circuit every thirty-three Gregorian years; Gregorian years are used in this book.

# Country Profile

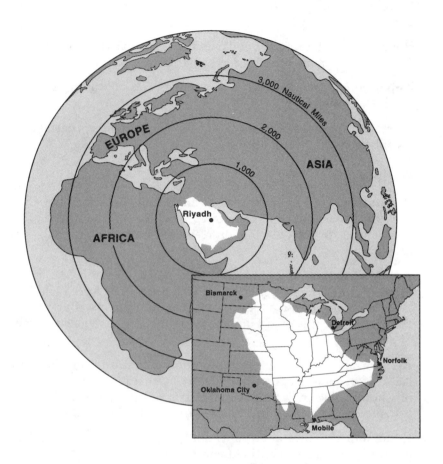

## Country

**Formal Name:** Kingdom of Saudi Arabia.

**Short Form:** Saudi Arabia.

**Term for Nationals:** Saudi(s) or Saudi Arabian(s); adjectival forms—Saudi or Saudi Arabian.

**Capital:** Riyadh.

**NOTE**—The Country Profile contains updated information as available.

# Geography

**Size:** Estimates vary between 2,149,690 and 2,240,000 square kilometers.

**Boundaries:** Most land boundaries not demarcated, some not defined; twelve nautical miles territorial limit.

**Topography:** No rivers or permanent bodies of water. Highest peak 3,133 meters.

**Climate:** Hot desert climate except for Asir Province; coastal cities subject to high humidity.

# Society

**Population:** Figures vary; 1992 Saudi census, published December 1992, gave total population of 16.9 million, of whom 12.3 million Saudi nationals, 4.6 million resident foreigners. Annual rate of growth in 1992 was 3.3 percent.

**Ethnic Groups and Languages:** All Saudis are Arab Muslims, as are over half the foreigners. In 1990 foreign work force included large numbers of Egyptians, Yemenis, Jordanians, Bahrainis, Pakistanis, Indians, and Filipinos, in that order. Arabic language of all Saudis.

**Religion:** Strict Wahhabi interpretation of Sunni Islam, the official faith of about 95 percent of Saudis. Remainder are Shia, most of whom reside in vicinity of Al Ahsa and Al Qatif in Eastern Province. Public worship by non-Muslims prohibited.

**Education and Literacy:** Education system experienced massive growth in 1970s and 1980s. Attendance not compulsory. Females accounted for close to 44 percent of public school student total of 2.6 million in 1989. About 130,000 students in 1989 enrolled in nonvocational institutions of higher learning, 9,000 in vocational institutions; about 4,000 enrolled abroad. Literacy estimated at 62 percent of those over age fifteen in 1990, 73 percent for males and 48 percent for females.

**Health:** Infant mortality declining, twenty-one per 1,000 births in Ministry of Health hospitals in 1990. Immunization of infants and young children compulsory. Health care facilities underwent huge expansion in 1970s and 1980s. Official policy to provide comprehensive medical care free or at nominal fee. Introduction of epidemic control system in 1986 eliminated cholera, plague, and yellow fever. Incidence of malaria and bilharzia reduced to 1.6 and 1.9

percent respectively of total 1988 population. Despite trachoma campaigns, disease remained a major cause of blindness.

## Economy

**Budget:** Latest available budget is for FY 1993 (December 31, 1992, to December 30, 1993). Revenues: SR169 billion (US$45.2 billion); expenditures: SR197 billion (US$52.6 billion); budget deficit: SR28 billion (US$7.5 billion). Persistent budget deficits since early 1980s; estimated government domestic debt at end 1992 was SR213 billion (US$57.0 billion).

**Gross Domestic Product (real GDP–1990 prices):** US$100.5 billion; US$10,338 per capita in 1992, up from US$9,933 per capita in 1990. Rapid rise in oil production and earnings combined with post-Persian Gulf War private sector financed mini-boom caused GDP to rise 12.9 percent in 1991.

**Oil Industry:** Largest crude oil producer in the world (8.4 million barrels per day in 1992) and largest crude oil exporter (7.0 million barrels per day in 1992). World's largest crude oil reserves (261 billion barrels at end 1990, about 25.8 percent of the world's reserves) and reserves to current production ratio of 83.6 years. Rapidly increased production and exports following United Nations embargo on Iraq and Kuwait in August 1990. Began major production-capacity expansion plan in 1989 with intent to raise sustainable crude oil output capacity to between 10.5 million and 11 million barrels per day by 1995. Also initiated refinery upgrading program in 1991.

**Industry:** Including manufacturing, utilities, and construction, industrial sector accounted for 21 percent of GDP in 1990. Government-funded industrial capacity grew sharply in 1980s. Major nonoil refining industries concentrated in petrochemical and chemicals sector. In early 1990s, private sector developing domestic light manufacturing. Petrochemical production capacity slated to increase 40 percent by 1995 compared with 1990.

**Agriculture:** After decade of massive government incentives, agricultural sector accounted for about 10 percent of GDP in 1990, up from under 1 percent of GDP in 1982. Rapid growth in output led to some food self-sufficiency (particularly food grains) but caused depletion of scarce underground water resources.

**Inflation:** Early 1990s inflation estimates 3.5 percent per annum.

**Fiscal Year (FY):** December 31 to following December 30, as of 1986.

**Exports:** Total exports rose from US$27.7 billion in 1989 to US$44.4 billion in 1990 and increased to US$51.7 billion in 1991. Higher crude oil exports main reason for increase, but since mid-1980s exports of chemicals and other manufactured goods have grown to just under US$2 billion per annum.

**Imports:** Total imports rose rapidly in early 1990s spurred by domestic investment boom. Despite increase of imports to US$24.1 billion in 1990 (from US$21.1 billion in 1989) and further increases to US$34.6 billion in 1991, import level sharply down from early 1980s oil-boom period. Major imports consumer goods, industrial inputs, and transport items. Military imports, estimated at US$10 billion in FY 1990 and 1991, not included in these figures.

## Transportation and Communications

**Roads:** About 100,000 kilometers, of which in 1991 over 35,000 kilometers paved and 65,000 kilometers improved earth. Trans-Arabian Highway, a multilane expressway, crossed peninsula from Ad Dammam to Jiddah via Riyadh and Mecca.

**Railroads:** 571 kilometers standard gauge (1.435 meters) from Riyadh to port at Ad Dammam; also shorter rail line linking Riyadh and Al Hufuf.

**Ports:** Jiddah, principal port, handled 60 percent of cargo. Ad Dammam, second largest port, and Ras Tanura handled most of the kingdom's petroleum exports. Al Jubayl, Yanbu al Bahr, and Jizan smaller ports.

**Airports:** Three international airports in Jiddah, Riyadh, and Dhahran.

**Telecommunications:** Good modern system with radio-relay, co-axial cable, and satellite facilities; network expanding. 1.6 million telephones in 1991; more than forty AM radio, and more than 100 television stations; five International Telecommunications Satellite Corporation (Intelsat) and two Arab Satellite Communications Organization (Arabsat) ground stations.

## Government and Politics

**Government:** Absolute monarchy that based legitimacy on strict interpretation of Islamic law. King head of state and head of government; no written constitution or elected legislature. Crown prince deputy prime minister; other royal family members headed important ministries and agencies. Political system highly centralized;

judiciary and local officials appointed by king through Ministry of Justice and Ministry of Interior.

**Politics:** Political parties, labor unions, and professional associations banned. Informal political activity centered around estimated 4,000 princes of Al Faisal branch of Al Saud ruling family. On important policy matters, king sought consensus among senior princes of major Al Saud clans. King also consulted senior ulama (religious scholars) of Al ash Shaykh family and leaders of main tribal families. Western-educated professional and technocratic elite had restricted influence through alliances with various Saudi princes.

**Foreign Relations:** Founding member of United Nations (UN), League of Arab States, Organization of the Islamic Conference, and Gulf Cooperation Council (GCC). Participated in UN specialized agencies, World Bank, Nonaligned Movement, Organization of the Petroleum Exporting Countries, and Organization of Arab Petroleum Exporting Countries. Security, Arab nationalism, and Islam main foreign policy concerns. Objective to prevent radical Arab nationalist or radical Islamic movements from threatening stability of Arabian Peninsula. Most active Arab participant in war against Iraq, 1991. Historically had close ties with United States, despite differences over Israel. Closest regional allies fellow members of GCC and Egypt.

## National Security

**Armed Forces:** Consisted of army, navy, air force, and air defense force, plus Saudi Arabian National Guard, although latter primarily for internal security. Estimated strengths in 1992: army—73,000; navy—11,000, including 1,500 marines; air force—18,000; air defense force—4,000; national guard—55,000 active, 20,000 tribal levies. Four regular armed forces recruited volunteers; national guard used system of tribal levies.

**Military Units:** Army in 1992 included eight brigades—two armored, five mechanized, one airborne. Field artillery battalions and antiaircraft batteries (gun and missile) provided fire support. Navy deployed vessels in Persian Gulf and Red Sea, primarily from major bases at Al Jubayl and Jiddah. Air force had six fighter/ground-attack, five air defense, one reconnaissance, one early warning, three transport, and two helicopter squadrons. Air defense force had surface-to-air missile batteries.

**Equipment:** Most armor and other weaponry in army and national guard of United States manufacture. Naval vessels primarily from United States, France, and Germany. Navy had four French-manufactured frigates and four United States-manufactured corvettes, and attack craft (missile- and torpedo-armed). Combat aircraft mostly United States F–15s and F–5s, plus British Tornadoes.

**Foreign Military Relations:** Member of GCC. Special military relationship with United States since late 1940s. Many foreign corporations, particularly British, French, and United States, had contracts for supply of hardware, construction of military facilities, maintenance of equipment, and training of personnel.

**Police:** Police and security forces controlled by central government through Ministry of Interior. Saudi Arabian National Guard most prominent internal security force, subordinated directly to king. Coast Guard, Investigation, Special Security Force, and Public Security directorates operated under Ministry of Interior. Public Security Police, nationwide police force, and Frontier Force also under Ministry of Interior.

**Paramilitary Forces:** Saudi Arabian National Guard, Coast Guard, Frontier Force, and Special Security Force considered paramilitary.

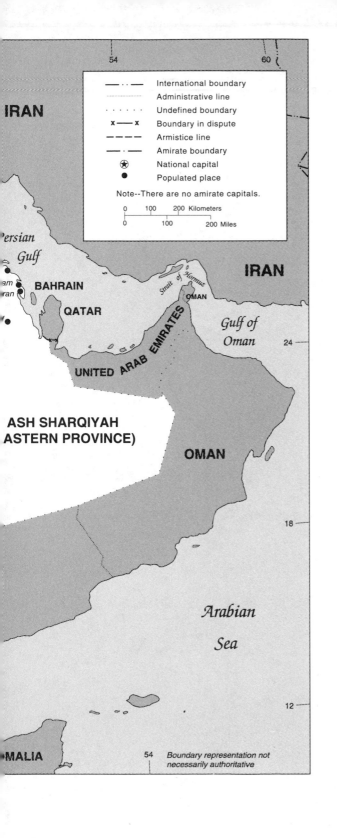

IRAN

| | International boundary |
|---|---|
| | Administrative line |
| | Undefined boundary |
| x —— x | Boundary in dispute |
| – – – – | Armistice line |
| — · — | Amirate boundary |
| ⊛ | National capital |
| ● | Populated place |

Note--There are no amirate capitals.

0   100   200 Kilometers

0   100   200 Miles

*Persian*

*Gulf*

IRAN

*am* ●
*ran*

**BAHRAIN**

OMAN

**QATAR**

Strait of Hormuz

UNITED ARAB EMIRATES

*Gulf of*
*Oman*

24

**ASH SHARQIYAH**
**(ASTERN PROVINCE)**

**OMAN**

18

*Arabian*

*Sea*

12

●MALIA

54   *Boundary representation not*
*necessarily authoritative*

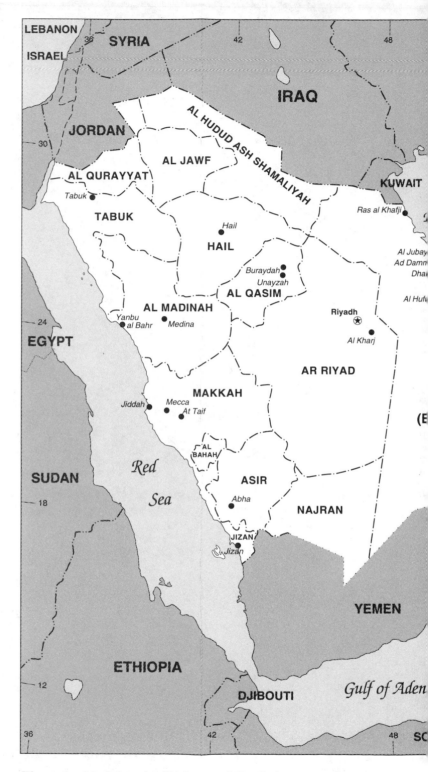

*Figure 1. Administrative Divisions of Saudi Arabia, 1992*

# Introduction

SAUDI ARABIA OBSERVED in 1992 the sixtieth anniversary of its existence as a state and the tenth anniversary of King Fahd ibn Abd al Aziz Al Saud's accession to the throne. Rather than adopting the title of *king,* Fahd was styled in Arabic Khadim al Haramayn, or "custodian of the two holy mosques," thereby stressing the Islamic aspect of his governance. In this regard, he echoed the partnership between the religious and political elements of society established in 1744 by Muhammad ibn Saud, the amir (see Glossary) in Ad Diriyah near Riyadh, and Muhammad ibn Abd al Wahhab, the shaykh who had come to the area to promote the doctrine of the oneness of God in true Islam. As a result of this cooperation and based on the strict Hanbali interpretation of Islamic law, political rule was the province of the House of Saud (Al Saud), whose leader was also given the title of *imam,* and religious authority was in the hands of the Al ash Shaykh (the family of *the* shaykh, Muhammad ibn Abd al Wahhab). This arrangement, however, did not give unchecked political power to the ruler because in accordance with the precepts of Abd al Wahhab, based on the political theory of Taqi ad Din ibn Taimiya, secular authority must conform to divine law and produce civil order in order to be legitimate.

Historically, the collaboration of the Al Saud and the Al ash Shaykh resulted in Al Saud dominion in Najd, the central region of the Arabian Peninsula, for more than two centuries, except for the brief period from 1891 to 1902 when the Al Rashid exiled the Al Saud to Kuwait. Because it has never been subjected to foreign rule and the consequent dissolution of its homogeneity, Najd has exerted an unusually strong influence on the jurisdiction of the Al Saud. In addition, because the region lacked large cities and the strong leadership they could provide, an interdependent relationship developed among Najdi towns, which paid tribute, and tribes, which provided protection. Traditionally, Najdi political power lay with the tribal shaykhs, who, when they became amirs, or governors of a wider area, endeavored to dissociate themselves from their tribal roles because they were ruling a more diverse population.

The prominence of the Al Saud is reflected in the name *Saudi Arabia;* the country is the only one to be named for the ruling family. The present kingdom of Saudi Arabia derives its existence from the campaigns of its founder, Abd al Aziz ibn Abd ar Rahman Al Saud, who initially captured Riyadh with his beduin followers in 1902. Thereafter, with the aid of the Ikhwan, or brotherhood, a fervent group of Wahhabi beduin warriors, he retook the rest of Najd, defeating the Al Rashid forces at Hail in the north in 1921, and in 1924 conquering the Hijaz, including Mecca and Medina. Chosen as king of the Hijaz and Najd in 1927, Abd al Aziz was obliged to defeat the Ikhwan militarily in 1929 because in their zeal the Ikhwan had encroached on the borders of neighboring states, thereby arousing the concern of Britain, in particular. In 1932 Abd al Aziz proclaimed the Kingdom of Saudi Arabia, which covered an area approximating the territory of the present state. The discovery of oil in 1938 ultimately transformed the kingdom and the lives of its inhabitants. During his reign, however, Abd al Aziz sought to obtain "the iron of the West without its ideas," as the king phrased it; he sought to make use of Western technology but at the same time to maintain the traditional institutions associated with Islamic and Arab life.

Upon Abd al Aziz's death in 1953, his son Saud ibn Abd al Aziz Al Saud succeeded to the throne. Saud proved to be an ineffective ruler and a spendthrift, whose luxurious life-style, together with that of the advisers with whom he surrounded himself, rapidly led to the depletion of the kingdom's treasury. As a result, the Al Saud obliged Saud in 1958, and again in 1962, to give his brother, Crown Prince Faisal ibn Abd al Aziz Al Saud, executive power to conduct foreign and domestic affairs. In 1964 the royal family, with the consent of the ulama, or religious leaders, deposed Saud and made Faisal king, appointing Khalid ibn Abd al Aziz Al Saud, another brother, as crown prince.

Faisal, a devout Muslim, sought to modernize the kingdom, especially in regard to economic development, education, and defense, while simultaneously playing a key role in foreign policy. For instance, during the October 1973 War between Israel and the Arab states of Syria, Jordan, and Egypt, Faisal helped to initiate an oil embargo against those countries that supported Israel; the embargo led to the tripling of oil prices. He supported the education of girls and the opening of government television stations to promote education. Tragically, Faisal was assassinated in 1975 by a deranged nephew.

Crown Prince Khalid ibn Abd al Aziz became king (and de facto prime minister) immediately; his brother, Fahd ibn Abd al Aziz Al Saud, served as deputy prime minister and another brother, Abd Allah ibn Abd al Aziz Al Saud, as second deputy prime minister. Khalid dealt primarily with domestic affairs, stressing agricultural development. He also visited all the gulf states, and took a keen interest in settling Saudi Arabia's outstanding boundary disputes, including that of the Al Buraymi Oasis with the United Arab Emirates (UAE) in 1975. (The area near Al Buraymi disputed with Oman had been resolved in 1971.) Fahd became the principal spokesman on foreign affairs and oil policy. Khalid's reign was an eventful one; it saw the attempt by strict Islamists (also known as fundamentalists), who criticized the corrupting influence of Western culture on the royal family, to take over the Grand Mosque in Mecca in 1979, riots by Eastern Province Shia (see Glossary) also in 1979 and 1980, and the formation of the Gulf Cooperation Council (GCC) in 1981.

Upon Khalid's death in 1982, Fahd assumed the throne, with Abd Allah becoming crown prince. Fahd soon faced the impact on the kingdom of the fall in oil revenues, which ended in the 1986 oil price crash. Recognizing the need for a more united Arab front, particularly in view of the deteriorating economic situation, he reestablished diplomatic relations with Egypt in 1987; relations had been broken in 1978 as a result of Anwar as Sadat's signing of the Camp David Accords, creating a separate peace between Egypt and Israel. Fahd also played a mediating role in the Lebanese civil war in 1989, bringing most of the members of the Lebanese National Assembly to At Taif to settle their differences.

To understand the forces that have shaped Saudi Arabia in the early 1990s, one must consider the roles of geographic factors, tribal allegiance and beduin life, Islam, the Al Saud, and the discovery of oil. Tribal affiliation has been the focus of identity in the Arabian Peninsula, approximately 80 percent of which is occupied by Saudi Arabia. Well into the present century, several great deserts, including the Rub al Khali, one of the largest in the world, cut tribal groups off from one another and isolated Najd, particularly, from other areas of the country. As a result, a high degree of cultural homogeneity developed among the inhabitants; the majority follow Sunni Wahhabi Islam and a patriarchal family system. Only about 5 percent of the Saudi population adheres to the Shia sect. The Shia, in general, represent the lowest socioeconomic group in the country, and their grievances over their status have led to protest demonstrations in the 1970s, and again in 1979–80, that have resulted in government actions designed to better their lot.

Saudi tribal allegiance and the beduin heritage have been weakened, however, since the mid-twentieth century by the increased role of a centralized state, by the growth of urbanization, and by the industrialization that has accompanied the finding of oil. At the same time, the impact of Islam on different elements of the population has varied. Many of the educated younger technocrats have felt a need to adapt Islamic institutions to fit the demands of modern technology. Other young people, more conservatively inclined, as well as a number of their elders and those with a more traditional beduin life-style, have deplored the alienation from Muslim values and the corruption that they believe Western ways and the presence, according to 1992 census figures, of some 4.6 million foreigners (in contrast to an indigenous population of 12.3 million) have brought into the kingdom. Their activist Islamism was reflected in the 1979 attempt by extremists to take over the Grand Mosque in Mecca and by other aspects of the Islamic revival, such as the prominent wearing of the *hijab,* or long black cloak and veil by women, and the more active role of the Committees for the Propagation of Virtue and Prevention of Vice (*mutawwiin*) in enforcing standards of public morality. The government found itself caught between these two trends. On the one hand, it feared the extremism of some of the traditionalists, which could well undermine the economic, education, and social development programs that the government had been implementing and which also constituted a threat to internal security. On the other hand, as guardian of the holy places of Islam, the sites of the annual pilgrimage for Muslims the world over, the government needed to legitimate itself as an "Islamic government."

The government therefore has sought to achieve political and social compromises. Repeated announcements have been made regarding the royal family's intention to create a consultative council, first proposed by King Faisal in 1962, as a means of giving a greater voice to the people. On August 20, 1993, Fahd announced the appointment of sixty men to the Consultative Council. Members of the council were primarily religious and tribal leaders; government officials, businessmen, and retired military and police officers were also included. An additional small step was King Fahd's decree of March 1992 establishing a main, or basic, code of laws that regularizes succession to the throne (the king chooses the heir apparent from among the sons and grandsons of Abd al Aziz) and sets forth various administrative procedures concerning the state. Fahd also issued a decree concerning the provinces, or regions, of the kingdom. Each region is to have an amir, a deputy, and a consultative council composed of at least ten persons appointed by the amir for a four-year term. The code does not, however, protect individual rights in the Western sense, as many professionals and technocrats had desired. Rather, it says that "the state protects human rights in accordance with the Islamic sharia."

The Saudi concept of legitimacy is akin to the beduin concept of tribal democracy in which the individual exchanges views with the tribal shaykh. Saudi rulers and most traditionalists reject

Western participatory democracy, because the latter establishes the people as the source of decision rather than the will of God as found in the sharia and as interpreted by the ulama. Moreover, in their view, democracy lacks the stability that a Muslim form of government provides. For these reasons, the government has tended to repress dissent and jail dissidents. Such repression applied to students and religious figures who belonged to such organizations as the Organization of Islamic Revolution in the Arabian Peninsula, active in January and February 1992 in criticizing the ruling family and the government.

Socially, the education of girls, although placed under the supervision of the religious authorities, has led over the four decades that girls' schools have existed to a considerable number of women graduates who were seeking employment in various sectors and who increasingly were making their presence felt. This trend occurred at a time of rising unemployment for Saudi males, particularly for graduates in the field of religious studies, and posed a further potential source of dissidence. In addition, growing urbanization was tending to increase the number of nuclear as opposed to extended families, thereby breaking down traditional social structures. There were also indications that drug smuggling and drug use were rising; twenty of the forty executions that occurred between January 1 and May 1, 1993, were drug related.

The Al Saud played the central role in achieving the needed compromises in the political, social, and foreign affairs fields, as well as in directing the economy with the support of the technocrats and the merchants. The control exercised by the Al Saud is demonstrated by the fact that as of 1993 the amirs, or governors, of all fourteen of Saudi Arabia's regions were members of the royal family. Some members of the family, such as King Fahd and his full brothers Sultan, Nayif, and Salman, were considered to be, however, more aligned with the modernizers; King Fahd's half brother Crown Prince Abd Allah, was more of a traditionalist. Specifically, the crown prince enjoyed the support of the tribal elements and headed the Saudi Arabian National Guard, a paramilitary body composed largely of beduin soldiers that served as a counterbalance to the regular armed forces, which were headed by Minister of Defense and Aviation Amir Sultan ibn Abd al Aziz Al Saud. The nation's police force reported to Minister of Interior Amir Nayif ibn Abd al Aziz Al Saud.

The crown prince was also considered closer than the king to the religious establishment, or the ulama. Thirty to forty of the most influential ulama, mainly members of the Al ash Shaykh, constituted the Council of Senior Ulama, seven of whose members were dismissed by the king in December 1992 on the pretext of "poor health." The actual reason for their dismissal was their failure to condemn July criticisms (published in September) of the government by a group of religious scholars who called themselves the Committee for the Defense of Rights under the Sharia. The king named ten younger and more progressive ulama to replace them.

In a further move, in July 1993 the king named Shaykh Abd al Aziz ibn Baz general mufti of the kingdom with the rank of minister and president of the Administration of Scientific Research and Fatwa. Abd al Aziz ibn Baz was also appointed to preside over the new eighteen-member Higher Ulama Council. Based on Abd al Aziz ibn Baz's advice, instead of the Ministry of Pilgrimage Affairs and Religious Trusts, the king created two new ministries: the Ministry of Islamic Affairs, Endowments, Call, and Guidance and the Ministry of Pilgrimage; this action gave the religious sector an additional voice in the Council of Ministers.

In addition to holding conservative domestic views, the crown prince was more oriented than Fahd toward the Arab world. After the Iraqi invasion of Kuwait in 1990, however, he joined the king and other more pro-Western members of the royal family in asking the United States to send forces to the kingdom.

In the foreign policy arena, Saudi Arabia historically has sought to walk a narrow line between East and West. Because of its strong commitment to Islam, the kingdom abhorred the atheist policy of the former Soviet Union and therefore tended to be somewhat pro-Western concerning defense matters. However, Saudi Arabia also strongly opposed what it considered to be the pro-Zionist policy of the United States with regard to Israel and the rights of the Palestinians. At one time, the kingdom had relatively close relations with Jordan, a fellow monarchy, but Jordan's failure to support Saudi Arabia in the 1991 Persian Gulf War soured those relations and resulted in the expulsion from the kingdom of thousands of Palestinians and Jordanians. In the war, Saudi Arabia also experienced a lack of support by Sudan and Yemen, both of which countries it had aided substantially. In 1993 relations with Yemen were somewhat tense because the kingdom expelled about 1 million Yemenis, as well, during the Persian Gulf War. In addition, as of late 1992, Saudi Arabia had revived a dispute with Yemen over an oil-rich border area.

Initially, Saudi Arabia saw both Iran and Iraq as neighbors posing potential threats. After the Persian Gulf War, however, Saudi Arabia's concern over containing Iraq increased, and the kingdom set aside some of its reservations about Iran's form of Shia Islam and began to normalize relations. Despite some border disagreements with its Persian Gulf neighbors, for example, Qatar in 1992 and early 1993, the kingdom's concern for regional security caused its closest relations to be with other members of the GCC; certain tensions existed in the organization, nevertheless, because of Saudi Arabia's position as the "big brother."

Saudi Arabia had taken the lead in 1970 in establishing the Organization of the Islamic Conference to bring together all Muslim countries. In addition, the kingdom followed a policy of supporting Islamic countries in Africa and Asia and providing military aid to Muslim groups opposing secular governments in Afghanistan, Ethiopia, and, formerly, in the People's Democratic Republic of Yemen (now part of Yemen).

Saudi Arabia's concern for regional security and its active role in supporting the GCC were understandable in view of its relatively small population and the resultant constraint on the size of its armed forces. To compensate for these limitations, the kingdom consistently has endeavored to buy the most up-to-date military matériel and especially to concentrate on developing its air force and air defense system. For more than twenty-five years, Saudi Arabia has had the highest ratio of military expenditures in relation to military personnel of any developing country. Following the Persian Gulf War, the kingdom increased its 1993 defense expenditures 14 percent over those of 1992. Defense purchases included at least 315 United States M1A2 main battle tanks to upgrade matériel of the ground forces as well as seventy-two United States F–15C Eagles and forty-eight British Tornadoes for the air force. Furthermore, the Saudi navy was considered of good quality in relation to naval forces of the region, and the navy's facilities were excellent. In spite of these policies, Saudi Arabia recognized its vulnerability because it has the world's largest oil reserves and extensive oil-processing facilities.

The discovery of oil in commercial quantities in 1938 was the major catalyst that transformed various aspects of the kingdom. The huge revenues from the sale of oil and the payments received from foreign companies involved in developing concessions in the country enabled the government to launch large-scale development programs by the early 1970s. Such programs initially focused on creation of infrastructure in the areas of transportation, telecommunications, electric power, and water. The programs also addressed the fields of education, health, and social welfare; the expansion and equipping of the armed forces; and the creation of petroleum-based industries. From this beginning, the government expanded its programs to drill more deep wells to tap underground aquifers and to construct desalination plants. These water sources, in turn, enabled ventures to make the country more nearly self-sufficient agriculturally; in many instances, however, such undertakings seriously depleted groundwater.

In pursuit of industrial diversification, the government created the industrial cities of Al Jubayl in the Eastern Province and Yanbu al Bahr (known as Yanbu) on the Red Sea (see fig. 1). The government also encouraged the establishment of nonoil-related industries, anticipating the day when Saudi Arabia's oil and gas resources would be depleted. Furthermore, the kingdom also has some promising copper, lead, zinc, silver, and gold deposits that have received little exploitation.

The kingdom's economic plans, including the Fifth Development Plan (1990–95), continued to emphasize training the indigenous labor force to handle technologically advanced processes and hence to enable Saudi Arabia to reduce the number of its foreign workers. The fifth plan also encouraged the creation of joint industrial enterprises with GCC member states and other Arab and Islamic countries and the development of industrial relations with foreign countries in order to attract foreign capital and transfer technology.

Saudi Arabia's economic goals were reflected in the national budget announced for 1993, which set expenditures at US$52.6 billion and revenues at US$45.1 billion, thereby reducing the deficit from US$8.0 billion in 1992 to US$7.5 billion in 1993. The continued existence of a deficit, which has characterized the Saudi economy since 1983, was a source of concern to some observers. Major budgetary expenditure items were US$9.1 billion for education (including funds to establish six new colleges and 800 new schools), US$8.2 billion for public organizations (not further identified), and more than US$3.7 billion for health and social development (including funds for setting up 500 new clinics). Another major expenditure announced in March 1993 was that substantial funds, most of which would be obtained from private borrowing, would be invested in oil facilities in order to raise the kingdom's oil production capacity to between 10.5 and 11 million barrels per day by 1995 and its total refining capacity to 210,000 barrels per day.

The major event affecting Saudi Arabia and other gulf states in the early 1990s was clearly the Persian Gulf War. The effect of that war on the kingdom has yet to be assessed. Financially, the cost of the war for the area as a whole has been estimated by the Arab Monetary Fund at US$676 billion for 1990 and 1991. This figure does not, however, take account of such factors as the ecological impact of the war, the loss of jobs and income for thousands of foreign workers employed in Saudi Arabia and elsewhere in the gulf, and the slowdown effect on the growth of the economies of Saudi Arabia and the gulf states. In most instances, these economies had been growing at a good rate before the war, which tended to deplete or eliminate any accumulated financial reserves.

More difficult to measure, however, was the social impact of the war. Many foreign observers had speculated that the arrival in the kingdom of more than 600,000 foreign military personnel, including women in uniform, would bring about significant changes in Saudi society. However, military personnel tended to be assigned to remote border areas of the country and were little seen by the population as a whole. The net effect of their presence was therefore minimal in the opinion of a number of knowledgeable Saudis.

As Saudi Arabia entered the final years of the twentieth century, there were signs, however, that the expression of public dissent, once unthinkable, was becoming more commonplace. Such dissent was usually couched within an Islamic framework, but nonetheless it represented a force with which the Al Saud had to reckon. King Fahd, now seventy-two, had succeeded thus far in balancing the demands of modernists and traditionalists domestically and in pursuing a policy of moderation internationally. Some observers wondered, however, how much longer Fahd would be able to rule and how adaptable the more conservative Crown Prince Abd Allah would be as Fahd's successor.


August 23, 1993                                Helen Chapin Metz

# Chapter 1. Historical Setting

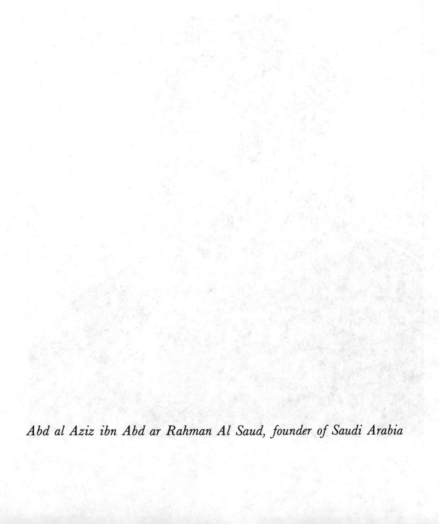

*Abd al Aziz ibn Abd ar Rahman Al Saud, founder of Saudi Arabia*

ABD AL AZIZ ibn Abd ar Rahman Al Saud rose to prominence in the Arabian Peninsula in the early twentieth century. He belonged to the Saud family (the Al Saud—see Glossary), who had controlled parts of Arabia during most of the nineteenth century. By the late nineteenth century, however, the rival Al Rashid family had forced the Al Saud into exile in Kuwait. Thus, it was from Kuwait that Abd al Aziz began the campaign to restore his family to political power. First, he recaptured Najd, a mostly desert region in the approximate center of the peninsula and the traditional homeland of the Al Saud. During the mid-1920s, Abd al Aziz's armies captured the Islamic shrine cities of Mecca and Medina. In 1932, he declared that the area under his control would be known as the Kingdom of Saudi Arabia.

Abd al Aziz's new realm was a very poor one. It was a desert kingdom with few known natural resources and a largely uneducated population. There were few cities and virtually no industry. Although the shrines at Mecca and Medina earned income from the Muslim pilgrims who visited them every year, this revenue was insufficient to lift the rest of the kingdom out of its near-subsistence level.

All this changed, however, when United States geologists discovered oil in the kingdom during the 1930s. Saudi Arabia's exploitation of its oil resources transformed the country into a nation synonymous with great wealth. Wealth brought with it enormous material and social change.

Perhaps because of the great upheaval since the 1932 oil discovery, history and origins were very important to Saudi Arabia. Although the country owed its prominence to modern economic realities, Saudis tended to view life in more traditional terms. The state in 1992 remained organized largely along tribal lines. Islam continued to be a vital element in Saudi statecraft.

The tendency to draw inspiration from the past was an essential part of the Saudi state. The historical parallels between the Kingdom of Saudi Arabia and its Arab and Islamic past were striking. In conquering Arabia, for instance, Abd al Aziz brought together the region's nomadic tribes in much the same way that his great-grandfather, Muhammad ibn Saud, had done more than a century earlier.

## The Setting of Saudi Arabia

The title, the Kingdom of Saudi Arabia, uses the word *kingdom*, which is not an Islamic term. However, given the significance of religion in Saudi Arabia, it is clear that Saudis believe that ultimate authority rests with God (Allah). The Saudi ruler is Allah's secular representative and bases political legitimacy on his religious credentials (see The King, ch. 4).

The term *Saudi* refers to the Al Saud family, the royal house of Saudi Arabia, whose eponym is Saud ibn Muhammad ibn Muqrin. Saud himself was not a significant figure, but his son, Muhammad ibn Saud (literally, Muhammad, the son of Saud), conquered most of the Arabian Peninsula in the early eighteenth century. In the almost two centuries since then, Muhammad ibn Saud's family has grown tremendously, and in 1992 the ruling house of Saudi Arabia had more than 4,000 male members.

The term *Arabia*—or the Arabian Peninsula—refers to a geographic region whose name is related to the language of the majority of its indigenous inhabitants. Before the era of the Muslim conquests in the mid-seventh century, some Arabic-speaking peoples also lived in Palestine, Syria, and Iraq, and Christian Arab buffer states were established north of the peninsula between the Sassanid and Byzantine empires. As a result of the Muslim conquests, however, people of the peninsula spread out over the wider region that today is known as the "Arab world," and the Arabic language became the region's dominant language.

The desert is the most prominent feature of the Arabian Peninsula. Although vast, arid tracts dominate Saudi Arabia, the country also includes long stretches of arid coastline along the Persian Gulf and the Red Sea and several major oases in the Eastern Province (see fig. 1). Accordingly, the Saudi environment is not uniform, and the differences between coastal and desert life have played their part in Arabian history. People living on the water have had more contact with other groups and thus have developed more cosmopolitan outlooks than those living in the interior.

Saudi Arabia is the largest country on the Arabian Peninsula. It shares the Persian Gulf and Red Sea coasts with such countries as the Persian Gulf states and Jordan; hence there are cultural and historical overlaps with its neighbors. Many of these countries rely on the authority of a single family—whether the ruler calls himself a king, as in Saudi Arabia and Jordan, or an amir, as in the gulf states. Tribal loyalties also play an important role in these countries, and large portions of their populations have only recently stopped living as nomads.

Several important factors, however, distinguish Saudi Arabia from its neighbors. Unlike other states in the area, Saudi Arabia has never been under the direct control of a European power. Moreover, the Wahhabi movement that began in Saudi Arabia has had a greater impact on Saudi history than on any other country. Although the religious fervor of Wahhabism affected populations of such neighboring states as present-day Qatar, only in Saudi Arabia was it an essential element in the formation of the modern state.

## The Pre-Islamic Period

The bodies of water on either side of the Arabian Peninsula provided relatively easy access to the neighboring river-valley civilizations of the Nile and the Tigris-Euphrates. Once contact was made, trading could begin, and because these civilizations were quite rich, many goods passed between them.

The coastal people of Arabia were well-positioned to profit from this trade. Much of the trade centered around present-day Bahrain and Oman, but those tribes living in the southwestern part of the peninsula, in present-day Yemen and southern Saudi Arabia, also profited from such trade. The climate and topography of this area also permitted greater agricultural development than that on the coast of the Persian Gulf.

Generous rainfall in Yemen enabled the people to feed themselves, while the exports of frankincense and myrrh brought wealth to the area. As a result, civilization developed to a relatively high level in southern Arabia by about 1000 B.C. The peoples of the area lived in small kingdoms or city states, of which the best known is probably Saba, which was called Sheba in the Old Testament. The prosperity of Yemen encouraged the Romans to refer to it as Arabia Felix (literally, "happy Arabia"). Outside of the coastal areas, however, and a few centers in the Hijaz associated with the caravan trade, the harsh climate of the peninsula, combined with a desert and mountain terrain, limited agriculture and rendered the interior regions difficult to access. The population most likely subsisted on a combination of oasis gardening and herding, with some portion of the population being nomadic or seminomadic.

The material conditions under which the Arabs lived began to improve around 1000 B.C. About this time, a method for saddling camels had been developed to transport large loads. The camel was the only animal that could cross large tracts of barren land with any reliability. The Arabs could now benefit from some of the trade that had previously circumvented Arabia.

The increased trans-Arabian trade produced two important results. One was the rise of cities that could service the trains of camels moving across the desert. The most prosperous of these— Petra in Jordan, associated with the Nabatean Kingdom, and Palmyra in Syria, for example—were relatively close to markets in the Mediterranean region, but small caravan cities developed within the Arabian Peninsula as well. One of the ancient cities that formed part of the Nabatean Kingdom from about 25 B.C. to the end of the first century A.D. was Madain Salin, the ruins of which still exist. The most important of these caravan cities was Mecca, which also owed its prosperity to certain shrines in the area that were visited by Arabs from all over the peninsula.

Some Arabs, particularly in the Hijaz, held religious beliefs that recognized a number of gods as well as a number of rituals for worshiping them. The most important of these beliefs involved the sense that certain places and times of year were sacred and must be respected. At those times and in those places, warfare, in particular, was forbidden, and various rituals were required. Foremost of these was the pilgrimage, and the best known pilgrimage site was Mecca.

The second result of the Arabs' increased involvement in trade was the contact it gave them with the outside world. In the Near East, the Persians and the Romans were the great powers in the centuries before the advent of Islam, and the Arab tribes that bordered these territories were drawn into their political affairs. After A.D. 400, both empires paid Arab tribes not only to protect their southern borders but also to harass the borders of their adversaries.

In the long term, however, it was the people that traveled with the camel caravans and their ideas that were most important. By A.D. 500, the traditional ritual of Arab worship was but one of a number of religious options. The Sabaeans of southern Arabia followed their own system of beliefs, and these had some adherents in the interior. Followers of pagan beliefs, as well as Hanifs, who were mentioned in the Quran and believed to be followers of an indigenous monotheistic religion, were widespread in the peninsula. In addition, the area had well-established communities of Christians and Jews. Along the gulf coast were Nestorians, while in Yemen Syrian Orthodox and smaller groups of Christians were to be found among beduin and in monasteries that dotted the northern Hijaz. In the sixth century, shortly before the birth of Muhammad, the city of Najran, in what is now southwestern Saudi Arabia, had a Christian church with a bishop, monks, priests, nuns, and laity, and was ruled by a Jewish king. Jews were an important part not only of the Yemeni population, but also of the oases communities in the region of Medina.

## The Early Islamic Period, 622–700

The Saudis, and many other Arabs and Muslims as well, trace much of their heritage to the birth of the Prophet Muhammad in

*Ancient Nabatean tomb,*
*Madain Salih*
*Courtesy*
*Saudi Arabian*
*Information Office*

A.D. 570. The time before Islam is generally referred to as "the time of ignorance" (of God).

Muhammad was born in Mecca at a time when the city was establishing itself as a trading center. For the residents of Mecca, tribal connections were still the most important part of the social structure. Muhammad was born into the Quraysh, which had become the leading tribe in the city because of its involvement with water rights for the pilgrimage. By the time of Muhammad, the Quraysh had become active traders as well, having established alliances with tribes all over the peninsula. These alliances permitted the Quraysh to send their caravans to Yemen and Syria. Accordingly, the Quraysh represented in many ways the facilitators and power brokers for the new status quo in Arabian society.

Tribes consisted of clans that had various branches and families, and Muhammad came from a respectable clan, the sons of Hashim, but from a weak family situation. Muhammad's father Abd Allah had died before his son was born, leaving the Prophet without a close protector. The Prophet was fortunate, however, that his uncle Abu Talib was one of the leaders of the Hashimite clan; his connection to Abu Talib gave Muhammad a certain amount of protection when he began to preach in 610 against the Meccan leadership.

Everything we know about Muhammad's life comes from Muslim historiography. The Prophet worked for Abu Talib in the

7

caravan business, giving him the opportunity to travel beyond Arabia. Travel gave the Prophet contact with some of the Christian and Jewish communities that existed in Arabia; in this way he became familiar with the notion of scripture and the belief in one God. Despite this contact, tradition specifies that Muhammad never learned to read or write. As a child, however, he was sent to the desert for five years to learn the beduin ways that were slowly being forgotten in Mecca.

Muhammad married a rich widow when he was twenty-five years old; although he managed her affairs, he would occasionally go off by himself into the mountains that surrounded Mecca. On one of these occasions, Muslim belief holds that the angel Gabriel appeared to Muhammad and told him to recite aloud. When Muhammad asked what he should say, the angel recited for him verses that would later constitute part of the Quran, which means literally "the recitation." Muslims believe that Muhammad continued to receive revelations from God throughout his life, sometimes through the angel Gabriel and at other times in dreams and visions directly from God.

For a while, Muhammad told only his wife about his experiences, but in 613 he acknowledged them openly and began to promote a new social and spiritual order that would be based on them. Muhammad's message was disturbing to many of the Quraysh for several reasons. The Prophet attacked traditional Arab customs that permitted lax marriage arrangements and the killing of children. More significant, however, was the Prophet's claim that there was only one God because in condemning the worship of idols he threatened the pilgrimage traffic from which the Quraysh profited.

By 618 Muhammad had gained enough followers to worry the city's leaders. The Quraysh hesitated to harm the Prophet because he was protected by his uncle, but they attacked those of his followers who did not have powerful family connections. To protect these supporters, Muhammad sent them to Ethiopia, where they were taken in by the Christian king who saw a connection between the Prophet's ideas and those of his own religion. Following his uncle's death in 619, however, Muhammad felt obliged to leave Mecca. In 622 he secretly left the city and traveled about 320 kilometers north to the town of Yathrib. In leaving Mecca, Muhammad chose to abandon the city where he had grown up to pursue his mission in another place; thus, the event often has been used to illustrate a genuine commitment to duty and sacrifice. This emigration, or *hijra* (see Glossary), marks the beginning of the Islamic calendar. Muslims use a lunar calendar, which means that their twelve-month year is shorter than a solar one.

The Quraysh were unwilling to allow Muhammad to remain un-opposed in Yathrib, and various skirmishes and battles occurred, with each side trying to enlist the tribes of the peninsula in its campaigns. Muhammad eventually prevailed, and in 630 he returned to Mecca, where he was accepted without resistance. Subsequently he moved south to strongholds in At Taif and Khaybar, which surrendered to him after lengthy sieges.

By his death in 632, Muhammad enjoyed the loyalty of almost all of Arabia. The peninsula's tribes had tied themselves to the Prophet with various treaties but had not necessarily become Muslim. The Prophet expected others, particularly pagans, to submit but allowed Christians and Jews to keep their faiths provided they paid a special tax as penalty for not submitting to Islam.

After the Prophet's death, most Muslims acknowledged the authority of Abu Bakr (died in 634), an early convert and respected elder in the community. Abu Bakr maintained the loyalty of the Arab tribes by force; and in the battles that followed the Prophet's death, which came to be known as the apostasy wars, it became essentially impossible for an Arab tribesman to retain traditional religious practices. Arabs who had previously converted to Judaism or Christianity were allowed to keep their faith, but those who followed the old polytheistic practices were forced to become Muslims. In this way, Islam became the religion of most Arabs.

The Prophet had no spiritual successor inasmuch as God's revelation (the Quran) was given only to Muhammad. There were, however, successors to the Prophet's temporal authority, and they were called caliphs (successors or vice regents). Caliphs ruled the Islamic world until 1258, when the last caliph and all his heirs were killed by the Mongols. For the first thirty years, caliphs managed the growing Islamic empire from Yathrib, which had been renamed Madinat an Nabi ("the city of the Prophet") or Al Madinah al Munawwarah ("the illuminated city"). These names are usually shortened simply to Medina—"the city."

Within a short time, the caliphs had conquered a large empire. At the conclusion of the apostasy wars, the Arab tribes united behind Islam and channeled their energies against the Byzantine and Persian empires. Arab-led armies pushed quickly through both of these empires and established Arab control from present-day Spain to Pakistan.

The achievements of Islam were great and various, but after 656 these achievements ceased to be controlled from Arabia. After the third caliph, Uthman, was assassinated in 656, the Muslim world was split, and the fourth caliph, Ali (murdered in 660) spent much of his time in Iraq. After Ali, the Umayyads established a hereditary line of caliphs in Damascus. The Umayyads were overthrown in 750 by the Abbasids, who ruled from Baghdad. By the latter part of the seventh century, the political importance of Arabia in the Islamic world had declined.

## The Middle Ages, 700–1500

Until about 900, the centers of Islamic power remained in the Fertile Crescent, a semicircle of fertile land stretching from the southeastern Mediterranean coast around the Syrian Desert north of the Arabian Peninsula to the Persian Gulf and close to the Arabian heartland. After the ninth century, however, the most significant political centers moved farther and farther away—to Egypt and India, as well as to what is now Turkey and the Central Asian republics. Intellectual vitality eventually followed political power, and, as a result, Islamic civilization was no longer centered in Mecca and Medina in the Hijaz.

Mecca remained the spiritual focus of Islam because it was the destination for the pilgrimage that all Muslims were required, if feasible, to make once in their lives. The city, however, lacked political or administrative importance even in the early Islamic period. This role devolved on Medina instead, which had been the main base for the Prophet's efforts to gain control of the shrines in Mecca and to bring together the tribes of the peninsula. After the Prophet's death, Medina continued to be an administrative center and developed into something of an intellectual and literary one as well. In the seventh and eighth centuries, for instance, Medina became an important center for the legal discussions that would lead to the codification of Islamic law. Orthodox (Sunni—see Glossary) Islam recognizes four systems, or schools, of law. One of these, the school of Malik ibn Anas, which originated with the scholars of Medina in the late eighth century, is observed today in much of Africa and Indonesia. The three other Sunni law schools (Hanafi, Shafii, and Hanbali) developed at about the same time, but largely in Iraq.

Arabia was also the site for some of the conflicts on which the sectarian divisions of Islam are based (see Religion, ch. 2). A major Islamic sect, the Shia (from Shiat Ali, or "party of Ali"—see Glossary), is still represented in Saudi Arabia but forms a larger percentage of the populations in Iraq and Iran.

One Shia denomination, known as the Kharijite movement, began in events surrounding the assassination of Uthman, the third caliph, and the transfer of authority to Ali, the fourth caliph. Those people who believed Ali should have been the legitimate successor to the Prophet refused to accept the authority of Uthman.

*Al Munis village, near Az Zahran al Janub, showing the hills of
southwestern Saudi Arabia in the background*
*Courtesy* Aramco World

Muawiyah in Syria challenged Ali's election as caliph, leading to
a war between the two and their supporters. Muawiyah and Ali
eventually agreed to an arbitrator, and the fighting stopped. Part
of Ali's army, however, objected to the compromise, claiming Muawiyah's family were insincere Muslims. So strong was their protest against compromise that they left Ali's camp (the term *khariji*
literally means "the ones who leave") and fought a battle with their
former colleagues the next year.

The most prominent quality of the Kharijite movement was opposition to the caliph's representatives and particularly to Muawiyah, who became caliph after Ali. Although the Kharijites were
known to some Muslims as bandits and assassins, they developed
certain ideals of justice and piety. The Prophet Muhammad had
been sent to bring righteousness to the world and to teach the Arabs
to pray and to distribute their wealth and power fairly. According
to the Kharijites, whoever was lax in following the Prophet's directives should be opposed, ostracized, or killed.

The Kharijite movement continued to be significant on the Persian Gulf coast from the ninth century through the eleventh century and survived in the twentieth century in the more moderate
form of Ibadi Islam. The uncompromising fanaticism of the original

11

Kharijites resembled the fervor that enabled Arab armies to conquer so much territory in the seventh century. This same spirit helped the Al Saud succeed at the end of the eighteenth century and again at the beginning of the twentieth.

The mainstream Shia sect originated in circumstances similar to those of the Kharijite movement. The Shia believed that Ali should have succeeded the Prophet as leader of the Muslim community. They were frustrated three times, however, when the larger Muslim community selected first Abu Bakr, next Umar (died in 644), and then Uthman as caliph. Ali finally became caliph in 656.

The dispute between Ali and Muawiyah was never resolved. Muawiyah returned to Syria while Ali remained in Iraq, where he was assassinated by a Kharijite follower in 660. Muawiyah assumed the caliphate, and Ali's supporters transferred their loyalty to his two sons, Hasan and Husayn. When Muawiyah's son, Yazid, succeeded his father, Husayn refused to recognize his authority and set out for Iraq to raise support. He was intercepted by a force loyal to Yazid. When Husayn refused to surrender, his entire party, including women and children, was killed at Karbala in southeastern Iraq.

The killing of Husayn provided the central ethos for the emergence of the Shia as a distinct sect. Eventually, the Shia would split into several separate denominations based on disputes over who of Ali's direct male descendants should be the true spiritual leader. The majority came to recognize a line of twelve leaders, each known as imam (see Glossary), beginning with Ali and ending with Muhammad al Muntazar (Muhammad, the awaited one). These Shia, who are often referred to as "Twelvers," claimed that the Twelfth Imam did not die but disappeared in 874. They believe that he will return as the "rightly guided leader," or mahdi, and usher in a new, more perfect order.

Twelver Shia reverence for the imams has encouraged distinctive rituals. The most important is Ashura, the commemoration of the death of Husayn. Other practices include pilgrimages to shrines of Ali and his relatives. According to strict Wahhabi Sunni interpretations of Islam, these practices resemble the pagan rituals that the Prophet attacked. Therefore, observance of Ashura and pilgrimages to shrines have constituted flash points for sectarian problems between the Saudi Wahhabis and the Shia minority in the Eastern Province.

The Shia minority in Saudi Arabia, like the Shia in southern Iraq, traces its origin to the days of Ali. A second Shia group, the Ismailis, or the Seveners, follow a line of imams that originally challenged the Seventh Imam and supported a younger brother,

Ismail. The Ismaili line of leaders has been continuous down to the present day. The current imam, Sadr ad Din Agha Khan, who is active in international humanitarian efforts, is a direct descendant of Ali.

Although present-day Saudi Arabia has no indigenous Ismaili communities, an important Ismaili center existed between the ninth and eleventh centuries in Al Hufuf, in eastern Arabia. The Ismailis of Al Hufuf were strong enough in 930 to sack the major cities of Iraq. They also attacked Mecca and removed the sacred stone of the Kaaba, the central shrine of the Islamic pilgrimage. The pilgrimage was suspended for several years and resumed only after the stone was replaced, following the caliph's agreement to pay the Ismailis a ransom.

Under normal circumstances, Muslims visited Mecca every year to perform the pilgrimage, and they expected the caliph to keep the pilgrimage routes safe and to maintain control over Mecca and Medina as well as the Red Sea ports providing access to them. When the caliph was strong, he controlled the Hijaz, but after the ninth century the caliph's power weakened and the Hijaz became a target for any ruler who sought to establish his authority in the Islamic world. In 1000, for instance, an Ismaili dynasty controlled the Hijaz from Cairo.

External control of the Hijaz gave the region extensive contact with other parts of the Muslim world. In this regard, the Hijaz differed greatly from the region immediately to the east, Najd.

Najd was relatively isolated. It was more arid and barren than the Hijaz and was surrounded on three sides by deserts and separated from the Hijaz by mountains. All overland routes to the Hijaz passed through Najd but it was easier to go around Najd by sea. As the caliphs in Baghdad became less powerful, the road between Baghdad and Mecca that led across Najd declined in importance. After the thirteenth century, pilgrimage traffic was more likely to move up the Red Sea toward Egypt and so bypass Najd.

So there were two faces of Arabia. To the west was the Hijaz, which derived a cosmopolitan quality from the foreign traffic that moved continually through it. In the east was Najd, which remained relatively isolated. During the eighteenth century, Wahhabi ideas, vital to the rise of the Al Saud, originated in Najd.

## The Al Saud and Wahhabi Islam, 1500–1818

The Al Saud originated in Ad Diriyah, in the center of Najd, close to the modern capital of Riyadh. In about 1500, ancestors of Saud ibn Muhammad took over some date groves, one of the few forms of agriculture the region could support, and settled there.

Over time the area developed into a small town, and the clan that would become the Al Saud came to be recognized as its leaders.

The rise of Al Saud is closely linked with Muhammad ibn Abd al Wahhab (1703–87), a Muslim scholar whose ideas form the basis of the Wahhabi movement. He grew up in Uyaynah, an oasis in southern Najd, where with his grandfather he studied Hanbali Islamic law, one of the strictest Muslim legal schools. While still a young man, he left Uyaynah to study with other teachers, the usual way to pursue higher education in the Islamic world. He studied in Medina and then went to Iraq and to Iran.

To understand the significance of Muhammad ibn Abd al Wahhab's ideas, they must be considered in the context of Islamic practice. There is a difference between the established rituals clearly defined in religious texts that all Muslims perform and popular Islam. The latter refers to local practice that is not universal.

The Shia practice of visiting shrines is an example of a popular practice. The Shia continued to revere the imams even after their death and so visited their graves to ask favors of the imams buried there. Over time, Shia scholars rationalized the practice and it became established.

Some of the Arabian tribes came to attribute the same sort of power that the Shia recognized in the tomb of an imam to natural objects such as trees and rocks. Such beliefs were particularly disturbing to Muhammad ibn Abd al Wahhab. In the late 1730s, he returned to the Najdi town of Huraymila and began to write and preach against both Shia and local popular practices. He focused on the Muslim principle that there is only one God and that God does not share his power with anyone—not imams, and certainly not trees or rocks. From this unitarian principle, his students began to refer to themselves as *muwahhidun* (unitarians). Their detractors referred to them as ''Wahhabis''—or ''followers of Muhammad ibn Abd al Wahhab,'' which had a pejorative connotation.

The idea of a unitary god was not new. Muhammad ibn Abd al Wahhab, however, attached political importance to it. He directed his attack against the Shia. He also sought out local leaders, trying to convince them that his teaching was an Islamic issue. He expanded his message to include strict adherence to the principles of Islamic law. He referred to himself as a ''reformer'' and looked for a political figure who might give his ideas a wider audience.

Lacking political support in Huraymila, Muhammad ibn Abd al Wahhab returned to Uyaynah where he won over some local leaders. Uyaynah, however, was close to Al Hufuf, one of the Twelver Shia centers in eastern Arabia, and its leaders were understandably alarmed at the anti-Shia tone of the Wahhabi message. Partly as a result of their influence, Muhammad ibn Abd al Wahhab was obliged to leave Uyaynah and headed for Ad Diriyah. He had earlier made contact with Muhammad ibn Saud, the leader in Ad Diriyah at the time, and two of Muhammad's brothers had accompanied him when he destroyed tomb shrines around Uyaynah.

Accordingly, when Muhammad ibn Abd al Wahhab arrived in Ad Diriyah, the Al Saud was ready to support him. In 1744 Muhammad ibn Saud and Muhammad ibn Abd al Wahhab swore a traditional Muslim oath in which they promised to work together to establish a state ruled according to Islamic principles. Until that time, the Al Saud had been accepted as conventional tribal leaders whose rule was based on longstanding but vaguely defined authority.

Muhammad ibn Abd al Wahhab offered the Al Saud a clearly defined religious mission to which to contribute their leadership and upon which they might base their political authority. This sense of religious purpose remained evident in the political ideology of Saudi Arabia in the 1990s.

Muhammad ibn Saud began by leading armies into Najdi towns and villages to eradicate various popular and Shia practices. The movement helped to rally the towns and tribes of Najd to the Al Saud-Wahhabi standard. By 1765 Muhammad ibn Saud's forces had established Wahhabism—and with it the Al Saud political authority—over most of Najd.

After Muhammad ibn Saud died in 1765, his son, Abd al Aziz, continued the Wahhabi advance. In 1802 the Al Saud-Wahhabi armies attacked and sacked Karbala, including the Shia shrine that commemorates the death of Husayn. In 1803 they moved to take control of Sunni towns in the Hijaz. Although the Wahhabis spared Mecca and Medina the destruction they visited upon Karbala, they destroyed monuments and grave markers that were being used for prayer to Muslim saints and for votive rituals, which the Wahhabis considered acts of polytheism (see Wahhabi Theology, ch. 2). In destroying the objects that were the focus of these rituals, the Wahhabis sought to imitate Muhammad's destruction of pagan idols when he reentered Mecca in 630.

While the Al Saud remained in Najd, the world paid them scant attention. Capturing the Hijaz, however, brought the Al Saud empire into conflict with the rest of the Islamic world. The popular and Shia practices to which the Wahhabis objected were important to other Muslims, the majority of whom were alarmed that shrines were destroyed and access to the holy cities restricted.

Moreover, rule over the Hijaz was an important symbol. The Ottoman Turks, the most important political force in the Islamic world at the time, refused to concede rule over the Hijaz to local leaders. At the beginning of the nineteenth century, the Ottomans were not in a position to recover the Hijaz, because their forces were weak and overextended. Accordingly, the Ottomans delegated the recapture of the Hijaz to their most ambitious client, Muhammad Ali, the semi-independent commander of their garrison in Egypt. Muhammad Ali, in turn, handed the job to his son Tursun, who led a force to the Hijaz in 1816; Muhammad Ali later joined his son to command the force in person.

Meanwhile, Muhammad ibn Abd al Wahhab had died in 1792, and Abd al Aziz died shortly before the capture of Mecca. The movement had continued, however, to recognize the leadership of the Al Saud and so followed Abd al Aziz's son, Saud, until 1814; after Saud died in 1814, his son, Abd Allah, ruled. Accordingly, it was Abd Allah ibn Saud ibn Abd al Aziz who faced the invading Egyptian army.

Tursun's forces took Mecca and Medina almost immediately. Abd Allah chose this time to retreat to the family's strongholds in Najd. Muhammad Ali decided to pursue him there, sending out another army under the command of his other son, Ibrahim. The Wahhabis made their stand at the traditional Al Saud capital of Ad Diriyah, where they managed to hold out for two years against superior Egyptian forces and weaponry. In the end, however, the Wahhabis proved no match for the Egyptian forces, and Ad Diriyah—and Abd Allah with it—fell in 1818.

## Nineteenth-Century Arabia

The modern history of Arabia is often broken into three periods that follow the fortunes of the Al Saud. The first begins with the alliance between Muhammad ibn Saud and Muhammad ibn Abd al Wahhab and ends with the capture of Abd Allah. The second period extends from this point to the rise of the second Abd al Aziz ibn Saud, the founder of the modern state; the third consists of the establishment and present history of the Kingdom of Saudi Arabia.

In the Egyptians' attempt to establish control over the peninsula, Muhammad Ali removed members of the Al Saud from the area. Following orders from the Ottoman sultan, he sent Abd Allah to Istanbul—where he was publicly beheaded—and forced other members of the family to leave the country. A few prominent members of the Al Saud found their way to Egypt.

The Egyptians turned next to the symbol of the Al Saud rule, the city of Ad Diriyah. They razed its walls and buildings and destroyed its palm groves so that the area could not support any agricultural settlement for some time. The Egyptians then sent troops to strategic parts of the peninsula to tighten their grip on it. They garrisoned Al Qatif, a port on the Persian Gulf that supplied some of the important centers in eastern Arabia and maintained various forces along the Red Sea coast in the west (see fig. 2).

In the Hijaz, Muhammad Ali restored the authority of the *ashraf* (sing., sharif—see Glossary), who had ruled the area from Mecca since the tenth century. However, Turki ibn Abd Allah, the uncle of one of the penultimate rulers (Saud), upset Egyptian efforts to exercise authority in the area. Turki had fought at Ad Diriyah but managed to escape the Egyptians when the town fell in 1818. He hid for two years among loyal forces to the south and, after a few unsuccessful attempts, recaptured Ad Diriyah in 1821. From the ruins of Ad Diriyah, Turki proceeded to Riyadh, another Najdi city, which eventually became the new Al Saud base. Forces under Turki's control reclaimed the rest of Najd in 1824.

Turki's relatively swift retaking of Najd showed the extent to which the Al Saud-Wahhabi authority had been established in the area over the previous fifty years. The successes of the Wahhabi forces had done much to promote tribal loyalty to the Al Saud. But the Wahhabi principles of the Al Saud rule were equally compelling. After Muhammad ibn Abd al Wahhab's death in 1792, the Al Saud leader assumed the title of *imam*. Thus, Al Saud leaders were recognized not just as shaykhs or leaders, but as Wahhabi imams, political and religious figures whose rule had an element of religious authority.

Turki and his successors ruled from Riyadh over a wide area. They controlled the region to the north and south of Najd and exerted considerable influence along the western coast of the Persian Gulf. This area was no state but a large sphere of influence that the Al Saud held together with a combination of treaties and delegated authority. In the Jabal Shammar to the north, for instance, the Al Saud supported the rule of Abd Allah ibn Rashid with whom Turki maintained a close alliance. Later, Turki's son Faisal cemented this alliance by marrying his son, Talal, to Abd Allah's daughter, Nura. Although this family-to-family connection worked well, the Al Saud preferred to rely in the east on appointed leaders to rule on their behalf. In other areas, they were content to establish treaties under the terms of which tribes agreed to defend the family's interests or to refrain from attacking the Al Saud when the opportunity arose.

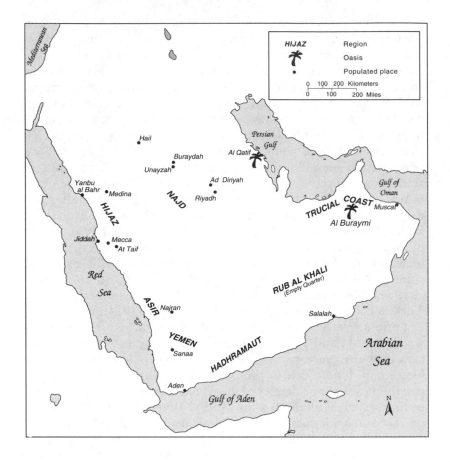

*Figure 2. Nineteenth-Century Arabia*

Within their sphere of influence, the Al Saud could levy troops for military campaigns from the towns and tribes under their control. Although these campaigns were mostly police actions against recalcitrant tribes, the rulers described them as holy wars (jihad), which they conducted according to religious principles. The tribute that the Al Saud demanded from those under their control also was based on Islamic principles. Towns, for instance, paid taxes at a rate established by Muslim law, and the troops that accompanied the Al Saud on raiding expeditions returned one-fifth of their booty to the Al Saud treasury according to sharia (Muslim law) requirements.

The collection of tribute was another indication of the extensive influence the Al Saud derived because of their Wahhabi connections.

Wahhabi religious ideas had spread through the central part of the Arabian Peninsula; as a result, the Al Saud influenced decisions even in areas not under their control, such as succession battles and questions of tribute. Their influence in the Hijaz, however, remained restricted. Not only were the Egyptians and Ottomans careful that the region not slip away again, but Wahhabi ideas had not found a receptive audience in western Arabia. Accordingly, the family was unable to gain a foothold in the Hijaz during the nineteenth century.

The Al Saud maintained authority in Arabia by controlling several factors. First, they could resist, or at least accommodate, Egyptian interference. After 1824 when the Egyptians no longer could maintain outright military control over Arabia, they turned to political intrigues. Turki, for instance, was assassinated in 1834 by a member of the Al Saud who recently had returned from Cairo. When Turki's son, Faisal, succeeded his father, the Egyptians supported a rival member of the family, Khalid ibn Saud, who with Egyptian assistance controlled Najd for the next four years.

Muhammad Ali and the Egyptians were severely weakened after the British and French defeated their fleet off the coast of Greece in 1827. This action prevented the Egyptians from exerting much influence in Arabia, but it left the Al Saud with the problem of the Ottomans, whose ultimate authority Turki eventually acknowledged. Because the challenge to the sultan had helped end the first Al Saud empire in 1818, later rulers chose to accommodate the Ottomans as much as they could. The Al Saud eventually became of considerable financial importance to the Ottomans because they collected tribute from the rich trading state of Oman and forwarded much of this to the *ashraf* in Mecca, who relayed it to the sultan. In return, the Ottomans recognized the Al Saud authority and left them alone for the most part.

The Ottomans, however, sometimes tried to expand their influence by supporting renegade members of the Al Saud. When two of Faisal's sons, Abd Allah and Saud, vied to take over the empire from their father, Abd Allah enlisted the aid of the Ottoman governor in Iraq, who used the opportunity to take Al Qatif and Al Hufuf in eastern Arabia. The Ottomans eventually were driven out, but until the time of Abd al Aziz they continued to look for a relationship with the Al Saud that they could exploit.

One of the reasons the Ottomans were unsuccessful was the growing British interest in Arabia. The British government in India considered the Persian Gulf to be its western flank and thus increasingly became concerned about the trade with the Arab tribes on the eastern coast. The British were also anxious about potentially hostile

19

Ottoman influence in an area so close to India and the planned Suez Canal. As a result, the British came into increasing contact with the Al Saud. As Wahhabi leaders, the Al Saud could exert some control over some of the tribes on the gulf coast, and they were simultaneously involved with the Ottomans. During the period from the 1830s to the 1880s, the Al Saud leaders began to play off the Ottomans and British against each other.

Whereas the Al Saud were largely successful in handling these two powers in the Persian Gulf, they did not do so well in managing their family affairs. The killing of Turki in 1834 touched off a long period of fighting. Turki's son, Faisal, held power until he was expelled from Riyadh by Khalid and his Egyptian supporters. Then, Abd Allah ibn Thunayyan (from yet another branch of the Al Saud) seized Riyadh. He could maintain power only briefly in the early 1840s, however, because Faisal, who had been taken to Cairo and then escaped, retook the city in 1845.

Faisal ruled until 1865, lending some stability to Arabia. Upon his death, however, fighting started again, and his three sons—Abd Allah, Abd ar Rahman, and Saud—as well as some of Saud's sons each held Riyadh on separate occasions (see fig. 3). The political structure of Arabia was such that each leader had to win the support of various tribes and towns to conduct a campaign. In this way, alliances were constantly formed and reformed, and the more often this occurred, the more unstable the situation became.

This instability accelerated the decline of the Al Saud after the death of Faisal. While the Al Saud were bickering among themselves, however, the family of Muhammad ibn Rashid, who controlled the area around the Jabal Shammar, had been gaining strength and expanding its influence in northern Najd. In 1891 Muhammad ibn Rashid, the grandson of the leader with whom Turki had first made an alliance, was in a position to enhance his own power. He removed the sons of Saud ibn Faisal from Riyadh and returned the city to the nominal control of their uncle, Abd ar Rahman. Muhammad put effective control of the city, however, into the hands of his own garrison commander, Salim ibn Subhan. When Abd ar Rahman attempted to exert real authority, he was driven out of Riyadh. Thus, the Al Saud, along with the young Abd al Aziz, were obliged to take refuge with the amir of Kuwait.

## The Rise of Abd al Aziz, 1890–1926

The founder of the modern state of Saudi Arabia lived much of his early life in exile. In the end, however, he not only recovered the territory of the first Al Saud empire, but made a state out of it. Abd al Aziz did this by maneuvering among a number of forces. The first was the religious fervor that Wahhabi Islam continued to inspire. His Wahhabi army, the Ikhwan (brotherhood—see Glossary), for instance, represented a powerful tool, but one that proved so difficult to control that the ruler ultimately had to destroy it. At the same time, Abd al Aziz had to anticipate the manner in which events in Arabia would be viewed abroad and allow foreign powers, particularly the British, to have their way.

Abd al Aziz established the Saudi state in three stages, namely, by retaking Najd in 1905, defeating the Al Rashid at Hail in 1921, and conquering the Hijaz in 1924. In the first phase, Abd al Aziz acted as tribal leaders had acted for centuries: while still in Kuwait, and only in his twenties, Abd al Aziz rallied a small force from the surrounding tribes and began to raid areas under Al Rashid control north of Riyadh. Then in early 1902, he led a small party in a surprise attack on the Al Rashid garrison in Riyadh.

The successful attack gave Abd al Aziz a foothold in Najd. One of his first tasks was to establish himself in Riyadh as the Al Saud leader and the Wahhabi imam. Abd al Aziz obtained the support of the religious establishment in Riyadh, and this relatively swift recognition revealed the political force of Wahhabi authority. Leadership in this tradition did not necessarily follow age, but it respected lineage and, particularly, action. Despite his relative youth, by taking Riyadh Abd al Aziz had showed he possessed the qualities the tribes valued in a leader.

From his seat in Riyadh, Abd al Aziz continued to make agreements with some tribes and to do battle with others. He eventually strengthened his position so that the Al Rashid were unable to evict him. By the middle of the first decade of the twentieth century, the Ottoman governor in Iraq recognized Abd al Aziz as an Ottoman client in Najd. The Al Saud ruler accepted Ottoman suzerainty because it improved his political position. Nevertheless he made concurrent overtures to the British to rid Arabia of Ottoman influence. In 1913, and without British assistance, Abd al Aziz's armies drove the Ottomans out of Al Hufuf in eastern Arabia and thereby strengthened his position in Najd as well.

About this time, the Ikhwan movement began to emerge among the beduin, spreading Wahhabi Islam among the nomads. Stressing the same strict adherence to religious law that Muhammad ibn Abd al Wahhab had preached, Ikhwan beduin gradually abandoned their traditional way of life in the desert and moved to a form of agricultural settlement called *hujar* (see Glossary). The word was related to the term *hijra* that refers to the Prophet's emigration from Mecca to Medina in 622, conveying the sense that one who settles in a *hujar* moves from a place of unbelief to a place of belief. By

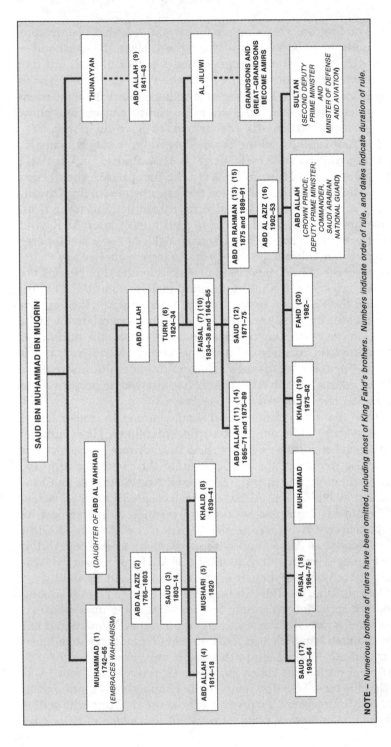

*Figure 3. Abbreviated Genealogy of the House of Saud with Order and Duration of Rule, 1992*

22

moving to the *hujra,* the Ikhwan intended to take up a new way of life and dedicate themselves to enforcing a rigid Islamic orthodoxy. Once in the *hujra,* the Ikhwan became extremely militant in enforcing upon themselves what they believed to be correct sunna (custom) of the Prophet, enjoining public prayer, mosque attendance, and gender segregation and condemning music, smoking, alcohol, and technology unknown at the time of the Prophet. They attacked people who refused to conform to Wahhabi interpretations of correct Islamic practice and tried to convert Muslims by force to their version of Wahhabism.

The Ikhwan looked eagerly for the opportunity to fight non-Wahhabi Muslims—and non-Muslims as well—and they took Abd al Aziz as their leader in this. By 1915 there were more than 200 *hujra* in and around Najd and at least 60,000 Ikhwan waiting for a chance to fight. This force provided Abd al Aziz with a powerful weapon, but his situation demanded that he use it carefully. In 1915 Abd al Aziz had various goals: he wanted to take Hail from the Al Rashid, to extend his control into the northern deserts in present-day Syria and Jordan, and to take over the Hijaz and the Persian Gulf coast. The British, however, had become more and more involved in Arabia because of World War I, and Abd al Aziz had to adjust his ambitions to British interests.

The British prevented the Al Saud from taking over much of the gulf coast where they had established protectorates with several ruling dynasties. They also opposed Abd al Aziz's efforts to extend his influence beyond the Transjordanian, Syrian, and Iraqi deserts because of their own imperial interests. To the west, the British were allied with the *ashraf* who ruled the Hijaz from their base in Mecca. The British actually encouraged the Sharif of Mecca to revolt against the Ottomans and so open a second front against them in World War I.

In this situation, Abd al Aziz had no choice but to focus his attentions on Hail. This action caused problems with the Ikhwan because, unlike Mecca and Medina, Hail had no religious significance and the Wahhabis had no particular quarrel with the Al Rashid who controlled it. The *ashraf* in Mecca, however, were another story. The Wahhabis had long borne a grudge against the *ashraf* because of their traditional opposition to Wahhabism. The ruler, Sharif Hussein, had made the situation worse by forbidding the Ikhwan to make the pilgrimage and then seeking non-Muslim, British help against the Muslim Ottomans.

In the end, Abd al Aziz was largely successful in balancing the Ikhwan's interests with his own limitations. In 1919 the Ikhwan completely destroyed an army that Hussein had sent against them near the town of Turabah, which lay between the Hijaz and Najd. The Ikhwan so completely destroyed the troops of the Sharif that no forces were left to defend the Hijaz, and the entire area cowered under the threat of a Wahhabi attack. In spite of this, Abd al Aziz restrained the Ikhwan and managed to direct them toward Hail, which they took easily in 1921. The Ikhwan went beyond Hail, however, and pushed into central Transjordan where they challenged Hussein's son, Abd Allah, whose rule the British were trying to establish after the war. At this point, Abd al Aziz again had to rein in his troops to avoid further problems with the British.

In the matter of the Hijaz, Abd al Aziz was rewarded for his patience. By 1924 Hussein had grown no stronger militarily and had been weakened politically. When the Ottoman sultan, who had held the title of caliph, was deposed at the end of World War I, Sharif Hussein took the title for himself. He had hoped that the new honor would gain him greater Muslim support, but the opposite happened. Many Muslims were offended that Hussein should handle Muslim tradition in such cavalier fashion and began to object strongly to his rule. To make matters worse for Hussein, the British were no longer willing to prop him up after the war. Abd al Aziz's efforts to control the Ikhwan in Transjordan as well as his accommodation of British interests in the gulf had proved to them that he could act responsibly.

The Al Saud conquest of the Hijaz had been possible since the battle at Turabah in 1919. Abd al Aziz had been waiting for the right moment, and in 1924 he found it. The British did not encourage him to move into Mecca and Medina, but they also gave no indication that they would oppose him. So the Wahhabi armies took over the area with little opposition.

## Nation Building: The Rule of Abd al Aziz, 1926–53

The capture of the Hijaz complicated the basis of Abd al Aziz's authority. The Al Saud ruler was fundamentally a traditional Arab clan leader who held the loyalty of various tribes because of his spectacular successes. But Abd al Aziz was also a Wahhabi imam who held the intense loyalty of the Ikhwan. When he became the ruler of Mecca and Medina as well, Abd al Aziz took on the responsibilities of Khadim al Haramayn (custodian of the two holy mosques) and so assumed an important position in the wider Muslim world. Further, by maintaining his authority under pressure from the Western powers, Abd al Aziz had become the only truly independent Arab leader after World War I. Thus, he had a role to play in wider Arab politics as well.

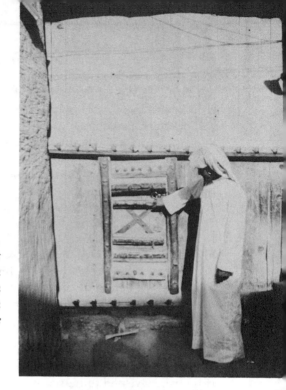

*Door of Al Mismak Palace,
Riyadh, site of Abd al Aziz's
attack in 1902 that began
his recovery of the kingdom
Courtesy Saudi Arabian
Information Office*

In establishing his state, Abd al Aziz had to consider the various constituencies that he served. He made some effort to gain world Muslim approval before he moved into the Hijaz. Once the Hijaz was under his control, he submitted to the world Muslim community, even if only rhetorically, the question of how the area should be ruled. When he received no response, he held an informal referendum in which the notables of the Hijaz chose him as their king. In the Hijaz, Abd al Aziz restrained the more fanatical of his Wahhabi followers and eventually won the support of the local religious authorities, or ulama.

Other Muslim countries were not at the time in a position to challenge Abd al Aziz. Most of the states lived under foreign rule or mandate, and two of the countries that did not, Persia and Turkey, were in the midst of secular reforms.

Abd al Aziz had problems at home, however. The first and most serious of these was the Ikhwan. The Ikhwan had no tolerance for the concessions to life in the twentieth century that Abd al Aziz was forced to make. They objected to machines, particularly those used for communication, such as the telegraph, as well as to the increasing presence of non-Muslim foreigners in the country. They also continued to object to some of the practices of non-Wahhabi Muslims.

Most important, the Ikhwan remained eager to force their message on everyone. This attitude led them to attack non-Wahhabi

25

Muslims, and sometimes Wahhabi Muslims as well, within Saudi Arabia and to push beyond its borders into Iraq. Whereas the first sort of attack challenged Abd al Aziz's authority, the second caused him problems with the British, who would not tolerate the violation of borders that they had set up after World War I. It was largely because of this second concern that Abd al Aziz found himself obliged to take on the Ikhwan militarily. When the Wahhabi forces continued to ignore his authority, he waged a pitched battle and defeated them in 1929.

The way that Abd al Aziz put down the Ikhwan demonstrated his ability to assemble a domestic constituency. Throughout their history, the Al Saud had no standing army; when the family had a military objective, it had simply assembled coalitions of tribes and towns, or such groups as the Ikhwan. In facing the Ikhwan, Abd al Aziz built support in the same way. He went out into the country and made his case in large and small local meetings. He talked not only to the people who would be fighting with him, but also to the religious authorities, seeking their advice and approval. If the ruler wished to battle the Ikhwan, could this be sanctioned by Islam? Or might the Ikhwan's demand to continue their jihad have greater justification?

In the late 1920s, the majority sided with Abd al Aziz, setting the foundation of the modern state. The ruler built on this foundation by taking into account the interests of various groups. He continued to consult the ulama and, if he disagreed with them, to work to change their opinion. One of the best examples of Abd al Aziz's method was his struggle to set up radio communications. Like the Ikhwan, the ulama first opposed radio as a suspect modern innovation for which there was no basis in the time of the Prophet. Only when Abd al Aziz demonstrated that the radio could be used to broadcast the Quran did the ulama give it their approval.

Abd al Aziz was careful not to make more enemies than necessary—and he tried to make those enemies he had into friends. This aim was demonstrated in his handling of his main rivals of the 1914–24 period, the Al Rashid of Hail and the Sharif of Mecca. After conquering Hail, Abd al Aziz reestablished the marriage links that his ancestor, Turki, had first forged between the two families by marrying three of the Al Rashid widows into his family. He made a similar effort to gain the favor of the Hashimites after taking the Hijaz. Rather than expelling the family as a future threat, Abd al Aziz gave some of its members large tracts of land, enabling them to stay in the area and prosper.

Abd al Aziz also assured himself the continued loyalty of those groups who had been allied with him by granting them what favors

*Mountain outcropping in the southwest*
*Beduin with their flocks and traditional tents*
*Courtesy* Aramco World

he could, with difficulty, however, because the new Saudi kingdom had little money in its first twenty years. Najd had never been prosperous, and during the previous century its leaders had become almost dependent on the British to help them through recurring periods of famine. The British had been helpful throughout World War I, but when the political situation in Arabia stabilized, they became less inclined to support Abd al Aziz.

The conquest of the Hijaz and the pilgrimage revenues that went with it considerably improved Abd al Aziz's fortune. With the worldwide depression in the 1930s, however, pilgrimage traffic dropped, and Saudi income from the pilgrimage was reduced by more than half. Accordingly, there was little that Abd al Aziz could do except to hand out what money he had in the traditional tribal manner. As many as 2,000 people would eat daily at Abd al Aziz's table, but this largess was the extent of the services that his government could provide.

The event that was to change Saudi Arabia dramatically was the discovery of massive oil reserves in the kingdom. Oil was first found on the Iranian side of the gulf before World War I and then in Bahrain shortly afterward. Geologists suspected that they would find oil in the Eastern Province of Saudi Arabia as well; so in the early 1930s, British and United States companies competed for the rights to explore for oil. Standard Oil Company of California (Socal) was the firm that won and struck small pockets of oil fairly quickly. By the end of the decade, Socal discovered enormous deposits that were close to the surface and thus inexpensive to extract (see Brief History, ch. 3).

## The Reigns of Saud and Faisal, 1953–75

Upon Abd al Aziz's death in 1953 he was succeeded by his son, Saud. Saud had been designated crown prince some years before in a political act that went back to the days of Muhammad ibn Saud and Muhammad ibn Abd al Wahhab. The new King Saud did not prove to be a leader equal to the challenges of the times. He was a spendthrift even before he became king, and this tendency became a more crucial issue when he controlled the kingdom's purse strings. Saud paid huge sums to maintain tribal acquiescence to his rule in return for recruits for an immense palace guard, the White Army, so-called because they wore traditional Arab dress rather than military uniforms. Revenues could not match Saud's expenditures for the tribes, subsidies to various foreign groups, and his personal follies. By 1958 the riyal (for value of the riyal—see Glossary) had to be devalued nearly 80 percent, despite annual oil revenues in excess of US$300 million.

Dissatisfaction grew over wasteful expenditures, the lack of development of public projects and education institutions, and the low wages of the growing labor force. Privileged classes had been unknown in the early days of Abd al Aziz's reign; his first palace was made of the same sun-dried mud bricks that the peasants used, shaykhs and beduin herdsmen called each other by their first names, and the clothing of rich and poor was quite similar.

Dissatisfaction came from many sources, chief of which were a few of the more liberal princes and the sons of the rising middle class educated abroad. In an effort to discourage the formation of critical attitudes, college students abroad were forbidden to major in law, political science, or related areas. Further evidence of discontent was reflected in 1956 when Arabian American Oil Company (Aramco) Saudi workers called a second strike, the first having occurred in 1953. Saud issued a royal decree in June 1956 forbidding further strikes under penalty of dismissal.

In foreign relations, Saud followed the inclinations of his father; he promoted Arab unity and, in cooperation with Gamal Abdul Nasser of Egypt, demanded the liberation of Palestine. Saudi Arabia's ties with Egypt had been strengthened by a mutual defense pact in October 1955. Together Nasser and Saud assisted in financing an effort to discourage Jordan from joining the Western-sponsored Baghdad Pact. When French, British, and Israeli forces invaded Egypt in 1956 as a result of Nasser's nationalization of the Suez Canal, Saud granted the equivalent of US$10 million to Egypt, severed diplomatic relations with Britain and France, and placed an embargo on oil shipments to both countries.

United States-Saudi relations also declined during the early years of Saud's reign. Nationalists criticized the leasing of Dhahran's air base to the United States, calling it a concession to Western imperialism. In 1954 the United States Point Four economic aid mission was terminated.

Saudi policy toward the United States became more favorable following United States condemnation of the British, French, and Israeli attack on Egypt in 1956. During Saud's successful 1957 visit to the United States, in a conference with President Dwight D. Eisenhower, Saud supported the Eisenhower Doctrine and agreed to a five-year renewal of the lease of the air base at Dhahran.

But as Western relations improved, those with Egypt worsened. Egypt and Saudi Arabia had been drawn together because of their mutual interest in opposing foreign intervention in the Arab world. Beyond that point, all similarity of objectives vanished. Nasser had deposed a king in Egypt and was encouraging revolutionary attitudes in other Arab countries. His notions of Arab unity were abhorrent to Saud and to many Saudis who wished to preserve an independent kingdom. Furthermore, the Egyptians trafficked with the Soviet Union, from whom the Saudis had declined an arms offer and with whom they had suspended diplomatic recognition because of their opposition to atheism. The presence of large numbers of Egyptian military attachés and teachers in Saudi Arabia caused concern among the Saudis that, at the very least, unacceptable views would circulate. Saudi officials were surprised when Syria and Egypt merged in 1958 to form the United Arab Republic. Yet the shock generated by news of the union paled before the subsequent disclosures of an alleged conspiracy by Saud to subvert the venture and to assassinate Nasser.

The embarrassed senior members of the royal family had also become increasingly unhappy over Saud's tendency to appoint his inexperienced young sons to major government positions rather than older, more seasoned family members. They feared that such appointments indicated a plan to transfer the succession to his offspring as opposed to the traditional practice of selecting the most senior and experienced family member as leader. These fears, combined with their concern over Saud's profligate spending and the alleged assassination plot, increased family dissatisfaction to the point that senior members of Al Saud pressured Saud to relinquish power to Faisal.

On March 24, 1958, Saud issued a royal decree giving Faisal executive powers in foreign and internal affairs, including fiscal planning. As a result of Faisal's initiation of an austerity program in 1959 that included a reduction of subsidies to the royal family, the budget was balanced, currency stabilized, and embarrassing national debts paid.

The reductions in the royal household budget incensed Saud and his circle, and a dispute arising out of Saud's desire to give full control of a Hijaz oil refinery to one of his sons made Faisal's position increasingly precarious. In January 1961, Faisal and his Council of Ministers tendered their resignations.

Saud assumed the post of prime minister and made another brother, the progressive Talal, minister of finance and national economy. A new cabinet was formed composed of many Western-educated commoners. Talal, concluding that Saud had misrepresented his intentions to engage his support, departed for Cairo, taking several air force officers and their airplanes with him. Civil war broke out in Yemen in September 1962, and Egyptian forces arrived to buttress the revolutionaries against the Saudis, who supported the overthrown royalist government.

Faisal was reappointed as deputy prime minister and minister of foreign affairs in March 1962, and exercised executive power on behalf of Saud, who was in the United States for medical treatment. In October 1962, the ulama and many princes urged Faisal to accept the post of monarch, but he declined, citing a promise to his father to support Saud. Instead, Faisal again became prime minister, named Khalid deputy prime minister, and formed a government. He took command of the armed forces and quickly restored their loyalty and morale.

The following month, Faisal announced a ten-point plan for reform. Projected changes in the government included promises to create a consultative council, establish local government, and form an independent judiciary with a supreme judicial council composed of secular and religious members. He pledged to strengthen Islam and to reform the Committees for the Propagation of Virtue and Prevention of Vice (also known as the Committees for Public Morality, or *mutawwiin*). Progress was to be ensured by the regulation of economic and commercial activities, and there was to be a sustained effort to develop the country's resources. Social reforms would include provisions for social security, unemployment compensation, educational scholarships, and the abolition of slavery. Consultations between Faisal and President John F. Kennedy led to promises of United States support of Faisal's plans for reform and of Saudi Arabia's territorial integrity. Diplomatic relations were reestablished with Britain and France, and debts to them were repaid.

Faisal's projects and the budgetary allowance necessary to modernize the armed forces for their engagement in Yemen meant that the king's personal income had to be cut. In March 1964, a royal decree endorsed by the royal family and the ulama reduced Saud's powers and his personal budget. The response from Saud, who had been on an extended and expensive tour of Europe with a large entourage, was outrage. Saud tried to garner support for a return to power, but the royal family and ulama held firm. On November 2, 1964, the ulama issued a final *fatwa,* or religious decree, on the matter. Saud was deposed, and Faisal was declared king. This decision terminated almost a decade of external and internal pressure to depose Saud and to assert the power and integrity of conservative forces within the Al Saud.

During his reign, Saud had largely cut himself off from the citizenry, relying heavily on his advisers, many of whom were primarily concerned with acquiring personal wealth and power. Faisal, in contrast, despite working long hours on affairs of state, made himself available to the public daily in the traditional majlis, followed by a meal open to anyone. During the times he had acted as prime minister for Saud, Faisal had strengthened the power of the Council of Ministers and in 1954 had been primarily responsible for the creation of the ministries of commerce and industry and of health (see The Council of Ministers, ch. 4).

As king (1964–75), Faisal set himself the task of modernizing the kingdom. He directed his first two official acts toward safeguarding the nation from potential internal and external threats that could thwart development. In the first month of Faisal's reign, the Al Saud designated Khalid, a half brother of Faisal, crown prince, thus avoiding the kind of family power politics over succession that had nearly destroyed Saudi hegemony in the past. Faisal charged Sultan, another half brother serving as minister of defense and aviation, with modernizing the army and establishing an air defense system to protect the nation and its petroleum reserves from potential external and internal threats.

The king substantially increased funds to the King Abd al Aziz University in Jiddah and opened the University of Petroleum and Minerals in Dhahran. The emphasis on education resulted from Faisal's feeling that foreign influence was unavoidable as long as the population remained undereducated and unable to assume the country's many demanding positions. Faisal reorganized the kingdom's planning agency as the Central Planning Organization to develop priorities for economic development. As a consequence, oil revenues were invested to stimulate growth.

Troubled by the spread of republicanism that challenged the legitimacy of the Al Saud, Faisal called an Islamic summit conference in 1965 to reaffirm Islamic principles against the rising tide of modern ideologies. Faisal was dedicated to Islamic ideals that he had learned in the house of his maternal grandfather, a direct descendant of Abd al Wahhab, the eighteenth-century initiator of the revival of religious orthodoxy in Arabia (see The Al Saud and Wahhabi Islam, 1500–1818, this ch.). Faisal was raised in a Spartan atmosphere, unlike most of his half brothers, and was encouraged by his mother to develop values consonant with tribal leadership. Faisal's religious idealism did not diminish his secular effectiveness. For him, political leadership was a religious act that demanded thoughtfulness, dignity, and integrity. Respect for Faisal increased in the Arab world based on the remarkable changes within Saudi Arabia, his reputation as a stalwart enemy of Zionism, and his rapidly increasing financial power.

Faisal proceeded cautiously but emphatically to introduce Western technology. He was continually forced to deal with the insistent demands of his Westernized associates to move faster and the equally vociferous urgings of the ulama to move not at all. He chose the middle ground, not merely in a spirit of compromise to assuage the two forces, but because he earnestly believed that the correct religious orientation would mitigate the adverse effects of modernization. For example, in 1965 the first Saudi television broadcasts offended some Saudis. One of Faisal's nephews went so far as to lead an assault on one of the new studios and was later killed in a shoot-out with the police. Such a family tragedy did not, however, cause Faisal to withdraw his support for the television project.

Faisal's reign initiated a massive education program. Expenditures for education increased to an annual level of approximately 10 percent of the budget. Vocational training centers and institutes of higher education were built in addition to the more than 125 elementary and secondary schools built annually. Women's demands, increasingly vocalized, led to the establishment of elementary schools for girls. These schools were placed under religious control to pacify those who were opposed to education for women. Health centers also multiplied (see Education; Health, ch. 2).

Regional affairs within the peninsula, with the exception of Yemen, primarily concerned boundary disputes. In August 1965, Saudi Arabia and Jordan reached a final determination of their boundaries. In 1965 Saudi Arabia also agreed on border delineations with Qatar. The Continental Shelf Agreement with Iran in October 1968 established the separate rights of Iran and Saudi Arabia in the Persian Gulf, and an agreement was reached to discourage foreign intervention there. The formation of the United Arab Emirates (UAE) in 1971 did not receive official recognition until the settlement of the long-standing Al Buraymi Oasis dispute in 1975.

Saudi Arabia's largest problem within the peninsula remained the settlement of the Yemen crisis. Egyptian aircraft bombed royalist installations and towns in southern Saudi Arabia in November 1962. Saudi Arabia responded by closing its two Egyptian banks, an action countered by Egypt's sequestration of all Saudi Arabian property holdings in Egypt. In August 1965, Faisal and Nasser agreed at Jiddah to an immediate cease-fire, the termination of Saudi aid to the royalists, and the withdrawal of Egyptian forces. In 1965 at Harad in Yemen, Saudi Arabia and Egypt sponsored a meeting of Yemeni representatives from the opposing sides. The conference became deadlocked, and hostilities resumed after the promised Egyptian troop withdrawals commenced. The royalists claimed extensive victories. The Egyptians, incensed at what they believed was renewed Saudi intervention, announced that they would not withdraw their remaining troops.

*Sand dunes in the Rub al Khali, or Empty Quarter,
with exploration party in the foreground
Courtesy* Aramco World

Saud, then living in Egypt, personally gave US$1 million to republicans of the Yemen Arab Republic (YAR—North Yemen) and made broadcasts from its capital and from Cairo, stating his intention to return to rule "to save the people and land of Saudi Arabia." A series of terrorist bomb attacks in Saudi Arabia against residences of the royal family and United States and British personnel led to the arrests of a group, including seventeen Yemenis, accused of the sabotage. They were found guilty and were publicly beheaded in accordance with the law. Egyptian and Saudi disagreements over Yemen were not resolved until the Khartoum Conference of August 1967.

In the aftermath of the June 1967 War between Israel and various Arab states, the disputes between Arab governments took second place to what the Arabs called the "alien threat" of Israel. Faisal's influence at Arab conferences continued to increase, his position strengthened by the enormous revenues with which he could make good his commitments, and by his irreproachable reputation as a pious Muslim. Faisal's pan-Islamic pronouncements took concrete form during the June 1967 War, when an Islamic nation, Jordan, received a direct threat to its existence and that same "infidel power," Israel, seized and retained Jerusalem, the third holiest city of Islam.

At the Khartoum Conference, Kuwait, Libya, and Saudi Arabia agreed to set up a fund equivalent to US$378 million to be distributed among countries that had suffered from the June 1967 War. The Saudi contribution would be US$140 million. The monies were intended not only to ease this situation but also to buttress their political bargaining power. Egypt no longer could continue expensive commitments to the war in Yemen, and Nasser and Faisal agreed to a compromise proposed by Sudan for financial and economic withdrawals in Yemen. The conferees agreed neither to recognize nor to make peace with Israel and to continue to work for the rights of Palestinians.

A fire in the Al Aqsa Mosque in Jerusalem on August 21, 1969, prompted the Islamic Summit Conference of September 1969 in Rabat, Morocco. Representatives agreed to intensify their efforts to ensure the prompt withdrawal of Israeli military forces in the occupied lands and to pursue an honorable peace.

Having increased economic power, Saudi Arabia in July 1973 threatened to reduce oil deliveries if the United States did not seek to equalize its treatment of Egypt and Israel. The threat was realized during the October 1973 War between Israel and Egypt and Syria, when the Organization of Arab Petroleum Exporting Countries imposed a general rise in oil prices and an oil embargo on major oil consumers that were either supporters of Israel or allies of its supporters. The embargo was a political protest aimed at obtaining Israeli withdrawal from occupied Arab territory and recognition of the rights of the Palestinian people.

At an Arab conference held in Algiers in November 1973, Saudi Arabia agreed with all the participants except the representative of Jordan to recognize the Palestine Liberation Organization (PLO) as the legitimate representative of the Palestinian people. Jordan's King Hussein refused to participate but was encouraged by Faisal to attend the follow-up conference in October 1974 in Rabat. At this meeting, Hussein gave his reluctant agreement to the proposal that the PLO should be the negotiators with Israel over the establishment of a Palestinian entity in the territory occupied by Israel. In return Saudi Arabia promised Hussein US$300 million a year for the next four years.

As a result of the 1973 agreements that tripled the price of crude oil in response to the October 1973 War, Saudi Arabia acquired vastly increased revenues to devote to domestic programs. However, Faisal's failing health, overwork, and age prevented him from formulating a coherent development plan before he was assassinated on March 25, 1975. He was shot by his nephew, a disgruntled brother of the nephew killed in the 1965 television station incident.

## The Reign of Khalid, 1975–82

Following the assassination, Crown Prince Khalid immediately succeeded to the throne and received the oaths, formal pledges of support from the family and tribal leaders, within the traditional three days. Fahd, the minister of interior, was named crown prince, as expected.

Khalid's preparation for ruling a modern state included accompanying Faisal on foreign missions and representing Saudi Arabia at the United Nations. He was a quiet but influential figure within the royal family. He was known, for instance, to have rallied the family to support Faisal in the ouster of Saud in 1964. The calm strength and consistency that he displayed during this delicate and potentially dangerous crisis in many ways typified his reign. Although he ruled quietly, he ruled effectively and was considerably more than the figurehead many had expected him to be.

Khalid's leadership style was remarkably different from Faisal's. He was more liberal in terms of informing the press of the rationale behind foreign policy decisions. Although he largely used the same policy-making team as Faisal had, he allowed them greater latitude in decision making within their separate portfolios. In regional affairs, he permitted the governors considerably more autonomy and even authorized their use of discretionary funds. Above all, he valued consensus and the team approach to problem solving.

The new king's first diplomatic coup was the conclusion in April 1975 of a demarcation agreement concerning the Al Buraymi Oasis, where the frontiers of Abu Dhabi, Oman, and Saudi Arabia meet. Claims and counterclaims over this frontier area had exacerbated relations among the three states for years. The successful conclusion of negotiations under Khalid's aegis added to his stature as a statesman among knowledgeable observers of the peninsula political scene.

In April 1976, Khalid made state visits to all the gulf states in the hope of promoting closer relations with his peninsular neighbors. These early visits, in retrospect, probably laid the foundation for the later establishment of the Gulf Cooperation Council (GCC). Coinciding with Khalid's visits to neighboring states, Iran called for a formal, collective security arrangement of the shaykhdoms of the Persian Gulf. This proposal, although not summarily rejected, was received with great coolness by the Saudi government, as wary of Iran's hegemonistic pretensions as of Iraq's.

Probably the most sensitive areas of Saudi Arabia's relations with its neighbors during Khalid's reign were its relations with the YAR and the People's Democratic Republic of Yemen (PDRY—South Yemen). Despite the establishment of relations with the YAR after the conclusion of its civil war in 1967 and massive Saudi aid, relations remained strained and marked by mutual distrust. The YAR government objected to Saudi subsidies to Yemeni tribes critical of it and felt that Saudi Arabia considered North Yemen a convenient buffer state to protect the kingdom against the PDRY, a major recipient of Soviet arms.

In a reorganization of the Council of Ministers in late 1975, Khalid named Crown Prince Fahd deputy prime minister and designated Abd Allah (another half brother and the commander of the Saudi Arabian National Guard) as second deputy prime minister (see The Royal Family, ch. 4; Saudi Arabian National Guard, ch. 5).

Fahd, who had already participated in major decisions, became chief spokesman for the kingdom and a major architect of Saudi economic development, foreign affairs, and oil policy. In 1976 a major concern of the Saudi government was the civil war in Lebanon. Although strongly committed to the official Saudi position that opposed outside intervention or interference in Lebanese affairs, Fahd nevertheless was instrumental in setting up a League of Arab States (Arab League) peacekeeping force. Despite this increasing reliance on Fahd, the strains of office began to tell on Khalid, forcing him to return to the United States for successful open-heart surgery in Cleveland, Ohio.

Much of the kingdom's attention in the late 1970s and early 1980s was focused on the construction of the Yanbu al Bahr and Al Jubayl industrial complexes, to diversify the kingdom's industrial base (see Non-Oil Industrial Sector, ch. 3). In addition to expanding industrial and petroleum facilities, one of Khalid's major domestic accomplishments was his emphasis on agricultural development (see Modern Agriculture, ch. 3).

In the field of foreign affairs, United States-Saudi relations continued to be cordial under Khalid, although Saudi Arabia remained frustrated by perceived United States intransigence in the settlement of the Palestinian problem. In a January 1978 meeting with President Jimmy Carter in Riyadh, the king insisted that peace in the area could be achieved only by the complete Israeli withdrawal from occupied territories, as well as self-determination and resettlement rights for the Palestinians.

Another topic reportedly discussed in Riyadh during this meeting was Soviet penetration and growing influence through arms sales and treaties of friendship with the two Yemens. Five months after the Riyadh meeting, Khalid asked Carter to sell advanced fighter planes to Saudi Arabia to assist in countering communist aggression in the area. The first delivery of the sixty F–15s under the agreement approved by Carter arrived in the kingdom in January 1982. The sale and delivery of the F–15s, the subsequent United States release of sophisticated equipment to enhance the capabilities of the aircraft, and the negotiations resulting in the approval of the airborne warning and control system (AWACS) aircraft owed much to Khalid's insistence on Saudi Arabia's being treated as a full partner in all United States-Saudi areas of joint concern.

The Iranian Islamic Revolution of 1979 caused major Saudi concern about its neighbors in the region. Moreover, as a result of the peace treaty between Egypt and Israel known as the Camp David Accords, on March 26, 1979, Khalid broke relations with Egypt and led in seeking Arab economic sanctions against Egypt.

Some thought in 1979 that traditionalism was no longer a strong force in Saudi Arabia. This idea was disproved when 500 dissidents invaded and seized the Grand Mosque in Mecca on November 20, 1979. The leader of the dissidents, Juhaiman al Utaiba, a Sunni, was from one of the foremost families of Najd. His grandfather had ridden with Abd al Aziz in the early decades of the century, and other family members were among the foremost of the Ikhwan. Juhaiman said that his justification was that the Al Saud had lost its legitimacy through corruption, ostentation, and mindless imitation of the West—virtually an echo of his grandfather's charge in 1921 against Abd al Aziz. Juhaiman's accusations against the Saudi monarchy closely resembled Ayatollah Sayyid Ruhollah Musavi Khomeini's diatribes against the shah of Iran.

The Saudi leadership was stunned and initially paralyzed by the takeover. The Grand Mosque surrounds the Kaaba, symbol of the oneness of God. The courtyard is one of the sites where the hajj, the fifth pillar of Islam, is enacted (see Pilgrimage, ch. 2). Because of the holiness of the place, no non-Muslims may enter the city of Mecca. Furthermore, all holy places come under a special injunction in Islam. It is forbidden to shed blood there or to deface or to pollute them in any way. Despite careful planning on Juhaiman's part, a guard was shot dead by one of the nervous dissidents. Such a desecration is a major violation under Islamic law and merits crucifixion for the convicted offender.

Juhaiman's party included women as well as men, other peninsular Arabs, and a few Egyptians. A score of the dissidents were unemployed graduates of the kingdom's seminary in Medina. They had provisions for the siege they expected as well as extensive supplies of arms.

The government's initial attempts to rout the dissidents were stymied. Before any military move could be authorized, the ulama had to issue a dispensation to allow the bearing of arms in a holy place. When the religious problems were solved by announcement of the ulama's ruling, logistical problems bogged down the efforts of the military and the national guard for several days. Finally, two weeks later the military effort succeeded and the dissidents were dislodged. All the surviving males were eventually beheaded in the squares of four Saudi cities.

Far from discounting the efforts of the rebels, the leaders examined themselves and their policies more closely. Khalid, particularly, was sensitive to their complaints. Many of the dissidents had come from two of the tribes that traditionally have been recruited for the national guard. Khalid had spent much time with these people in the desert.

Compounding the problems for the regime were Shia riots in Al Qatif, in the Eastern Province, two weeks after the siege of the Grand Mosque. Many of the rioters bore posters with Khomeini's picture. Although these were not the first Shia protests in the kingdom (others had occurred in 1970 and 1978 in response to discriminatory treatment of Shia by the government), the December rioters had become emboldened by Khomeini's triumphal return to Iran in early 1979. Up to 20,000 national guard troops were immediately moved into the Eastern Province. Several demonstrators were killed and hundreds reportedly arrested.

Almost visibly shaken by the takeover of the mosque and the Shia disturbances, the Saudi leadership announced in the aftermath of these events that a consultative council (*majlis ash shura*) soon would be formed. The Shia disturbances in the Eastern Province encouraged the government to take a closer look at conditions there. Although it was clear that the Shia had been inspired by Khomeini, it was also obvious that repression and imprisonment were stopgap solutions and as likely to promote greater resistance as to quell it. Further, the Shia lived in the area of the kingdom most vulnerable to sabotage, where numerous oil and gas pipelines crisscross the terrain. Aramco had refused to discriminate against the Shia in hiring practices and had a preponderance of Shia employees. This policy resulted from the location of Aramco's activities and also because Aramco employment offered the Shia the best chance for mobility.

Compared with other towns in the Eastern Province, the predominantly Shia towns of Al Qatif and Al Hufuf were neglected areas. The Shia lacked decent schools, hospitals, roads, and sewerage and had inadequate electrification and water supplies. Violent Shia demonstrations occurred once again in February 1980, and, although they were as harshly repressed as the previous ones, the deputy minister of interior, Amir Ahmad ibn Abd al Aziz Al Saud, was directed to draw up a comprehensive plan to improve the standard of living in Shia areas. His recommendations, which were immediately accepted and implemented, included an electrification project, swamp drainage, the construction of schools and a hospital, street lighting, and loans for home construction.

In early November 1980, a week before Ashura—the most important Shia religious observance, which commemorates the death of Husayn—the government announced a new US$240 million project for Al Qatif. Also shortly before Ashura, Fahd ordered the release of 100 Shia arrested in the November 1979 and February 1980 disturbances. Five days after Ashura, which was peaceful, Khalid toured the area—the first such visit by a Saudi monarch. Co-optation, which served the Saudi leadership so well with the general populace, also seemed the palliative for the Shia problem.

After the troubles of 1979 and 1980, the Saudi leadership began to take a more assertive role in world leadership. Saudi Arabia obtained agreement on the kingdom as the site of the meeting of the Organization of the Islamic Conference in January 1981. Hosting the conference of thirty-eight Muslim heads of state was seen as a vehicle for refurbishing the Saudi image of "custodian of the two holy mosques.'' Also, the kingdom wished to present an alternative to the Islamic radicalism of Libya's Muammar al Qadhafi and Iran's Khomeini, both of whom had caused Saudi Arabia concern in the previous two years.

Shortly after the conference, the Saudi leadership announced the formation of the GCC project long favored by Khalid. Khalid and Fahd had been campaigning actively for such an organization for some time. The GCC included the six states of the peninsula that have similar political institutions, social conditions, and economic resources: Bahrain, Kuwait, Oman, Qatar, Saudi Arabia, and the United Arab Emirates. The aim of the GCC, as it was formally announced at its first summit in May 1981, was to coordinate and unify economic, industrial, and defense policies.

In the late 1970s, Saudi Arabia faced a host of regional problems. In addition to the Palestinian problem, early in Khalid's reign the civil war in Lebanon began. In December 1979, the Soviet Union invaded Afghanistan, and in September 1980 Iraq attacked Iran over suzerainty of the Shatt al Arab waterway. Saudi Arabia feared the conflict between Iran and Iraq might spread down the Persian Gulf. Furthermore, because Iraq and Iran were so engaged, a unique opportunity existed of forming an alliance that excluded them both. The two Yemens, who registered their outrage at exclusion from the GCC, continued to be among serious Saudi concerns. The Soviet Union appeared to be increasing its influence in both Yemeni nations.

One month after the GCC second summit meeting in Riyadh, the Shia attempted a coup d'état in Bahrain in December 1981. The insurgents, most of whom were captured, included Shia from Kuwait and Saudi Arabia, reminding the Saudis of one of their potential causes of discontent.

In another regional development, the Saudis were angry at the Syrians for having signed a Treaty of Friendship and Cooperation with the Soviet Union. The Saudis, however, remained conciliatory in the hope of maintaining the facade of Arab unity and also so that they could function as mediators. In December 1980, when Jordanian and Syrian troops faced each other ready for confrontation, Amir Abd Allah was sent to avert a crisis. Abd Allah, whose mother hailed from a Syrian tribe and who maintained excellent personal relations there, was successful.

Fahd was especially active in advancing Saudi foreign policy objectives. He is credited with averting an escalation of tensions between Algeria and Morocco in May 1981. His major effort in 1980 and 1981 was in devising some alternative to the divisive Camp David Accords, which had isolated Egypt. Before there could be a Saudi-Egyptian rapprochement, a face-saving resolution to Egypt's agreement with Israel was necessary to preserve Saudi Arabia's legitimacy as an Arab mediator.

In August 1981, prior to Egyptian president Anwar as Sadat's departure for the United States to discuss the resumption of the peace process, Fahd proposed his own peace plan to resolve the Arab-Israeli conflict. The Fahd Plan, as it became known, stressed the necessity for a comprehensive settlement that included the creation of a Palestinian state and Arab recognition of Israel's right to exist in exchange for Israeli withdrawal from the West Bank and the Gaza Strip. Although the plan was endorsed by the PLO, dissident Palestinians, Libya, and Syria rejected it, leading to an early close of the Arab Summit in Fez, Morocco, in November 1981 (see Arab Nationalism, ch. 4).

## The Reign of Fahd, 1982–

Fahd, already the major spokesman for the Saudi regime, became even more active as Khalid's health steadily deteriorated. This visibility and experience stood him in good stead when Khalid died after a short illness on June 14, 1982; Fahd immediately assumed power, and Abd Allah, head of the national guard, became crown prince. One of the first problems that the new king faced was a 20 percent drop in oil revenues, as a result of a world oil surplus that developed by 1982 (see Economic Policy Making, ch. 3). Despite the fall in revenues, until the oil price crash of 1986 Saudi Arabia did not make significant changes in the oil policies it followed beginning in the oil boom years from 1974 onward.

The reduction in Saudi Arabia's wealth has not decreased its influence in the Arab world. The kingdom, and Fahd in particular, have played a mediating role in inter-Arab conflicts. Saudi Arabia continued, for instance, its efforts to stop the fighting in Lebanon. In 1989 King Fahd brought most of the Lebanese National Assembly, both Christian and Muslim deputies, to the Saudi resort city of At Taif. At the time, the assembly had been unable to meet in Lebanon because of military clashes and political violence. Once in At Taif, however, the Lebanese deputies voted on a plan for reform and were eventually able to elect a new president. Fahd's actions did not solve the problems in Lebanon, but they helped to end a particular stage of the conflict.

In November 1987, Saudi Arabia reestablished diplomatic relations with Egypt. King Fahd visited Egypt in March 1989 and received an enthusiastic welcome on the streets of Cairo. His visit signified the end of Egypt's temporary isolation within the Arab world. Although Egypt was the country of Nasser, one of the most charismatic figures of the modern Arab world, the visit of a Saudi king symbolized Egypt's return to the Arab family.

\* \* \*

The best and most accessible book on Saudi Arabia before 1984 is Robert Lacey's *The Kingdom: Arabia and the House of Saud.* Lacey begins essentially with Abd al Aziz's rise to power, the establishment of the modern state, and the difficulties faced by Abd al Aziz's successors. A more analytical discussion of comparable material is found in Christine Moss Helms's *The Cohesion of Saudi Arabia.* Information on Abd al Aziz's relationship with the Ikhwan exists in John S. Habib's *Ibn Sa'ud's Warriors of Islam.*

The leading book for the history of Al Saud before Abd al Aziz is R. Bayly Winder's *Saudi Arabia in the Nineteenth Century.* For the period of Muhammad ibn Saud and Muhammad ibn Abd al Wahhab, see George Rentz's article, "Wahhabism and Saudi Arabia." Little has been written on Arabia in medieval times. Much information exists, however, on the early Islamic period; the principal Western author on the subject is W. Montgomery Watt. Anyone interested in a Muslim presentation of the subject should consider Mohamed Hassanein Haykal's *The Life of Muhammad.* For the period before Islam, see the first two chapters of Philip K. Hitti's *History of the Arabs.* (For further information and complete citations, see Bibliography.)

# Chapter 2. The Society and Its Environment

*The Royal Mosque, Jiddah*

SAUDI ARABIA IN THE 1990s was a society of contrasts. After three decades of intense modernization, the country's urban infrastructure was highly developed and technologically sophisticated. Excellent hospitals, clinics, schools, colleges, and universities offered free medical care and education to Saudi citizens. Shopping malls displayed Paris fashions; supermarkets sold vegetables flown in from the Netherlands; restaurants offered Tex-Mex, Chinese, or haute cuisine; and amusement centers with separate hours for male and female patrons dotted the urban landscape. Suburban neighborhoods with single-family houses and swimming pools hidden behind high walls ringed commercial districts, and satellite communications made a telephone call from Riyadh to New York as fast and as clear as a call to New York from Connecticut.

Massive oil revenues had brought undreamed-of wealth to the kingdom. Affluence, however, proved a two-edged sword. The dilemma that Saudis faced in the 1990s was to preserve their cultural and religious heritage while realizing the advantages that such wealth might bring. The regime sought to acquire Western technology while maintaining those values that were central to Saudi society.

It was not an easy quest. The country has its roots in Wahhabism (see Glossary), an eighteenth-century reform movement that called for a return to the purity and simplicity of the early Islamic community. It was the alliance between the Wahhabi religious reformers and the House of Saud (Al Saud) that provided the Arabs of the peninsula with a new and compelling focus for their loyalties and helped to forge the unification of the peninsula under the leadership of Abd al Aziz ibn Abd ar Rahman Al Saud.

The kingdom was rooted in religion-based conservatism stemming from the Wahhabi reform movement. The strength of conservative opinion grew even as the pace of economic change increased. Religious conservatives and modernizers disagreed on what kinds of technology might be used appropriately and how best to use the kingdom's vast wealth. The dichotomy between the two was at the heart of much of the country's political affairs. There was, nonetheless unanimous accord that Saudi Arabia's modernization— whatever form it might take—reflect its Islamic values.

Massive urbanization and the altered economic situation have fueled both the forces of change and conservatism. Urbanization brought with it new social groups—students, technical experts, and a vast corps of foreign workers among them. The government has made every effort to insulate the population from the influence of the foreign community; the task grew more difficult as the number of non-Saudis in the work force increased. Expansion of educational and economic opportunities polarized those who had pursued secular studies and those who had pursued religious studies.

Saudi Arabia stood with one foot firmly placed among the most highly developed nations of the world, yet the other foot lagged behind. Almost one-third of the population lived in rural areas very distant from developed urban centers, some living as nomadic and seminomadic herdsmen, and some as oasis agricultural workers. Other families were divided, caught between the devaluation of local products and the rising cost of living that accompanied development. Men went to distant towns to work as drivers, laborers, or soldiers in the Saudi Arabian National Guard, and women were left to tend family plots and livestock and raise children. Medical care and schooling were available to much of the population but were often located far from rural areas. For many rural people, lack of knowledge, a lack of incentive, illiteracy, physical distance, and bureaucratic obstacles limited access to the resources of Saudi Arabia's burgeoning society.

Saudi Arabia's population also presented a picture of cultural contrasts. On the one hand, Saudi people felt a strong, almost tangible conviction in the rightness of trying to live one's life according to God's laws as revealed through the Quran and the life of the Prophet Muhammad. On the other hand, the interpretation of what it meant to live according to God's laws had assumed different meanings to different groups of people: some wished to adjust traditional values to the circumstances of the present; others wished to adjust the circumstances of the present to traditional values. In no aspect of Saudi society was this tension more manifest than in the question of the role of women. The conservative view favored complete separation of women from men in public life, with the education of women devoted to domestic skills, whereas the liberal view sought to transform ''separation values'' into ''modesty values,'' allowing the expansion of women's opportunities in work and education.

Politically, the early 1990s saw unprecedented expressions of political dissidence born of the economic imbalances and shifting social boundaries produced by the development process. In petitions to the king for reform in the political system and political sermons in the mosques, Saudis have sought representation in government decision making. They have begun to ask who should control the fruits of oil production, who should decide the allocation of resources, and whose version of the just society should be rendered into law? But among opposition voices there was another contrast: some demanded representation to ensure that the governing system would enforce sharia (Islamic law), whereas others demanded representation to ensure protection for the individual from arbitrary religious or political judgments.

The Persian Gulf War of 1991 has exacerbated these contrasts: as Saudi Arabia becomes more dependent on the United States militarily, the need to assert cultural independence from the West becomes proportionately greater. As Saudi Arabia abandons traditional alliances in the Arab world in favor of closer ties with the West, the need to assert its leadership as a Muslim nation among the Muslim nations of the world becomes greater. In the early 1990s, tradition and Westernization coexisted in uneasy balance in Saudi Arabian society.

## Geography

The kingdom occupies 80 percent of the Arabian Peninsula. Most of the country's boundaries with the United Arab Emirates (UAE), Oman, and the Republic of Yemen (formerly two separate countries: the Yemen Arab Republic, or North Yemen, and the People's Democratic Republic of Yemen, or South Yemen) are undefined, so the exact size of the country remains undetermined. The Saudi government estimate is 2,217,949 square kilometers. Other reputable estimates vary between 2,149,690 square kilometers and 2,240,000 square kilometers. Less than 1 percent of the total area is suitable for cultivation, and in the early 1990s population distribution varied greatly among the towns of the eastern and western coastal areas, the densely populated interior oases, and the vast, almost empty deserts.

### External Boundaries

Saudi Arabia is bounded by seven countries and three bodies of water. To the west, the Gulf of Aqaba and the Red Sea form a coastal border of almost 1,800 kilometers that extends south to Yemen, then follows a mountain ridge for approximately 320 kilometers to the vicinity of Najran. This section of the border with Yemen was demarcated in 1934 and is one of the few clearly defined borders with a neighboring country. The Saudi border running southeast from Najran, however, is still undetermined (see fig. 1). The undemarcated border became an issue in the early 1990s, when oil was discovered in the area and Saudi Arabia objected to the commercial exploration by foreign companies on behalf of Yemen. In the summer of 1992, representatives of Saudi

Arabia and Yemen met in Geneva to discuss settlement of the border issue.

To the north, Saudi Arabia is bounded by Jordan, Iraq, and Kuwait. The northern boundary extends almost 1,400 kilometers from the Gulf of Aqaba on the west to Ras al Khafji on the Persian Gulf. In 1965 Saudi Arabia and Jordan agreed to boundary demarcations involving an exchange of small areas of territory that gave Jordan some essential additional land near Aqaba, its only port.

In 1922 Abd al Aziz ibn Abd ar Rahman Al Saud (r. 1902–53) and British officials representing Iraqi interests signed the Treaty of Mohammara, which established the boundary between Iraq and the future Saudi Arabia. Later that year, the Al Uqair Convention signed by the two parties agreed to the creation of a diamond-shaped Iraq-Saudi Arabia Neutral Zone of approximately 7,000 square kilometers, adjacent to the western tip of Kuwait, within which neither Iraq nor Saudi Arabia would build permanent dwellings or installations. The agreement was designed to safeguard water rights in the zone for beduin of both countries. In May 1938, Iraq and Saudi Arabia signed an additional agreement regarding the administration of the zone. Forty-three years later, Saudi Arabia and Iraq signed an agreement that defined the border between the two countries and provided for the division of the neutral zone between them. The agreement effectively dissolved the neutral zone.

The boundary between Abd al Aziz's territories of Najd and the Eastern Province and the British protectorate of Kuwait was first regulated by the Al Uqair Convention in 1922. In an effort to avoid territorial disputes, another diamond-shaped Divided Zone of 5,790 square kilometers directly south of Kuwait was established. In 1938 oil was discovered in Kuwait's southern Burqan fields, and both countries contracted with foreign oil companies to perform exploration work in the Divided Zone. After years of discussions, Saudi Arabia and Kuwait reached an agreement in 1965 that divided the zone geographically, with each country administering its half of the zone. The agreement guaranteed that the rights of both parties to the natural resources in the whole zone would continue to be respected (see Brief History, ch. 3) after each country had annexed its half of the zone in 1966.

Saudi Arabia's eastern boundary follows the Persian Gulf from Ras al Khafji to Qatar, whose border with Saudi Arabia was never delineated following a 1965 agreement. The Saudi border with the state of Oman, on the southeastern coast of the Arabian Peninsula, runs through the Empty Quarter (Rub al Khali). The border demarcation was defined by a 1990 agreement between Saudi Arabia and

Oman that included provisions for shared grazing rights and use of water resources. The border through Al Buraymi Oasis, located near the conjunction of the frontiers of Oman, Abu Dhabi (one of the emirates of the UAE), and Saudi Arabia has triggered extensive dispute among the three states since the Treaty of Jiddah in 1927. In a 1975 agreement with Saudi Arabia, Abu Dhabi accepted sovereignty over six villages in the Al Buraymi Oasis and the sharing of the rich Zararah oil field. In return, Saudi Arabia obtained an outlet to the Persian Gulf through Abu Dhabi.

Saudi Arabia's maritime claims include a twelve-nautical-mile territorial limit along its coasts. The Saudis also claim many small islands as well as some seabeds and subsoils beyond the twelve-nautical-mile limit.

## Topography and Natural Regions

The Arabian Peninsula is an ancient massif composed of stable crystalline rock whose geologic structure developed concurrently with the Alps. Geologic movements caused the entire mass to tilt eastward and the western and southern edges to tilt upward. In the valley created by the fault, called the Great Rift, the Red Sea was formed. The Great Rift runs from the Dead Sea along both sides of the Red Sea south through Ethiopia and the lake country of East Africa, gradually disappearing in the area of Mozambique, Zambia, and Zimbabwe. Scientists analyzing photographs taken by United States astronauts on the joint United States-Soviet space mission in July 1975 detected a vast fan-shaped complex of cracks and fault lines extending north and east from the Golan Heights. These fault lines are believed to be the northern and final portion of the Great Rift and are presumed to be the result of the slow rotation of the Arabian Peninsula counterclockwise in a way that will, in approximately 10 million years, close off the Persian Gulf and make it a lake.

On the peninsula, the eastern line of the Great Rift fault is visible in the steep and, in places, high escarpment that parallels the Red Sea along the Gulf of Aqaba and the Gulf of Aden. The eastern slope of this escarpment is relatively gentle, dropping to the exposed shield of the ancient landmass that existed before the faulting occurred. A second lower escarpment, the Jabal Tuwayq, runs north to south through the area of Riyadh.

The northern half of the region of the Red Sea escarpment is known as the Hijaz and the more rugged southern half as Asir. In the south, a coastal plain, the 'Tihamah, rises gradually from the sea to the mountains. Asir extends southward to the borders of mountainous Yemen. The central plateau, Najd, extends east

51

to the Jabal Tuwayq and slightly beyond. A long, narrow strip of desert known as Ad Dahna separates Najd from eastern Arabia, which slopes eastward to the sandy coast along the Persian Gulf. North of Najd a larger desert, An Nafud, isolates the heart of the peninsula from the steppes of northern Arabia. South of Najd lies one of the largest sand deserts in the world, the Rub al Khali (see fig. 4).

### The Hijaz and Asir

The western coastal escarpment can be considered two mountain ranges separated by a gap in the vicinity of Mecca. The northern range in the Hijaz seldom exceeds 2,100 meters, and the elevation gradually decreases toward the south to about 600 meters around Mecca. The rugged mountain wall drops abruptly to the sea with only a few intermittent coastal plains. There are virtually no natural harbors along the Red Sea. The western slopes have been stripped of soil by the erosion of infrequent but turbulent rainfalls that have fertilized the plains to the west. The eastern slopes are less steep and are marked by dry river beds (wadis) that trace the courses of ancient rivers and continue to lead the rare rainfalls down to the plains. Scattered oases, drawing water from springs and wells in the vicinity of the wadis, permit some settled agriculture. Of these oases, the largest and most important is Medina.

South of Mecca, the mountains exceed 2,400 meters in several places with some peaks topping 3,000 meters. The rugged western face of the escarpment drops steeply to the coastal plain, the Tihamah lowlands, whose width averages only sixty-five kilometers. Along the seacoast is a salty tidal plain of limited agricultural value, backed by potentially rich alluvial plains. The relatively well-watered and fertile upper slopes and the mountains behind are extensively terraced to allow maximum land use.

The eastern slope of the mountain range in Asir is gentle, melding into a plateau region that drops gradually into the Rub al Khali. Although rainfall is infrequent in this area, a number of fertile wadis, of which the most important are the Wadi Bishah and the Wadi Tathlith, make oasis agriculture possible on a relatively large scale. A number of extensive lava beds (*harrat*) scar the surfaces of the plateaus east of the mountain ranges in the Hijaz and Asir and give evidence of fairly recent volcanic activity. The largest of these beds is Khaybar, north of Medina.

### Najd

East of the Hijaz and Asir lies the great plateau area of Najd. This region is mainly rocky plateau interspersed by small, sandy deserts and isolated mountain clumps. The best known of the mountain groups is the Jabal Shammar, northwest of Riyadh and just south of the An Nafud. This area is the home of the pastoral Shammar tribes, which under the leadership of the Al Rashid were the most implacable foes of the Al Saud in the late nineteenth and early twentieth centuries. Their capital was the large oasis of Hail, now a flourishing urban center.

Across the peninsula as a whole, the plateau slopes toward the east from an elevation of 1,360 meters in the west to 750 meters at its easternmost limit. A number of wadis cross the region in an eastward direction from the Red Sea escarpment toward the Persian Gulf. There is little pattern to these remains of ancient riverbeds; the most important of them are Wadi ar Rummah, Wadi as Surr, and Wadi ad Dawasir.

The heart of Najd is the area of the Jabal Tuwayq, an arc-shaped ridge with a steep west face that rises between 100 and 250 meters above the plateau. Many oases exist in this area, the most important of which are Buraydah, Unayzah, Riyadh, and Al Kharj. Outside the oasis areas, Najd is sparsely populated. Large salt marshes (*sabkah*) are scattered throughout the area.

### Northern Arabia

The area north of the An Nafud is geographically part of the Syrian Desert. It is an upland plateau scored by numerous wadis, most tending northeastward toward Iraq. This area, known as Badiyat ash Sham, and covered with grass and scrub vegetation, is extensively used for pasture by nomadic and seminomadic herders. The most significant feature of the area is the Wadi as Sirhan, a large basin as much as 300 meters below the surrounding plateau, which is the vestige of an ancient inland sea. For thousands of years, some of the heavily traveled caravan routes between the Mediterranean and the central and southern peninsula have passed through the Wadi as Sirhan. The most important oases in the area are Al Jawf and Sakakah, just north of the An Nafud.

### Eastern Arabia

East of the Ad Dahna lies the rocky As Summan Plateau, about 120 kilometers wide and dropping in elevation from about 400 meters in the west to about 240 meters in the east. The area is generally barren, with a highly eroded surface of ancient river gorges and isolated buttes.

Farther east the terrain changes abruptly to the flat lowlands of the coastal plain. This area, about sixty kilometers wide, is generally featureless and covered with gravel or sand. In the north is

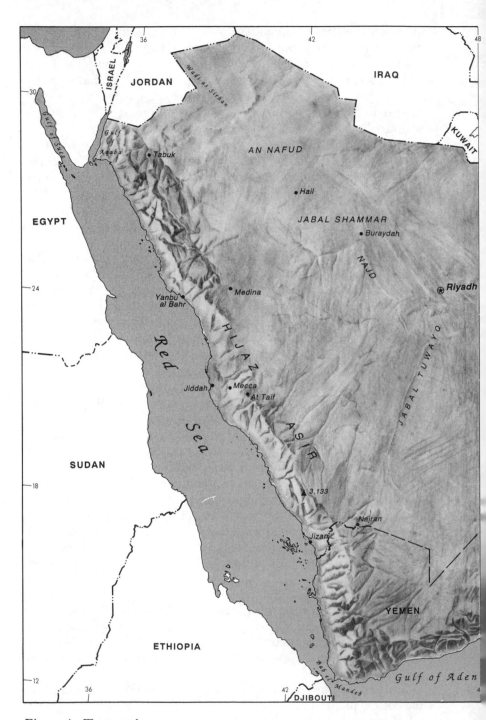

*Figure 4. Topography*

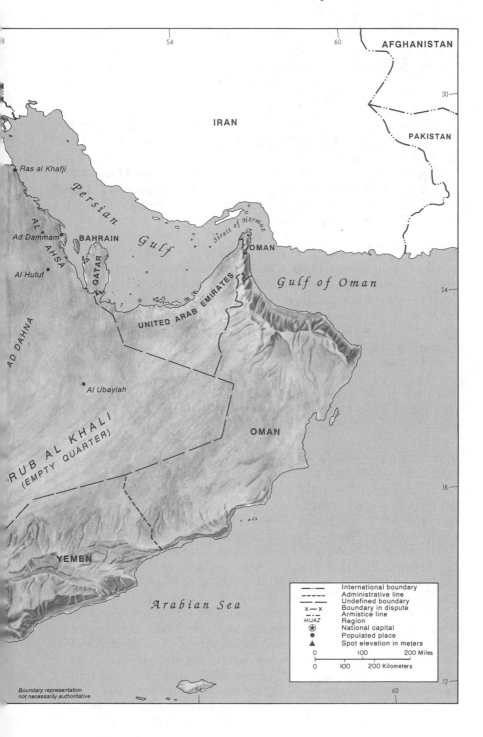

the Ad Dibdibah graveled plain and in the south the Al Jafurah sand desert, which reaches the gulf near Dhahran and merges with the Rub al Khali at its southern end. The coast itself is extremely irregular, merging sandy plains, marshes, and salt flats almost imperceptibly with the sea. As a result, the land surface is unstable; in places water rises almost to the surface, and the sea is shallow, with shoals and reefs extending far offshore. Only the construction of long moles at Ras Tanura has opened the Saudi coast on the gulf to seagoing tankers.

Eastern Arabia is sometimes called Al Ahsa, or Al Hasa, after the great oasis, one of the more fertile areas of the country. Al Ahsa, the largest oasis in the country, actually comprises two neighboring oases, including the town of Al Hufuf.

### The Great Deserts

Three great deserts isolate Najd from north, east, and south as the Red Sea escarpment does from the west. In the north, the An Nafud—sometimes called the Great Nafud because An Nafud is the term for desert—covers about 55,000 square kilometers at an elevation of about 1,000 meters. Longitudinal dunes—scores of kilometers in length and as much as ninety meters high, and separated by valleys as much as sixteen kilometers wide—characterize the An Nafud. Iron oxide gives the sand a red tint, particularly when the sun is low. Within the area are several watering places, and winter rains bring up short-lived but succulent grasses that permit nomadic herding during the winter and spring.

Stretching more than 125 kilometers south from the An Nafud in a narrow arc is the Ad Dahna, a narrow band of sand mountains also called the river of sand. Like the An Nafud, its sand tends to be reddish, particularly in the north, where it shares with the An Nafud the longitudinal structure of sand dunes. The Ad Dahna also furnishes the beduin with winter and spring pasture, although water is scarcer than in the An Nafud.

The southern portion of the Ad Dahna curves westward following the arc of the Jabal Tuwayq. At its southern end, it merges with the Rub al Khali, one of the truly forbidding sand deserts in the world and, until the 1950s, one of the least explored. The topography of this huge area, covering more than 550,000 square kilometers, is varied. In the west, the elevation is about 600 meters, and the sand is fine and soft; in the east, the elevation drops to about 180 meters, and much of the surface is covered by relatively stable sand sheets and salt flats. In places, particularly in the east, longitudinal sand dunes prevail; elsewhere sand mountains as much as 300 meters in height form complex patterns. Most of the area is totally waterless and uninhabited except for a few wandering beduin tribes.

## Water Resources

In the absence of permanent rivers or bodies of water, rainfall, groundwater, desalinated seawater, and very scarce surface water must supply the country's needs. In eastern Arabia and in the Jabal Tuwayq, artesian wells and springs are plentiful. In Al Ahsa a number of large, deep pools are constantly replenished by artesian springs as a result of underground water from the eastern watershed of the Jabal Tuwayq. Such springs and wells permit extensive irrigation in local oases. In the Hijaz and Asir, wells are abundant, and springs are common in the mountainous areas. In Najd and the great deserts, watering places are comparatively fewer and scattered over a wide area. Water must be hoisted or pumped to the surface, and even where water is plentiful, its quality may be poor.

Modern technology has located and increased the availability of much of the underground water. Saudi Arabian Oil Company (Saudi Aramco) technicians have determined that very deep aquifers lie in many areas of northern and eastern Arabia and that the Wasia, the largest aquifer in Saudi Arabia, contains more water than the Persian Gulf. The Saudi government, Saudi Aramco, and the United Nations (UN) Food and Agriculture Organization (FAO) have made separate and joint efforts to exploit underground water resources. In the past, improperly drilled wells have reduced or destroyed any good they might have served by leaching the lands they were drilled to irrigate. Successive agricultural projects, many of which were designed primarily to encourage beduin settlement, have increased water resource exploitation. In the early 1990s, large-scale agricultural projects have relied primarily on such underground aquifers, which provided more than 80 percent of the water for agricultural requirements. In fiscal year (FY—see Glossary) 1987, about 90 percent of the total water demand in the kingdom was consumed by agriculture.

## Climate

With the exception of the province of Asir with its towns of Jizan on the western coast and Najran, Saudi Arabia has a desert climate characterized by extreme heat during the day, an abrupt drop in temperature at night, and slight, erratic rainfall. Because of the influence of a subtropical high-pressure system and the many fluctuations in elevation, there is considerable variation in temperature and humidity. The two main extremes in climate are felt between the coastal lands and the interior.

Along the coastal regions of the Red Sea and the Persian Gulf, the desert temperature is moderated by the proximity of these large bodies of water. Temperatures seldom rise above 38°C, but the relative humidity is usually more than 85 percent and frequently

100 percent for extended periods. This combination produces a hot mist during the day and a warm fog at night. Prevailing winds are from the north, and, when they blow, coastal areas become bearable in the summer and even pleasant in winter. A southerly wind is accompanied invariably by an increase in temperature and humidity and by a particular kind of storm known in the gulf area as a *kauf.* In late spring and early summer, a strong northwesterly wind, the *shamal,* blows; it is particularly severe in eastern Arabia and continues for almost three months. The *shamal* produces sand-storms and dust storms that can decrease visibility to a few meters.

A uniform climate prevails in Najd, Al Qasim Province, and the great deserts. The average summer daytime temperature is 45°C, but readings of up to 54°C are common. The heat becomes intense shortly after sunrise and lasts until sunset, followed by comparatively cool nights. In the winter, the temperature seldom drops below 0°C, but the almost total absence of humidity and the high wind-chill factor make a bitterly cold atmosphere. In the spring and autumn, temperatures average 29°C.

The region of Asir is subject to the southwest monsoon, usually occurring from May through October. An average of 300 millimeters of rainfall occurs during this period—60 percent of the annual total. Additionally, in Asir and the southern Hijaz condensation caused by the higher mountain slopes contributes to the total rainfall.

For the rest of the country, rainfall is low and erratic. The entire year's rainfall may consist of one or two torrential outbursts that flood the wadis and then rapidly disappear into the soil to be trapped above the layers of impervious rock. This is sufficient, however, to sustain forage growth. Although the average rainfall is 100 millimeters per year, whole regions may not experience rainfall for several years. When such droughts occur, as they did in the north in 1957 and 1958, affected areas may become incapable of sustaining either livestock or agriculture.

## The Environment and the 1991 Persian Gulf War

The Persian Gulf War of 1991 brought serious environmental damage to the region. The world's largest oil spill, estimated at as much as 8 million barrels, fouled gulf waters and the coastal areas of Kuwait, Iran, and much of Saudi Arabia's Persian Gulf shoreline. In some of the sections of the Saudi coast that sustained the worst damage, sediments were found to contain 7 percent oil. The shallow areas affected normally provide feeding grounds for birds and feeding and nursery areas for fish and shrimp. Because the plants and animals of the seafloor are the basis of the food chain, damage to the shoreline has consequences for the whole shallow-water ecosystem, including the multimillion-dollar Saudi fisheries industry.

The spill had a severe impact on the coastal area surrounding Madinat al Jubayl as Sinaiyah, the major industrial and population center newly planned and built by the Saudi government. The spill threatened industrial facilities in Al Jubayl because of the seawater cooling system for primary industries and threatened the supply of potable water produced by seawater-fed desalination plants. The Al Jubayl community harbor and Abu Ali Island, which juts into the gulf immediately north of Al Jubayl, experienced the greatest pollution, with the main effect of the spill concentrated in mangrove areas and shrimp grounds. Large numbers of marine birds, such as cormorants, grebes, and auks, were killed when their plumage was coated with oil. In addition, beaches along the entire Al Jubayl coastline were covered with oil and tar balls.

The exploding and burning of approximately 700 oil wells in Kuwait also created staggering levels of atmospheric pollution, spewed oily soot into the surrounding areas, and produced lakes of oil in the Kuwaiti desert equal in volume to twenty times the amount of oil that poured into the gulf, or about 150 million barrels. The soot from the Kuwaiti fires was found in the snows of the Himalayas and in rainfall over the southern members of the Commonwealth of Independent States (former Soviet Union), Iran, Oman, and Turkey. Residents of Riyadh reported that cars and outdoor furniture were covered daily with a coating of oily soot. The ultimate effects of the airborne pollution from the burning wells have yet to be determined, but samples of soil and vegetation in Ras al Khafji in northern Saudi Arabia revealed high levels of particles of oily soot incorporated into the desert ecology. The UN Environmental Programme warned that eating livestock that grazed within an area of 7,000 square kilometers of the fires, or 1,100 kilometers from the center of the fires, an area that included northern Saudi Arabia, posed a danger to human health. The overall effects of the oil spill and the oil fires on marine life, human health, water quality, and vegetation remained to be determined as of 1992. Moreover, to these two major sources of environmental damage must be added large quantities of refuse, toxic materials, and between 173 million and 207 million liters of untreated sewage in sand pits left behind by coalition forces.

# Population

## Saudis and Non-Saudis

Estimates of the population holding Saudi citizenship have varied widely. Official figures published by the Saudi government indicated

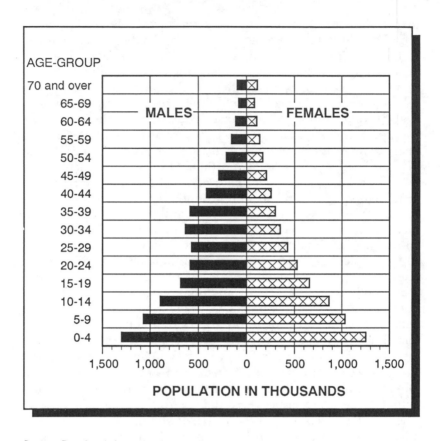

AGE-GROUP

| | MALES | FEMALES |
| 70 and over | | |
| 65-69 | | |
| 60-64 | | |
| 55-59 | | |
| 50-54 | | |
| 45-49 | | |
| 40-44 | | |
| 35-39 | | |
| 30-34 | | |
| 25-29 | | |
| 20-24 | | |
| 15-19 | | |
| 10-14 | | |
| 5-9 | | |
| 0-4 | | |

1,500   1,000   500   0   500   1,000   1,500

**POPULATION IN THOUSANDS**

Source: Based on information from United Nations, *The Sex and Age Distributions of Population,* New York, 1990, 320.

*Figure 5. Population by Age and Sex, 1990*

a population of 14,870,000 in 1990 (see fig. 5). In the same year, however, estimates by one Western source inside the kingdom were as low as 6 million. United Nations estimates were slightly less than the official Saudi figure. Based on the official Saudi figure, at the 1990 rate of growth a population of 20 million was projected by the year 2000. The 1992 Saudi census indicated an indigenous population of 12.3 million people and a growth rate of 3.3 percent.

In addition to the population holding Saudi citizenship, there were large numbers of foreign residents in the kingdom. In 1985 the number of foreigners was estimated at 4,563,000, with a total foreign work force of 3,522,700. In 1990 the number of foreigners had risen to 5,300,000. In 1990 the greatest number of foreign workers came from Arabic-speaking countries, chiefly Egypt, followed by Yemen, Jordan, Syria, Kuwait, and Palestinians, then Pakistan, India, the Philippines, Sri Lanka, and the Republic of Korea (South Korea). About 180,000 came from European countries and 92,000 from North America. Between 1985 and 1990, the number of foreigners employed in the economy rose, in contrast to the substantial decline expected and called for in the Fourth Development Plan (1985–90) (see Five-Year Plans, ch. 3). This increase was reflected in the number of residence permits issued to foreigners, which rose from 563,747 in 1985 to 705,679 in 1990. A goal of Saudi planners continued to be a reduction in the number of foreign workers, and the Fifth Development Plan (1990–95) projected a 1.2 percent annual decline over five years, or a drop of almost 250,000 foreign workers. The 1992 census gave the number of resident foreigners as 4.6 million.

Whether such a decline could occur, or had already begun to occur in 1992, was questionable. From an economic point of view, there were difficulties in increasing the number of Saudi citizens in the work force. One difficulty was that potential Saudi workers for low-skilled and other jobs were becoming less competitive with foreigners in the private sector labor market. Wages of non-Saudi workers had been adjusted downward since the early 1980s, and, with a ready supply of non-Saudis willing to work in low-skilled occupations, the wage gap between Saudis and non-Saudi workers was widening. In addition, as the government recognized, Saudi secondary school and university graduates were not always as qualified as foreign workers for employment in the private sector. Although the Riyadh-based Institute of Public Administration offered training programs to increase the competitiveness of Saudi nationals, the programs had difficulty attracting participants.

Social constraints on the employment of women (7 percent of the work force in 1990) also hampered indigenization of the work force. Government and private groups actively sought ways to expand the areas in which women might work. The issue became more pressing as the number of female university graduates continued to increase at a faster rate than the number of male graduates.

Although such economic and social pressures have militated against increasing the number of Saudi nationals in the work force, the desired decline in foreign labor may have occurred as a result of new residency requirements imposed in the summer of 1990 to encourage the departure of Yemenis, the second largest segment of the foreign labor population. As a punitive response to the government of Yemen's sympathy with Iraq, the Saudi government issued a decree requiring Yemenis, who were previously exempt from regulations governing foreigners' doing business in the kingdom, to obtain residence permits. Subsequently, about 1 million Yemenis left the country. Only three weeks after the decree was issued, the Riyadh Chamber of Commerce announced that there were almost 250,000 jobs, especially in the area of small retail businesses, available for young Saudis as a result of the regulation of foreign residence visas. It was unclear in 1992 whether the types of employment and businesses vacated by Yemenis would prove attractive to Saudi job seekers, or whether these jobs would be recirculated into the foreign labor market.

## Diversity and Social Stratification

The Saudi population is characterized by a high degree of cultural homogeneity and by an equally high degree of social stratification. The territory that in 1992 constituted the Kingdom of Saudi Arabia consisted of four distinct regions and diverse populations. Each region has sustained some measure of nomadic and semi-nomadic population: as recently as 1950, at least one-half the total population of the kingdom was estimated to be nomadic. Tribal identities were paramount among the nomadic population and among those in towns and villages who recognized a tribal affiliation. The Eastern Province had a substantial Shia (see Glossary) population with cultural links to Iran, Bahrain, and other places in the gulf region, as well as an Indian, Yemeni, and black African component (see Shia, this ch.). Asir was more closely linked to Yemen than to Saudi Arabia both by population and geography. Najd was geographically divided into three regions, with town centers that functioned almost as independent city-states until the early twentieth century. Until the era of development began in the 1960s, Najd remained relatively isolated, located as it was in the center of the peninsula in the midst of three deserts and a mountain chain, but its towns, too, had populations linked to the gulf, the Hijaz, and Africa.

By contrast, the Hijaz, being home to the holy sites of Islam and host to pilgrimage traffic, was directly tied historically into the Ottoman bureaucratic system. The populations of Mecca, Medina, and Jiddah have been infused for centuries by descendants of foreign Muslims who had come for the pilgrimage and stayed. Mecca had substantial Indian and Indonesian communities, and Jiddah had descendants of Persians and Hadramis (from Hadramaut, or Aden), as well as Africans and people from other parts of the Arabic-speaking world. The cities of the Hijaz benefited by donations from pious Muslims throughout the world and became major centers of Islamic scholarship and learning. Jiddah was virtually without peer as the commercial center in the kingdom until the 1960s, and in all the Hijaz towns, mercantile families comprised a powerful elite.

Social stratification was linked to this population diversity. Tribal affiliation constituted a major status category based on bloodline. At the top of the tribal status category were the *qabila*, families that could claim purity of descent from one of two eponymous Arab ancestors, Adnan or Qahtan, and could therefore claim to possess *asl*, the honor that stemmed from nobility of origin. To some extent, tribal status could be correlated to occupation, yet manual labor in general, but particularly tanning hides and metal work, was considered demeaning for individuals of *qabila* status. *Qabila* families considered themselves distinct from and distinctly superior to *khadira*, nontribal families, who could not claim *qabila* descent. *Khadira* include most tradesmen, artisans, merchants, and scholars, and constituted the bulk of the urban productive population of pre-oil Arabia. Marriage between individuals of *qabila* and *khadira* status was not normally considered. The claim to *qabila* status was maintained by patrilineal descent; therefore, *qabila* families were concerned to observe strict rules of endogamy (marriage back into the paternal line) so that status might be maintained and children, who were considered to belong to the family of the father, not the mother, would not suffer the taint of mixed blood. Within the *qabila* status group, however, there were status differentials, some groups being considered inferior precisely because they had once intermarried with *khadira* or an *abd* (slave) and were unable to claim purity of descent. The *abd* was at the bottom of the tribal-linked status hierarchy in the past. Black Africans were imported into the peninsula in large numbers to be sold as slaves until the late nineteenth century. Although slavery was not formally abolished until 1962, intermarriage between *khadira* and the black population has been extensive and has blurred social distinctions between the two. In contemporary Saudi Arabia, new status categories based on education and economic advantage began to undermine the importance of tribal affiliation to status and were having an homogenizing effect on this barrier to social integration.

An additional status category based on bloodline was that of *ashraf*, those who claimed descent from the Prophet Muhammad. The *ashraf* (sing., sharif—see Glossary) were significant in the Hijaz but far less so in Najd.

These status categories based on blood have at times in the past and were in the 1990s being transcended by status groups based on religion, commerce, professions, and political power. Religious authority, for example, constituted an additional category of status. The ulama historically have represented a powerful intellectual elite of judges, scholars, imams, notaries, and preachers. Prestige still strongly adhered to religious scholarship and especially to the groups of scholars whose religious authority was recognized by the rulers and who were employed in the government bureaucracy (see Islamism in Saudi Arabia, this ch.; The Ulama, ch. 4). To some extent, as secular education became more valued and greater economic rewards accrued to those with technical and administrative skills, the status of the ulama declined.

Merchants constituted an additional elite status category based on wealth. Many of the traditional merchant class, especially merchants from the Hijaz and the Eastern Province, lost influence as Saudi rulers ceased borrowing from them and began to compete with them, using oil resources to create a new merchant class favoring Najdis. The rulers also used preferential recruitment for administrative personnel from Najdi tribes, who in turn used their position to favor other Najdis and Najdi businesses. The result has been the creation of powerful administrative and commercial classes supplanting older elite groups based outside Najd.

The interest and status of these groups may overlap others. In the Hijaz, members of an elite group known as the *awaali* (first families) claimed group solidarity based on past family connections; their association was actually distinguished by wealth and life-style, and the circle of families was constantly in flux. Families who belonged to the group came from diverse backgrounds and included descendants of religious scholars, merchants, and pilgrimage guides.

The Shia of the Eastern Province were near the low end of the social ladder in relation to the fruits of development and access to sources of power. According to literature produced outside Saudi Arabia, Shia opposition groups were active inside the kingdom and constituted the majority of the political prisoners in Saudi jails. Shia were generally disparaged in society by the Wahhabi (see Glossary) antipathy in which their rituals were held. The status of Shia, however, was in flux: they began to be drawn into positions of responsibility in government service and since the 1980s have received an increased share of government funding for development.

## Cultural Homogeneity and Values

The population was characterized by a high degree of cultural homogeneity. This homogeneity was reflected in a common Arabic language and in adherence to Sunni (see Glossary) Wahhabi Islam, which has been fostered within the political culture promoted by the Saudi monarchy (see Wahhabi Theology, this ch.). Above all, the cultural homogeneity of the kingdom rested in the diffusion of values and attitudes exemplified in the family and in Arabian tribal society, in particular the values and attitudes regarding relations within the family and relations of the family with the rest of society.

The family was the most important social institution in Saudi Arabia. For Saudis generally, the family was the primary basis of identity and status for the individual and the immediate focus of individual loyalty, just as it was among those who recognized a tribal affiliation. Families formed alignments with other families sharing common interests and life-styles, and individuals tended to socialize within the circle of these family alliances. Usually, a family business was open to participation by sons, uncles, and male cousins, and functioned as the social welfare safety net for all members of the extended family.

The structure of the family in Saudi Arabia was generally compatible with the structure of tribal lineage. Families were patrilineal, the boundaries of family membership being drawn around lines of descent through males. Relations with maternal relatives were important, but family identity was tied to the father, and children were considered to belong to him and not to the mother. At its narrowest, a family might therefore be defined as comprising a man, his children, and his children's children through patrilineal descent.

Islamic laws of personal status remained in force in Saudi Arabia without modification, and the patrilineal character of the family was compatible with and supported by these Islamic family laws. Marriage was not a sacrament but a civil contract, which had to be signed by witnesses and which specified an amount of money (*mehr*) to be paid by the husband to the wife. It might further include an agreement for an additional amount to be paid in the event of divorce. The amount of the *mehr* averaged between 25,000 and 40,000 Saudi riyals (for value of the riyal—see Glossary) in the early 1990s, although some couples rejected the *mehr* altogether, stipulating only a token amount to satisfy the legal requirement necessary to validate the marriage contract. The contract might also add other stipulations, such as assuring the wife the right of divorce if the husband should take a second wife. Divorce could usually only be instigated by the husband, and because by law children belonged to the father, who could take custody of them after a certain age (the age varied with the Islamic legal school, but was usually seven for boys and puberty for girls), legally a wife and mother could be detached from her children at the wish of her husband.

When women married, they might become incorporated into the household of the husband but not into his family. A woman did not take her husband's name but kept the name of her father

65

because legally women were considered to belong to the family of their birth throughout their lives. Many in Saudi Arabia interpreted the retention of a woman's maiden name, as well as her retention of control over personal property as allowed under Islamic law, as an indication of women's essential independence from a husband's control under the Islamic system. Legally, a woman's closest male relative, such as a father or brother, was obligated to support her if she were divorced or widowed. Divorce was common.

According to Islamic law, men are permitted to marry as many as four wives. Among the adult generation of educated, Western-oriented elites, polygyny was not practiced. Polygyny was common, however, among some groups, such as the religiously conservative and the older generation of the royal family. In the cities, polygynous households were seen among recent migrants from rural areas. For a family of means, a polygynous housing arrangement usually entailed a separate dwelling unit for each wife and her children. These units might be completely separate houses or houses within a walled family compound, in which case the compound might include a separate house that the men of the family shared and used for male gatherings, such as meals with guests or business meetings.

Because the prerogatives of divorce, polygyny, and child custody lay with the husband, women in Saudi Arabia appeared to be at a considerable disadvantage in marriage. However, these disadvantages were partially offset by a number of factors. The first was that children were attached to mothers, and when children, especially sons, were grown, their ties to the mother secured her a place of permanence in the husband's family. Second, marriages were most often contracted by agreement between families, uniting cousins, or individuals from families seeking to expand their circle of alliances and enhance their prestige, so that a successful marriage was in the interest of, and the desire of, both husband and wife. In addition, Islamic inheritance laws guaranteed a share of inheritance to daughters and wives, so that many women in Saudi Arabia personally held considerable wealth. Because women by law were entitled to full use of their own money and property, they had economic independence to cushion the impact of divorce, should it occur. Most important, custody of children was in practice a matter for family discussion, not an absolute regulated by religion. Furthermore, judges of the sharia courts, according to informal observations, responded with sympathy and reason when women attempted to initiate divorce proceedings or request the support of the court in family-related disputes.

Families in Saudi Arabia, like families throughout the Middle East, tended to be patriarchal, the father in the family appearing as an authoritarian figure at the top of a hierarchy based on age and sex. Undergirding the patriarchal family were cultural and religious values that permeated the society as a whole, and that found their clearest expression in tribal values and practices. Families shared a sense of corporate identity, and the esteem of the family was measured by the individual's capacity to live up to socially prescribed ideals of honor.

The values and practices inherent in these ideals, as well as adherence to Islam, were at the heart of the cultural homogeneity among the diverse peoples—tribal and nontribal—of the kingdom. The society as a whole valued behavior displaying generosity, selflessness, and hospitality; deference to those above in the hierarchy of the family; freedom from dependence on others and mastery over one's emotions; and a willingness to support other family members and assume responsibility for their errors as well. An example of the sense of corporate responsibility binding Arabian families may be seen in an incident that occurred in the 1970s in a Hijazi village. Although this incident occurred among beduin who were recently settled, the group solidarity illustrated was applicable to the Arabian family in general as well as to those united by tribal affiliation. An automobile accident took the life of a young boy, and the driver of the car was obligated to pay compensation to the boy's father. The family of the driver, although indigent, was able to borrow the money from a local merchant and present it to the boy's father in a ceremony "to forgive." Afterward, delegated members of the tribe assumed the responsibility of collecting money toward repayment of the compensation from all the people in the tribe, who happened to include close relatives of the boy who was killed. In this way, all parties to the tragedy were satisfied that the best interests of the extended family/tribal group had been served in serving the interests of an individual member.

Chastity and sexual modesty were also very highly valued. Applied primarily to women, these values not only were tied to family honor but also were held to be a religious obligation. Specific Quranic verses enjoin modesty upon women and, to a lesser degree, upon men; and women are viewed as being responsible for sexual temptation (*fitna*). Although this attitude is ancient in the Middle East and found to some degree throughout the area in modern times, it has taken on religious significance in Islam through interpretations of Muslim theologians.

The veiling and separation of women were considered mechanisms to ensure sexual modesty and avoid *fitna*. In practice, the effect of veiling and separation also ensured the continuing dependence of women on men. Some families adopted more liberal standards than others in defining the extent of veiling and separation, but the underlying value of sexual modesty was almost universal. Because the separation of women from unrelated men was accepted as a moral imperative, most activities of a woman outside her home required the mediation of a servant or a man; for example, if a woman should not be seen, how could she apply for a government housing loan in an office staffed by men? In fact, how could she get to the government office without a servant or a man to take her, because women were not allowed to drive. The continuing dependence of women on men, in effect, perpetuated the family as a patriarchal unit. Control of women ensured female chastity and thus family honor as well as the patrilineal character of the family. In Saudi society in general, the role of women was basic to maintaining the structure of the family and therefore of society.

## Structure of Tribal Groupings

Almost all nomadic people are organized in tribal associations, the exceptions being the *saluba,* the tinkers and traders of the desert, and black beduin, descendants of former slaves. Not all tribal people, however, are beduin because urban and agricultural peoples may maintain tribal identities.

Structurally, tribal groups are defined by common patrilineal descent that unites individuals in increasingly larger segments. The lineage is the unit that shares joint responsibility for avenging the wrongs its members may suffer and, conversely, paying compensation to anyone whom its members have aggrieved. Although tribes may differ in their status, all lineages of a given tribe are considered equal. Water wells, aside from the newer deep wells drilled by the government, are held in common by lineages. Among nomads, lineage membership is the basis of summer camps; all animals, although owned by individual households, bear the lineage's brand. The lineage is the nexus between the individual and the tribe. To be ostracized by one's lineage leaves the individual little choice but to sever all tribal links; it is to lose the central element in one's social identity.

Above the level of lineage, there are three to five larger segments that together make up the tribe. Donald Cole, an anthropologist who studied the Al (see Glossary) Murrah, a tribe of camel-herding nomads in eastern and southern Arabia, notes that four to six patrilineally related lineages are grouped together in a clan (seven clans comprise the Al Murrah tribe). However the subdivisions of a tribe are defined, they are formed by adding larger and larger groups of patrilineally related kin. The system permits lineages to locate themselves relative to all other groups on a "family tree."

In practice, effective lineage and tribal membership reflect ecological and economic constraints. Among nomads, those who summer together are considered to be a lineage's effective membership. On the individual level, adoption is, and long has been, a regular occurrence. A man from an impoverished lineage will sometimes join his wife's group. His children will be considered members of their mother's lineage, although this contravenes the rules of patrilineal descent.

The process of adjusting one's view of genealogical relationships to conform to the existing situation applies upward to larger and larger sections of a tribe. Marriages and divorces increase the number of possible kin to whom an individual can trace a link and, concomitantly, of the ways in which one can view potential alliances and genealogical relationships. The vicissitudes of time, the history of tribal migrations, the tendency of groups to segment into smaller units, the adoption of client tribes by those stronger, a smaller tribe's use of the name of one more illustrious—all tend to make tenuous the tie between actual descent and the publicly accepted view of genealogy. At every level of tribal organization, genealogical "fudging" brings existing sociopolitical relationships into conformity with the rules of patrilineal descent. The genealogical map, therefore, is as much a description of extant social relations as a statement of actual lines of descent.

## Tribe and Monarchy

The rise of the centralized state has undercut tribal autonomy, and sedentarization has undermined the economic benefits of tribal organization, but in the 1990s the tribe remained a central focus of identity for those claiming a tribal affiliation. Contemporary tribal leadership continued to play a pivotal role in relations between individuals and the central government, particularly among those who were recently settled or still nomadic.

The tribal leader, the shaykh (see Glossary), governs by consensus. Shaykhs acquire influence through their ability to mediate disputes and persuade their peers toward a given course of action. The qualities their position demands are a detailed grasp of tribal affairs, a reputation for giving good advice, and generosity. Shaykhs are essentially arbitrators; the process of resolving disputes reflects the tribe's egalitarian ethos. Shaykhs do not lead discussions but carefully ascertain everyone's opinion on a given question. Consensus is necessary before action is taken. To force a decision is to undermine one's influence; leaders are effective only as long as they conform to the tribe's expectations.

Tribal leaders in the past brokered relationships among competing tribes and clans. Raiding was a mechanism of economic redistribution that conferred status on strong and successful raiding clans. Tribes or lineages could opt out of the round of raiding and counterraiding by seeking the protection of a stronger, more militarily oriented group. The protected paid their protector an agreed sum (*khuwa*), in return for which their lives and property were to be spared. The shaykh who accepted *khuwa* was obliged to safeguard those who paid it or compensate them for whatever damages they incurred. As with the booty of raiding, the shaykh who accepted the payment could only guarantee this influence by distributing it to his fellow tribesmen. These client-patron relationships based on payment of protection money were undermined by Abd al Aziz in the 1920s when he released weaker tribes from obligations to stronger ones and made himself the sole source of wealth redistributed from the spoils of raiding, and then later from oil profits.

The working relationship between the monarchy and tribal leaders is viewed in much the same framework as the traditional relationship between the shaykh and tribal members. In fact, the same framework of the relationship between tribal shaykh and tribal members is the model for the ideal relationship between the monarchy and all Saudi citizens. Just as the tribal shaykh was expected to mediate disputes and assure the welfare of his group by receiving tribute and dispensing largess, governors in the provinces and the king himself continue the custom of holding an open audience (majlis—see Glossary) at which any tribesman or other male citizen could gain a hearing. The largess of the shaykh was dispensed not as direct handouts of food or clothing, as in the past, but through the institutions of the state bureaucracy in the form of free medical care, welfare payments, grants for housing, lucrative contracts, and government jobs.

The tribes of Arabia acknowledged the political authority of the Saudi monarchy as being above the tribal group. Loyalty to the state was not a matter of nationality or still less an abstract notion of citizenship; it was a matter of loyalty to the Al Saud (see Glossary) and to the royal family as the focus of the Islamic nation. In a study of the Al Murrah, Nicholas Hopkins notes that "The Al Murrah make a distinction between al-Dawlah (the state or bureaucracy) and al-Hukumah (the Saudi royal family or governors); they are loyal to the latter and fearful of the former, but fear that the state is taking over the government." Most tribes were affiliated with the Al Saud through marriage ties as the product of Abd al Aziz's deliberate policy of cementing ties between himself and the tribal groups. In the 1970s and 1980s, the political alliance between tribe and state was reinforced by marrying tribal women to government officials and Saudi princes. According to a 1981 study carried out among the Al Saar beduin in southern Arabia, these marriages were encouraged by tribal leaders because they were seen as a means of ensuring continuing access to government leaders.

Tribal solidarity has been institutionalized and tribal ties to both *dawlah* and *hukumah* have been cemented through the national guard. The amir of the Al Murrah tribal unit studied by Hopkins was the head of a national guard unit composed mainly of Al Murrah, and most Al Murrah families in the unit under study had at least one family member serving in the national guard. Through the national guard, former nomads received training and the potential for high-level careers, as well as instruction in military sciences, and housing, health, and social services for dependents and families. The government also provided water taps and markets in cities, towns, and villages that were used in marketing livestock. Also provided were veterinary services, subsidized fodder, and buildings for storage.

## Beduin Economy in Tradition and Change

The word *beduin* is derived from the Arabic word *bawaadin* (sing., *baadiya*), meaning nomads, and is usually associated with a camel-herding life in the desert. The word, therefore, describes an occupation and is not synonymous with the word *tribe* (*qabila*), despite the fact that the two are often used interchangeably. The word *bawaadin*, furthermore, not only refers to camel-herding but also is an elastic term that is understood in relation to *hadar*, or settled people. People from the city, for example, are likely to view villagers as part of the *bawaadin*, but the villager considers only the nomadic people as *bawaadin*. Villagers and nomads, on the other hand, make a distinction between shepherds who tend sheep and goats, staying close by the village, and the beduin who raise camels. ''While the physical boundary between the desert and the sown is strikingly sharp in the Middle East . . '' notes Donald Cole, ''the boundary between nomadic pastoralist and sedentary farmer is less precise.'' Beduin and farmers are united in a single social system. Each relies on the other for critical goods and services to sustain a way of life; they share substantial cultural unity. Tribal loyalties transcend differences in livelihood; many tribes have both sedentary and nomadic branches.

There is a nomadic-sedentary continuum: at one extreme are completely settled farmers and merchants; at the other are camel herders who produce primarily for their own consumption and have little recourse to wage labor. A host of finely graded distinctions exist between the two extremes. Wealthy beduin frequently established a branch of the family in an oasis with commercial and agricultural investments. Individual households moved along the continuum as their domestic situation changed. Part of the family might settle to attend school, while others maintained the family's flocks.

Among nomads there is a dichotomy—as well as a status differential—between those who herd sheep and goats and those who herd camels. Because sheep and goats are more demanding in their need for water and thus more limited in their migrations, their herders migrate shorter distances and have greater contact with the oasis population. Camels, on the other hand, can endure much longer periods without water, and camel herders are thereby able to range much more widely than other pastoralists. Camel-herding tribes were usually the most powerful militarily and had more status than other herders.

Alliances between beduin and townsmen have historically been a defining feature of the politics of the peninsula. Just as beduin could opt out of raiding a particular town, the town could pay an agreed *khuwa,* the payment being the exchange of a portion of their surplus production for a guarantee of peace.

At the same time that town and village relied on nomad protection, nomads themselves relied on the sedentary populace for sustenance and diverse services. Nomadism has never been a self-contained system. Even camel-herding beduin relied on the oasis population for a variety of needs. Their diet was supplemented with dates, grains, and, more recently, processed foods together with such essentials as tent fibers and tent pins. Further, the sedentary population provided medical care when home remedies failed, as well as education facilities and religious leadership. Farmers who owned animals entrusted them to nomads' care and the nomads in turn received the animals' milk; beduin left their date palms in the farmers' hands in return for a portion of the harvest.

Development policies in Saudi Arabia have encouraged the sedentarization of most nomadic groups in the kingdom. The percentage of fully nomadic people is unknown, but it was certainly declining in the early 1990s. Those who continued to maintain their livestock faced economic difficulties in spite of government assistance. The rise in the cost of living in Saudi Arabia, coupled with the decline in the commercial value of camels and other

*Beduin father and son*
*Courtesy Saudi Aramco*
*Beduin driving camels*
*Courtesy* Aramco World

73

livestock, occasioned a need for greater cash income. Consequently, beduin men had begun migrating to the cities for wage work, often as drivers of cars, trucks, and tractors. They frequently left their families behind to tend the animals.

A study among Al Saar beduin shows that urban migration of men resulted in increased work for women and, at the same time, denied them the economic benefits of government programs designed to improve the welfare of nomadic families. With the family together, women generally tended only the sheep and goats; men herded the camels. In addition to caring for animals, producing food, and caring for the household, nomadic women also engaged in crafts, primarily weaving household textiles, such as mats, tent cloth, tent dividers, and sacks to contain their belongings.

The women in the study were left alone with children and had total responsibility for caring for all the animals, camels as well as sheep and goats, while their husbands remained in the towns as much as six months at a time. However, because they were not entitled to a separate citizenship card, being listed as dependents on their husbands' citizenship cards, they were unable to apply for livestock subsidies or for land or home loans issued through government-run service centers near their summer grazing areas. Similarly, women were denied use of the pickup truck, now ubiquitous among nomadic families and indispensable for transporting wood and water and for transportation between the encampment and the herds as well as to government service centers. Although the burden of labor was left to women, they could use trucks only in the desert where they could not be seen by government authorities because women were not allowed to drive.

One result of the increased burden on women has been the social reorganization of labor based on the combined efforts of women. Women with infants tended to carry out traditional female work of child care and food preparation, whereas older women, widows, and women without infants cared for the herds and also sold their animals at the service stations, another task traditionally the responsibility of men.

# Religion

## Early Development of Islam

The vast majority of the people of Saudi Arabia are Sunni Muslims. Islam is the established religion, and as such its institutions receive government support. In the early seventh century, Muhammad, a merchant from the Hashimite branch of the ruling Quraysh tribe in the Arabian town of Mecca, began to preach the first of a series of revelations that Muslims believe were granted him by God through the angel Gabriel. He stressed monotheism and denounced the polytheism of his fellow Meccans.

Because Mecca's economy was based in part on a thriving pilgrimage business to the Kaaba, the sacred structure around a black meteorite, and the numerous pagan shrines located there, Muhammad's vigorous and continuing censure eventually earned him the bitter enmity of the town's leaders. In 622 he was invited to the town of Yathrib, which came to be known as Medina (the city) because it was the center of his activities. The move, or *hijra* (see Glossary), known in the West as the hegira, marks the beginning of the Islamic era. The Muslim calendar, based on the lunar year, begins in 622. In Medina, Muhammad—by this time known as the Prophet—continued to preach, defeated his detractors in battle, and consolidated both the temporal and spiritual leadership of all Arabia in his person before his death in 632.

After Muhammad's death, his followers compiled those of his words regarded as coming directly from God into the Quran, the holy scripture of Islam. Other sayings and teachings of his and his companions as recalled by those who had known Muhammad, became the hadith (see Glossary). The precedent of his personal deeds and utterances was set forth in the sunna. Together the Quran, the hadith, and the sunna form a comprehensive guide to the spiritual, ethical, and social life of an orthodox Sunni Muslim.

During his life, Muhammad was both spiritual and temporal leader of the Muslim community; he established Islam as a total, all-encompassing way of life for individuals and society. Islam historically recognizes no distinction between religion and state, and no distinction between religious and secular life or religious and secular law. A comprehensive system of religious law (the sharia—see Glossary) developed during the first four centuries of Islam, primarily through the accretion of precedent and interpretation by various judges and scholars. During the tenth century, however, legal opinion began to harden into authoritative doctrine, and the figurative *bab al ijtihad* (gate of interpretation) gradually closed, thenceforth limiting flexibility in Sunni Islamic law.

After Muhammad's death, the leaders of the Muslim community chose Abu Bakr, the Prophet's father-in-law and one of his earliest followers, as caliph, or successor. At the time, some persons favored Ali, the Prophet's cousin and husband of his daughter Fatima, but Ali and his supporters (the so-called Shiat Ali or Party of Ali) eventually recognized the community's choice. The next two caliphs—Umar, who succeeded in 634, and Uthman, who took power in 644—were acknowledged by the entire community.

When Ali finally succeeded to the caliphate in 656, Muawiyah, governor of Syria, rebelled in the name of his murdered kinsman Uthman. After the ensuing civil war, Ali moved his capital to Mesopotamia, where a short time later he, too, was murdered.

Ali's death ended the period in which the entire community of Islam recognized a single caliph. Upon Ali's death, Muawiyah proclaimed himself caliph from Damascus. The Shiat Ali, however, refused to recognize Muawiyah or his line, the Umayyad caliphs; in support of a caliphate based on descent from the Prophet, they withdrew and established a dissident sect known as the Shia.

Originally political in nature, the differences between the Sunni and Shia interpretations gradually assumed theological and metaphysical overtones. Ali's two sons, Hasan and Husayn, became martyred heroes to the Shia and repositories of the claims of Ali's line to mystical preeminence among Muslims. The Sunnis retained the doctrine of the selection of leaders by consensus, although Arabs and members of the Quraysh, Muhammad's tribe, predominated in the early years.

Reputed descent from the Prophet continued to carry social and religious prestige throughout the Muslim world in the early 1990s. Meanwhile, disagreements among Shia over who of several pretenders had a truer claim to the mystical powers of Ali produced further schisms. Some Shia groups developed doctrines of divine leadership far removed from the strict monotheism of early Islam, including beliefs in hidden but divinely chosen leaders with spiritual powers that equaled or surpassed those of the Prophet himself. The main sect of Shia became known as Twelvers because they recognized Ali and eleven of his direct descendants (see The Middle Ages, 700–1500, ch. 1).

The early Islamic polity was intensely expansionist, fueled both by fervor for the new religion and by economic and social factors. Conquering armies and migrating tribes swept out of Arabia, spreading Islam. By the end of Islam's first century, Islamic armies had reached far into North Africa and eastward and northward into Asia.

Although Muhammad had enjoined the Muslim community to convert the infidel, he had also recognized the special status of the "people of the book," Jews and Christians, whose scriptures he considered revelations of God's word that contributed in some measure to Islam. Inhabiting the Arabian Peninsula in Muhammad's time were Christians, Jews, and Hanifs, believers in an indigenous form of monotheism who are mentioned in the Quran. Medina had a substantial Jewish population, and villages of Jews dotted the Medina oases. Clusters of Christian monasteries were located in the northern Hijaz, and Christians were known to have visited seventh-century Mecca. Some Arabic-speaking tribal people were Christian, including some from the Najdi interior and the Ghassanids and Lakhmids on the Arabian borderlands with the Byzantine Empire. Najran, a city in the southwest of present-day Saudi Arabia, had a mixed population of Jews, Christians, and pagans, and had been ruled by a Jewish king only fifty years before Muhammad's birth. In sixth-century Najran, Christianity was well established and had a clerical hierarchy of nuns, priests, bishops, and laity. Furthermore, there were Christian communities along the gulf, especially in Bahrain, Oman, and Aden (in present-day Yemen).

Jews and Christians in Muslim territories could live according to their religious law, in their communities, and were exempted from military service if they accepted the position of *dhimmis,* or tolerated subject peoples. This status entailed recognition of Muslim authority, additional taxes, prohibition on proselytism among Muslims, and certain restrictions on political rights.

## Tenets of Islam

The *shahada* (testimony) succinctly states the central belief of Islam: "There is no god but God (Allah), and Muhammad is his Prophet." This simple profession of faith is repeated on many ritual occasions, and its recital in full and unquestioning sincerity designates one a Muslim. The God of Muhammad's preaching was not a new deity; Allah is the Arabic term for God, not a particular name. Muhammad denied the existence of the many minor gods and spirits worshiped before his prophecy, and he declared the omnipotence of the unique creator, God. Islam means submission to God, and one who submits is a Muslim. Being a Muslim also involves a commitment to realize the will of God on earth and to obey God's law.

Muhammad is the "seal of the Prophets"; his revelation is said to complete for all time the series of biblical revelations received by Jews and Christians. Muslims believe God to have remained the same throughout time, but that men strayed from his true teaching until set right by Muhammad. Prophets and sages of the biblical tradition, such as Abraham (Ibrahim), Moses (Musa), and Jesus (Isa), are recognized as inspired vehicles of God's will. Islam, however, reveres as sacred only the message, rejecting Christianity's deification of Christ. It accepts the concepts of guardian angels, the Day of Judgment, general resurrection, heaven and hell, and eternal life of the soul.

The duties of the Muslim—corporate acts of worship—form the five pillars of Islamic faith. These are *shahada,* affirmation of the faith; *salat,* daily prayer; *zakat,* almsgiving; *sawm,* fasting during the month of Ramadan; and hajj, pilgrimage to Mecca. These acts of worship must be performed with a conscious intent, not out of habit. *Shahada* is uttered daily by practicing Muslims, affirming their membership in the faith and expressing an acceptance of the monotheism of Islam and the divinity of Muhammad's message.

The believer is to pray in a prescribed manner after purification through ritual ablutions at dawn, midday, midafternoon, sunset, and nightfall. Prescribed bows and prostrations accompany the prayers, which the worshiper recites facing Mecca. Prayers imbue daily life with worship, and the day is structured around religious observance. Whenever possible, men pray in congregation at the mosque under a prayer leader. On Fridays, the practice is obligatory. Women may attend public worship at the mosque, where they are segregated from the men, but women most frequently pray at home. A special functionary, the muezzin, intones a call to prayer to the entire community at the appropriate hours; those out of earshot determine the proper time from the position of the sun.

In the early days of Islam, the authorities imposed a tax on personal property proportionate to one's wealth; this tax was distributed to the mosques and to the needy. In addition, free-will gifts were made. Although still a duty of the believer, almsgiving in the twentieth century has become a more private matter. Properties contributed by pious individuals to support religious activities are usually administered as a religious foundation, or waqf (see Glossary).

The ninth month of the Muslim calendar is Ramadan, a period of obligatory fasting that commemorates Muhammad's receipt of God's revelation, the Quran. Fasting is an act of self-discipline that leads to piety and expresses submission and commitment to God. Fasting underscores the equality of all Muslims, strengthening sentiments of community. During Ramadan all but the sick, weak, pregnant or nursing women, soldiers on duty, travelers on necessary journeys, and young children are enjoined from eating, drinking, or smoking during the day. Official work hours often are shortened during this period, and some businesses close for all or part of the day. Because the lunar calendar is eleven days shorter than the solar calendar, Ramadan revolves through the seasons over the years. When Ramadan falls in the summertime, a fast imposes considerable hardship on those who must do physical work. Each day's fast ends with a signal that light is insufficient to distinguish a black thread from a white one. Id al Fitr, a three-day feast and holiday, ends the month of Ramadan and is the occasion of much visiting.

Finally, Muslims at least once in their lifetime should, if possible, make the hajj to the holy city of Mecca to participate in special rites held during the twelfth month of the lunar calendar. The Prophet instituted this requirement, modifying pre-Islamic custom to emphasize sites associated with Allah and Abraham, father of the Arabs through his son Ismail (also known as Ishmael). The pilgrim, dressed in two white, seamless pieces of cloth (*ihram*) performs various traditional rites (see Pilgrimage, this ch.) These rites affirm the Muslim's obedience to God and express intent to renounce the past and begin a new righteous life in the path of God. The returning male pilgrim is entitled to the honorific "hajj" before his name and a woman the honorific "hajji." Id al Adha, the feast of sacrifice, marks the end of the hajj month.

The permanent struggle for the triumph of the word of God on earth, jihad, represents an additional duty of all Muslims. This concept is often taken to mean holy war, but most Muslims see it as a struggle in the way of God. Besides regulating relations between the individual and God, Islam regulates the relations of one individual to another. Aside from specific duties, Islam imposes a code of ethical conduct encouraging generosity, fairness, honesty, and respect. It also explicitly propounds guidance as to what constitutes proper family relations and it forbids adultery, gambling, usury, and the consumption of carrion, blood, pork, and alcohol.

A Muslim stands in a personal relationship to God; there is neither intermediary nor clergy in orthodox Islam. Men who lead prayers, preach sermons, and interpret the law do so by virtue of their superior knowledge and scholarship rather than because of any special powers or prerogatives conferred by ordination. Any adult male versed in the prayer form is entitled to lead prayers—a role referred to as imam (see Glossary).

During the formative period of Islamic law, four separate Sunni schools developed and survived. These schools differ in the extent to which they admit usage of each of the four sources of law: the Quran, the sunna or custom of the Prophet, reasoning by analogy, and the consensus of religious scholars. The Hanafi school, named after Imam Abu Hanifa, predominates in the territories formerly under the Ottoman Empire and in Muslim India and Pakistan; it relies heavily on consensus and analogical reasoning in addition to the Quran and sunna. The Maliki school, named after Malik ibn Anas, is dominant in upper Egypt and West Africa;

developed in Medina, it emphasizes use of hadith that were current in the Prophet's city. The school of Muhammad ibn Idris ash Shafii, prevailing in Indonesia, stresses reasoning by analogy.

The fourth legal school is that of Ahmad ibn Hanbal (d. 855), which is the school adhered to in Saudi Arabia. The Hanbali school has attracted the smallest following because it rejects the use of analogy as well as the consensus of judicial opinion except as recorded by the jurists of the first three centuries of Islam. However, an important principle in Hanbali thought is that things are assumed to be pure or allowable unless first proved otherwise.

## Wahhabi Theology

The political and cultural environment of contemporary Saudi Arabia has been influenced by a religious movement that began in central Arabia in the mid-eighteenth century. This movement, commonly known as the Wahhabi movement, grew out of the scholarship and preaching of Muhammad ibn Abd al Wahhab, a scholar of Islamic jurisprudence who had studied in Mesopotamia and the Hijaz before returning to his native Najd to preach his message of Islamic reform.

Muhammad ibn Abd al Wahhab was concerned with the way the people of Najd engaged in practices he considered polytheistic, such as praying to saints; making pilgrimages to tombs and special mosques; venerating trees, caves, and stones; and using votive and sacrificial offerings. He was also concerned by what he viewed as a laxity in adhering to Islamic law and in performing religious devotions, such as indifference to the plight of widows and orphans, adultery, lack of attention to obligatory prayers, and failure to allocate shares of inheritance fairly to women.

When Muhammad ibn Abd al Wahhab began to preach against these breaches of Islamic laws, he characterized customary practices as *jahiliyah,* the same term used to describe the ignorance of Arabians before the Prophet. Initially, his preaching encountered opposition, but he eventually came under the protection of a local chieftain named Muhammad ibn Saud, with whom he formed an alliance. The endurance of the Wahhabi movement's influence may be attributed to the close association between the founder of the movement and the politically powerful Al Saud in southern Najd (see The Al Saud and Wahhabi Islam, 1500–1818, ch. 1).

This association between the Al Saud and the Al ash Shaykh, as Muhammad ibn Abd al Wahhab and his descendants came to be known, effectively converted political loyalty into a religious obligation. According to Muhammad ibn Abd al Wahhab's teachings, a Muslim must present a *bayah,* or oath of allegiance, to a

Muslim ruler during his lifetime to ensure his redemption after death. The ruler, conversely, is owed unquestioned allegiance from his people so long as he leads the community according to the laws of God. The whole purpose of the Muslim community is to become the living embodiment of God's laws, and it is the responsibility of the legitimate ruler to ensure that people know God's laws and live in conformity to them.

Muhammad ibn Saud turned his capital, Ad Diriyah, into a center for the study of religion under the guidance of Muhammad ibn Abd al Wahhab and sent missionaries to teach the reformed religion throughout the peninsula, the gulf, and into Syria and Mesopotamia. Together they began a jihad against the backsliding Muslims of the peninsula. Under the banner of religion and preaching the unity of God and obedience to the just Muslim ruler, the Al Saud by 1803 had expanded their dominion across the peninsula from Mecca to Bahrain, installing teachers, schools, and the apparatus of state power. So successful was the alliance between the Al ash Shaykh and the Al Saud that even after the Ottoman sultan had crushed Wahhabi political authority and had destroyed the Wahhabi capital of Ad Diriyah in 1818, the reformed religion remained firmly planted in the settled districts of southern Najd and of Jabal Shammar in the north. It would become the unifying ideology in the peninsula when the Al Saud rose to power again in the next century.

Central to Muhammad ibn Abd al Wahhab's message was the essential oneness of God (*tawhid*). The movement is therefore known by its adherents as *ad dawa lil tawhid* (the call to unity), and those who follow the call are known as *ahl at tawhid* (the people of unity) or *muwahhidun* (unitarians). The word *Wahhabi* was originally used derogatorily by opponents, but has today become commonplace and is even used by some Najdi scholars of the movement.

Muhammad ibn Abd al Wahhab's emphasis on the oneness of God was asserted in contradistinction to *shirk,* or polytheism, defined as the act of associating any person or object with powers that should be attributed only to God. He condemned specific acts that he viewed as leading to *shirk,* such as votive offerings, praying at saints' tombs and at graves, and any prayer ritual in which the supplicant appeals to a third party for intercession with God. Particularly objectionable were certain religious festivals, including celebrations of the Prophet's birthday, Shia mourning ceremonies, and Sufi mysticism. Consequently, the Wahhabis forbid grave markers or tombs in burial sites and the building of any shrines that could become a locus of *shirk.*

The extensive condemnation of *shirk* is seen in the movement's iconoclasm, which persisted into the twentieth century, most notably with the conquest of At Taif in the Hijaz. A century earlier, in 1802, Wahhabi fighters raided and damaged one of the most sacred Shia shrines, the tomb of Husayn, the son of Imam Ali and grandson of the Prophet, at Karbala in Iraq. In 1804 the Wahhabis destroyed tombs in the cemetery of the holy men in Medina, which was a locus for votive offerings and prayers to the saints.

Following the legal school of Ahmad ibn Hanbal, Wahhabi ulama accept the authority only of the Quran and sunna. The Wahhabi ulama reject reinterpretation of Quran and sunna in regard to issues clearly settled by the early jurists. By rejecting the validity of reinterpretation, Wahhabi doctrine is at odds with the Muslim reformation movement of the late nineteenth and twentieth centuries. This movement seeks to reinterpret parts of the Quran and sunna to conform with standards set by the West, most notably standards relating to gender relations, family law, and participatory democracy. However, ample scope for reinterpretation remains for Wahhabi jurists in areas not decided by the early jurists. King Fahd ibn Abd al Aziz Al Saud has repeatedly called for scholars to engage in *ijtihad* to deal with new situations confronting the modernizing kingdom.

The Wahhabi movement in Najd was unique in two respects: first, the ulama of Najd interpreted the Quran and sunna very literally and often with a view toward reinforcing parochial Najdi practices; second, the political and religious leadership exercised its collective political will to enforce conformity in behavior. Muhammad ibn Abd al Wahhab asserted that there were three objectives for Islamic government and society; these objectives have been reaffirmed over the succeeding two centuries in missionary literature, sermons, *fatwa* (see Glossary) rulings, and in Wahhabi explications of religious doctrine. According to Muhammad ibn Abd al Wahhab the objectives were "to believe in Allah, enjoin good behavior, and forbid wrongdoing."

Under Al Saud rule, governments, especially during the Wahhabi revival in the 1920s, have shown their capacity and readiness to enforce compliance with Islamic laws and interpretations of Islamic values on themselves and others. The literal interpretations of what constitutes right behavior according to the Quran and hadith have given the Wahhabis the sobriquet of "Muslim Calvinists." To the Wahhabis, for example, performance of prayer that is punctual, ritually correct, and communally performed not only is urged but also is publicly required of men. Consumption of wine is forbidden to the believer because wine is literally forbidden in the

Quran. Under the Wahhabis, however, the ban extended to all intoxicating drinks and other stimulants, including tobacco. Modest dress is prescribed for both men and women in accordance with the Quran, but the Wahhabis specify the type of clothing that should be worn, especially by women, and forbid the wearing of silk and gold, although the latter ban has been enforced only sporadically. Music and dancing have also been forbidden by the Wahhabis at times, as have loud laughter and demonstrative weeping, particularly at funerals.

The Wahhabi emphasis on conformity makes of external appearance and behavior a visible expression of inward faith. Therefore, whether one conforms in dress, in prayer, or in a host of other activities becomes a public statement of whether one is a true Muslim. Because adherence to the true faith is demonstrable in tangible ways, the Muslim community can visibly judge the quality of a person's faith by observing that person's actions. In this sense, public opinion becomes a regulator of individual behavior. Therefore, within the Wahhabi community, which is striving to be the collective embodiment of God's laws, it is the responsibility of each Muslim to look after the behavior of his neighbor and to admonish him if he goes astray.

To ensure that the community of the faithful will "enjoin what is right and forbid what is wrong," morals enforcers known as *mutawwiin* (literally, "those who volunteer or obey") have been integral to the Wahhabi movement since its inception. *Mutawwiin* have served as missionaries, as enforcers of public morals, and as "public ministers of the religion" who preach in the Friday mosque. Pursuing their duties in Jiddah in 1806, the *mutawwiin* were observed to be "constables for the punctuality of prayers . . . with an enormous staff in their hand, [who] were ordered to shout, to scold and to drag people by the shoulders to force them to take part in public prayers, five times a day." In addition to enforcing male attendance at public prayer, the *mutawwiin* also have been responsible for supervising the closing of shops at prayer time, for looking out for infractions of public morality such as playing music, smoking, drinking alcohol, having hair that is too long (men) or uncovered (women), and dressing immodestly.

In the first quarter of the century, promoting Wahhabism was an asset to Abd al Aziz in forging cohesion among the tribal peoples and districts of the peninsula. By reviving the notion of a community of believers, united by their submission to God, Wahhabism helped to forge a sense of common identity that was to supersede parochial loyalties. By abolishing the tribute paid by inferior tribes to militarily superior tribes, Abd al Aziz undercut traditional hierarchies of power and made devotion to Islam and to himself as the rightly guided Islamic ruler the glue that would hold his kingdom together. In the early 1990s, unity in Islam of the Muslim *umma* (community) under Al Saud leadership was the basis for the legitimacy of the Saudi state.

The promotion of Islam as embracing every aspect of life accounted in large measure for the success of Wahhabi ideology in inspiring the zealotry of the Ikhwan movement. Beginning in 1912, agricultural communities called *hujar* (collective pl.) were settled by beduin who came to believe that in settling on the land they were fulfilling the prerequisite for leading Muslim lives; they were making a *hijra,* "the journey from the land of unbelief to the land of belief." It is still unclear whether the Ikhwan settlements were initiated by Abd al Aziz or whether he co-opted the movement once it had begun, but the settlements became military cantonments in the service of Abd al Aziz's consolidation of power. Although the Ikhwan had very limited success in agriculture, they could rely on a variety of subsidies derived from raids under the aegis of Abd al Aziz and provisions disbursed directly from his storehouses in Riyadh.

As newly converted Wahhabi Muslims, the Ikhwan were fanatical in imposing their zealotry for correct behavior on others. They enforced rigid separation of the sexes in their villages, for example, and strict attention to prayers, and used violence in attempting to impose Wahhabi restrictions on others. Their fanaticism forged them into a formidable fighting force, and with Ikhwan assistance, Abd al Aziz extended the borders of his kingdom into the Eastern Province, Hail, and the Hijaz. Ultimately, the fanaticism of the Ikhwan undermined their usefulness, and they had to be reckoned with; the Ikhwan Rebellion (1928–30) marked their eclipse (see The Ikhwan Movement, ch. 5).

In the 1990s, Saudi leadership did not emphasize its identity as inheritor of the Wahhabi legacy as such, nor did the descendants of Muhammad ibn Abd al Wahhab, the Al ash Shaykh, continue to hold the highest posts in the religious bureaucracy. Wahhabi influence in Saudi Arabia, however, remained tangible in the physical conformity in dress, in public deportment, and in public prayer. Most significantly, the Wahhabi legacy was manifest in the social ethos that presumed government responsibility for the collective moral ordering of society, from the behavior of individuals, to institutions, to businesses, to the government itself.

## Shia

Shia are a minority in Saudi Arabia, probably constituting about 5 percent of the total population, their number being estimated from a low of 200,000 to as many as 400,000. Shia are concentrated primarily in the Eastern Province, where they constitute perhaps 33 percent of the population, being concentrated in the oases of Qatif and Al Ahsa. Saudi Shia belong to the sect of the Twelvers, the same sect to which the Shia of Iran and Bahrain belong. The Twelvers believe that the leadership of the Muslim community rightfully belongs to the descendants of Ali, the son-in-law of the Prophet, through Ali's son Husayn (see Early Development of Islam, this ch.). There were twelve such rightful rulers, known as Imams, the last of whom, according to the Twelvers, did not die but went into hiding in the ninth century, to return in the fullness of time as the messiah (mahdi) to create the just and perfect Muslim society.

From a theological perspective, relations between the Shia and the Wahhabi Sunnis are inherently strained because the Wahhabis consider the rituals of the Shia to be the epitome of *shirk* (polytheism; literally ''association''), especially the Ashura mourning celebrations, the passion play reenacting Husayn's death at Karbala, and popular votive rituals carried out at shrines and graves. In the late 1920s, the Ikhwan (Abd al Aziz ibn Abd ar Rahman Al Saud's fighting force of converted Wahhabi beduin Muslims) were particularly hostile to the Shia and demanded that Abd al Aziz forcibly convert them. In response, Abd al Aziz sent Wahhabi missionaries to the Eastern Province, but he did not carry through with attempts at forced conversion. Government policy has been to allow Shia their own mosques and to exempt Shia from Hanbali inheritance practices. Nevertheless, Shia have been forbidden all but the most modest displays on their principal festivals, which are often occasions of sectarian strife in the gulf region, with its mixed Sunni-Shia populations.

Shia came to occupy the lowest rung of the socioeconomic ladder in the newly formed Saudi state. They were excluded from the upper levels of the civil bureaucracy and rarely recruited by the military or the police; none was recruited by the national guard. The discovery of oil brought them employment, if not much of a share in the contracting and subcontracting wealth that the petroleum industry generated. Shia have formed the bulk of the skilled and semiskilled workers employed by Saudi Aramco. Members of the older generation of Shia were sufficiently content with their lot as Aramco employees not to participate in the labor disturbances of the 1950s and 1960s.

In 1979 Shia opposition to the royal family was encouraged by the example of Ayatollah Sayyid Ruhollah Musavi Khomeini's revolutionary ideology from Iran and by the Sunni Islamist (sometimes seen as fundamentalist) groups' attack on the Grand Mosque in Mecca in November. During the months that followed, conservative ulama and Ikhwan groups in the Eastern Province, as well as Shia, began to make their criticisms of government heard. On November 28, 1979, as the Mecca incident continued, the Shia of Qatif and two other towns in the Eastern Province tried to observe Ashura publicly. When the national guard intervened, rioting ensued, resulting in a number of deaths. Two months later, another riot in Al Qatif by Shia was quelled by the national guard, but more deaths occurred. Among the criticisms expressed by Shia were the close ties of the Al Saud with and their dependency on the West, corruption, and deviance from the sharia. The criticisms were similar to those levied by Juhaiman al Utaiba in his pamphlets circulated the year before his seizure of the Grand Mosque. Some Shia were specifically concerned with the economic disparities between Sunnis and Shia, particularly because their population is concentrated in the Eastern Province, which is the source of the oil wealth controlled by the Sunni Al Saud of Najd. During the riots that occurred in the Eastern Province in 1979, demands were raised to halt oil supplies and to redistribute the oil wealth so that the Shia would receive a more equitable share.

After order was restored, there was a massive influx of government assistance to the region. Included were many large projects to upgrade the region's infrastructure. In the late 1970s, the Al Jubayl project, slated to become one of the region's largest employers, was headed by a Shia. In 1992, however, there were reports of repression of Shia political activity in the kingdom. An Amnesty International report published in 1990 stated that more than 700 political prisoners had been detained without charge or trial since 1983, and that most of the prisoners were Shia (see Prison Conditions, ch. 5).

## Islamism in Saudi Arabia

The decade of the 1980s was characterized by the rise of ultraconservative, politically activist Islamic movements in much of the Arab world. These Islamist movements, labeled *fundamentalist* in the West, sought the government institutionalization of Islamic laws and social principles. Although Saudi Arabia already claimed to be an Islamic government whose constitution is the Quran, the kingdom has not been immune to this conservative trend.

In Saudi Arabia, the 1960s, and especially the 1970s, had been years of explosive development, liberal experimentation, and openness to the West. A reversal of this trend came about abruptly in

1979, the year in which the Grand Mosque in Mecca came under attack by religiously motivated critics of the monarchy, and the Islamic Republic of Iran was established. Each of these events signaled that religious conservatism would have to be politically addressed with greater vigor. Although the mosque siege was carried out by a small band of zealots and their actions of shooting in the mosque appalled most Muslims, their call for less ostentation on the part of the Saudi rulers and for a halt to the cultural inundation of the kingdom by the West struck a deep chord of sympathy across the kingdom. At the same time, Ayatollah Khomeini's call to overthrow the Al Saud was a direct challenge to the legitimacy of the monarchy as custodian of the holy places, and a challenge to the stability of the kingdom with its Shia minority.

In the years following these events, the rise of the ultraconservative periphery has caused the vast center of society to shift in a conservative direction, producing greater polarity between those who are Western-oriented and the rest of society. The 1991 Persian Gulf War marked another dramatic shift toward conservative sentiment, and this conservative trend continued to gain momentum in the early 1990s.

The conservative revival has been manifest in literature, in individual behavior, in government policies, in official and unofficial relations with foreigners, in mosque sermons, and in protest demonstrations against the government. The revival was also apparent in increased religious programming on television and radio, and an increase in articles about religion in newspapers.

On an individual level, some Saudi citizens, especially educated young women, were expressing the revivalist mood by supplementing the traditional Saudi Islamic *hijab* (literally curtain or veil), a black cloak, black face veil, and hair covering, with long black gloves to hide the hands. In some cases, women who formerly had not covered their faces began to use the nontransparent covering once worn mainly by women of traditional families. Some, especially younger, university-educated women, wore the *hijab* when traveling in Europe or the United States to demonstrate the sincerity of their belief in following the precepts of Islam.

In the Hijaz, another expression of the Islamic revival was participation in the ritual celebration of popular Islamic holidays. Some elite Hijazi families, for example, have revived the *mawlid,* a gathering for communal prayer on the occasion of the Prophet's birthday, or to celebrate a birth, mourn a death, bless a new house, or seek God's favor in fulfillment of some wish, such as cure of an illness or the birth of a child. *Mawlid* rituals, especially when performed by women, were suppressed by Abd al Aziz when he conquered the Hijaz because they incorporated intercession and the Wahhabis considered them the equivalent of polytheism.

Reacting to the revivalist mood, the government has backed the *mutawwiin* in responding to calls for controls over behavior perceived as non-Islamic. In November 1990, a group of forty-seven women staged a demonstration to press their claim for the right to drive. The *mutawwiin* demanded that the women be punished. The government confiscated the women's passports, and those employed as teachers were fired. The previously unofficial ban on women's driving quickly became official. As a further indication of the growing conservatism, considerable criticism of the women's behavior in asking for the right to drive came from within the women's branch of the university in Riyadh.

Religiously sanctioned behavior, once thought to be the responsibility of families, was being increasingly institutionalized and enforced. Women, for example, were usually prevented from traveling abroad unless accompanied by a male chaperon (*mahram*), a marked shift from the policy of the late 1970s, when a letter granting permission to travel was considered sufficient. This rule has compounded the difficulties for women wishing to study abroad: a 1982 edict remained in force that restricted scholarships for women to those whose father, husband, or brother was able to remain with them during the period of study.

State funding has increased for the nationwide organization of *mutawwiin* that is incorporated into the civil service bureaucracy. Once responsible primarily for enforcing the attendance of men in the mosque at prayer time, the tasks of the *mutawwiin* since the 1980s have come to include enforcing public abstinence from eating, drinking, and smoking among both Muslims and non-Muslims in the daylight hours during Ramadan. The *mutawwiin* (also seen as Committees for the Propagation of Virtue and Prevention of Vice or Committees for Public Morality) are also responsible for seeing that shops are closed at prayer time and that modest dress is maintained in public. Foreign women were under increased pressure to wear clothing that covered the arms and legs, and men and women who were unrelated might be apprehended for traveling together in a car. In the early 1980s, an offending couple might have received an official reprimand, but in the early 1990s they might experience more serious consequences. In 1991, for example, a Saudi citizen who gave a foreign female coworker a ride home was sentenced to a public flogging and his coworker subsequently was deported.

The rise in conservatism also can be seen in measures taken to obstruct non-Muslim religious services. Non-Muslim services have long been discouraged, but never prohibited, in Arabia. Even at the height of the Wahhabi revival in the 1920s, Christian missionary doctors held prayer services in the palace of Abd al Aziz. In the 1960s, 1970s, and 1980s, Christian religious services were held regularly in private houses and in housing compounds belonging to foreign companies, and these services were usually ignored by *mutawwiin* as long as they did not attract public attention or encourage proselytism. With the end of the Persian Gulf War, however, *mutawwiin* began to enforce a ban on non-Muslim worship and punished offenders. In 1991, for example, a large number of *mutawwiin* accompanied by uniformed police broke up a Christian service in Riyadh and arrested a number of participants, including children.

The most significant indicator of the growing shift toward conservatism was the willingness of the state to silence opposition groups. For example, in May 1991, more than 400 men from the religious establishment and universities, including Saudi Arabia's most prominent legal scholar, Shaykh Abd al Aziz ibn Baz, petitioned the king to create a consultative council, a request to which the king responded favorably in February 1992. In their petition, however, the signatories asked not only for more participation in decision making, but also for a revision of all laws, including commercial and administrative regulations, to conform with the sharia. They asked for the creation of Islamic banks and an end to interest payments in established banks, as well as the redistribution of wealth, protection for the rights of the individual, censure of the media so that they would serve Islam and morality, and the creation of a strong army so that the kingdom would not be dependent on the West. The requests represented a combination of apparently liberal petitions (a consultative council, redistribution of wealth) with a conservative religious bent.

In a follow-up to the petition, a number of the signatories wrote a letter stating that funds for religious institutions were being cut back, that the institutions were not being given the resources to create jobs, and that their *fatwas* were being ignored. The letter further claimed that those who signed the original petition had had their passports confiscated and were being harassed by security personnel even though "they had committed no other crime than giving advice to the Guardian." This affair suggested that the government was sufficiently concerned about the increasingly conservative mood to shift its strategy from merely co-opting the conservative agenda to suppressing its extreme voices.

In another incident, a movement called Islamic Awakening, which had a growing following in religious colleges and universities, attempted to hold a public demonstration in early 1991, but participants were threatened with arrest if they did so. At the same time, the government arrested a well-known activist in the Islamic Awakening while he was preaching a sermon in a Riyadh mosque.

Factors contributing to the increased attraction of Islamic conservatism included the problem of impending loss of identity caused by overwhelming Westernization. As secular education, population mobility, the breakup of extended family households, and the employment of women chipped away at cherished institutions of family and society, religion was a refuge and a source of stability (see Cultural Homogeneity and Values, this ch.).

Another factor was disaffection with the existing economic system in the face of rising unemployment. During the rapid expansion of the 1970s, employment in the public sector was virtually assured for Saudi citizens with technical skills and for those with a Western education. By the end of the decade, however, those positions, especially in education and in the ministries, came under pressure from increasing numbers of university graduates with rising expectations that no longer could be fulfilled in public sector employment. In addition, in the 1990s a growing number of young men educated in Islamic colleges and universities were unemployed; their acquired knowledge and skills were becoming more irrelevant to the demands of the economy and bureaucratic infrastructure, even within the judiciary where traditionally Islamic scholarship was most highly valued.

An additional factor lay in the monarchy's continuing need to maintain legitimacy as an "Islamic government." As long as the ruling family believes it must continue to prove itself a worthy inheritor of the legacy on which the kingdom was founded, it will be obliged to foster religious education and the Islamic political culture in which the kingdom's media are steeped. A lesser factor in the rise of conservatism may be widespread sympathy with the sense of being victimized by the West, as evidenced, for example, in the continuing displacement of Palestinians in the occupied territories and southern Lebanon.

Islam remained the primary cohesive ideology in the kingdom, the source of legitimacy for the monarchy, and the pervasive system for moral guidance and spirituality. The nature of the Islamic society Saudi Arabia wished to have in the future, however, was one of the important and passionately debated issues in the kingdom in the early 1990s. The ultraconservative moral agenda appealed on an emotional level to many Saudi citizens. But the desire to expand the jurisdiction of sharia law and to interfere with the banking system was also a source of concern for many people.

*Hajj, or pilgrimage, terminal, at King Abd al Aziz International Airport, Jiddah*
*Courtesy* Aramco World

Because nearly all Saudis have reaped material benefits from state-funded development, people were hesitant to jeopardize those benefits and the political stability that allowed development. Some have suggested that the new system of basic laws was a clear signal that the monarchy was firmly committed to liberalization and no longer felt compelled to tolerate conservative excesses. Close assessment of the implications of the basic laws suggested, however, that the monarchy was making no substantive changes and, in effect, was taking no chances to risk disturbing the balance among competing religious persuasions in the kingdom.

## Pilgrimage

The hajj, or pilgrimage to Mecca, occurs annually between the eighth and thirteenth days of the last month of the Muslim year, Dhu al Hijjah. The hajj represents the culmination of the Muslim's spiritual life. For many, it is a lifelong ambition. From the time of embarking on the journey to make the hajj, pilgrims often experience a spirit of exaltation and excitement; the meeting of so many Muslims of all races, cultures, and stations in life in harmony and equality moves many people deeply. Certain rites of pilgrimage may be performed any time, and although meritorious, these constitute a lesser pilgrimage, known as *umra*.

Improved transportation and accommodations have increased dramatically the number of visitors who enter the kingdom for

91

pilgrimage. In 1965 almost 300,000 Muslims came from abroad to perform the rites of pilgrimage, primarily from other Arab and Asian countries. By 1983 that number had climbed to more than 1 million. In addition to those coming from abroad, each year 600,000 to 700,000 people living in the kingdom join in the hajj rituals. In 1988 and 1989, a total of 1.5 million pilgrims attended the hajj, representing a drop of about 200,000 in the number of foreign pilgrims, probably the result of a temporary ban on Iranian pilgrims instituted after a violent confrontation with Saudi police. In the hajj season of 1992, the Saudi press claimed a record of 2 million pilgrims.

The Ministry of Pilgrimage Affairs and Religious Trusts handles the immense logistical and administrative problems generated by such a huge international gathering. The government issues special pilgrimage visas that permit the pilgrim to visit Mecca and to make the customary excursion to Medina to visit the Prophet's tomb. Care is taken to assure that pilgrims do not remain in the kingdom after the hajj to search for work.

An elaborate guild of specialists assists the hajjis. Guides (*mutaw-wifs*) who speak the pilgrim's language make the necessary arrangements in Mecca and instruct the pilgrim in the proper performance of rituals; assistants (*wakils*) provide subsidiary services. Separate groups of specialists take care of pilgrims in Medina and Jiddah. Water drawers (*zamzamis*) provide water drawn from the sacred well.

In fulfilling the commandment to perform the hajj, the pilgrim not only obeys the Prophet's words but also literally follows in his footsteps. The sacred sites along the pilgrimage route were frequented by Muhammad and formed the backdrop to the most important events of his life. It is believed, for example, that he received his first revelation at Jabal an Nur (Mountain of Light) near Mina.

The *haram,* or holy area of Mecca, is a sanctuary in which violence to people, animals, and even plants is not permitted. The word *haram* carries the dual meaning of forbidden and sacred. As a symbol of ritual purification, on approaching its boundaries the male pilgrim dons an *ihram,* two white seamless pieces of cloth. Women wear a white dress and head scarf and may choose to veil their faces, although it is not required. Once properly attired, pilgrims enter a state of purity in which they avoid bathing, cutting hair and nails, violence, arguing, and sexual relations.

Approaching Mecca, pilgrims shout, "I am here, O Lord, I am here!" They enter the Grand Mosque surrounding the Kaaba, a cube-shaped sanctuary first built, according to Muslim tradition, by Abraham and his son Ismail. The Kaaba contains a black stone believed to have been given to Abraham by the angel Gabriel, according to some sources, and by others, to have been simply part of the structure of the original Kaaba. In pre-Islamic times, the Kaaba was the object of pilgrimage, housing the idols of the pagan *jahiliyah,* the age of ignorance, and, according to Islamic tradition, was cleansed by Muhammad of idols and rededicated to the worship of the one God.

On the eighth day, the pilgrims go to Mina, a plain outside Mecca, spending the night in prayer and meditation. On the morning of the ninth day, they proceed to the Plain of Arafat where they perform the central ritual of the hajj, the standing (*wuquf*). The congregation faces Mecca and prays from noon to sundown. Muhammad delivered his farewell sermon from a hill above the plain called the Mount of Mercy, or Mount Arafat, during his final pilgrimage. In performing *wuquf,* the pilgrim figuratively joins those the Prophet addressed. It is believed that the pilgrim leaves Arafat cleansed of sin.

A cannon sounds at sunset, and all rush to Muzdalifah, where they toss pebbles at one of three stone pillars representing Satan. Satan, in Islamic tradition, tempted Abraham not to sacrifice Ismail as God commanded. Ismail stoned Satan in response to the temptation, an act that symbolizes for the Muslim Ismail's total submission to the will of God, for he went as a willing victim to the sacrifice. In the stoning, pilgrims renounce evil and declare their willingness to sacrifice all they have to God. Following the stoning, each pilgrim buys a camel, sheep, or goat for sacrifice in imitation of Abraham, and the excess meat is distributed to the poor. The sacrifice is duplicated by Muslims the world over, who celebrate the day as Id al Adha, the major feast of the Muslim year. The sacrifice ends the hajj proper. The pilgrim may then bathe, shave, cut his hair, and resume normal clothing.

Lastly, the pilgrims go to the Grand Mosque in Mecca. In the sanctuary, the pilgrims walk around the Kaaba seven times and point to the stone or kiss it as a symbol of the continuity of Islam over time and of the unity of believers. They then pray in the Place of Abraham, the spot within the mosque where the patriarch prayed. During this time, the pilgrims may also reenact the running between the hills of Safa and Marwa and may drink from the sacred well of Zamzam, commemorating the frantic search by Hagar to find water for her son Ismail, and the opening of the well of Zamzam by the angel Gabriel, which saved the future father of the Arabs. These rites constitute the *umra.* Some pilgrims conclude their pilgrimage with a visit to the Prophet's Mosque in Medina.

The rite of pilgrimage not only has special significance in the life of Muslims but also has profound political significance for the

Saudi monarchy. The king has claimed for himself the title Khadim al Haramayn, or "custodian of the two holy mosques," a title that complements the Saudi claim to legitimacy. To prove themselves worthy of the title, Saudi monarchs must show that they are capable not only of defending the interests of Arabian Muslims but also of defending the holy sites of Islam for the benefit of Muslims the world over. The Saudis have therefore invested heavily over the years in facilitating the arrival, transportation, feeding, and accommodation of pilgrims arriving annually for the rites of the hajj. New airport buildings, road networks, water supplies, and public health facilities have been provided. Much publicity has accompanied government contributions to the comfort of pilgrims. The government distributes bottled water, juices, and boxed lunches during the climbing of Mount Arafat; stations ambulances staffed with first-aid teams in strategic locations; shows health education videos on airplanes and ships bringing pilgrims; and relieves pilgrims of the task of having to slaughter their sacrificial animal. The Islamic Development Bank now sells vouchers for sacrificial animals, which are chosen by the pilgrim and then slaughtered, processed, and frozen for distribution and sale in slaughterhouses in Mina.

Since the late 1980s, the Saudis have been particularly energetic in catering to the needs of pilgrims. In 1988 a US$15 billion traffic improvement scheme for the holy sites was launched. The improvement initiative resulted partly from Iranian charges that the Saudi government was incompetent to guard the holy sites after a 1987 clash between demonstrating Iranian pilgrims and Saudi police left 400 people dead. A further disaster occurred in 1990, when 1,426 pilgrims suffocated or were crushed to death in one of the new air-conditioned pedestrian tunnels built to shield pilgrims from the heat. The incident resulted from the panic that erupted in the overcrowded and inadequately ventilated tunnel, and further fueled Iranian claims that the Saudis did not deserve to be in sole charge of the holy places. In 1992, however, 114,000 Iranian pilgrims, close to the usual level, participated in the hajj.

To symbolize their leadership of the worldwide community of Muslims as well as their guardianship of the holy sites, Saudi kings address the pilgrimage gathering annually. The Saudis also provide financial assistance to aid selected groups of foreign Muslims to attend the hajj. In 1992, in keeping with its interests in proselytizing among Muslims in the newly independent states of the former Soviet Union, the Saudi government sponsored the pilgrimage for hundreds of Muslims from Azerbaijan and Tadzikistan.

*Muslim pilgrims praying on Mount Arafat*
*Courtesy* Aramco World

## Education

Education has been a primary goal of government in Najd since the late eighteenth century, when the Wahhabi movement encouraged the spread of Islamic education for all Muslim believers. Because the purpose of Islamic education was to ensure that the believer would understand God's laws and live his or her life in accordance with them, classes for reading and memorizing the Quran along with selections from the hadith were sponsored in towns and villages throughout the peninsula. At the most elementary level, education took place in the *kuttab*, a class of Quran recitation for children usually attached to a mosque, or as a private tutorial held in the home under the direction of a male or female professional Quran reader, which was usually the case for girls. In the late nineteenth century, nonreligious subjects were also taught under Ottoman rule in the Hijaz and Al Ahsa Province, where *kuttab* schools specializing in Quran memorization sometimes included arithmetic, foreign language, and Arabic reading in the curriculum. Because the purpose of basic religious learning was to know the contents of holy scripture, the ability to read Arabic text was not a priority, and illiteracy remained widespread in the peninsula. In 1970, in comparison to all countries in the Middle East and North Africa, the literacy rate of 15 percent for men and 2 percent for women in Saudi Arabia was lower only in Yemen. For this reason, the steep rise in literacy rates—by 1990 the literacy rate for men had risen to 73 percent and that for women to 48 percent—must be seen as an achievement.

Students who wished to pursue their studies beyond the elementary level could attend an informal network of scholarly lectures (*halaqat*) offering instruction in Islamic jurisprudence, Arabic language, Quranic commentaries (*tafsir*), hadith, literature, rhetoric, and sometimes arithmetic and history. The most prestigious ulama in Arabia received specialized training at Al Azhar mosque in Cairo, or in Iraq. In Saudi Arabia, higher studies in religious scholarship were formalized in 1945 with the establishment of the At Taif School of Theology (Dar al Tawhid). In the early 1990s, there were two university-level institutions for religious studies, the Islamic University of Medina and the Imam Muhammad ibn Saud Islamic University in Riyadh.

Since the 1920s, a small number of private institutions has offered limited secular education for boys, but it was not until 1951 that an extensive program of publicly funded secondary schools was initiated. In 1957 the first university not dedicated to religious subjects, Riyadh University, subsequently renamed King Saud

University, was established. The Ministry of Education, which administered public educational institutions for boys and men, was set up in 1954. Publicly funded education for girls began in 1960 under the inspiration of then Crown Prince Faisal and his wife Iffat.

Initially, opening schools for girls met with strong opposition in some parts of the kingdom, where nonreligious education was viewed as useless, if not actually dangerous, for girls. This attitude was reflected in the ratio of school-age boys to girls in primary school enrollments: in 1960, 22 percent of boys and 2 percent of girls were enrolled. Within a few years, however, public perceptions of the value of education for girls changed radically, and the general population became strongly supportive. In 1981 enrollments were 81 percent of boys and 43 percent of girls. In 1989 the number of girls enrolled in the public school system was close to the number of boys: almost 1.2 million girls out of a total of 2.6 million students, or 44 percent. School attendance was not compulsory for boys or girls (see table 2, Appendix.)

By 1989 Saudi Arabia had an education system with more than 14,000 education institutions, including seven universities and eleven teacher-training colleges, in addition to schools for vocational and technical training, special needs, and adult literacy. The system was expanding so rapidly that in 1988–89 alone, 950 new schools were opened to accommodate 400,000 new students. General education consisted of kindergarten, six years of primary school, and three years each of intermediate and secondary (high) school. All instruction, books, and health services to students were provided free by the government, which allocated nearly 20 percent of its expenditures, or US$36.3 billion, to human resources under the Fourth Development Plan (1985–90). The Fifth Development Plan (1990–95) proposed a total expenditure of about US$37.6 billion.

Administratively, two organizations oversaw most education institutions in the kingdom. The Ministry of Education supervised the education of boys, special education programs for the handicapped, adult education, and junior colleges for men. Girls' education was administered by the Directorate General of Girls' Education, an organization staffed by ulama, working in close cooperation with the Ministry of Education. The directorate general oversaw the general education of girls, kindergartens and nurseries for both boys and girls, and women's literacy programs, as well as colleges of education and junior colleges for girls. The Ministry of Higher Education was the authority overseeing the kingdom's colleges and universities.

Public education, at both the university and secondary-school level, has never been fully separated from its Islamic roots. The education policy of Saudi Arabia included among its objectives the promotion of the "belief in the One God, Islam as the way of life, and Muhammad as God's Messenger." At the elementary-school level, an average of nine periods a week was devoted to religious subjects and eight per week at the intermediate-school level. This concentration on religious subjects was substantial when compared with the time devoted to other subjects: nine periods for Arabic language and twelve for geography, history, mathematics, science, art, and physical education combined at the elementary level; six for Arabic language and nineteen for all other subjects at the intermediate level. At the secondary level, the required periods of religious study were reduced, although an option remained for a concentration in religious studies.

For women, the goal of education as stated in official policy was ideologically tied to religion: "The purpose of educating a girl is to bring her up in a proper Islamic way so as to perform her duty in life, be an ideal and successful housewife and a good mother, ready to do things which suit her nature such as teaching, nursing and medical treatment." The policy also recognized "women's right to obtain suitable education on equal footing with men in light of Islamic laws." In practice, educational options for girls at the precollege level were almost identical to those for boys. One exception was that, at all levels of precollege education, only boys took physical education, and only girls took home economics.

Inequalities of opportunity existed in higher education that stemmed from the religious and social imperative of gender segregation. Gender segregation was required at all levels of public education, but was also demanded in public areas and businesses by religiously conservative groups as well as by social convention. Because the social perception was that men would put the knowledge and skills acquired to productive use, fewer resources were dedicated to women's higher education than to men's. This constraint was a source of concern to economic planners and policy makers because training and hiring women not only would help solve the difficulties of indigenizing the work force, but also would help to satisfy the rising expectations of the thousands of women graduating from secondary schools, colleges, and universities.

The concern was compounded by the fact that women as a group have excelled academically over males in secondary schools, and the number of female graduates has outstripped the number of males, even though the number of girls entering school was considerably lower than the number of boys. The number of female secondary level graduates has increased more than tenfold, from 1,674 in 1975 to 18,211 in 1988. Calculated as a combination of

*Chemistry class,*
*Al Mubarraz School,*
*Eastern Province*
*Courtesy* Aramco World

*Recess at a girls' school*
*Courtesy Saudi Aramco*

the hours invested in those who drop out or repeat classes and those who graduate, it took an average of eighteen pupil years to produce a male graduate of general education, as opposed to fifteen pupil years to produce a female graduate. Under conditions existing in the early 1990s, the problem can only become more acute because the Fifth Development Plan projected 45,000 female secondary school graduates in 1995 and only 38,000 male graduates.

This increase in women graduates has not been met by a commensurate increase in higher education opportunities. Despite substantial expansion of college and university programs for women, they remained insufficient to serve the graduates who sought admission. The Fifth Development Plan cited higher education for women as a major issue to be addressed, and Saudi press reports in 1992 indicated that there was discussion of creating a women's university.

A major objective for education in the Fourth Development Plan and the Fifth Development Plan has been to develop general education to deal with technological changes and rapid developments in social and economic fields. The ultimate goal was to replace a portion of Saudi Arabia's huge foreign labor force (79 percent of the total in 1989) with indigenous workers. In the late 1980s, a high rate of student dropouts and secondary school failures precluded the realization of these goals. (In 1990 the ratios of the number of students at the primary, intermediate, and secondary levels to the total number of students stood at 69.6, 20.5, and 9.9 percent, respectively.) The dropout problem was far more acute with boys than with girls. One means of addressing the dropout problem was a program initiated in 1985 called ''developed secondary education,'' designed to prepare students for university study as well as for practical participation in the work force. In this program, the student was allowed to select two-thirds of his or her study plan from courses that had practical applications or genuine appeal to the student's own interests and abilities. After completing a required general program consisting of courses in religion, mathematics, science, social studies, English, Arabic, and computers, students elected a course of study in one of three concentrations: Islamic studies and literature, administrative science and humanities, or the natural sciences.

Another goal in both the Fourth Development Plan and the Fifth Development Plan has been to indigenize the secondary teacher corps. At the end of the 1980s, about 40 percent were foreigners, mostly from other Arabic-speaking countries, and almost half of that percentage were Egyptian. In the early 1980s, there had been steep gains in the number of Saudis teaching at all levels, especially at the elementary level. This gain resulted from the increase during the 1970s of institutes for training teachers and the greater material incentives for careers in education, stipulated in a royal decree of 1982. Nonetheless, training schools for teachers had trouble attracting candidates, especially males; male enrollment declined slightly, whereas female enrollment nearly tripled. In 1984 there were about 12,000 women enrolled in the seven female colleges of education located in Riyadh, Jiddah, Mecca, Medina, Buraydah, Abha, and Tabuk. The challenge of attracting Saudis to the teaching profession was being met in the early 1990s by a plan to abolish the training institutes for secondary teachers and shift the enrollment to junior colleges. This move would allow graduates the opportunity to complete a university education for a bachelor's degree and thus draw more potential candidates to the teaching profession.

Government funding for higher education has been particularly munificent. Between 1983 and 1989, the number of university students increased from approximately 58,000 to about 113,000, a 95 percent increase. Equally dramatic was the increase in the number of women students at the university level: from 20,300 to 47,000 during the same period, or a 132 percent increase. In 1989 the number of graduates from all of the kingdom's colleges and universities was almost the same for men and women: about 7,000 each.

The new campus of King Saud University in Riyadh, built in the early 1980s, was designed to accommodate 25,000 male students; the original university buildings in central Riyadh were converted into a campus for the women's branch of the university. King Saud University included colleges of administrative sciences, agriculture, arts, dentistry, education, engineering, medical sciences, medicine, pharmacy, and science. Of these, the only course of study that excluded women was engineering, on the premise that a profession in engineering would be impossible to pursue in the context of sex-segregation practices. In the early 1990s, the university offered postgraduate studies in sixty-one specializations, and doctorates in Arabic, geography, and history. In 1984 there were 479 graduate students, including 151 women.

The University of Petroleum and Minerals (King Fahd University) in Dhahran, founded in 1963, offered undergraduate and graduate degree programs in engineering and science, with most programs of study offered in English. Also in Dhahran was King Faisal University, founded in 1976, with colleges of agricultural sciences and foods, architecture, education, medicine, and veterinary medicine. In 1984 some 40 percent of its 2,600 students were women.

In progress in 1992 was the expansion of King Abd al Aziz University in Jiddah. Founded in 1968, the university in 1990 had about 15,000 undergraduate students, of whom about one-third were women. It consisted of nine colleges, including arts and sciences, environmental studies, marine sciences, medicine, and meteorology. The university's expansion plans, funded by an investment of US$2 billion, called for the addition of colleges of education, environmental design, pharmacy, and planning and technology. The completed expansion should accommodate 25,500 students, with a medical complex to include a hospital, a health services center, and a medical research facility.

The establishment and growth of faculties of arts and sciences, medicine, and technology have been accompanied by the growth in religious institutes of higher learning. The Islamic University of Medina, founded in 1961, had an international student body and faculty that specialized in Islamic sciences. In 1985 the university had 2,798 students including several hundred graduate students. The Islamic University also had a college preparatory program that specialized in teaching the Arabic language and religion; in 1985 there were 1,835 students, all but 279 of them foreign.

At least two of the universities founded for religious instruction have integrated secular subjects and practical training into their curriculum. The Imam Muhammad ibn Saud Islamic University, established in 1974, produced qualified Muslim scholars, teachers, judges, and preachers. The university specialized in such classical studies as Arabic language and Islamic jurisprudence. It also offered newer approaches to the study of Islam, with courses in state policy in Islam, Islamic sects, and Islamic culture and economics. In addition, practical subjects such as administration, information and mass media, library sciences, psychology, and social service were offered. In 1986 enrollment numbered 12,000 students with an additional 1,000 in graduate programs. More than 1,500 of these students were women. Umm al Qura University, originally a college of sharia with an institute to teach Arabic to non-Arabs, had grown to include colleges of agricultural sciences, applied sciences, engineering, and social sciences. Of its 7,500 undergraduate students in 1984, 51 percent, or 3,800, were women.

The expansion of the university system in Saudi Arabia has enabled the kingdom to limit financial support for study abroad. Such restrictions had long been the desire of some conservatives, who feared the negative influences on Saudi youth from studying abroad. Since the mid- to late 1980s, the number of Saudi students going abroad to study has dropped sharply. In the 1991–92 school year,

*Royal Technical Institute,*
*Riyadh*
*Courtesy* Aramco and Its World

only 5,000 students were reported studying abroad; there were slightly more than 4,000 the previous year, with half of those study-ing in the United States. These figures contrasted with the approx-imately 10,000 students studying abroad in 1984. As in the past, students going abroad to study received substantial financial as-sistance. Students selected to receive government funding to study abroad in 1992 received allowances for tuition, lodging, board, and transportation; those intending to study science or technology received an additional stipend. A male student also was encouraged through financial incentives to marry before leaving Saudi Arabia and to take his wife and children with him. The incentives, including an offer of tuition payment that allowed the wife to pursue a course of study as well, addressed concerns about moral temptations and cultural confusions that might arise from living alone abroad. As an additional buffer against such potential problems, an orienta-tion program in Islamic and foreign cultures was offered at Imam Muhammad ibn Saud Islamic University for students about to go abroad.

Women going abroad to study were a particular concern for the ulama in the Department of Religious Research, Missionary Ac-tivities, and Guidance. In 1982 government scholarships for women to study abroad were sharply curtailed. Enforcement of the *mahram* rule, whereby women were not allowed to travel without their closest male relative as a chaperon, discouraged prospective students from

103

studying abroad. In 1990 there were almost three times as many men studying abroad on government scholarships as there were women, whereas in 1984 more than half were women.

The expansion of formal religious education programs in a technologically modernizing society has created some economic dislocations and some degree of social polarization between those equipped primarily with a religious education and those prepared to work in the modern economic sector. Opportunities for government employment in religious affairs agencies and the judiciary have been shrinking as traditional areas of religious authority have given way to new demands of the modernizing and developing state. At the same time, unemployment was becoming a problem in the society at large. In the private sector, for example, where most of the employment growth was expected from 1990 to 1995, employment was projected to increase by 213,500, but at the same time the Saudi indigenous labor force was expected to increase by 433,900. Consequently, the growing number of graduates in religious studies—in 1985, 2,733 students in the Islamic University of Medina and more than 8,000 in Muhammad ibn Saud University in Riyadh—was a potential source of disaffection from the state and its modernizing agenda.

## Health

Saudi Arabia has committed vast resources (US$16.4 billion in the years 1985 to 1990) to improving medical care for its citizens, with the ultimate goal of providing free medical care for everyone in the kingdom. In 1990 the number of hospitals operated by the government and the private sector together stood at 258, with a capacity of 36,099 beds. Of these hospitals, 163 were run by the Ministry of Health and sixty-four by the private sector. In addition, other government agencies, such as the national guard, the Ministry of Interior, and the Ministry of Defense and Aviation, operated hospitals and clinics for their staffs and families. There were also teaching hospitals attached to the medical faculties of universities in the kingdom (see table 3, Appendix).

King Fahd Medical City outside Riyadh was a US$534 million project. It was to include five hospitals of different specializations, with a capacity of 1,400 beds in addition to outpatient clinics, and was expected to be completed in the early 1990s. To provide personnel for the expanding medical facilities, which in 1992 were staffed largely by foreign physicians, nurses, technicians, and administrators, the government has encouraged medical education in the kingdom and has financed medical training abroad. Four of the kingdom's seven universities offered medical degrees and operated well-equipped hospitals. Saudi universities also had colleges of nursing, pharmacology, and other fields related to the delivery of medical care.

One objective of medical planning was to sponsor cutting-edge research in the kingdom. There were some reported successes. The King Saud University College of Pharmacology developed a drug effective in stabilizing blood sugar in diabetics, and heart surgeons at the Armed Forces Hospital Heart Center in Riyadh performed innovative open-heart surgery on an infant. At the College of Sciences of King Saud University, scientists have used radioactive isotopes to determine the effect of antibiotics on body functions. The King Khalid Eye Specialist Hospital, staffed by foreign doctors, was a world center for the treatment of eye disorders.

Whereas advanced medical research and some of the most sophisticated medical care available anywhere in the world were concentrated in Riyadh and a few major cities, medical care at the most basic level was limited in the countryside. In the early 1990s, a key objective of the Ministry of Health was to facilitate the delivery of primary care to rural areas by establishing primary health-care centers that provided basic services and dispensed medicines. For every four or five primary centers, which numbered 1,668 in 1990, there was to be one diagnostic and maternity center (there were ninety-eight centers in 1990). The large specialist hospitals located in cities were intended as referral hospitals for sophisticated medical treatment such as transplants, cancer treatment, surgery, and complicated diagnoses.

For the primary centers to be effective, health education has had to become an essential part of the centers' mission. In some areas, basic hygiene was unknown, as was the principle of contagion. The rural population and others who had had little or no exposure to observable benefits of modern medicine tended to view preventive measures and medicines with caution. According to a common traditional view, illness was not related to human behavior, such as poor sanitation habits, but was caused by spiritual agents, such as the jinn, the evil eye, or the will of God. Prevention and treatment of disease, therefore, lay in appealing to the spiritual agent responsible, using means such as prayer to God, votive offerings, or amulets to ward off the evil eye.

Before the introduction of modern medicine, local practitioners specialized in a variety of treatments, such as exorcism for mental illness, setting of broken bones, herbal remedies for many ailments, and cauterization. Cauterization involved heating a stick or nail until it was red-hot and then applying it to the area believed to be affected; this procedure was used to treat almost any affliction, from coughs to abscesses to convulsions. Recourse to local healers was declining as access to more effective health care and health education became available.

Infant mortality rates for the kingdom remained high in the early 1980s, with an estimated 118 deaths per 1,000 live births. By contrast, based only on deliveries of infants in hospitals of the Ministry of Health, the infant mortality rate (children stillborn or died during birth) was low, declining in 1990 to 21 per 1,000 in 1990 from 25 per 1,000 in 1986. Death rates have declined as well, from 20 per 1,000 in 1965, to 10.7 per 1,000 between 1975 and 1980, down to 7.6 per 1,000 between 1985 and 1990.

In 1990 the World Health Organization certified that Saudi Arabia was free from the quarantine diseases of cholera, plague, and yellow fever. Compulsory immunization of infants and young children and the introduction in 1986 of an epidemic control system to facilitate communication on outbreaks of communicable diseases have contributed to the successful eradication of these diseases. Poliomyelitis, however, has persisted, and the Ministry of Health has set a target date of the year 2000 to eliminate the disease.

Malaria remained a problem in the Tihamah southern coastal plain, especially in Jizan, Asir, and Al Qunfudhah, which was on the coast in northern Asir. In 1988 the disease affected 1.6 percent of the total population, down from the 4.2 percent recorded eight years earlier. This drop was attributed mainly to measures taken to eliminate breeding grounds for mosquitoes and spraying with insecticides. Bilharzia was a continuing problem in Jizan, Al Bahah, Asir, Najran, Medina, Al Jawf, Hail, and At Taif. The incidence of the disease was lowered from 8.4 percent in 1980 to 1.9 percent in 1988, but efforts to eliminate infestations of the bilharzia parasite and to prevent reinfestation were a continuing challenge. Cases of leishmaniasis have occurred in almost every province with the expansion of agricultural lands, which provide breeding grounds for disease-carrying flies. In 1988 the reported number of cases (under 15,000) was small, but the disease was being studied to prevent its spread. Trachoma was considered one of the main causes of blindness in the kingdom despite programs designed to combat the disease.

## Urbanization and Development

The family and religious values have profound implications for future development and for policy planning. Family values, and the corresponding behaviors of individuals, have been institutionalized by the state in the process of centralizing control and allocating resources. Many of the state-supported restrictions on women,

*Public playground, Abha*
*Courtesy Saudi Arabian Information Office*

for example, did not exist in the 1960s and 1970s. They were the product of attempts to reconcile family and religious values with opportunities and objectives that have grown out of the development process and of increased religious conservatism. Over the past two decades, one striking outgrowth of Saudi development has been rapid migration of the population to the cities. In the early 1970s, an estimated 26 percent of the population lived in urban centers. In 1990 that figure had risen to 73 percent. The capital, Riyadh, had about 666,000 inhabitants according to the 1974 census (the most recent official census). By 1984 the population, augmented by the removal of the diplomatic missions from Jiddah to Riyadh, was estimated at about 1.8 million.

Urbanization, education, and modernization were having profound effects on society as a whole, but especially on the family. The urban environment fostered new institutions, such as women's charitable societies, that facilitated associations and activities for women outside the family network. Urban migration and wealth were breaking up the extended family household, as young couples left hometowns and established themselves in single-family homes. Education for women also was encouraging the rise of the nuclear family household: a study in Ad Dammam carried out in 1980 showed that of a sample of 100 salaried women, 91 percent

107

of whom had a high-school or university education, fully 90 percent lived in nuclear family households. By contrast, in a sample of rural women who were 91 percent illiterate, only half lived in a nuclear family unit. The same study showed that the more educated, salaried women had an average of two children, as opposed to rural women with an average of 4.6 children. As the level of education rose, the age of first marriages rose as well: 79 percent of the salaried women were over the age of sixteen (and most over the age of nineteen) when first married, whereas 75 percent of rural women were married between the ages of ten and twelve.

In spite of the limitations imposed by sex-segregation values, and in spite of the small proportion of women in the work force relative to men (7 percent in 1990), the number of working women—and the kinds of places in which they worked—were growing. In the early 1990s, women were employed in banks, including banks exclusively for women, in utility and computer operations, in television and radio programming, and in some ministries. They worked as clerical assistants, journalists, teachers and administrators in girls' schools, university professors, and as social workers. In medicine, women served as doctors, pharmacists, and, more recently, as nurses. In 1992 there were almost 3,100 Saudi women trained and employed as nurses, or 10 percent of the total number of nurses employed in the kingdom. This number represented a dramatic change in the attitudes of some families, not only toward the profession, but about the limits of sex segregation. In the 1970s, nursing was disparaged as a profession for women because of the presumed contact it entailed with male doctors and patients; nursing programs in Saudi Arabia thus could not recruit female Saudi students.

By the 1990s, women had proved themselves competent to succeed in employment that had been culturally perceived as men's work, and in the academic field they had shown that they could be more successful than men (see Education, this ch.). Women had also carved out for themselves positions of respect outside the family, whereas previously an aspect of respect for women came from being unknown outside the family.

The practices of veiling and separation, and the values underlying these practices, however, were not being dislodged. There was little expressed desire for such change because the practices were grounded in fundamental family values, religiously sanctioned and institutionalized by the government. The premise that women, from a moral standpoint, should not associate with unrelated men was the basis for all Saudi regulations on the behavior of women, including the separation of boys and girls in the education system, the requirement that women have a male chaperon to travel, that women hire a male manager as a requirement for obtaining a commercial license, that women not study abroad without a male chaperon, not check into a hotel alone, and not drive a car in the kingdom.

There was a link between tribal-family values, religion, and state power that made intelligible the outcome of the women's driving demonstration of November 1990. If, in fact, society held as a basic moral premise that a woman should not be seen by any man outside her own family, how could the same society allow her to drive a car, when anyone passing by could see her face? The position of the ulama as stated in a *fatwa* by the head of the Department of Religious Research, Missionary Activities, and Guidance was that women should not be allowed to drive because Islam supported women's dignity. The *fatwa* did not say that Islam forbade women's driving—Saudi Arabia was the only Muslim country that forbade women to drive—but said that because Islam supported women's dignity, a Muslim government must protect women from the indignity of driving. The state could not easily abrogate such rulings of the ulama because these rulings responded to the family-tribal values and the interpretations of Islam that were at the heart of Saudi society. The general public response was supportive of the ulama and the actions of the state. Indeed, there was a broad consensus of support for such rulings precisely because they corresponded to the values of modesty and sex segregation that were enmeshed in religion and in the honor of the family.

Changes being wrought through urbanization and development were having disturbing consequences for the traditional notion of the family and its values. They brought closely held religious values into question. For men, the consequences were particularly unsettling because these changes brought their position of control and protection of the family into question. Education, urbanization, and modernization placed women in areas of public space where, culturally, they should not be, for public space was space reserved for men. The physical world around Saudis was changing. Social groupings were realigning, status categories were shifting, and economic dislocations were altering people's income expectations. In such a fluctuating world, for both men and women, clinging to traditional attitudes about women in the family was an expression of a desire for stability in the society at large. The development policies of the 1970s and 1980s had, in effect, planted the seeds of a cultural backlash, seeds that were coming into flower in the early years of the decade of the 1990s.

\* \* \*

The classic work on Arabian beduin is H.R.P. Dickson's *The Arab of the Desert*. For information on beduin today, see especially William Lancaster's *The Rwalla Bedouin Today* and Donald Cole's numerous publications, including *Nomads of the Nomads*. Motoko Katakura in *Bedouin Village* writes about issues of beduin settlement. Some of the best anthropological studies available on Saudi Arabia, such as *Arabian Oasis City: The Transformation of 'Unayzah,* have been prepared by Soraya Altorki and Donald Cole. On gender issues, see the work of Aisha Mohamed Almana, Soraya Altorki, and Eleanor Doumato. Deborah Amos's book *Lines in the Sand* contains a chapter on gender issues during the Persian Gulf War.

John Esposito's books on Islam, such as *Islam: The Straight Path* and *The Islamic Threat: Myth or Reality?* are among the best and most readable. James P. Piscatori's work on Islamism, *Islamic Fundamentalisms and the Gulf Crisis,* contains information pertinent to Saudi Arabia, as does "Transforming Dualities: Tribe and State Formation in Saudi Arabia" by Joseph Kostiner. John S. Habib's *Ibn Sa'ud's Warriors of Islam* remains the best reference for the Ikhwan movement. Edward Mortimer in *Faith and Power* and George Rentz in "Wahhabism and Saudi Arabia" write on the Wahhabi movement. Christine Moss Helms's *The Cohesion of Saudi Arabia* is not only valuable on the formation of the Saudi state, but also on geography, ecology, and human settlement.

In Alan Richards's and John Waterbury's book, *A Political Economy of the Middle East,* Saudi Arabia may be seen in relation to other Middle Eastern countries. J.S. Birks and C.A. Sinclair discuss issues of economy and development in *Saudi Arabia into the '90s.* (For further information and complete citations, see Bibliography.)

# Chapter 3. The Economy

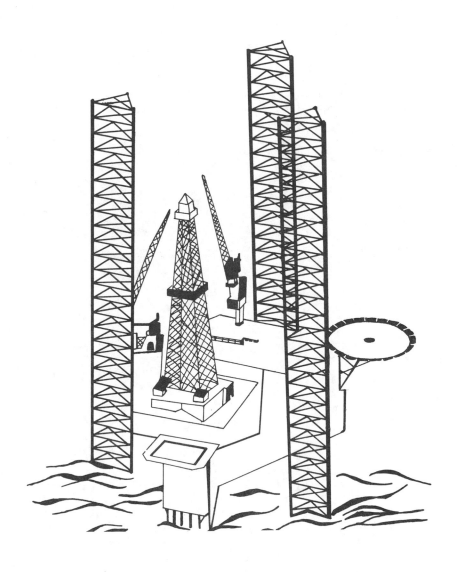

*Offshore drilling platform*

THE DEVELOPMENT of the Saudi Arabian economy has gone hand in hand with the establishment and expansion of the Saudi state during the last fifty years. The process of building the state, fortified by oil revenues distributed through the modern institutions of bureaucracy, worked to unify this economically diverse country. So pervasive has been the influence of these relatively young institutions that few vestiges of the old economy survive unchanged.

Before the discovery of oil in the Arabian Peninsula, it would have been difficult to speak of a unified entity such as the Saudi Arabian economy. Before the 1930s, the region that would later come under the control of the Saudi state was composed of several regions that lived off specific resources and differentiated human activities. The western province, the Hijaz, for example, depended chiefly on subsistence agriculture, some long-distance trade, and the provision of services to pilgrims traveling to the holy cities of Mecca and Medina. A plantation economy that grew dates and other cash crops dominated the Eastern Province (also known as Al Ahsa, Al Hasa, and Ash Sharqiyah). An extremely hostile environment determined geographical separation of peoples. Because permanent habitation could exist only where there was water—at natural springs and wells—the long distances between water sources isolated clusters of people and hampered travel. The difficulty of travel also discouraged penetration from the outside, as did the lack of readily exploitable natural resources.

The discovery of oil in the Eastern Province in 1938 came just six years after another major development: the establishment of the Kingdom of Saudi Arabia, which unified a number of diverse areas of the peninsula under one ruler. Moreover, the rebuilding of Europe after World War II and its need for cheap, reliable sources of oil greatly enhanced the position of the newly established Saudi Arabian oil industry. The combination of these three events formed the basis of the current structure of the Saudi economy.

The quantum jump in revenues that flowed into the treasury of Abd al Aziz ibn Abd ar Rahman Al Saud (ruled 1932–53) fortified his position and allowed the king to exert greater political and economic control over the territories he had conquered. At the apex of the economy was the state with all the mechanisms needed to ensure the rule of the Saud family (Al Saud). The state became the widespread agent of economic change, replacing the traditional economy with one that depended primarily on the state's outlays.

The conjuncture of these events also thrust Saudi Arabia, by virtue of its location and its enormous oil assets, into the center of the West's strategic concerns. At first the issue was the reconstruction of Europe; later, however, the steady flow of oil from the kingdom would be regarded as essential for international economic stability. In this sense, Saudi oil production and investment policies have assumed paramount importance to the industrialized world and, more recently, the developing world. This importance of oil to the West, particularly to the United States, could not have been more clearly underscored than it was by the Iraqi invasion of Kuwait in August 1990 and may have been a key reason for the massive military effort marshaled to expel Iraq from Kuwait. After the Persian Gulf War (1991), Saudi Arabia's standing in the world oil market increased because it was the only major oil-producing country that had significant excess capacity of crude oil production and thereby a strong influence on international oil supplies and prices.

Maintaining this position in the international oil market has been the basis of Saudi economic policy in the early 1990s and was likely to remain so in the near future. Despite Saudi attempts to diversify the economy, developing a self-perpetuating nonoil sector has proved more difficult than earlier Saudi planners had envisioned. This is not to say that the government has not raised the average Saudi citizen's standard of living to one of the highest levels in the world and established for most of its inhabitants world-class infrastructural and social services. But sustaining real income growth still depended primarily on government spending, which was largely facilitated by oil revenues. Therefore, the government could not afford to neglect the oil sector, the primary engine of economic growth.

Developing the oil sector was crucial to domestic political stability, and it was the kingdom's importance as an oil producer that guaranteed its protection during the gulf crisis. During the early 1990s, it was becoming clear that with the expected decline of oil production from the republics of the former Soviet Union, combined with the stagnating output in other debt-ridden and geologically constrained Organization of the Petroleum Exporting Countries (OPEC) and non-OPEC oil producers, Saudi Arabia had the chance to obtain a disproportionate share of any net increment of crude oil demand over the coming years.

Saudi Arabia had set out to meet this challenge with a major capacity-expansion plan for its oil industry. First, the Saudi Arabian Oil Company (Saudi Aramco, the national oil company) accelerated plans to push sustainable domestic crude oil production capacity by 1995 to between 10.5 million and 11 million barrels per day (bpd—see Glossary) from 8.4 million bpd in 1992, with an increased share of lighter grades of crude oil produced. Second, the Saudi Arabian Marketing and Refining Company (Samarec) planned to upgrade its refineries to meet the new environmental standards in the West and growing domestic demand. Third, following its acquisition of downstream (see Glossary) assets in the United States and the Republic of Korea (South Korea), the kingdom planned to purchase refining capacity closer to key consuming markets. Although shrouded in secrecy that made details obscure, this strategy seemed designed to obtain or increase Saudi Arabia's market share.

During the 1970s and early 1980s, the sharp increase in oil prices relieved the chronic financial constraints that had plagued the Saudi state since its inception. Massive oil revenues, combined with delays in using the funds and the Saudi economy's limited absorptive capacity, created large financial surpluses in both the private and government sectors of the economy. The vast majority of these assets were invested in international financial institutions and in Western government securities.

After 1982 government authorities were obliged to change their emphasis from managing surpluses to coping with growing budgetary and balance-of-payments shortfalls. With the downturn in oil prices beginning in 1982, oil revenues to the kingdom began to recede. Given the huge investment expenditures to which it was already committed, the government was forced to finance large budget and current account deficits of the external balance of payments through foreign asset drawdowns. At first, the small decline in oil prices was considered a necessary "cooling off" period and a chance to review the investment program begun fifteen years earlier. Facing an ever-worsening international oil supply glut, the burden of reducing oil output under OPEC's newly installed quota system fell largely on Saudi Arabia. The kingdom's oil revenues therefore took a double blow—reduced prices and reduced exports—not to mention the devaluation of the United States dollar, the currency in which oil is sold on international markets. By late 1985, responding to domestic concerns, Saudi Arabia sharply boosted oil output in an attempt to regain its market share and to impose production discipline on other OPEC members. This policy led directly to the oil price crash of 1986.

The replacement in 1986 of well-known Minister of Petroleum and Mineral Resources Ahmad Zaki Yamani by Hisham Muhi ad Din Nazir, and King Fahd ibn Abd al Aziz Al Saud's personal intervention in the kingdom's oil affairs, were followed by a more commercial approach to oil exports that was designed to maintain Saudi Arabia's world market share. Greater OPEC discipline and a revival in world demand, stimulated by lower oil prices and rapid economic growth in Asia, helped return some buoyancy to the oil markets after 1986. Nonetheless, oil revenues in the late 1980s remained at 25 percent to 30 percent of levels during the early 1980s and proved insufficient to cover government expenditures and offset imports, thus perpetuating budget and external payment deficits. The authorities further reduced foreign assets and attempted to stanch capital flight (aggravated by the short-lived Iranian military thrusts into Iraq in 1986 and 1987 and the "tanker war" of 1987) and to induce the repatriation of private capital through the sale of government bonds. This strategy stemmed the hemorrhage. By early 1990, following the end of the Iran-Iraq War two years earlier, increased oil output and higher oil prices combined with improving private sector confidence to revive an economy that had contracted for several years in a row.

In the two months following the Iraqi invasion of Kuwait in 1990, all government efforts at restoring confidence in the economy since the 1986 price crash evaporated, precipitating another large outflow of private capital and a virtual standstill in domestic investment. But as oil prices and Saudi output soared to replace embargoed Iraqi and Kuwaiti oil, and with the arrival of the United Nations (UN) coalition forces, calm returned to the economy, helped no doubt by substantial expenditures related to the war effort. After the war, the repatriation of private funds and renewed economic confidence created what some journalists called a "miniboom." Despite budgetary problems at home and international economic problems, promising regional trade prospects emerged. Such prospects consisted of new markets in Iran, Central Asia, and South Asia, as well as the reconstruction of Kuwait, that opened new opportunities for Saudi businessmen.

The Persian Gulf War was disastrous for government finances, however. Higher oil revenues were insufficient to cover the estimated US$60 billion that the war cost the Saudi government. The authorities had to deplete the last of the financial reserves remaining from the oil-boom days of the early 1980s. In mid-1992, official external assets stood at the minimum needed for ensuring confidence in the Saudi currency, the riyal, and for maintaining prudent reserves. Although budgetary and external deficits had been sharply reduced, the government was forced to borrow on the international market and to reduce subventions to government enterprises, such as Saudi Basic Industries Corporation (Sabic) and Saudi Aramco, forcing such firms to seek capital overseas.

The status of government accounts in the aftermath of the Persian Gulf War clouded the prospects for smooth financing of the three major expenditure categories on the ruling family's priority list for the 1990s: the oil-sector capacity-expansion plan, major increases in defense and arms purchases, and the maintenance of public investments to sustain the domestic standard of living. The options faced by the government to alleviate its financial constraints were limited, especially on the oil revenue front, and debt financing would be clearly unsustainable over the medium term. During the 1990s, therefore, the government will probably strive for financial maneuverability by reducing the dependence of the private sector on government funds and by attempting to diversify budget revenue sources.

## Economic Policy and the Structure of the Economy
### Fundamental Factors That Transformed the Economy

For thousands of years, the economy of the Arabian Peninsula was determined by autonomous clusters of people living near wells and oases. Most of the population was engaged in agriculture, including nomads who raised livestock by moving their animals to the limited forage produced by infrequent rains. However, the inability of pastoral nomads to provide for their communities solely on the basis of pastoral activities forced them to create multiple resource systems. Such systems took the form of protection services for merchant caravans and pilgrims, control over small oases, and, to a lesser extent, direct cultivation. In the settled areas, local craftsmen produced a few items needed by those living near or visiting the scattered sources of water. Production was limited to serve very small markets and existed essentially on a subsistence level. Trade was limited primarily to camel caravans and the annual influx of pilgrims visiting the holy places in the Hijaz. In the principal cities, such as Jiddah and Mecca, several large merchant families settled permanently and prospered, especially after the late nineteenth-century development of the Hejaz Railway. The growth in international trade associated with European colonial expansion also benefited these merchants and attracted numerous families from as far away as the Eastern Province of Arabia, Persia, the Levant, and Turkey.

The most profound agent of change for the economy of Saudi Arabia was the discovery of huge reserves of oil by a United States company in 1938. Initially, the newly established oil industry had only an indirect impact on this primitive economy. The establishment of the Arabian American Oil Company (Aramco, predecessor of Saudi Aramco) and the oil towns around the oil fields triggered major changes in the economy of the kingdom, especially in the Eastern Province. Development of the oil fields required ancillary construction of modern ports, roads, housing, power plants, and water systems. Saudi workers had to be trained in new skills. In addition, the concentration of oil field employees and the range of services the oil company and employees needed opened new economic opportunities on a scale previously unseen by local merchants, contractors, and others. Aramco provided technical, financial, and logistical support to local entrepreneurs to shed the many support activities it had initially assumed. The discovery of oil ended the kingdom's isolation and introduced new ways to organize the production and distribution of goods and services.

Although the oil industry's creation produced a profound impression on the kingdom's economy, economic structural change was well under way before oil was discovered. Abd al Aziz Al Saud's quest to consolidate his family's control over the territories by establishing a modern state had begun to transform the traditional economy. One of the pivotal policies pursued by the king was sedentarization of the beduin, largely for political and security reasons. As part of the creation of the Ikhwan (see Glossary) movement, Abd al Aziz encouraged the establishment of a series of agricultural communities (*hujar*—see Glossary), designed to relieve the beduin groups comprising this unified military force of providing for their livelihoods (see Nation Building: The Rule of Abd al Aziz, 1926–53, ch. 1). The *hujar* never succeeded in becoming self-sufficient, however, requiring the government to supplement basic necessities. Once the Ikhwan movement was disbanded, some tribesmen returned to their original occupations, but a significant number joined the White Army (so-called because members wore beduin attire not military uniform), which later became the Saudi Arabian National Guard, or moved to the cities to seek employment (see The Ikhwan Movement, ch. 5). Moreover, in 1925 the government abolished the exclusive rights of tribes to their *dira* (tribal grazing land) and further accelerated the transformation. The final blow to the traditional tribal economy was dealt many years later. A law adopted in 1968 distributed swaths of land in various parts of the country to individuals, thereby breaking the centuries-old communal control over land. Inevitably, this distribution of lands led to land ownership patterns that mainly benefited tribal leaders and, finally, to the growth in land sales to nontribal members.

## Economic Policy Making

The economic philosophy of the Saudi Arabian royal family has not changed since the reign of Abd al Aziz, but the economic role of the government has grown tremendously. The stated goal of Saudi rulers has been to improve the economic conditions of the country's citizens while retaining the society's Islamic values. Imbedded in this social contract, however, is the issue of political control. The Al Saud recognized that the key to political power in the kingdom lay in replacing the old economy with lucrative new economic opportunities for the country's citizenry.

In the early stages of the kingdom, the only nontraditional economic opportunities for Saudi citizens were linked to employment in the military, distribution of land, and some modest contracts and commissions. Abd al Aziz had limited means. His revenue was adequate to allow only minimal government functions, not to undertake economic and social projects. Development of the country's oil resources resulted in some wage payments to Saudis and local purchases of goods and services by foreign oil companies, but the impact on the Saudi economy was initially minor. The main beneficiary of oil exports was the ruling family and its tribal allies. Until the 1970s, oil income increased slowly, and the government usually operated under financial constraint. The government's economic decisions were largely those of determining priorities among alternative uses of limited resources. Government structure and subsidiary economic organizations also evolved slowly. In 1952 the Saudi Arabian Monetary Agency (SAMA) was created to serve as the central bank, and in 1962 the General Petroleum and Mineral Organization (Petromin) was formed.

### *Economic Policy During the Oil Boom, 1974–85*

In the early 1970s, the economic situation changed dramatically. Oil exports expanded substantially, royalty payments and taxes on foreign oil companies increased sharply, and oil-exporting governments, including the kingdom, began setting and raising oil export prices. Saudi Arabia's revenues per barrel of oil (averaged from total production and oil revenues) quadrupled from US$0.22 in 1948 to US$0.89 in 1970. By 1973, the price had reached US$1.56 and soared to US$10 and higher in 1974 following the Arab oil embargo introduced to pressure Western supporters of Israel during the October 1973 War. In 1982 the average export price per barrel of oil reached well above US$30. Between 1973 and 1980, government oil revenues jumped from US$4.3 billion to US$101.8 billion. At last the higher oil revenues gave Saudi officials the means to make major structural changes in the economy.

The society encompassed factions eager to promote the modernization program, as well as some elements within the royal family and the religious community who feared the social consequences of rapid economic transformation. Others, mainly from the technocratic elite, were concerned about the economic consequences of such a rapid expansion in expenditures. One choice facing policymakers in the early 1970s was whether to restrict oil production to a level that was adequate to finance limited economic and social development or to allow production at a level that would meet world demand for crude oil. Choosing a relatively high production level would force a decision on whether to use resulting revenues for rapid domestic economic and social development or long-term investments abroad. There were other policy choices. Those people who wanted to keep oil in the ground, except for that needed for limited development, argued strongly that this policy would best preserve the country's resources for future generations.

The choices appear to have been made by 1974 at the latest, although the decision-making process was not always clear or discernible. One issue was clear, however: domestic economic policy did not drive oil production and export policies. The Al Saud pledged to keep oil flowing at moderate prices, commensurate with world needs, arguing that the kingdom was as dependent on the stability and prosperity of consuming nations as those nations were on Saudi oil. Moreover, if Saudi Arabia wanted to ensure that oil would remain the energy source of choice, moderate prices were essential. In addition to framing the issue in purely economic terms, the decision had a geopolitical dimension: since World War II the kingdom had linked itself with the West and was eager to honor its pledge as a loyal ally on the international and regional level. This position was also reflected in its relations with Aramco. Saudi officials argued that the kingdom had avoided nationalization, opting instead for a gradual takeover of foreign oil companies operating within Saudi borders. Despite these attempts to moderate oil prices, the supply-and-demand fundamentals of the international oil market combined with the changes in ownership of downstream assets to raise international oil prices, creating enormous pressures on the domestic front to invest rising oil revenues in developing the country's economic and social infrastructure.

By the mid-1970s, the government had decided to use most of the growing oil revenues for a massive development effort. An important part of that effort was to industrialize, largely by investing in processing plants that used the country's hydrocarbon resources. This policy meant at least a decade of very large investments to build the plants and the necessary infrastructure. It meant financing and building the gas-gathering system, the pipelines for gas and crude oil to bring the raw material to the two chosen main industrial sites—Al Jubayl (or Jubail) and Yanbu al Bahr (known as Yanbu)—and building the industrial sites themselves. The development effort also included many other projects, such as the huge and costly airports at Riyadh and Jiddah, hospitals, schools, industrial plants, roads, and ports. By the mid-1980s, the massive expenditures totaled US$500 billion.

The decision to increase the country's oil and gas resource development through downstream investments in refineries and petrochemical plants was logical considering the country's resource endowment. Three factors motivated such a strategy. First, downstream investments were capital-intensive, which fitted Saudi Arabia's small population and large oil revenues. Second, more value-added income would be extracted and retained, thereby maximizing Saudi revenues through the export of more refined petroleum products instead of crude oil. Moreover, the natural gas that had been largely wasted before the 1980s would be processed and used.

Third, some Saudi planners saw industrialization as another opportunity to widen the sphere of economic activity for foreign and domestic private firms. Participation of foreign private sector firms was crucial from the outset. Saudi Arabia invited several international oil companies to invest in joint ventures in the new export refineries built in the kingdom during the late 1970s and early 1980s. Furthermore, participation by international petrochemical companies was necessary to obtain the technology needed. There was also the issue of access to the markets of the West: Saudi planners anticipated regulatory and trade problems by exporting petrochemicals to markets that already had made substantial investments in the petrochemical industry. Saudi planners therefore hoped that, with the help of foreign multinationals, they could fit Saudi petrochemical output into international distribution networks.

On the domestic front, the state would build the basic industries, the crucial first step in the chain of industrial processing. Through loans and other incentives, the state would foster the growth of specific private sector industries that would be at the lower end of the industrial process. Over a period, the planners anticipated that the state-owned conglomerates might be partially privatized.

A large part of the funds spent on development programs were intended to promote private sector investment and to support future consumption. Starting in the mid-1970s, the government decided that an adequate infrastructure was essential to the kingdom's future development. Providing this infrastructure included revamping and building electricity, water, sewerage, desalination, and telecommunication systems. Moreover, it entailed creating airports and ports and laying a vast network of roads. In terms of generating and distributing electric power, the government assisted private companies building and operating its electricity network through concessionary capital loans and continuing operating subsidies. Apart from upgrading distribution facilities for water, the government built several desalination plants and drilled wells, built dams, and installed pumps. Telecommunications were quickly brought to international standards, allowing Saudi Arabia to handle all its communication needs in local and international telephone, telegraph, maritime, and television distribution services, via cable, satellite, and terrestrial transmission systems. Under King Faisal ibn Abd al Aziz Al Saud (1964–75), there was a massive increase in government spending on education to an annual level of about 10 percent of the budget.

Saudi planners also saw the need for a subsidy program to supplement direct government outlays. The major reason was income distribution. Although direct grants to average citizens would have been most efficient, the logistics involved would have been difficult. Conversely, waiting for the oil expenditures to reach this economic and social objective might have created additional social tensions. Therefore, the government adopted a widespread subsidy program for utilities, fuels, agriculture, social services (both private and public), the industrial sector, and several other areas. Beyond income distribution, the rationale of the subsidy program was the need to promote nonoil development through cheap loans, technical assistance, industrial and agricultural incentives, and preferential buying of domestic products by the government. The subsidy program was also designed to improve education and health services.

The massive development effort entailed many risks. The size of the effort and the technology involved required the participation of a huge number of foreign workers for a long period, with the potential of disrupting the society. The pace of modernization was also economically disruptive. Some observers questioned whether Saudi refineries and petrochemical plants would be efficiently managed and prove competitive within a reasonable time. By the early 1980s, the country encountered economic and social tensions—such as the inflation of the mid-1970s, the takeover of the Grand Mosque in Mecca in November 1979, and disturbances in the Eastern Province in 1979–80—that dissipated only late in the 1980s.

Another risk of the massive development effort was the loss of control over expenditures or inadequate justification of investments.

The sudden easing of financial constraints in the mid-1970s permitted consideration of projects deemed too lavish or too large earlier. The forced development of the capital at Riyadh was a sentimental and political decision that required large expenditures to bring such necessities as water, electricity, communications, and housing inland to a capital far from the economic centers of the country. The huge airports at Riyadh and Jiddah (built at a reported cost of US$3.2 billion and more than US$5 billion, respectively) were architectural monuments, but whether they were a wise use of the patrimony of future generations was unclear.

The rapid rise of public purchases and contracts after 1974 caused foreign businessmen to flock to the kingdom. Because Saudi agents were usually essential, foreign businessmen frequently paid them large fees, to be recovered in the contract they were seeking. The Saudi business sector viewed these practices from a perspective different from that of some outside observers: agent fees and influence peddling were called corruption by visiting journalists but were judged less harshly domestically, although there was some unease. Some Saudis criticized agent fees frequently granted to the wealthy, especially people related to the royal family. The perceived costs, combined with growing criticism at home, eventually prompted the government to restrict the use of agents and fees on some defense contracts and to take other measures to control costs.

Looking back at this huge effort in the early 1990s after several years of stagnant public investment, the picture was mixed. On the one hand, the infrastructure had stood the test of time and provided the citizenry with world-class facilities. On the other hand, maintaining these investments, some of which lacked a direct financial payback, despite their more general economic uses, has been costly. More problematic may be the public perception that authorities, having fostered such dependency on government largess, found it extremely difficult to reduce services.

Several other infrastructure problems became apparent. First, the vast majority of expenditures were concentrated in a few cities, predisposing these metropolitan areas to more rapid economic growth. Second, infrastructural support systems were programmed at an early stage of the country's development, rendering some obsolete in the early 1990s. Third, some of the facilities seemed to have been built as an end in themselves, leading to unnecessary waste and continuing maintenance costs.

The most entrenched problem from the period of rapid development of the mid-1970s to the early 1980s stemmed from the government's willingness to subsidize production, consumption, and investment. The objectives for subsidies were threefold: encouraging nonoil economic activity, meeting social goals, and distributing income. The subsidy program may have created greater problems than were earlier anticipated. Saudi planners never thought that oil revenues would constrain expenditures to the extent that they did in the late 1980s and early 1990s. Efficiency requires that subsidies be applied directly at the source. Most Saudi production subsidies have been indirect subsidies, which have reduced the cost to consumers of electricity and other industrial inputs, leading to unnecessary waste. The industrial sector has thereby become a relatively inefficient producer and has made little effort to wean itself from government assistance.

Nowhere was this problem more prevalent than in the agricultural sector where national security was the original objective in raising output. Saudi Arabia became self-sufficient in several major food grains but the cost to the budget and the ecology could not be justified. First, international experience has shown that if a food embargo were to be imposed, such an embargo has generally failed unless accompanied by a major military campaign. Second, savings on food purchased from overseas could easily have been invested in inventory to safeguard against an external threat. Third, no social benefit emanated from such a program. Agricultural employment continued to decline, and large conglomerates, rather than peasant farmers, profited from most subsidies. Fourth, subsidies could have been related to more appropriate production methods that promoted water conservation.

### Economic Policy after the 1986 Oil-Price Crash

The general thrust of Saudi economic policy underwent a fundamental change after the oil price crash of 1986. The serious depletion of foreign assets, combined with the extensive decline in oil revenues, necessitated a revised economic policy. The depreciation of the United States dollar on international financial markets also hurt Saudi purchasing power abroad. The kingdom's external terms of trade deteriorated rapidly because oil exports were largely denominated in United States dollars, and the bulk of Saudi imports came from countries whose currencies were appreciating relative to the United States dollar.

Reappraisal of the development program became necessary. The most urgent task was shoring up government finances, yet domestic constraints allowed only a few options, especially in terms of raising nonoil revenues. Imposing an income tax, for example, was out of the question partly because of its political dangers in a country where it was an unknown procedure likely to raise questions of income distribution and taxation without representation. Also an income tax appeared impractical because the bureaucratic difficulties involved in collection would be more expensive than the intake would justify. King Fahd's short-lived idea of taxing foreign workers' income was retracted after a public outcry. The government froze some current account spending and cut capital spending, partly by delaying projects and also by canceling some programs. The private sector was informed that subsidies of vast capital expenditures had ended for the present, and, whereas certain major projects would be completed, the government's emphasis would shift to improving the efficiency and maintenance of its public assets. In addition, major defense contracts would include a provision whereby foreign equipment and service contractors would be required to allocate 35 percent of the cost of their projects or services for industrial investments in Saudi Arabia.

### Economic Policy in the 1990s

The government's attempts to deal with the chronic budget deficits, largely through expenditure retrenchment, depletion of foreign assets, and the sale of development bonds, generally helped stabilize its financial situation by the late 1980s (see table 4, Appendix). It became clear by 1989 that the economy had weathered some of the other problems, such as the spate of bankruptcies of private companies, the growth of bad banking debts, and the massive outflow of private capital to overseas financial centers that followed the oil-price crash of 1986. During 1989 and 1990, economic planners had renewed optimism. New plans were made to put the oil and nonoil sectors of the economy on a surer footing. The perceived recovery in international oil consumption and prices provided regional policymakers the opportunity to resume spending to promote economic growth. As a result, two major initiatives became the basis of Saudi economic policy.

First, Saudi Arabia unveiled plans to raise crude oil production capacity to between 10.5 million and 11 million bpd by 1995. With the restructuring of the General Petroleum and Mineral Organization (Petromin), the creation of Samarec, which was given control over most of the kingdom's oil refineries, and the announcement of a major plan to upgrade domestic and export refineries, a comprehensive picture emerged of the government's effort to promote oil investments. Another indication of Riyadh's intentions came in 1989 when Saudi Aramco purchased 50 percent of Star Enterprises in the United States, a joint venture with Texaco that signaled Saudi Arabia's pursuit of geographically diversified downstream projects.

Second, the government was not eager to continue its expansionist fiscal policies. Despite moderately higher oil prices, military outlays, oil-capacity expansion plans, and current expenditures accounted for the bulk of total spending and did not permit a fiscal boost. However, because the nonoil private sector remained largely dependent on government spending, the sharp cutbacks in capital outlays hindered economic diversification. In light of this failure, the government adopted two policies to reorient and revive the private sector.

Financial sector reform was the government's main option. Since 1988 SAMA had made great strides in bolstering commercial bank balance sheets through mergers, debt write-offs, and injection of funds to prevent failures. Subsequently, banking regulations and supervision were tightened and compliance with international capital adequacy requirements enforced. The authorities also encouraged banks to take a more active role in financing private sector investments. The idea of opening a Riyadh stock exchange received renewed interest: the government sanctioned the establishment of the exchange in early 1990 and hinted it could be an appropriate venue for selling government assets.

Protectionism as a policy also gained some popularity during this period. Partly motivated by the impasse in Gulf Cooperation Council (GCC) negotiations with the European Economic Community (EEC), but mainly to protect domestic private investment, Saudi Arabia began enforcing some restrictive tariff and nontariff barriers that had been instituted in the mid-1980s. Under the guise of conforming to GCC-wide levels, Saudi Arabia raised its tariff rates to 20 percent on most items, with certain industrial items gaining protection at higher rates. The government also began enforcing nontariff regulations such as preference for nationally produced commodities and the continued application of preference for local contractors, as well as quality standards that favored local production. In addition, the kingdom assiduously protected domestic banks from foreign competition by barring the sale of any foreign financial products and services.

The Iraqi invasion of Kuwait halted the miniboom that these policies had fostered. In the immediate wake of the invasion, the government faced two tasks. First, it had to deal with the massive outflow of assets from the domestic banking sector by liquidating the commercial banks (which lost more than 12 percent of their deposits within the first month of the crisis), encouraging a repatriation of private assets, and restoring the confidence of foreign creditors, who had canceled lines of credit as a precautionary measure. The monetary authorities reversed most of the hemorrhage caused by the loss of confidence in the Saudi riyal. Second, the government was obliged to raise oil output to levels unseen since the early 1980s. Saudi Aramco had to respond to a serious crisis without an adequate assessment of its overall production capacity. It quickly became apparent that Saudi Arabia had sufficient capacity to replace the bulk of the 4.5 million to 5 million bpd of Iraqi and Kuwaiti oil embargoed by the UN. Output rose rapidly to 8.5 million bpd, which restored some calm to the international oil market; however, by the end of 1990, oil prices were nearly double those in June 1990.

Supporting the United States-led multinational forces, however, placed an enormous burden on the government's budget. Because the deficits for 1990 and 1991 reached record levels, the fiscal authorities were forced again to engage in further external asset drawdowns, increased volumes of development bond sales, and a novel feature: external borrowing from commercial banks and export credit agencies. Saudi Arabia was a prominent member of the World Bank (see Glossary) but because of the nation's high per capita income, it was not entitled to borrow from that organization. Most of the major projects envisaged before August 1990 were preserved, however. But external borrowing had gained credence as the means to fund not only budgetary shortfalls but also the capital programs of major public enterprises. Notably, Saudi Aramco did not scale back its crude-oil capacity expansion plan. Rather, it appeared that new ways of financing were being sought from foreign commercial banks, multinational companies, and the domestic private sector. Sabic also moved to raise capital overseas, while Saudi Consolidated Electric Company (Sceco), the electricity conglomerate, requested foreign suppliers to help finance its expansion program.

The fiscal crisis did not cause economic problems for the private sector because the government's reduction of its budgeted expenditures was slight. Moreover, domestic government spending in support of the war effort surged, and many Saudi companies benefited from war-related contracts. Also, as a result of Operation Desert Shield and Operation Desert Storm, the more than 600,000 troops of the multinational forces increased domestic spending on consumer goods. This spending offset the effects of the fall in the number of foreign workers after the government expelled more than 1 million Yemenis, Palestinians, Sudanese, and Iraqis following the Iraqi invasion of Kuwait. The miniboom, which was interrupted by the Iraqi invasion, was revived by this increase in government spending, and then received further stimulus by three other factors. First, the protection of the kingdom by United States forces and the perception that this would continue enhanced private sector confidence in the government. The private sector again repatriated capital, and the stock market boomed, with share issues rising to unprecedented levels. Second, changing regional politics encouraged many firms, which had set up manufacturing and processing plants for the domestic market, to seek sales in Iran, Turkey, and Central Asia. Third, the government cut domestic fees and utility charges almost in half. This increased subsidy was targeted to lower- and middle-income Saudis but had the net effect of raising domestic disposable income. As a result, it was seen by some people as a serious attempt by the monarchy to head off growing domestic demands for political participation.

## Five-Year Plans

The kingdom first established a planning agency in 1958 in response to suggestions of International Monetary Fund (IMF— see Glossary) advisers. Planning was limited in the 1960s partly because of Saudi financial constraints. The government concentrated its limited funds on developing human resources, the transportation system, and other infrastructure aspects. In 1965 planning was formalized in the Central Planning Organization, and in the 1975 government reorganization it became the Ministry of Planning. The Ministry of Finance and National Economy controlled funding, however, and appeared to exert considerable influence over plan implementation.

The First Development Plan (1970–75) was drafted in the late 1960s and became effective on September 2, 1970, at the start of the fiscal year (FY—see Glossary). Drafted during a period of fiscal constraint, gross domestic product (GDP—see Glossary) was to increase by 9.8 percent per year (in constant prices) and show the greatest increase in the nonoil sectors. Planned budget allocations for the five years were US$9.2 billion, 45 percent of which was to be spent on capital projects. Planned expenditures were concentrated on defense, education, transportation, and utilities. The unanticipated great expansion of crude oil production, accompanied by large increases in revenues per barrel, contributed to an exceptionally high rate of economic growth, far beyond the planners' expectations. Nonoil real GDP increased by 11.6 percent per year. As oil revenues grew, budget allocations increased, totaling about US$27 billion for the five years; actual budget expenditures amounted to US$21 billion.

The Second Development Plan (1975–80) became effective on July 9, 1975, at the start of the fiscal year. The plan contained numerous social goals similar to those of the first plan, but it also set forth goals that reflected decreased fiscal constraints. Social goals included the introduction of free medical service, free education and vocational training, interest-free loans and subsidies for the purchase of homes, subsidized prices for essential commodities, interest-free credit for people with limited incomes, and extended social security benefits and support for the needy. The plan also outlined several economic goals and programs. GDP was to grow at an average rate of 10 percent a year. The nonoil sector's real planned rate of increase was 13.3 percent per year; the oil sector's projected rate of growth was 9.7 percent, although actual growth would depend on world markets.

The government's planned expenditures totaled almost US$142 billion, plus additional private investment. As the size of oil revenues became clearer during the plan's preparation, the final investment figure was more than double the initial sum. The planners acknowledged that spending of this magnitude would create various problems, and they anticipated shortfalls in actual spending. The largest share of planned government expenditure, 23 percent, was allocated for continuing development of ports, roads, and other infrastructure. Expansion of industry, agriculture, and utilities received 19 percent of expenditures, and defense and human resource development—essentially education—each received 16 percent.

The planners were correct in anticipating problems. An increasing flood of imports after 1972 proved too great for the transportation system to handle. Ports, where ships waited for four to five months to unload, were bottlenecks, but storage and distribution from the ports were also inadequate. Government spending contributed to the problems. By 1976 the clogged ports, an acute housing shortage, skyrocketing construction costs, and a growing manpower shortage caused prices to accelerate at what some observers estimated at about 50 percent a year, although the official cost-of-living index did not reflect these rates.

By 1977 second plan projects and ad hoc measures, such as the government's spending less than planned, had relieved many problem areas. Construction of additional ports, which contributed to almost a fivefold increase in the number of ship berths, and paved roads, which increased by 63 percent to more than 22,000 kilometers as well as other substantial additions to the transportation and communications system occurred during the second plan period. More than 200,000 housing units were built over the five years.

Actual government expenditures during the second plan reached US$200 billion, about 40 percent above the planned figure and almost ten times the level of the first plan. As the transportation bottlenecks were removed, annual budget expenditures increased. Expenditures for salaries and other operating costs increased more rapidly than expected, whereas capital investments rose more slowly than budgeted. Over the course of the plan, between 20 percent and 33 percent of national income was devoted to investment. The private sector accounted for 27 percent of fixed capital formation; government ministries and agencies outside of the oil and gas sector invested 61 percent, and the public oil sector accounted for 12 percent. The bulk of fixed capital formation was in construction.

Despite the massive increase in government expenditures, overall real GDP growth at 9.2 percent average per annum was below the planned 10 percent rate. This lower growth resulted from a slower-than-anticipated growth in petroleum production, a function of international market conditions and political factors. Nonoil GDP grew at an average annual rate of 14.8 percent per year compared with a planned rate of 13.3 percent. The producing components grew at 16.6 percent per year on average (the plan rate was 13 percent), with most components outpacing their targets. The following components all exceeded their targets: agriculture, manufacturing, utilities, and services (including trade, transport, and finance). Construction paralleled the planned growth rate, and mining other than oil and public sector projects did not meet targets.

The Third Development Plan (1980–85) took effect May 15, 1980. The third plan featured a modest rise in government expenditures reflecting stabilization of oil revenues and a desire to avoid inflation and disruptions to society from an unduly rapid pace of development. The planners expected construction activity to decline, but unfinished projects were to be completed and industry developed. Lower construction levels were expected to require only a small increase in the number of foreign workers. However, requirements for highly skilled workers and technicians, Saudi and foreign, to operate and maintain plants and equipment were expected to require shifts in the composition of the work force.

Total planned government civilian development expenditures during the third plan amounted to US$213 billion, plus an additional US$25 billion for administrative and subsidy costs. Third plan expenditures were categorized differently, making comparisons with the second plan difficult. Civilian development expenditures planned for 1980–85 were US$79 billion for the economy, primarily industry (37 percent of the total in the third plan; 25 percent in the second plan), US$76 billion for infrastructure (36 percent in the third plan; 50 percent in the second plan), US$39 billion for human resource development (19 percent in the third plan; 16

percent in the second plan), and US$18 billion for social development (close to 9 percent in both plans).

The third plan coincided with the sharp downturn in Saudi oil production. The oil sector's output fell on average 14.2 percent per annum. As a result, during the five years of the plan the average annual real GDP growth rate declined 1.5 percent compared with a planned annual increase of 1.3 percent. The principal factors behind the continued positive rates of growth in the nonoil sector (6.4 percent on average per annum) were the relatively few cutbacks in government expenditures and the continuation of major infrastructure and industrial projects despite declining oil revenues. The nonoil manufacturing sector and utilities expanded at 12.4 percent and 18.6 percent, respectively, but at annual growth rates well below their targets. The construction sector contracted but only at half the rate planned. The agricultural sector grew rapidly, surging to 8.1 percent per annum. The service sector maintained its momentum during the third plan, with trade and government services leading the way. The transportation and finance subsectors, however, fell well below their targets.

The Fourth Development Plan (1985–90) budgeted total government outlays at SR1 trillion (for value of the riyal—see Glossary) or almost US$267 billion, of which about US$150 billion was budgeted for civilian development spending. Most cuts were to come from reduced expenditures on infrastructure and a shift to developing economic and human resources. Concern for preserving the government's new investments was reflected in increased budgeted spending on operations and maintenance. The plan also emphasized stimulating private sector investment and increasing economic integration with members of the GCC (see Collective Security under the Gulf Cooperation Council, ch. 5).

During the period of the fourth plan, oil revenues plummeted following the oil-price crash of 1986. Overall real rates of GDP growth averaged a positive 1.4 percent per annum, far below the 4 percent programmed. The revival in crude oil output from the low levels of 1986, however, boosted oil sector growth rates to 3.6 percent per annum. The sharp decline in external income caused lower rates of output expansion in the producing sectors. Construction and other mining sector growth rates fell by 8.5 and 1.9 percent, respectively. Other manufacturing continued to grow modestly at 1.1 percent per annum, but well below the 15.5 percent target. Trade, transport, and finance reflected the financial setbacks in the government's program with annual average production declines. Two surprises helped to offset the depressed growth rates: agriculture, which had shown steadily higher rates of output growth in the second and third plan, rose by 13.4 percent per annum on average during the fourth plan, nearly double its planned rate, and the utilities sector's ability to surpass its planned target of 5 percent per annum.

Constrained resources shaped the Fifth Development Plan (1990–95), with committed funds for the civilian program falling by nearly 30 percent to approximately US$105.4 billion for the period. The bulk of the cuts were in government investment in economic enterprises, transportation, and communications. Human resources development, health and social services, and municipality and housing all maintained their fourth-plan levels. Overall, the fifth plan called for consolidating the gains in infrastructure and social services of the previous twenty years and emphasized further economic diversification. The principal means for achieving this goal was expanding the productive base of the economy by encouraging private sector investment in agriculture and light manufacturing. The private sector was allowed to purchase shares in the larger industrial complexes and utilities. For example, Sabic may be further privatized as well as some downstream refining assets. In addition, there was greater emphasis on financial sector reform and development through the establishment of joint stock companies and the role of the stock market in trading shares and other financial instruments. Another objective of the plan was greater government efficiency in social and economic services.

Fifth-plan targets envisaged a 3.2 percent per annum growth rate. Oil sector output was expected to increase 2.2 percent per annum, while nonoil sector growth-rate targets were 3.6 percent. Agriculture, other manufacturing, utilities, and finance were to pace the economy while other sectors would show only modest growth rates of 2 percent to 4 percent per annum.

## Changing Structure of the Economy

Measuring the changing structure of the economy was difficult because of the lack of consistent data on the GDP structure (see table 5, Appendix). After the 1986 price crash and the shift from the use of the *hijra* (see Glossary) calendar as the basis for government fiscal year accounting, national accounts data were revised and were generally not comparable to pre-1984 data. Moreover, the base year used was extremely important: if the base year were 1980, when oil prices were at peak levels, the nonoil sector in 1986 accounted for 50 percent of real GDP; if the 1970 base year were used, nonoil GDP was closer to 75 percent of total output.

Since 1984 the relative share of nonoil GDP has fallen from 75.8 percent of overall real GDP (in 1970 prices) to 67.4 percent in 1990 (the latest year for which data were available in 1992). This fall in nonoil GDP share resulted from the steady growth in crude oil production, increases in gas output, and higher refinery throughput, which rose prior to the sharp increase in oil output in late 1990. In the nonoil sector, the agricultural sector has grown most during this period. Accounting for 7.5 percent of nonoil output in 1984, this sector had risen to more than 14.7 percent in 1990. The utilities sector has also gained, growing from 2.5 percent of nonoil production in 1984 to 4.6 percent in 1990. In contrast, manufacturing has remained relatively stable, rising from 8.1 percent of nonoil GDP in 1984 to 9.0 percent in 1990. In contrast, construction fell from 14.3 percent of nonoil GDP in 1984 to 9.2 percent in 1990. Services, comprising trade, transport, and social services, fell from more than 66.8 percent to 62.4 percent in the same period.

## Labor

The Saudi labor force has undergone tremendous change in the latter half of the twentieth century as a consequence of the demise of traditional means of livelihood linked to pastoral nomadism as a way of life for most of the people and the rise of a modern economy. A large number of Saudis moved from these older occupations into government service. Many foreign workers were also brought into the kingdom by the private sector. With the domestic labor force growing at an average of 5 percent annually between 1975 and 1985, despite an annual population growth among the highest in the world at 3.5 percent, foreign labor was still necessary. Estimates varied, but a reliable Western source indicated that total employment grew from more than 1.7 million in 1975 to 2.2 million in 1980. The domestic work force numbered 1 million people (58 percent of total employment) in 1975. By 1980 employment of foreigners had risen from 723,000 in 1975 to more than 1 million (or 46 percent of total employment).

Ministry of Planning estimates, providing a breakdown of the sectoral distribution of employment, showed a slightly different picture. According to these figures, the total work force was 2.9 million in FY 1979, of which 1.3 million workers were in producing sectors and 1.6 million were in the services sectors. Labor was concentrated in four main sectors: in FY 1979 agriculture accounted for 15.8 percent of the total work force, construction 20.4 percent, trade 10.6 percent, and community and social services, including government service, 34.1 percent. By FY 1989 the total labor force had risen to close to 5.8 million, with 2.1 million in production sectors and 3.7 million in service sectors. Agriculture's share had fallen to 9.9 percent, construction was down to 16.4 percent, whereas trade's share of the labor force rose to 15.6 percent and community and social services were up to 42.4 percent. These figures indicated the extent to which the government had a direct hand in the livelihood of the average Saudi.

## Oil and Gas Industry

Saudi Arabia is the world's most important oil producer. Given its relatively high production levels, accounting for nearly 13 percent of world output and 35 percent of total OPEC output in 1991, and, more significantly, its small domestic needs, the kingdom's dominance of international crude oil markets is unchallenged. Although reluctant to play the role, Saudi Arabia has become the "swing producer," balancing international oil demand and supply. Therefore, within limits, Saudi oil production policies can have a profound impact on international prices. Since the early 1970s, the kingdom has occasionally used this dominance to influence oil prices, usually to further its objectives of sustaining long-term oil consumption and ensuring economic stability in the industrialized world.

The oil sector is the key domestic production sector; oil revenues constituted 73 percent of total budgetary revenues in 1991. Precise statistics for expenditures on sector development were not available, but some estimates placed the annual figure at US$5 billion to US$7 billion, or less than 10 percent of total budgetary expenditures. Export oil revenues accruing to Saudi Aramco, a large portion of which is allocated to the budget, accounted for 90 percent of total exports in 1991. Only in the number of jobs was the oil sector relatively unimportant to the economy; the capital-intensive nature of the oil industry required few workers—less than 2 percent of the labor force in the early 1990s.

### Brief History

Abd al Aziz ibn Abd ar Rahman Al Saud, the first king of Saudi Arabia, had not gained control of the western part of the country when he granted the first oil concession in 1923. A British investment group, the Eastern and General Syndicate, was the recipient. The syndicate gambled on the possibility that it could sell the concession, but British petroleum companies showed no interest. The concession lapsed and was declared void in 1928.

Discovery of oil in several places around the Persian Gulf suggested that the peninsula contained petroleum deposits. Several major oil companies, however, were blocked from obtaining concessions there by what was known as the Red Line Agreement, which prohibited companies with part ownership of a company

*Pipelines, Ras Tanura refinery*
*Offshore pipelines, Ras Tanura*
*Courtesy* Aramco World

operating in Iraq from acting independently in a proscribed area that covered much of the Middle East. Standard Oil Company of California (Socal—later Chevron), which was not affected by the Red Line Agreement, gained a concession and found oil in Bahrain in 1932. Socal then sought a concession in Saudi Arabia that became effective in July 1933. Socal assigned its concession to its wholly owned operating subsidiary, California Arabian Standard Oil Company (CASOC). In 1936 Socal sold a part interest in CASOC to Texaco to gain marketing facilities for the crude discovered in its worldwide holdings. The name of the operating company in Saudi Arabia was changed to Arabian American Oil Company (Aramco) in January 1944. Two partners, Standard Oil Company of New Jersey (later renamed Exxon) and Socony-Vacuum (now Mobil Oil Company), were added in 1946 to gain investment capital and marketing outlets for the large reserves being discovered in Saudi Arabia. These four companies were the sole owners of Aramco until the early 1970s.

The original concession called for an annual rental fee of 5,000 British pounds (£) in gold or its equivalent until oil was discovered, a loan of £250,000 in gold to the Saudi government, a royalty payment of four shillings gold per net ton of crude production after the discovery of oil, and the free supply to the government of specific quantities of products from the refinery Aramco was to build after oil was discovered. (In 1933 the British pound was worth US$4.87; there were twenty shillings to the British pound.) The company received exclusive rights to explore for, produce, and export oil, free of all Saudi taxes and duties, from most of the eastern part of Saudi Arabia for sixty years. The terms granted by the government were liberal, reflecting the king's need for funds, his low estimate of future oil production, and his weak bargaining position.

The original concession agreement was modified many times. The first modification was made in 1939 after the discovery of oil in 1938. This change added to Aramco's concession area and extended the period to 1999 in return for payments substantially higher than those specified in the first agreement and for larger quantities of free gasoline and kerosene to be supplied by Aramco to the Saudi government. In 1950 a fifty-fifty profit-sharing agreement was signed, whereby a tax (called an income tax, but actually a tax on each barrel of oil produced) was levied by the government. This tax considerably increased government revenues. Further revisions increased the government's share—slowly until the 1970s and rapidly thereafter. At the beginning of 1982, Aramco's concession area amounted to about 220,000 square kilometers

(189,000 onshore and 31,000 offshore), having relinquished more than 80 percent of the original area of almost 1.3 million square kilometers.

Once the existence of oil in quantity was ascertained, the advantages of a pipeline to the Mediterranean Sea seemed obvious; it would save about 3,200 kilometers of sea travel and the transit fees of the Suez Canal. The Trans-Arabian Pipeline Company (Tapline), a wholly owned Aramco subsidiary, was formed in 1945, and the pipeline was completed in 1950. Many innovations were required to keep costs down and to make operations competitive with tankers. Tapline linked the Lebanese port of Az Zahrani, close to Sidon, to Al Qaysumah in Saudi Arabia (a distance of more than 1,200 kilometers), where it connected with a pipeline collecting oil from Aramco fields. Initial capacity was 320,000 bpd, but capacity was expanded, and the pipeline eventually handled 480,000 bpd in the mid-1970s. Tax problems with Saudi authorities and transit fees due Jordan, Iraq, and Lebanon plagued Tapline for many years. The line was damaged and out of operation several times in the 1970s. And as operating costs of Tapline increased, supertankers were reducing seaborne expenses. By 1975 Tapline was no longer used to export Saudi crude via Sidon. In 1982 the line was again damaged. In late 1983, Tapline filed formal notice to cease operations in Syria and Lebanon, although small amounts of crude would reportedly continue, albeit temporarily, to supply a refinery in Jordan.

From the very start, Aramco had to concern itself with more than just oil. Its company presidents were virtually United States ambassadors in Saudi Arabia and played a significant role in shaping United States-Saudi relations in the early days of the oil company. Moreover, the undeveloped infrastructure and facilities demanded that Aramco construct virtually everything it needed. A port to bring in equipment had to be built; water had to be found and delivered to work areas; and housing, hospitals, and offices had to be constructed to launch development. Few Saudis were familiar with machinery, local construction firms hardly existed, and the unavailability of most materials locally necessitated long supply lines.

Aramco adopted the long-range policy of training Saudis to take over as many tasks as possible. However, major management positions (culled from the ranks of the parent companies) were not intended to be relinquished and were not relinquished until Aramco could not resist government pressure to do so in the 1970s and 1980s. A wide variety of training programs, including sixty annual scholarships to foreign universities, and social service programs

137

were established by Aramco. Saudis, for example, were trained as doctors, supply experts, machinists, ship pilots, truck drivers, oil drillers, and cooks. Many of these Saudis later fanned out into the local economy to establish businesses and entered the growing bureaucracy in Jiddah and Riyadh. Others remained with Aramco and advanced in responsibility. Aramco was also one of the first foreign companies in Saudi Arabia to employ labor from a variety of countries other than the United States. By 1980 about 22,000 of the 38,000 Aramco employees (excluding some 20,000 workers employed by Aramco contractors), were Saudis. More than 45 percent of management and supervisory positions were occupied by Saudis. In 1982 Ali Naimi, who had started with Aramco at age eleven and had risen through the ranks, became first executive vice president in charge of operations; two years later, Naimi became the first Saudi president of Aramco. The United States presence declined over the years. By 1980 there were only 3,400 United States citizens with Aramco. The remaining work force consisted of nationals from about forty-four countries. In 1989 the total number of company employees was 43,248. Of these, 31,712 were Saudis whereas the United States work force had shrunk to 2,482, and other foreign workers were slightly more than 9,000.

To divest itself of supply and service sidelines, Aramco had always subcontracted work to local entrepreneurs and at times provided technical, financial, and material assistance. At the request of King Abd al Aziz, Aramco teams helped find water and develop agricultural projects. The Saudi government paid the company to build a modern port at Ad Dammam and to supervise the construction of a railroad linking the port to Riyadh.

In the 1970s, Aramco's activities expanded greatly. Part of the expansion was associated with the facilities needed for the more than threefold increase of crude oil production during the period. Well drilling, pipeline installation, and construction of gas-oil separation plants, storage tanks, and tanker-loading terminals accelerated tremendously. As the world's largest oil company, Aramco frequently had to design and build installations larger than those used elsewhere. During the 1970s, Aramco was also entrusted with developing a gas-gathering system (currently referred to as the master gas system), which reportedly cost between US$10 billion and US$15 billion for the first phase alone and was completed in 1982. The company was also charged with producing the Eastern Province's electricity supply through managing the regional electric power company.

In 1968 Minister of Petroleum and Mineral Resources Ahmad Zaki Yamani first publicly broached the idea of Saudi participation in Aramco. In December 1972, long negotiations were completed for the Saudi government to buy 25 percent ownership of Aramco, effective in 1973. Negotiations during 1973 resulted in Saudi participation increasing to 60 percent, effective the beginning of 1974. In 1976 arrangements for total ownership of Aramco were reached, and in 1980 payments to the four Aramco parent companies were completed. By 1988 Aramco was converted to a totally Saudi-owned company called Saudi Arabian Oil Company (Saudi Aramco). By the 1990s, Saudi Aramco had responsibility for all domestic exploration and development—its mandate was expanded to include all Saudi Arabia—engaging in downstream joint ventures overseas, purchasing on-land storage facilities closer to key consuming markets for its crude oil, and expanding its tanker subsidiary, Vela Marine International.

The General Petroleum and Mineral Organization (Petromin) was established in 1962 as a public corporation wholly owned by the Saudi government to develop industries based on petroleum, natural gas, and minerals by itself or in conjunction with other investors, foreign or domestic. Although its activities predominantly centered on the country's hydrocarbon resources, Petromin also explored for and developed other mineral resources.

Petromin's original charter suggested that it would eventually become the country's national oil company. After the mid-1960s, only Petromin received concessions for exploration and development. Petromin, however, assigned its rights, but not its concessions, to companies formed with foreign oil companies. A joint venture was formed with an Italian state company to explore part of the Rub al Khali, or Empty Quarter, but activity ceased in 1973 after the company failed to discover oil. In 1967 Petromin joined a number of foreign oil companies in an equally unsuccessful exploration of areas of the Red Sea claimed by the kingdom.

In the 1960s, Petromin became responsible for domestic distribution of petroleum products, partly by purchasing Aramco's local marketing facilities. It became part owner with private Saudi investors in domestic refineries in Jiddah and Riyadh. It also began marketing crude oil abroad and became involved in tanker transport. By 1975 some of Petromin's activities were curtailed as part of a ministerial reorganization. Among the reasons for limiting its scope were its unsuccessful attempts at further oil exploration, the incompetence of its operations, and the diffusion of its activities. A clearer distinction between its activities and those of Aramco also occasioned the restriction. Some businesses in which Petromin held part ownership, such as a fertilizer plant and a steel mill, as well as responsibility for the many large petrochemical plants that were in the study stage, were transferred to the new Ministry of Industry and Electricity.

Although its responsibilities shrank somewhat after 1975, Petromin's activities increased. It supervised the construction and became responsible for operation of the crude oil pipeline from the Eastern Province oil fields to the new industrial city of Yanbu on the Red Sea coast. In joint-venture partnerships with foreign oil companies, it rapidly expanded refining facilities for domestic use and export. Petromin had responsibility for the supply, storage, and distribution of domestic petroleum products, for which the demand was growing rapidly. Petromin marketed some crude oil and petroleum products abroad and exported natural gas liquids. It also continued exploration and drilling activities well into the 1980s.

By the late 1980s, however, the government had decided to create a company to take over Petromin's activities. The Saudi Arabian Marketing and Refining Company (Samarec) was created in 1988 to produce and market refined products in the kingdom and abroad. It assumed control of the joint ventures with foreign oil companies. Moreover, the government ordered Samarec to implement the major upgrading of domestic refineries, believed to cost well over US$5 billion during the first half of the 1990s.

Among the pivotal concessions Saudi Arabia awarded were those made to two small independent oil companies to explore for oil in the Divided Zone (see Glossary). In 1949 the Getty Oil Company (formerly Pacific Western Oil Corporation) was granted the right to explore in the Saudi share of the Divided Zone. Aramco had relinquished this area in 1948 partly because the ruler of Kuwait had won very favorable terms for a concession in his share of the Divided Zone, and Aramco did not want to match those terms (see External Boundaries, ch. 2).

Production from this concession (since the 1970s partly owned by Saudi Arabia) averaged 60,000 bpd during the 1980s. During the Persian Gulf War, production came to a halt because Getty's facilities were heavily damaged by the Iraqi occupying forces. The oil fields were mined while wells and gathering centers were seriously damaged or destroyed, as were the refinery and ten of fourteen crude oil storage tanks.

The second pivotal concession was granted in December 1957 by Saudi Arabia to the Arabian Oil Company (AOC), owned by Japanese business interests, giving exploration rights to the Divided Zone offshore area for two years, subject to extension. If oil were discovered in commercial quantities, an exploitation lease was to be granted for forty years. Subsequently, Saudi Arabia and Kuwait each became 10 percent owners of AOC. By the mid-1970s, Saudi

Arabia had increased its stake to 60 percent, and in the early 1990s still controlled the company.

During the 1980s, average production was 125,000 bpd. After Iraqi attacks on storage facilities and the removal of personnel during the Persian Gulf War, output was shut down; production returned to peak levels by early 1992.

## Oil Industry in the 1990s

### Structure and Organization

After two decades of organizational change, the reshaping of the oil industry in Saudi Arabia neared completion by the late 1980s. During the 1970s and early 1980s, the industry was transformed from one controlled by foreign oil companies (the Aramco parent companies) to one owned and operated by the government. Decisions made directly by the ruling family increasingly became a feature of the industry in the late 1970s. Saudi Arabia's participation in the Arab oil embargo in 1973 and foreign policy goals were features of this transition. In 1992 the government had title to all mineral resources in the country (except in the former Divided Zone, where both Kuwait and Saudi Arabia had interests in the natural resources of the whole zone). Through the Supreme Oil Council, headed by the king, and the Ministry of Petroleum and Mineral Resources the government initiated, funded, and implemented all investment decisions. It also controlled daily operations related to production and pricing.

On a functional level, the industry also underwent significant transformation. By the late 1980s, the major companies established by or taken over from foreign owners by the government were required to produce a particular product. For the most part, only one company controlled a certain industrial subsector, although there was some overlap. In the upstream part of the oil industry, all exploration, development, and production decisions within Saudi Arabia were controlled by Saudi Aramco. It managed the oil fields, pipelines, crude oil export facilities, and the master gas system throughout the country. Through its subsidiary Vela Marine International, Saudi Aramco controlled Saudi Arabia's tanker fleet. Because downstream investments overseas were an integral part of Saudi Arabia's crude oil marketing strategy, these have come under the control of Saudi Aramco. These downstream investments were joint-venture operations with foreign oil refiners. Saudi Aramco also operated the kingdom's largest oil refinery. In 1992 the refinery's output largely conformed to Samarec's specifications. Saudi Aramco was managed by a board of directors headed by the minister of petroleum and mineral resources and a senior management staff headed by a president, with the Supreme Oil Council having oversight. Most operational decisions were made by the professional staff except oil output decisions, instructions for which came from the king through the minister.

The downstream subsector of the oil industry was dominated by Samarec. Operated as a wholly government-owned refining and marketing company, Samarec took over Petromin's operation in 1988. Petromin still existed on paper, legally holding title with three foreign oil companies to the export refinery joint ventures at Al Jubayl on the gulf, and Yanbu and Rabigh on the Red Sea. In addition to managing these refineries, Samarec operated three wholly owned domestic refineries at Riyadh, Jiddah, and Yanbu. Samarec controlled the distribution of refined products within Saudi Arabia and managed the bulk plants, loading terminals, tanker fleet, and product pipelines. All export sales of refined products were also managed by the downstream company. During the Persian Gulf War, to augment domestic supplies of jet fuel and other products, Samarec bid for products in the Singapore market. The Petromin board of directors, headed by the minister of petroleum and mineral resources, set Samarec policy but operations were managed by a senior staff.

After the reorganization of Petromin, the government transferred the production and distribution of lubricating oils to two joint ventures with Mobil. Two new companies were established: Petromin Lubricating Oil Company (Petrolube) and Petromin Lubricating Oil Refining Company (Luberef). Luberef operated the kingdom's single base oil refinery (base oil is a byproduct of the refining process), while Petrolube ran three small lubricating oil blending plants. Three other smaller private sector plants also operated lubricating oil blending facilities.

### Crude Oil Production and Pricing Policy

The kingdom's oil policy was based on three factors: maintaining moderate international oil prices to ensure the long-term use of crude oil as a major energy source; developing sufficient excess capacity to stabilize oil markets in the short run and maintain the importance of the kingdom and its permanence to the West as a crucial source of oil in the long term; obtaining minimum oil revenues to further the development of the economy and prevent fundamental changes in the domestic political system.

Short-term oil policy in the early 1990s has been shaped by two major sequences of events. The first was Saudi Arabia's refusal

*Al Marjan gas-oil separation plant*
*Ras Tanura Sea Islands Number 3 and Number 4, with tankers*
*Courtesy* Aramco World

143

to play the role of "swing producer" in the mid-1980s, its subsequent bid to maintain its market share, and abandonment of the fixed oil price system after the 1986 price crash. The second was Iraq's invasion of Kuwait, the kingdom's replacement of most of the oil lost from these two OPEC members, and its ascendance as unchallenged leader within OPEC after August 1990. Both periods have shaped an oil policy that called for OPEC decisions to promote moderate and stable oil prices but not compromise the kingdom's demand for its market share. Before the Persian Gulf War, Saudi Arabia demanded about 25 percent of the OPEC production ceiling; after the Iraqi invasion of Kuwait the share rose to 35 percent.

Saudi Arabia's behavior in the oil market since 1986 demonstrated its attempts to ensure both goals. In the early 1980s, oil prices rose rapidly because of the breakdown of the old vertically integrated system of multinational oil companies, following nationalizations by producer governments during the 1970s. Other causes of the price rises were the disruption of Iranian exports during and after the Iranian Islamic Revolution in 1979, and the destruction of the Iranian and Iraqi oil sectors during the Iran-Iraq War of 1980–88, which exacerbated an already low level of spare production capacity. High oil prices in the early 1980s stimulated the rapid growth of non-OPEC oil supplies in the developing world, in Siberia, the North Sea, and Alaska.

As a result, oil prices began to drop in late 1982, forcing OPEC to institute a voluntary output reduction system by assigning individual quotas. The new system failed to stem the price slide, however. By 1985 spot oil (see Glossary) prices had fallen to about US$25 per barrel from an average of US$32 per barrel in the early 1980s.

Saudi Arabia's adherence to an official price system, which most OPEC members were abandoning, rendered the kingdom the swing producer. As a result, Saudi Arabia was forced to curtail output to ever lower levels. Other members "cheated" on their quotas by offering competitive prices, effectively pushing the entire burden of adjustment onto Saudi Arabia. In 1979–80, Saudi Arabia had peaked at a production of more than 10 million bpd; by 1986, that amount had reached a low point of 3 million bpd.

In early 1986, Saudi Arabia discontinued selling its oil at official prices and switched to a market-based pricing system called netback pricing—that guaranteed purchasers a certain refining margin. In doing so, Saudi Arabia recaptured a significant market share from the rest of OPEC. The sharp rise in crude oil supplies precipitated the crash of spot prices from an average of US$28 per barrel in 1985 to US$14 per barrel in 1986. The Saudis had used their "oil weapon"—significant excess capacity combined with adequate foreign financial reserves cushioning the blow of lower oil revenues—to establish some discipline in OPEC.

It did not take long before OPEC agreed to a new set of quotas tied to a price target of US$18 per barrel. By late 1986 and early 1987, prices rose to US$15 or US$16 per barrel for the OPEC basket (from well below US$10 per barrel in early 1986). To avoid a swing producer role, the Saudis imposed an important condition on other OPEC members: a guaranteed quota of approximately 25 percent of the total output ceiling, correlated to a US$18 per barrel price objective.

The latter became the center of controversy within the organization for much of the period before the Iraqi invasion of Kuwait. A revival in oil demand growth rates in the industrialized world between 1988 and 1990, partly aided by several years of low oil prices and double-digit annual consumption growth in the newly industrializing countries of East Asia, gave OPEC the chance to induce price increases above US$18 per barrel. Some members called for expanding OPEC's overall output ceiling by a smaller factor than the growth in anticipated demand, which would in effect push oil prices up, possibly back to their early 1980s level.

Whereas Saudi Arabia has always endeavored to maintain moderate oil prices, regional political and economic concerns have also motivated the kingdom not to depress prices too far, the 1986 Saudi-induced price crash notwithstanding. In 1988 and 1989, King Fahd publicly guaranteed that Saudi Arabia would work to achieve oil price stability at US$18 per barrel. There was one overwhelming reason for this policy: with the Iran-Iraq War cease-fire in 1988, the kingdom wanted to maintain oil prices at levels that would force Saddam Husayn to be concerned with rebuilding Iraq rather than threatening his neighbors. This objective was formally registered in the 1989 Nonaggression Pact that Riyadh signed with Baghdad.

The biggest battles in OPEC prior to 1990, however, were between Saudi Arabia and two of its gulf neighbors: Kuwait and the United Arab Emirates (UAE). Both refused to restrict production to their quota levels, and by early 1990 their serious overproduction contributed to mounting international crude oil inventories. By the second quarter of 1990, the oil traders in New York were pushing oil prices down.

Saddam Husayn's envoy, Saadun Hamadi, toured the gulf in June 1990 and halted the slide in prices as Iraq unveiled its own "oil weapon": the threat to invade Kuwait. Buttressing this threat by mobilizing 30,000 troops on the Kuwaiti border, Baghdad dictated an agreement at the OPEC ministerial meeting the following month. Although respecting Saudi Arabia's 25 percent market share, and allowing the UAE to raise its quota to 1.5 million barrels per day, OPEC set an overall ceiling of almost 22.5 million bpd and a compromise price of US$21 per barrel.

Saudi Arabia played a largely passive role at the July 1990 OPEC meeting in Geneva and conceded to Iraq's bid for dominance. Kuwait was clearly cowed: even before the meeting it reduced its oil output and appointed a new oil minister, Rashid Salim al Amiri, an unknown chemistry professor, to replace Ali Khalifa, the architect of Kuwait's downstream projects and its aggressive oil policies.

When it invaded Kuwait, Iraq provoked massive intervention by the United States into the gulf and ultimately lost its power within OPEC. Behind direct United States protection, Saudi oil production rose to 8.5 million bpd or 35 percent of OPEC's total output.

Operation Desert Storm allowed Riyadh to regain its status within OPEC. At each successive OPEC meeting until the gathering of ministers in February 1992, Saudi Arabia dictated the final agreements with virtually no opposition. The eleven active members were producing at capacity while prices remained relatively high. Between March and July 1991, both Iran and Saudi Arabia expertly sequenced the unloading of large stocks of oil in "floating storage" that had been built up as insurance during Operation Desert Shield. This action prevented an anticipated crash in oil prices during the spring and summer months of 1991. Part of the harmony within OPEC resulted from the opportunity Iran saw in being more cooperative with Saudi Arabia. For the West to see Iran as a "responsible" member of OPEC could help Iran attract investment for its oil and other industrial sectors.

Observers of OPEC, however, awaited the revival of the old dove-hawk battles. The February 12, 1992 OPEC meeting was held to discuss reinstatement of the July 1990 agreement, temporarily suspended after August 2, 1990. The hawks wanted to preserve the quota system and the reference price, which had been ignored in order to replace lost Iraqi and Kuwaiti output, raising oil prices to about US$21 per barrel for the OPEC basket. The expected return of Kuwait and Iraq to the oil market required a return to the preinvasion rules in order to prevent prices from falling sharply.

Saudi Arabia's aim at the February 1992 OPEC meeting was to eradicate the last vestiges of the 1990 agreement and its quota shares, especially the kingdom's share of about 25 percent. At the February 1992 meeting, OPEC members refused to blink at Saudi pressure. Iran particularly was willing to risk the improved relations it had forged with Saudi Arabia and absorb the oil price cut.

Saudi Arabia's income requirement in the wake of the Persian Gulf War would, Tehran suspected, keep the Saudis from forcing other OPEC members into accepting its objectives as it did in 1986. Technically, the final agreement reached was essentially what the Saudis wanted in the short run: a total production ceiling of almost 23 million bpd, a temporary quota of 35 percent of the ceiling, and the maintenance of price stability. They did not achieve their long-term objective: unanimous OPEC recognition of a 35 percent market share of all future OPEC output ceilings.

Longer-term Saudi policy imperatives for the 1990s were shaped by structural factors within OPEC and within the international oil market. Highest on the priority list was the decision to push domestic oil capacity to more than 10.5 million bpd sustainable capacity with a further 1.5 million to 2 million bpd surge capacity in times of emergency. Three factors prompted these expansion plans. Growth in world demand for oil over the preceding several years, combined with the Persian Gulf War, had pushed the kingdom and other OPEC countries to their production capacities. Expecting that demand would continue to grow and that most other exporters were constrained by diminishing oil reserves or financing problems, a rapid rise in capacity could capture any increase in demand that might occur. Second, in light of the post-1986 intra-OPEC market-share competition, oil capacity expansions have had a direct impact on the ability of individual members to jockey for quota increases. Third, the ability to raise output at will, in the event of an unforeseen price decline, helped stabilize total oil revenues, which constituted the bulk of domestic budgetary income.

Saudi Arabia's interest in moving downstream was also a priority of its oil policy. The drive to obtain overseas refining and storage facilities was designed to further two objectives related to security of supply. First, the kingdom wanted to obtain captive buyers of its crude, assuring stable prices and terms. Saudi Arabia would thus be more receptive to market conditions in consuming countries and avoid being closed out of certain countries. Gaining further profits from refining the crude was an associated reason for the move downstream overseas. Second, the kingdom sought to provide consuming countries with "reciprocal security measures," under which it would undertake to guarantee supply—through capacity additions or stocking arrangements abroad—in return for consumer countries' decisions to avoid taxes and import restrictions on oil. Few consuming countries, however, have responded favorably to such arrangements.

### Crude Oil Reserves and Production Capacity

Saudi Arabia has been described as the world "mother lode" of oil and gas reserves. Estimates for 1990 placed total oil reserves of the kingdom at 261 billion barrels. Saudi Aramco controlled all the reserves within the country's borders with the exception of reserves in the Divided Zone, which were controlled by Getty Oil Company and the Arabian Oil Company. Total oil reserves have risen steadily since oil was discovered in 1938. During the 1970s and 1980s, estimates of total oil reserves grew by nearly 91 percent from 137 billion barrels in 1972 (see table 6, Appendix). The comprehensive reassessment of existing reserves boosted Saudi Arabia's share of world reserves to 25.8 percent. At 1992 production levels, these oil reserves would allow oil production for almost eighty-four years.

Until the mid-1980s, all the oil that had been discovered had been found in the Eastern Province. Aramco had found forty-seven oil fields, including some during the 1970s in the Rub al Khali. The world's largest oil field, Al Ghawar, located in the Al Ahsa region of the Eastern Province, is 250 kilometers long and 35 kilometers wide at its greatest extent. The field is so vast that names have been given to separate subsections such as Ain Dar, Shadqam, Al Hawiyah, Al Uthmaniyah, and Harad. Discovered in 1948, the field began output in 1951. By 1990 Al Ghawar had 219 flowing wells. Saudi Arabia also possessed the world's largest offshore field, As Saffaniyah, located in the gulf near Kuwait and the Divided Zone. As Saffaniyah was discovered in 1951, began output in 1957, and by 1990 had 223 flowing wells. Of the four fields discovered before Al Ghawar—Ad Dammam, Abu Hadriyah, Abqaiq (also seen as Buqayq), and Al Qatif—only Abqaiq and Al Qatif were still producing in 1990. Abqaiq had forty-seven flowing wells. The major producing fields discovered after Al Ghawar, mainly in the 1960s and early 1970s, are offshore and include Manifah, Abu Safah, Al Barri, Az Zuluf, Al Marjan, and Al Khafji in the Divided Zone (see fig. 6). Saudi Arabia had a total of 789 flowing wells during 1990, up from 555 producing wells in 1983.

The quality of crude oil flowing from these wells is based on density (measured by gravity standards established by the American Petroleum Institute—API) and the amount of sulfur and wax it contains. Light crude oil is generally more desirable and commands a higher price because it yields more high-value products such as gasoline and jet fuel. Several Saudi fields, including those in the Divided Zone, contain heavier grades by international standards. Al Ghawar field produces crude ranging from API gravity 33 degrees to 40 degrees, which is considered light crude oil in the kingdom but is generally heavier than most international light crude oils. As Saffaniyah produces heavy crude oil with API gravity ranging from 27 degrees to 32 degrees.

The historical production pattern until the early 1980s contained greater proportions of light and very light crude oils. By the mid-1980s, government policy sought to adjust output between heavy and light crude oils to reflect actual users of each, so that the kingdom would not exhaust its supply of light crude oils. Estimates for 1991 showed that this balance was not achieved, however; Extra Light (from Al Barri field) and Arab Light (crudes from Abqaiq, Al Ghawar, Abu Hadriyah, Al Qatif, and others) recorded production levels close to 70 percent of total output of 8.2 million bpd, whereas Arab Medium (from Az Zuluf, Al Marjan, Al Kharsaniyah, and other fields) and Arab Heavy (from As Saffaniyah, Manifah, and other fields) production levels approached 11 percent and 19 percent, respectively. In the early 1990s, the consensus was that after capacity was expanded, the split between light and heavy grades would shift to 10 percent more heavy crude oils, despite recent discoveries of very light grades south of Riyadh. During the 1980s, technological developments in refining narrowed the differentials between light and heavy crudes. Therefore, the traditional price disadvantage that the Saudis faced was steadily being erased because of the more sophisticated refineries being brought on line.

Saudi crude oils also contain high sulfur levels. Crude from Al Ghawar has sulfur content ranging from about 1.9 percent to close to 2.2 percent by weight, which is generally considered high. As Saffaniyah crude's sulfur content is even higher at above 2.9 percent by weight. Sulfur compounds are undesirable, often contaminating crude oils and corroding processing facilities.

### Gas Reserves and Production Capacity

In the Saudi fields, dissolved gas is associated under pressure with the crude oil in the reservoir. When the reservoir is penetrated by a production well, the pressure causes the crude oil mixed with the associated gas to rise freely to the surface. In Al Ghawar field, for example, 15 cubic meters of gas are extracted for every barrel of oil, while As Saffaniyah field produces 26 cubic meters of gas for every crude oil barrel. In numerous gas-oil separation plants (GOSPs), the associated gas is separated from the crude oil. In addition, a number of fields containing only natural gas have been discovered. In the late 1970s, the government estimated total gas reserves, including associated gas, at 2.4 trillion cubic meters, or about 3 percent of known world gas deposits. By 1991 gas reserves

149

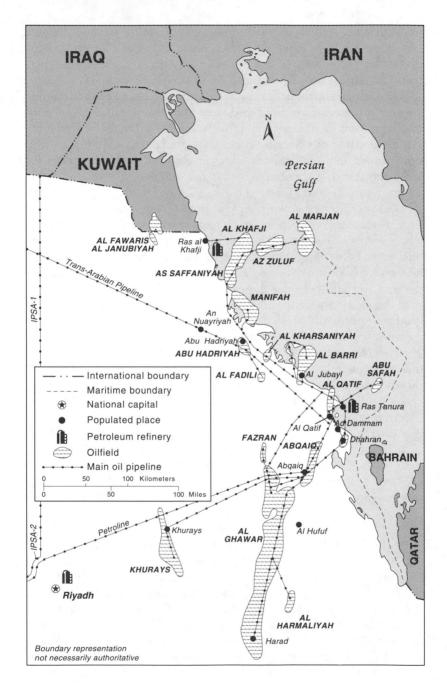

*Figure 6. Major Oil Fields, 1992*

in Saudi Aramco's fields were estimated at about 5.1 trillion cubic meters, while gas reserves in the Divided Zone were estimated at 170 billion cubic meters. The ratio of reserves to current production has remained relatively steady at 100 to 115 years since the mid-1980s.

### Crude Oil Production and Exports

During the 1980s, crude oil production fell from a peak of 9.9 million bpd in 1980, as Saudi Arabia boosted output to offset shortfalls in supply resulting from the beginning of the Iran-Iraq War, to 3.3 million bpd in 1985. Thereafter, and until the Iraqi invasion of Kuwait, a combination of moves by the kingdom and developments in international oil markets allowed for a steady increase in supply. Production rose to 4.9 million bpd in 1986 and reached in excess of 5.8 million bpd on the eve of the Iraqi invasion. To replace most of the 4.5 million bpd of embargoed Kuwaiti and Iraqi oil, Saudi Arabia raised output to 8.5 million bpd within three months. After the Persian Gulf War, market conditions and maintenance projects required modest declines in output to below 8 million bpd, but the kingdom's output in 1991 and 1992 averaged 8.4 million bpd. Divided Zone output, which was included in this figure, fell to zero immediately after the Persian Gulf War as a result of the war damage, but the Arabian Oil Company facilities resumed pumping at levels close to 350,000 bpd within a few months. Half of this output was attributed to Saudi Arabia. Getty Oil facilities in the Divided Zone did not resume pumping oil after the Persian Gulf War.

The bulk of Saudi Arabia's crude oil production was exported. In 1980, for example, crude oil exports totaled about 9.2 million bpd or 93 percent of production. By 1985, with lower production, exports fell to below 2.2 million bpd (see table 7, Appendix). Over the latter half of the 1980s, exports have risen steadily to average 3.3 million bpd in 1989, 4.8 million bpd in 1990, and 6.8 million bpd in 1991 and 1992. Direction of exports has also varied during the 1980s. In the early 1980s, the United States and Canada accounted for 15 percent of Saudi exports; by 1985 they accounted for only 6 percent. Lower oil prices and more aggressive pricing structures enabled Saudi Arabia to place greater quantities of oil in North America by the early 1990s when this market constituted almost one-third of Saudi crude oil sales overseas (see table 8, Appendix). By contrast, Western Europe's importance to Saudi Arabia as an importer of crude fell during the 1980s from 41 percent in 1981 to about 18 percent by 1990. Saudi Arabia has maintained its market presence in Asia, although the high levels of dependence of the mid-1980s have been reduced. Asia received 37 percent of Saudi crude oil exports in 1981, expanded its share to 68 percent by mid-decade, but with the kingdom's attempts to capture a greater share of the United States market, Asia imported a somewhat reduced 47 percent of Saudi crude oil exports by the early 1990s.

### Petroleum Refining Capacity, Production, Consumption, and Exports

Total refining capacity in the kingdom grew from fewer than 700,000 bpd in 1980 to roughly 1.9 million bpd in 1990. The significant capacity expansions during the 1980s were associated with the construction of three refineries: the Petromin/Mobil plant at Yanbu, which added 250,000 bpd; the 250,000-bpd Petromin/Shell plant at Al Jubayl; and the 325,000-bpd refinery at Rabigh. An 80,000-bpd increase to Saudi Arabia's largest refinery at Ras Tanura (530,000-bpd capacity after the increase), completed by 1987, also contributed to the overall increase. Damage to Saudi Arabia's refineries during the Persian Gulf War reduced capacity at Saudi Aramco's Ras Tanura refinery and at the AOC and Getty refineries in the Divided Zone. Total refining capacity during 1991 averaged 1.6 million bpd, but repairs during 1992 helped restore overall refinery capacity to 1.8 million bpd.

Domestic refined output grew steadily with the capacity expansions during the 1980s and early 1990s. Total production of refined petroleum averaged 1.2 million bpd in 1985, growing to more than 1.7 million bpd by 1990, representing an average capacity use of 84 percent in 1985 and 93 percent in 1990. The bulk of refined product output was naphtha and diesel oil; however, output of gasoline and lighter product grades grew more rapidly during the 1980s. This trend indicated both the construction of more sophisticated refineries and the upgrade of existing plants. Nonetheless, Saudi Arabia's refining capacity was of fairly low quality.

Domestic consumption of refined products grew rapidly in the first half of the 1980s. With economic retrenchment, however, consumption growth slowed markedly in the latter half of the 1980s. From 460,000 bpd in 1980, domestic consumption rose to 630,000 bpd by 1985 and stagnated at that level until military consumption during the Persian Gulf War boosted domestic demand to 840,000 bpd during 1991. A fall in consumption to 700,000 bpd was anticipated in 1992. Saudi Arabia became a major exporter of refined products after 1985. From a modest level of exports of 290,000 bpd in 1985, refined product sales reached 734,000 bpd in 1990 before falling to 610,000 bpd as a result of output retained domestically to fuel the foreign forces in the kingdom. A large proportion of exports have been directed to Asian markets, of which Japan alone accounted for one-third of Samarec's overseas sales.

## Master Gas System

The structure of the master gas system—a system of gas-gathering facilities and pipelines that collect associated gas as a by-product of oil and nonassociated gas—reflected both its original design and changes made during the latter half of the 1980s. At first it was anticipated that the master gas system would distribute and process gas produced in association with crude oil. However, declining crude oil output in the mid-1980s forced Saudi Aramco to supplement the system's gas feed by developing the kingdom's non-associated gas resources. The current structure of the master gas system consists of sixty GOSPs in Khurays, As Saffaniyah, Al Ghawar, and Az Zuluf fields; three gas-processing plants located at Al Barri, Shadqam, and Al Uthmaniyah; the east-west natural gas liquids (NGL) pipeline that feeds NGL from Shadqam to Yanbu; and two gas fraction plants at Yanbu and Al Juaymah. Saudi Aramco also added about 57 million cubic meters per day of nonassociated gas-gathering capacity to the master gas system. Furthermore, it installed facilities capable of producing up to almost 13 million cubic meters per day from the Abqaiq gas cap to meet peak demand, and 1.7 million cubic meters per day from the Qatif storage reservoir for emergency use. The system had the capacity to gather about 170 million cubic meters per day of unprocessed gas.

In 1992 the master gas system could produce about 600,000 bpd of NGL when operating at full capacity, which included 315,000 bpd of propane, 165,000 bpd of butane, and 120,000 bpd of natural gas. Saudi Arabia's refineries contributed another 40,000 bpd of liquid petroleum gas (LPG—propane and butane). The kingdom was the world's largest LPG exporter with a 30 percent market share of world seaborne trade in LPG.

Despite the impressive capabilities of the system, it had several shortcomings. The system lacked sufficient associated gas-gathering facilities; as a result, substantial amounts of gas were flared or used in reinjection. Furthermore, there were insufficient processing plants once the gas was collected. Therefore, only about 113 million cubic meters per day of a total of nearly 170 million cubic meters per day of raw gas was processed. Finally, the government's domestic pricing policy, whereby gas was available to customers at US$0.50 per million British thermal units, yielded insufficient revenues to finance further gas-processing facilities.

### Upstream Development Plans

In the early 1990s, Saudi Arabia was engaged in five major programs to raise production capacity of crude oil to 10 million bpd by the mid-1990s. The overall plan was originally scheduled for completion in 1998, but accelerated activity in the wake of the gulf crisis and the allocation of additional funds has moved the projected completion date to 1994. The cost of this program has jumped from US$13 billion to between US$17 billion to US$20 billion. The needs associated with the gulf crisis largely entailed activating existing capacity, which lay unused after output fell in the mid-1980s. This requirement involved recommissioning nearly 150 wells and 12 GOSPs. By the end of 1990, that effort yielded total sustainable capacity of 8.8 million bpd. In addition to the war effort, Saudi Aramco has been involved in bringing on-line a number of GOSPs in existing and known areas such as As Saffaniyah, Al Uthmaniyah, and Abqaiq, all in the Eastern Province. Finally, Saudi Aramco began development of its new light crude oil finds in the central region, with the expectation that it could produce 150,000 bpd of Arab Super Light from Al Hawtah field, south of Riyadh. Following Saudi Aramco's mandate to conduct such activities in the entire country, it has begun exploration in nontraditional areas such as the central region and along the Red Sea coast. Prior to the gulf crisis, AOC and Getty Oil had plans to step up their exploration and development activity. These have been revised in light of the damage to existing facilities sustained during the war.

### Downstream Development Plans

In addition to repairing damaged oil-refining facilities, mainly Saudi Aramco's Ras Tanura refinery, the government has ordered Samarec to undertake a US$5 billion program to upgrade refineries. This five-year program will endeavor to transform its relatively basic domestic refining system into a sophisticated system designed to produce a cleaner, lighter series of products featuring higher octane, lead-free gasoline. Although aimed primarily at meeting a growing internal demand, this development could position Saudi Arabia as a major exporter of gasoline by the end of the 1990s. Moreover, Samarec's refineries are being revamped to process more Arab Heavy crude oils, leaving a larger proportion of Arab Light for export. Concentrating on the Riyadh, Yanbu, and Jiddah refineries fully owned by Samarec, the first phase of the project will cost US$1.7 billion. Later phases may include upgrading the operation of the kingdom's most problem-prone refinery at Rabigh.

Two projects at the Petromin/Mobil plant to produce methyl tertiary-butyl ether (MTBE), an additive for unleaded gasoline, and an isomerization unit are also part of the downstream capacity-upgrading plans.

Downstream plans overseas call for acquiring 2 million to 2.5 million bpd of refining and marketing capacity abroad. Combined with current domestic refining capacity, such an expansion would allow the kingdom to refine roughly half of its crude oil output. In 1992 Saudi Aramco owned 50 percent of Star Enterprises, a joint venture with Texaco, in the United States. Star Enterprises operations included three refineries with combined refining capacity of 615,000 bpd. The company planned to upgrade one of the refineries at Port Arthur, Texas. It also had acquired significant distribution facilities, including 450 gas stations in Florida. In Asia Saudi Aramco had taken a 33 percent share in Ssangyong Oil Refining Company refinery in Onsan, South Korea, giving the oil exporter approximately 175,000 bpd in refining capacity for its exclusive use. Further downstream plans called for expansion in Europe and Japan.

### Hydrocarbon-Sector Transport and Storage Facilities

Pipelines usually provided the easiest and most efficient means of transporting oil and gas products. Expansion of the pipeline system was the major prerequisite for increased crude oil production and exports, for use of associated and nonassociated gas, and for increased refining and distribution of products. Saudi Arabia had four major pipelines serving the crucial transport needs of the country's hydrocarbon sector. In the 1980s and early 1990s, pipeline construction and expansion have been motivated by security concerns stemming from the two major wars fought in the gulf rather than for economic reasons. Therefore, development efforts have concentrated on moving crude oil, products, and export terminals to the western part of the country.

Two of the major crude oil pipelines crossing Saudi Arabia have been shut down. The Trans-Arabian Pipeline (Tapline), built in the 1950s to export oil to the Lebanese port of Az Zahrani on the Mediterranean Sea, ceased operations after the onset of the Lebanese civil war in the 1970s. Whereas small quantities of oil continued to be shipped to the Az Zarqa refinery in Jordan, this operation was also terminated in September 1990 as a result of Jordan's stance in the Persian Gulf War and its inability to meet Saudi Arabia's payment terms. The second pipeline that has been closed runs from the southern Iraqi border town of Az Zubayr to Saudi export terminals on the Red Sea. The Iraqis built the pipeline in two sections: the first, IPSA 1, was originally a spur to Petroline, Saudi Arabia's main oil transport artery, which allowed access to Petroline for further transport of Iraqi crude oil to Yanbu; the second, IPSA 2, built to parallel Petroline, ended at the export terminal at Ras al Muajjis near Yanbu. This pipeline, with capacity to transport more than 1.6 million bpd, opened in January 1990, but closed in August 1990 after the UN ordered an embargo on Iraqi exports. Moreover, the pipeline's two pump stations in southern Iraq suffered heavy damage during the Persian Gulf War.

Petroline runs from Abqaiq to Yanbu. Built in 1981 with the capacity to move more than 1.8 million bpd of crude oil, Petroline was expanded to handle 3.2 million bpd in 1987. The expansion consisted of laying a new pipeline parallel to the original. Further development plans call for additional capacity to raise overall throughput to 4.5 million bpd. This project will give Saudi Aramco greater flexibility to move different grades of crude oil to its western export terminals. Security concerns have largely motivated this expansion because the kingdom's foreign customers have shown less enthusiasm for lifting crude oil from the Red Sea port as a result of the higher cost of cargoes. Consequently, the actual carriage from Petroline has averaged only 1.5 million bpd. Saudi Arabia's other major pipeline is the east-west NGL pipeline. This pipeline runs from Shadqam to Yanbu, again parallel to Petroline, and can transport 270,000 bpd of NGL. Given the problems associated with the gas-gathering system, original plans to expand the pipeline to 490,000 bpd were shelved. Finally, a smaller pipeline, built in the 1940s, runs from Saudi Aramco's facilities in the Eastern Province to the refinery on Bahrain, transporting approximately 200,000 bpd of crude oil.

In the early 1990s, the kingdom had three main export terminals for crude oil with a number of smaller facilities closer to production units. The export terminals at Ras Tanura on the Persian Gulf were the largest in the world. Designed to export crude oil and LPG, the facilities included two piers and one sea island with a total of eighteen berths, which can accommodate ships of up to 550,000 deadweight tons (dwt). The facilities also included a tank farm with total storage capacity of 33 million barrels. Also on the Persian Gulf, thirty-three kilometers north of Ras Tanura, is the port of Al Juaymah. Tankers of up to 700,000 dwt could be accommodated at its six single-point moorings. Up to 4 million bpd of crude oil could be exported from Al Juaymah. Two additional berths were designed to export 200,000 cubic meters of LPG. Tank farm storage facilities had a capacity of 17.5 million barrels. The third Persian Gulf export terminal at Az Zuluf, located sixty-four kilometers offshore, served the Az Zuluf and Al Marjan fields with one single-point mooring.

Before the outbreak of the Persian Gulf War in 1991, AOC and Getty Oil operated two other Persian Gulf ports in the Divided Zone. AOC had four berths with varying capabilities located almost five and eleven kilometers offshore at Al Khafji. Offshore facilities at Mina Saud, managed by Getty Oil, serviced ships at shallower berths.

In 1981 Saudi Arabia opened the Red Sea port of Yanbu. Consisting of three offshore crude-oil berths, the port could handle tankers up to 550,000 dwt. In the early 1990s, total crude oil loading capacity stood at 2.6 million bpd with storage facilities holding as much as 6 million barrels. LPG export facilities included two berths that served ships with 200,000-cubic-meter capacity. By the end of 1992, expansion plans called for adding a fourth crude-oil berth that would increase the port's overall loading capacity to 3.9 million bpd. Connected to the IPSA 2 pipeline was the Red Sea port of Ras al Muajjis, south of Yanbu. Farther south at Rabigh, Saudi Arabia was completing a small port to serve the refinery. Nine berths capable of handling ships up to 312,000 dwt were under construction in 1992.

Both Saudi Aramco and Samarec maintained a fleet of tankers to export crude oil and products. In 1992 Saudi Arabia controlled forty-three vessels with a combined displacement of 7 million dwt. Vela Marine International, Saudi Aramco's shipping subsidiary, had twenty-eight ships in its fleet, of which it owned six and chartered the rest. Samarec's fleet consisted of fifteen ships, including four small crude-oil tankers and eleven clean-product tankers. Expansion plans in the early 1990s called for Vela Marine International to acquire twenty-one additional vessels at a projected cost of US$2 billion. In addition to the six very large crude carriers (VLCCs), each with a capacity of 280,000 dwt under construction in the early 1990s, Vela planned to add nine VLCCs and eight ultra-large crude carriers (ULCCs), each with a capacity of 350,000 dwt. The expansion of the fleet resulted from Saudi Aramco's desire to move as much as 70 percent of its crude exports on its own tankers, thereby reducing transport costs. Moreover, it sought marketing flexibility and floating storage facilities so as to improve the market balance of supply and demand.

## Non-Oil Industrial Sector

During the 1980s, the government established, virtually from scratch, a modern industrial sector. The industrialization process had two goals: first, the use of the kingdom's enormous gas production as industrial inputs to produce chemicals and petrochemicals for export and, second, the construction of energy-intensive industries, some for import-substitution purposes and others to meet infrastructural needs. The government also established state-of-the-art industrial cities and facilities to support its industrial program, including those at Al Jubayl and Yanbu.

By the early 1990s, the vast majority of these plants had been completed, and few major expansions were planned. Infrastructure requirements had largely stabilized and were adequate to meet the needs of the population and industry for much of the 1990s. Therefore, the government concentrated on maintenance and on improving productivity and efficiency. Moreover, with the onset of serious budgetary constraints, the government's role in advancing the domestic industrialization process grew more indirect. The government was forcing a number of state-owned industrial institutions to seek financing for their new capacity-expansion programs from nontraditional sources such as domestic and foreign commercial banks, stock markets, and private investors. In an ongoing attempt to encourage more private sector investment in manufacturing, particularly in light industries, local business received incentives in the form of production and consumption subsidies.

## Utilities

Most of Saudi Arabia's electric power-generating capacity was built during the 1970s and 1980s. Nonetheless, after the establishment of the first municipal power plant in 1950, the development of the industry occurred largely in the private sector. By 1980 about ninety-five private companies supplied electric service, leading to a totally decentralized system. Voltages and cycles differed between towns and even within towns, preventing consumers from standardizing equipment and appliances. Consumers suffered from chronic power failures, voltage fluctuations, and poor repair service. Hospitals and large plants often had their own generators. Planners estimated that only 54 percent of the potential demand for electricity had been met in 1978.

In the early 1970s, the government embarked on a twofold plan to organize the sector and to stimulate further investment. The system relied on private sector participation with strong government oversight and planning. Early attempts to standardize the system called for all new generators to be 60 Hertz with distribution voltages of 127 and 220 volts. In 1976 the first of a series of regional companies, Saudi Consolidated Electric Company (Sceco), was formed for the eastern region (Sceco-East). Ownership of the regional companies, which amalgamated their facilities under Sceco,

remained locally held. The government had some equity participation, but the regional companies retained administrative
autonomy. The government requested Aramco to manage Sceco-
East because of its large share of generating facilities and its management expertise. Regional companies for the central and southern
parts of the country were formed in 1979; Sceco-West was established in 1981. The goal was to link the generators in a region and
to improve planning and service. Eventually the regional companies would be tied together to form a nationwide grid. The
government-owned General Electricity Corporation, which served
rural areas, participated in the regional companies in areas where
it was active.

In addition, the government provided the private sector direct
financial assistance for building and operating generating plants
and distribution facilities under the Electric Utility Lending Program, administered by the Saudi Industrial Development Fund
(SIDF). The government provided consumption subsidies by paying
producers to sell their power below cost. The government also gave
the producer an implicit fuel subsidy on gas. Direct subsidies to
the sector peaked at SR2.75 billion in fiscal year 1984–85 but fell
in 1989 to SR210 million. Following a 1992 government decree,
subsidies were expected to rise again because electricity charges
to users were halved.

After the early 1960s, generating capacity expanded rapidly. By
1979 generating capacity amounted to 4,214 megawatts. By 1990
this capacity had quadrupled to 16,549 megawatts. Between 1975
and 1979, consumption of electricity increased 37 percent yearly
while the number of consumers rose 16 percent yearly. During the
1980s, the consumption growth rate slowed to 23.8 percent annually, with the number of consumers rising annually by 17 percent.
From 872,054 subscribers in 1980—representing 4 million people—
subscribers reached 2.4 million in 1990. Industry usage averaged
28.3 percent of electricity consumed, although in the Eastern
Province, given the location of country's major industrial complexes, industry demand accounted for more than 60 percent of electric consumption. Industrial users in the other regions consumed
less than 5 percent of total electricity generated.

Water consumption also rose rapidly during the 1970s and 1980s,
both by traditional sectors and by newly established urban and industrial users. In the early 1980s, a national water plan was for-
mulated when particularly serious problems were encountered. Lack
of sewage treatment was contaminating groundwater from wells
in the Eastern Province, and overpumping from wells in the central region near Riyadh drastically lowered the water table.

However, few substantive changes in water supply have been instituted, leading to a continued depletion of water resources. Saudi Arabia's water was supplied from three different sources: surface water (about 10 percent), underground aquifers (more than 80 percent), and desalination plants (5 percent). The nonrenewable sources continued to provide the bulk of water to users and were being depleted at an alarming rate. Efforts to supplement the available water supply have concentrated on building desalination plants. In 1980 fourteen plants were in operation with a combined capacity of 65 million cubic meters per year. Eight more plants were constructed during the decade, taking total capacity to more than 600 million cubic meters per year. By the end of the 1980s, output from these plants was approximately 500 million cubic meters per year.

Between 1980 and 1985, water consumption more than tripled, going from 190 million cubic meters to 574 million cubic meters. The consumption increase continued in the latter half of the decade, with water usage rising to 900 million cubic meters in 1990. Agriculture was the prime water user, accounting for 85 percent; its rate of consumption quadrupled from 1980 to 1985. Although data are lacking for the late 1980s and early 1990s, it appeared that usage continued to grow but at a slightly slower rate. The government's policy of providing water free to the sector, combined with new water-intensive methods of farming have been the main factors for this growth of water consumption.

The idea of importing water into Saudi Arabia was first presented in the early 1970s when Denmark's Royal Greenland Company was commissioned to perform a study on the feasibility of towing icebergs. The conclusion reached was that no technical problems were insurmountable, but that the cost was prohibitive. In the late 1980s, the Turkish government proposed a plan whereby two pipelines from Turkey would bring water (at a cost of about US$1 per cubic meter compared with US$5 to US$6 per cubic meter for producing desalinated water) to both the Eastern Province and the Hijaz. Security concerns have prevented the Saudis from moving further on these plans, however.

## Mining and Quarrying

By the early 1980s, promising deposits of metallic minerals had been found, largely in the western part of the country, but commercial mining was limited. Several international companies and other organizations, including the United States Geological Survey, were surveying and exploring for minerals. Commercial exploitation was being evaluated at some promising sites. The government

*Water tower, Buraydah, Al Qasim*
*Courtesy Saudi Arabian Information Office*
*Water from desalination plants, such as that above,*
*helps supplement limited groundwater.*
*Courtesy* Aramco World

owned all subsoil resources and permitted joint ventures with Petromin for exploration and mining activities. In fact, the government provided substantial assistance and incentives to foreign firms to develop mining.

The first mining project was the Mahd adh Dhahab gold mine about 280 kilometers northeast of Jiddah. The gold mine started commercial production in 1988, with a total capacity of 400 tons of ore a day with a ratio of 26 grams of gold and 90 grams of silver per ton. Petromin reached an agreement with a Swedish company to exploit the gold deposits at Shukhaybirat, northeast of Medina. The mine began operations in 1991, planning to produce 1,500 kilograms of gold annually together with silver. Furthermore, gold deposits were found at Hajar (north of Medina), Bir at Tawilah (southeast of At Taif), and Al Amar (southwest of Riyadh). Also in the early 1980s, iron ore deposits in Wadi Sawawin near the Gulf of Aqaba were under study to determine their economic potential. Ore containing copper, lead, zinc, silver, and gold was located in the Al Masani area about 200 kilometers northeast of Jiddah and showed promise. A pilot project began in the early 1980s to determine the feasibility of processing metal-rich mud from the bottom of the Red Sea. Lead, zinc, copper, silver, platinum, and cadmium appeared potentially exploitable. The country also has adequate nonmetallic minerals, such as clay, limestone, glass sand, and stone for the construction industry. These materials were exploited by private firms. Large gypsum deposits had been located near Yanbu and phosphorite had been found in several locations in the 1980s.

## Manufacturing

The government has played an instrumental role in developing the manufacturing sector. It had directly established in the basic industries sector industrial plants such as petrochemical, steel, and other large manufacturing enterprises. Also, it has developed manufacturing through direct loans, mainly by the SIDF and through industrial subsidies, offset programs, set-asides, preferential buying programs, and tariffs. In the 1980s, the bulk of private manufacturing investment was directed to plants that manufactured goods for the construction industry. With the decline of construction in the mid-1980s, there has been a shift to other light manufacturing including food processing, furniture making, and other consumer goods. This trend accelerated in the early 1990s.

Partly because of private sector reluctance to invest in manufacturing and partly because of growing oil revenues, the government was involved early in the 1960s in some basic industries. In the

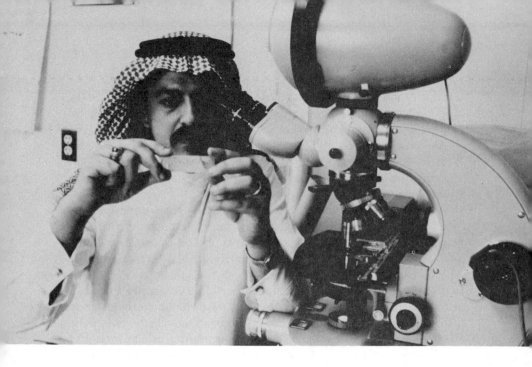

*Laboratory technician at work*
*Courtesy* Aramco World

late 1960s, Petromin established a steel-rolling mill in Jiddah using imported billets, a urea fertilizer plant in Ad Dammam with 49 percent private Saudi capital, and a sulfuric acid plant in the same location. In the early 1970s, as oil revenues grew, a coordinated plan emerged to collect and distribute gas that was flared to two yet-unbuilt industrial sites where it could be used in basic industries. The two sites selected were Al Jubayl and Yanbu.

In 1975 the Royal Commission for Al Jubayl and Yanbu was created. The commission was given authority to plan, construct, manage, and operate the infrastructure needed to support the basic industries the government intended to build and to satisfy the community needs of the work force employed in these industries. The commission was also to promote investment in secondary and supporting industries, to develop effective city government, and to train Saudis to take over as many jobs as possible. The commission received an independent budget to facilitate its work.

By 1990 there were sixteen primary industries, forty-six secondary enterprises, and approximately 100 support and light industrial units at Al Jubayl. Yanbu had attracted five primary industrial plants, twenty-five secondary plants, and seventy-five support and light units in 1990. Al Jubayl benefited from the massive petrochemical projects of the Saudi Basic Industries Corporation (Sabic), but both industrial sites saw substantial growth during the 1980s. Nonetheless, both locations suffered from overcapacity; for example, initial population projections called for 58,000 residents by 1985 in Al Jubayl, but by 1987 total residents barely reached 40,000. Revised forecasts estimated that there was substantial room for growth during the 1990s, and that no major capacity expansion would be necessary until the year 2000.

With the establishment of Sabic in 1976, the government undertook a major effort to create a domestic petrochemical industry that was designed to augment oil export earnings and to use abundantly available domestic resources, particularly associated gas supplies. The investments have been guided by a two-phase strategy. The first phase (1976–87) included a number of large capital-intensive and export-oriented petrochemical projects that have been completed. Its aim was to produce bulk products such as ethylene, polyethylene, melamine, methanol, and downstream products including derivatives of ethylene. Moreover, during this period, Sabic undertook the construction of plants to produce fertilizers (urea, sulfuric acid, and melamine), metals (steel rods and bars), supporting industrial products (nitrogen), and intermediate petrochemical products (vinyl chloride monomer, polyvinyl chloride, and MTBE). Sabic also acquired shares in two Saudi aluminum companies and expanded overseas by investing in a Bahraini petrochemical complex.

During the first phase, financing by joint-venture partners and funding from the government's Public Investment Fund (PIF) provided the bulk of support for these projects. Domestic and regional private sector participation was also allowed after 30 percent of the equity capital of Sabic (approximately SR3 billion) was sold to residents of Saudi Arabia and other GCC countries. In 1987 Sabic split each share into ten shares to mobilize investments from smaller investors.

In 1992 Sabic owned, either outright or with a minimum 50 percent stake, fifteen major industrial enterprises. Total output capacity was 13 million tons of various petrochemicals per year, up from 11.9 million tons per year in 1990 and 9.5 million tons per year in 1989. Although total sales have continued to rise, weaker international prices depressed profits during the late 1980s and early 1990s. During 1991 Sabic registered net profits of US$613 million. About 95 percent of Sabic's sales were exported; total exports approached US$4 billion per annum. Its success in rapidly increasing exports and capturing an international market share have made Sabic's petrochemical exports subject to nondiscriminatory restraint in both Europe and Japan, its main export markets. Both the EC and Japan have applied quantitative restrictions to Saudi exports. Moreover, urea exports from Saudi Arabia were subject to anti-dumping duties in the EEC, which no longer permitted preferential treatment under its General System of Preferences.

Future development plans, part of Sabic's second phase, were designed to maintain Saudi Arabia's 1992 international market share and raise domestic petrochemical capacity by 40 percent. By 1993 Sabic hoped to increase total petrochemical capacity to 20 million tons per year. Projects underway included the Eastern Petrochemical Company (Sharq), an equal-share joint venture with Japan's Mitsubishi Gas Company, which was planning a major increase in its capacity to produce ethylene glycol. The expansion program aimed to raise production to 660,000 tons per year from the 1991 level of 450,000 tons per year. Sharq also intended to increase its polyethylene production from 140,000 tons per year to 270,000 tons per year. Ibn Zahr, the Saudi-European Petrochemical Company, a joint venture in which Sabic had a 70 percent share and Finland's Neste, Italy's Eco Fuel, and the Arabian Petroleum Investment Corporation (Apicorp—owned by the Organization of Arab Petroleum Exporting Countries) each had 10 percent, intended to raise the output of MTBE from 550,000 tons per year. The company's polypropylene plant was to be expanded as well. The National Methanol Company (Ibn Sina) planned to double methanol production from the 640,000 tons annually in 1991 to 1.2 million tons. This plant was also expected to increase capacity of MTBE to 500,000 tons per year and possibly to 700,000 tons per year. The National Plastics Company (Ibn Hayyan), a joint venture with the South Korean Lucky Group (15 percent), planned to expand output of polyvinyl chloride from 200,000 tons to 300,000 tons per year. The National Industrial Gases Company was engaged in 1991 in doubling nitrogen production capacity from 219,000 tons per year to 438,000 tons per year, whereas oxygen production capacity was to increase from 438,000 tons per year to 876,000 tons per year. The Saudi Arabian Fertilizer Company completed a 500,000-tons-per-year anhydrous ammonia plant and a 600,000-tons-per-year granulated urea plant in 1992, and was expected to undertake further expansion throughout the 1990s. Because the available gas-based feedstock (ethane and methane) would be insufficient to meet requirements of the second phase, Sabic has invested in two flexible feedstock crackers with a total combined capacity of about 1 million tons. The crackers help reduce dependence on ethane and methane and allow the use of naphtha, liquefied petroleum gas, or propane as feedstock.

In Sabic's second-phase financing plans, retained profits and limited borrowing from the PIF, SIDF, and domestic commercial banks were expected to provide partial funding. Nonetheless, Sabic hoped to raise almost 30 percent of the planned US$3.5 billion to US$4 billion on the international market through syndicated borrowing. For example, Sharq's expansion plans called for approximately US$600 million in foreign borrowing, and Ibn Zahr was expected to raise US$500 million from foreign capital markets.

The private sector's role in industrialization has been largely restricted to light and medium-sized manufacturing units. However, some larger merchant families had established larger-scale chemical, secondary-stage petrochemical, and car or truck assembly plants. By 1981 Saudi Arabia had approximately 1,200 industrial plants of all sizes. At the end of the 1980s, this figure had doubled to about 2,000 units and had risen to 2,100 by 1991. Most private manufacturing concerns in the 1980s produced construction materials, including cement, insulation materials, pipes, bricks, and wood products. Judging from data available from the Ministry of Industry and Electricity, there has been a marked shift from this sort of production to downstream chemicals, food processing, and metals, machinery, and equipment manufacturing. The annual number of new licenses issued to companies in the chemical, rubber, and plastics sector rose from seven per year in 1987 to fifteen in 1990. Although this number constituted at most 20 percent of all licenses granted, the size of the firms was growing, judging from their authorized capital, which grew from 42 percent of total new investment planned to 90 percent. Trailing well behind this sector was the food-processing sector, which saw a rise in number of licenses between 1987 and 1990, but the volume of authorized capital declined, indicating smaller individual companies and more widespread participation. Metals and machinery manufacturing followed a pattern similar to chemical companies, with both the number of units and authorized capital growing during the four-year period.

The patterns of Saudi private manufacturing investment have conformed to government investments. Incentives offered to private businesses included interest-free loans from SIDF of up to 50 percent of the cost an industrial project, repayable within fifteen years. Exemptions from tariff duties on imported equipment, raw materials, spare parts, and other industrial inputs; land leases at significantly reduced prices; discriminatory buying practices by government agencies; and significant import protection were some of the other incentives provided.

# Transportation and Telecommunications

## Transportation

Saudi Arabia's extensive transportation system was almost completely built in the four decades following 1950. In that year, the country had no railroads, about 200 kilometers of paved roads, and no adequate air facilities. Most localities could be reached only by gravel roads or tracks interspersed with a few airstrips for small airplanes. By 1991 the country boasted an excellent system of expressways, paved roads, and airports that linked all the populated areas of the kingdom (see fig. 7).

Highways constituted the backbone of the Saudi transportation system. In 1991 there were about 100,000 kilometers of roads, 35,000 kilometers of which were paved. The country's chief route was the Trans-Arabian Highway, a multilane expressway that crossed the peninsula from Ad Dammam to Jiddah, passing through Riyadh and Mecca. Other expressways connected Jiddah with Medina, extended north from Ad Dammam toward the Kuwaiti border, and ringed the capital and Jiddah. Paved roads linked all other major urban areas. Paved roads crossed into all of Saudi Arabia's neighbors except Oman and a causeway connected with Bahrain. The Saudi Public Transportation Company, partly owned by the government, operated a fleet of more than 1,000 buses that provided regular service both between the country's cities and within them.

Railroads were only a minor element in the country's transportation system, and rail service was only reestablished in the early 1950s after a four-decade hiatus. The Ottoman Turks built the first railroad on the peninsula, the Hejaz Railway linking Damascus with Medina. Parts of this railroad were destroyed in World War I, and the line was abandoned. In 1951 a 571-kilometer, 1.435-meter standard-gauge rail line was built linking Ad Dammam to Riyadh. A second, shorter line between Riyadh and Al Hufuf was built in the early 1980s.

Because of the country's position as exporter of petroleum, ports played a major role in the transportation system. Jiddah was the kingdom's principal port, handling almost 60 percent of the goods moved by sea in 1988. Ad Dammam, serving the country's oil fields in the east, was the second-largest port for imports whereas Ras Tanura handled a major part of Saudi Arabia's petroleum exports. Al Jubayl on the Persian Gulf and Yanbu north of Jiddah, both of which were connected to large industrial complexes, were somewhat smaller. Jizan near the Yemeni border in the south was a lesser port serving the Asir agricultural region. Numerous harbors on both the Persian Gulf and the Red Sea served the fishing and coastal transportation sectors.

Large distances between urban areas and difficult terrain have made air travel an essential complement to Saudi Arabia's road network. In 1991 there were sixty-nine airports with paved runways. The country's three largest airports, King Abd al Aziz International in Jiddah, King Khalid International in Riyadh, and Dhahran International (King Fahd International in Ad Dammam was under construction, scheduled for completion in 1994), had large modern terminals, runways capable of handling large airplanes, and regularly scheduled international flights. The country counted more than 19 million air passengers in 1985, many of them pilgrims en route to Mecca. Saudi Arabian Airlines, the national airline, offered domestic service to more than twenty cities and an international network to almost four dozen destinations in Africa, Europe, Asia, and North America.

## Telecommunications

In 1991 Saudi Arabia had one of the most modern telecommunications systems in the world. An extensive system of microwave and coaxial cables crisscrossed the country and linked Saudi Arabia with Jordan, Kuwait, Bahrain, Qatar, the United Arab Emirates, and Yemen. Tropospheric-scatter radio linked the kingdom with Sudan and undersea coaxial cables extended from points on the west coast to Egypt and to Djibouti. Telephone service was entirely automatic, and international direct-distance dialing was available to all subscribers. In 1991 the country counted 1.6 million telephones or about eleven telephones per 100 inhabitants.

Eight satellite ground stations provided worldwide transmission of telephone, telex, data, ship-to-shore, and broadcast signals. Five satellite ground stations operated with the International Telecommunication Satellite Corporation (Intelsat) Atlantic Ocean and Indian Ocean satellites. In addition, two satellite ground stations in the Arab Satellite Communications Organization (Arabsat) network could simultaneously handle 8,000 telephone calls and seven separate television channels to the twenty-two member countries of the Arabsat system. Another satellite ground station was linked to the International Marine Satellite system that provided communications to ships at sea.

Broadcast facilities were scattered across the country and most locations could receive at least one radio station. More than 100 transmitters provided television service to all urban areas. Saudi Arabia had an estimated 5 million radio receivers and 4.5 million television sets in 1991.

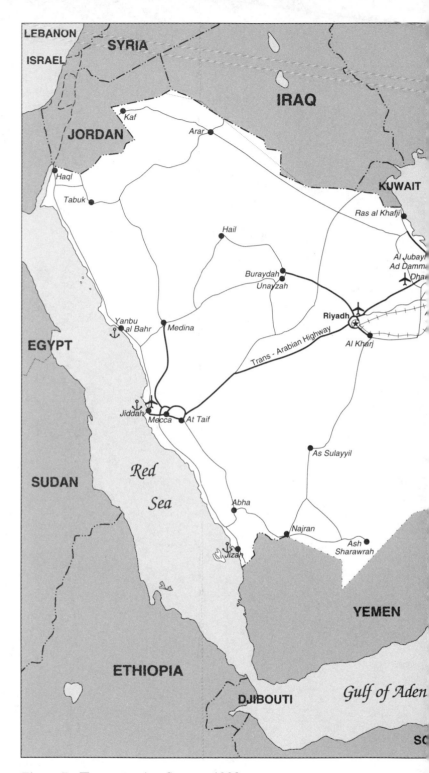

*Figure 7. Transportation System, 1992*

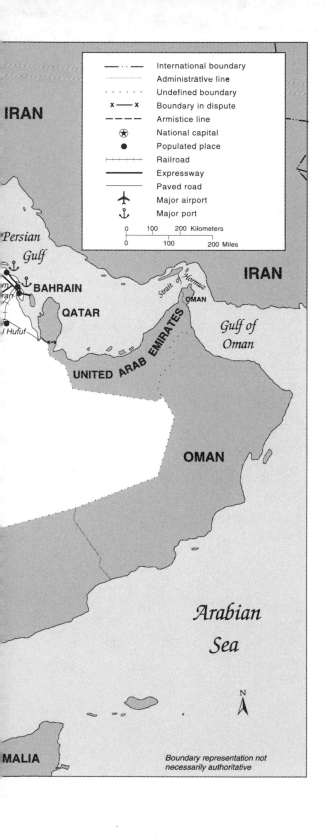

# Agriculture

During the 1970s and 1980s, the government undertook a massive restructuring of the agricultural sector. The stated objectives were food security through self-sufficiency and improvement of rural incomes. Although successful in raising domestic output of several important crops and foodstuffs through the introduction of modern agricultural techniques, the agricultural development program has not entirely met these objectives. In regard to self-sufficiency, the kingdom produced a sufficient surplus to export limited quantities of food. However, if the entire production process were considered, the import of fertilizers, equipment, and labor have made the kingdom even more dependent on foreign inputs to bring food to the average Saudi household.

Two patterns of income distribution emerged: traditional agricultural regions did not benefit from the development program, and the government's financial support led to the establishment of large-scale agricultural production units. Some of these were managed and operated by foreign entities and owned by wealthy individuals and large businesses. From an environmental viewpoint, the program had a less than satisfactory impact. Not only has it caused a serious drain on the kingdom's water resources, drawing mainly from nonrenewable aquifers, but it has also required the use of massive amounts of chemical fertilizers to boost yields. In 1992 Saudi agricultural strategy was only sustainable as long as the government maintained a high level of direct and indirect subsidies, a drain on its budget and external accounts.

## Traditional Agriculture and Pastoral Nomadism

In the past, the bulk of agricultural production was concentrated in a few limited areas. The produce was largely retained by these communities although some surplus was sold to the cities. Nomads played a crucial role in this regard, shipping foods and other goods between the widely dispersed agricultural areas. Livestock rearing was shared between the sedentary communities and nomads, who also used it to supplement their precarious livelihoods.

Lack of water has always been the major constraint on agriculture and the determining factor on where cultivation occurred. The kingdom has no lakes or rivers. Rainfall is slight and irregular over most of the country. Only in the southwest, in the mountains of Asir, close to the Yemen border and accounting for 3 percent of the land area, was rainfall sufficient to support regular crops. This region and the southern Tihamah coastal plains sustained subsistence farming. Cropping in the rest of the country was scattered

171

and dependent on irrigation. Along the western coast and in the western highlands, groundwater from wells and springs provided adequate water for self-supporting farms and, to some extent, for commercial production. Moving east Najd and An Nafud, in the central and northern parts of the interior, had enough groundwater to allow limited farming. The Eastern Province supported the most extensive plantation economy. The major oasis centered around Al Qatif, which enjoyed high water tables, natural springs, and relatively good soils.

Historically, the limited arable land and the near absence of grass-land forced those raising livestock into a nomadic pattern to take advantage of what forage was available. Only in summer, the year's driest time, did the nomad keep his animals around an oasis or well for water and forage. The beduin developed special skills that enabled them to know where rain had fallen and forage was available to feed their animals and where they could find water en route to various forage areas.

Traditionally, beduin were not self-sufficient but needed some food and materials from agricultural settlements. The near constant movement required to feed their animals limited other activities, such as weaving. The settled farmers and traders needed the nomads to tend their camels. Nomads would graze and breed animals belonging to sedentary farmers in return for portions of the farmers' produce. Beduin groups contracted to provide protection to the agricultural and market areas they frequented in return for such provisions as dates, cloth, and equipment. Beduin further supplemented their income by taxing caravans for passage and protection through their territory.

Beduin themselves needed protection. Operating in small independent groups of a few households, they were vulnerable to raids by other nomads and therefore formed larger groups, such as tribes. The tribe was responsible for avenging attacks on any of its members. Tribes established territories that they defended vigorously. Within the tribal area, wells and springs were found and developed. Generally, the developers of a water source, such as a well, retained rights to it unless they abandoned it. This system created problems for nomads because many years might elapse between visits to a well they had dug. If people from another tribe just used the well, the first tribe could frequently establish that the well was in territory where they had primary rights; but if another tribe improved the well, primary rights became difficult to establish. By the early twentieth century, control over land, water rights, and intertribal and intratribal relationships were highly developed and complex (see Beduin Economy in Tradition and Change, ch. 2).

*The Hijaz/Wadi Hanifah junction is an
example of the modern Saudi highway system.
Courtesy Saudi Arabian Information Office
Causeway to Bahrain under construction; it was completed in 1986.
Courtesy* Aramco World

## Modern Agriculture

Pastoral nomadism declined as a result of several political and economic forces. Sedenterization was a means of imposing political control over various tribal groupings in the Arabian Peninsula. New legal structures such as the 1968 Public Lands Distribution Ordinance created novel land relations and spurred the dissolution of the beduin way of life. The establishment of an activist modern state provided incentives for large numbers of Saudi citizens to enter the regular, wage-based, or urban commercial employment. Moreover, modern technology and new transport networks undermined the primitive services that the beduin offered the rest of the economy.

Until the 1970s, sedentary agriculture saw few changes and declined in the face of foreign imports, urban drift, and lack of investment. The use of modern inputs remained relatively limited. Introduction of mechanical pumping in certain areas led to a modest level of commercial production, usually in locations close to urban centers. Nevertheless, regional distribution of agricultural activity remained relatively unchanged, as did the average holding size and patterns of cultivation.

During the late 1970s and early 1980s, the government undertook a multifaceted program to modernize and commercialize agriculture. Indirect support involved substantial expenditures on infrastructure, which included electricity supply, irrigation, drainage, secondary road systems, and other transportation facilities for distributing and marketing produce. Land distribution was also an integral part of the program. The 1968 Public Lands Distribution Ordinance allocated 5 to 100 hectares of fallow land to individuals at no cost, up to 400 hectares to companies and organizations, and a limit of 4,000 hectares for special projects. The beneficiaries were required to develop a minimum of 25 percent of the land within a set period of time (usually two to five years); thereafter, full ownership was transferred. In FY 1989, the total area distributed stood at more than 1.5 million hectares. Of this total area 7,273 special agricultural projects accounted for just under 860,000 hectares, or 56.5 percent; 67,686 individuals received just under 400,000 hectares or 26.3 percent; 17 agricultural companies received slightly over 260,000 hectares, or 17.2 percent. Judging from these statistics, the average fallow land plot given to individuals was 5.9 hectares, 118 hectares to projects, and 15,375 hectares to companies, the latter being well over the limit of 400 hectares specified in the original plans.

The government also mobilized substantial financial resources to support the raising of crops and livestock during the 1970s and

*Riyadh television tower*
*Courtesy Saudi*
*Arabian Information Office*

*Arabsat tracking station,*
*Jabal al Ali, in northern*
*Saudi Arabia near Jordan*
*Courtesy* Aramco World

1980s. The main institutions involved were the Ministry of Agriculture and Water, the Saudi Arabian Agricultural Bank (SAAB) and the Grain Silos and Flour Mills Organization (GSFMO). SAAB provided interest-free loans to farmers; during FY 1989, for example, 26.6 percent of loans were for well drilling and casing, 23 percent for agricultural projects, and the balance for the purchase of farm machinery, pumps, and irrigation equipment. SAAB also provided subsidies for buying other capital inputs.

GSFMO implemented the official procurement program, purchasing locally produced wheat and barley at guaranteed prices for domestic sales and exports. The procurement price was steadily reduced during the 1980s because of massive overproduction and for budgetary reasons, but it was substantially higher than international prices. By the late 1980s, the procurement price for wheat, for example, was three times the international price. Although quantity restrictions were implemented to limit procurement, pressures from a growing farm lobby led to ceiling-price waivers. Moreover, the government encountered considerable fraud with imports being passed off as domestic production. To control this situation, the government has granted import monopolies for some agricultural products to the GSFMO, and procurement and import subsidies on certain crops have been shifted to encourage a more diversified production program. Finally, agricultural and water authorities provided massive subsidies in the form of low-cost desalinated water, and electric companies were required to supply power at reduced charges.

The program prompted a huge response from the private sector, with average annual growth rates well above those programmed. These growth rates were underpinned by a rapid increase in land brought under cultivation and agricultural production (see table 9, Appendix). Private investments went mainly into expanding the area planted for wheat. Between 1983 and 1990, the average annual increase of new land brought under wheat cultivation rose by 14 percent. A 35 percent increase in yields per ton during this period further boosted wheat output; total production rose from 1.4 million tons per year in FY 1983 to 3.5 million tons in FY 1989. Other food grains also benefited from private investment. For example, output growth rates for sorghum and barley accelerated even faster than wheat during the 1980s, although the overall amount produced was much smaller. During the 1980s, farmers also experimented with new varieties of vegetables and fruits but with only modest success. More traditional crops, like onions and dates, did not fare as well and their output declined or remained flat.

In the 1970s, increasing incomes in urban areas stimulated the demand for meat and dairy products, but by the early 1980s government programs were only partially successful in increasing domestic production. Beduin continued to raise a large number of sheep and goats. Payments for increased flocks, however, had not resulted in a proportionate increase of animals for slaughter. Some commercial feedlots for sheep and cattle had been established as well as a few modern ranches, but by the early 1980s much of the meat consumed was imported. Although the meat supply was still largely imported in the early 1990s, domestic production of meat had grown by 33 percent between 1984 and 1990, from 101,000 tons to 134,000 tons. This increase, however, masked the dominant role of traditional farms in supplying meat. Although new projects accounted for some of the rapid growth during the 1980s, a sharp decline of roughly 74 percent in beef stock production by specialized projects during 1989 resulted in only a 15 percent fall in meat output. This reversal also highlighted the problems in introducing modern commercial livestock-rearing techniques to the kingdom.

Commercial poultry farms, however, greatly benefited from government incentives and grew rapidly during the 1980s. Chickens were usually raised in controlled climatic conditions. Despite the doubling of output, as a result of the rapid rise in chicken consumption, which had become a major staple of the Saudi diet, domestic production constituted less than half of total demand. Egg production also increased rapidly during the 1980s. The numbers of broiler chickens increased from 143 million in 1984 to 270 million in 1990, while production of eggs increased from 1,852 million in 1984 to 2,059 million in 1990.

Fishing, however, was an underdeveloped aspect of the Saudi economy despite the abundance of fish and shellfish in coastal waters. The major reasons for the small size of this sector were the limited demand for fish and the comparative lack of fish marketing and processing facilities. Iraqi actions in releasing oil into the Persian Gulf during the Persian Gulf War caused appreciable damage to fish and wildlife in the gulf. Data concerning postwar catches were not available in late 1992, but in 1989 the Food and Agriculture Organization of the United Nations estimated Saudi Arabia's total catch at more than 53,000 tons.

## Money and Banking

Until the mid-twentieth century, Saudi Arabia had no formal money and banking system. To the degree that money was used, Saudis primarily used coins having a metallic content equal to their value (full-bodied coins) for storing value and limited exchange transactions in urban areas. For centuries foreign coins had served the local inhabitants' monetary needs. Development of banking was inhibited by the Quranic injunction against interest. A few banking functions existed, such as money changers (largely for pilgrims visiting Mecca), who had informal connections with international currency markets. A foreign bank was established in Jiddah in 1926, but its importance was minor. Foreign and domestic banks were formed as oil revenues began to increase. Their business consisted mostly of making short-term loans to finance imports, commercial trading, and businesses catering to pilgrims.

The government issued a silver riyal in 1927 to standardize the monetary units then in circulation. By 1950 the sharp increase in government expenditures, foreign oil company spending, and regulation of newly created private banking institutions necessitated more formal controls and policies. With United States technical assistance, in 1952 the Saudi Arabian Monetary Agency (SAMA) was created, designed to serve as the central bank within the confines of Islamic law.

The financial system has developed several layers intended to serve a number of multifaceted economic, exchange, and regulatory roles. At the apex was SAMA, which set the country's overall monetary policy. SAMA's functions also included stabilization of the value of the currency in an environment of openness with respect to exchange transactions and capital flows. The central bank used a number of monetary policy instruments for this purpose, including setting commercial-bank interest rates, which have been kept close to comparable dollar rates, the management of foreign assets, and the introduction of short- and medium-term government paper for budgetary and balance of payments purposes and to smooth fluctuations in domestic liquidity. SAMA also regulated commercial banks, exchange dealers, and money changers and has acted as the depository for all government funds; it paid out funds for purposes approved by the minister of finance and national economy.

SAMA's charter stipulated that it would conform to Islamic law. It could not be a profit-making institution and could neither pay nor receive interest. There were additional prohibitions, including one against extending credit to the government. This latter prohibition was dropped in 1955, when the government needed funds and SAMA financed about one-half of the government's debt that accrued in the late 1950s. From 1962 to 1983, the budget surplus did not require such action and all the government's debt was repaid. In 1988 SAMA was once again required to bolster government reserves, which had been sharply reduced to finance fiscal

*Modern cultivation techniques substantially increased
crop production beginning in the 1980s.
Courtesy Saudi Aramco
Fish market, Jizan
Courtesy Aramco World*

deficits, through the sale of Government Development Bonds. These bonds had varying short- and long-term maturities, with yields competitive with international interest rates. As a result of persistent government deficits, the stock of these bonds had grown to well over SR100 billion in 1991. Most of these bonds were placed with autonomous government institutions; however, close to 25 percent were purchased by domestic commercial banks.

In 1966 a major banking control law clarified and strengthened SAMA's role in regulating the banking system. Applications for bank licenses were submitted to SAMA, which submitted each application and its recommendations to the Ministry of Finance and National Economy. The Council of Ministers set conditions for granting licenses to foreign banks, however. The law also established requirements concerning reserves against deposits. Several restrictions continued to inhibit SAMA's implementation of monetary policy. It could neither extend credit to banks nor use a discount rate because these measures were forms of interest. SAMA had little flexibility in setting reserve and liquidity requirements for commercial banks. Its primary tool for expanding the credit base consisted in placing deposits in commercial banks.

By the 1980s, new regulations were introduced, based on a system of service charges instead of interest to circumvent Islamic restrictions. As of the early 1990s, banks were subject to reserve requirements. A statutory reserve requirement obliged each commercial bank to maintain a minimum of noninterest-bearing deposits with SAMA. Marginal reserve requirements applied to deposits exceeding a factor of the bank's paid-in capital and reserves. Moreover, banks had to hold additional liquid assets—such as currency, deposits with SAMA beyond the reserve accounts, and Government Development Bonds—equal to part of their deposit liabilities. SAMA used two other instruments to manage commercial bank liquidity. The Bankers' Security Deposit Account (BSDA) was a short-term instrument with low yield, rediscountable with SAMA and transferable to other banks. In November 1991, SAMA issued the first treasury bills, which were short-term, usable for both liquidity management and government deficit financing, and designed gradually to replace the BSDAs.

Twelve private commercial banks operated in the kingdom, providing full-service banking to individuals, and to private and public enterprises. Eight of the banks were totally Saudi-owned. Four were joint ventures with foreign banks. In 1975 the government adopted a program of Saudi participation in ownership of foreign banks operating in the kingdom. In December 1982, the last of the foreign banks merged with a Saudi bank. The commercial banks operated more than 1,000 branches throughout the country and a widespread network of automated teller machines. The range of bank activities grew markedly during the 1970s and 1980s. Beyond providing credit and deposit facilities, they engaged in securities trading, investment banking, foreign exchange services, government finance, and development of a secondary government bond-treasury bill market.

For years money exchangers remained an anomaly in the Saudi banking system. They had operated for centuries in Arabia, particularly for pilgrims to Mecca. Most were family businesses, some of which had grown very large since World War II, conducting most kinds of banking activities in many areas of the country. Although licensed, the money-exchange houses remained largely unregulated. Most money exchangers operated under sound business practices; however, a series of fraudulent and speculative practices in the 1980s prompted SAMA to establish regulations for money-exchange houses. One of the larger such operations was converted to a commercial bank in 1987.

Because commercial banks favored short-term lending to established firms and individuals, the government created special credit institutions to channel funds to other sectors and groups in the economy. The Saudi Arabian Agricultural Bank was formed in 1963 to provide development financing and subsidies to the agricultural sector. The Saudi Credit Bank was formed in 1971 to provide interest-free loans to low-income Saudis who could not obtain credit from commercial banks. The Public Investment Fund was created in 1973 to help finance large public ventures. The Saudi Industrial Development Fund was established in 1974 to provide interest-free, medium- and long-term financing of up to 50 percent of the cost of a private sector project. The Real Estate Development Fund, also founded in 1974, was designed to encourage private sector residential and commercial building, partly through interest-free loans to low- and medium-income Saudis for up to 70 percent of the cost of a home.

The government budget provided almost all the funds for these specialized credit institutions and continued to increase their capital requirements until the mid-1980s, when budgetary problems necessitated cutbacks. For the most part, these funds were self-financing during the latter half of the 1980s. A significant departure from such self-financing was the government's substantial subvention to the Real Estate Development Fund in 1991 to allow a one-year moratorium on payments, which was a gift by King Fahd to his citizens.

The Saudi financial system also consisted of three autonomous government institutions, included because of their significant role in providing financing for budgetary shortfalls, deposits with SAMA, and foreign currency holdings. These included the Pension Fund, the General Organization of Social Insurance, and the Saudi Fund for Development.

For much of the 1980s, the stock exchange, created in 1983, was largely viewed by domestic investors as a vehicle for long-term investments. Since the Persian Gulf War, this situation has changed markedly because the exchange has attracted investors seeking shorter-term investments. Share prices and trading volumes have grown sharply and by early 1992 had reached unprecedented levels, sparking fears of overvaluation. The official stock market index, which had remained relatively dormant in the late 1980s, and had dropped from 108.7 at the end of 1989 to 98.0 in late 1990, roughly doubled to 187.7 by the close of 1991. The value of shares traded grew from SR135 million at the end of 1990 to SR1.8 billion by the first quarter of 1992. The number of shares traded doubled from 15 million for the whole of 1989, to 29.2 million in 1991.

Three factors propelled this level of stock market activity. First, following the Persian Gulf War, confidence in the Saudi economy spurred by high oil prices and greater confidence in the regional geopolitical situation prompted domestic investors to repatriate foreign funds. Second, low international interest rates, combined with similar returns of domestic savings rates, increased the attractiveness of the stock exchange. Third, the number of companies trading on the exchange increased markedly as they attempted to boost domestic investment following several years of depressed economic conditions. Moreover, the tight government budget prompted some public enterprises to obtain capital on the domestic financial markets rather than from the state.

The Saudi stock exchange was not open to foreign investment and only shares of Saudi companies could be traded. The exception to the former rule was the right of citizens of GCC member states to purchase Sabic shares from 1984. In 1991 the Arab National Bank, partially funded by Jordanian capital, received permission to launch a stock fund, of which foreigners might purchase a portion. Despite growth in the stock market, the percentage of shares traded as a percentage of total market value of shares outstanding has been estimated as no more than 5 percent, very low by international standards. This lack of market depth resulted from the high proportion of shares owned by institutions rather than individuals and the concentration of ownership in a few hands.

# External Trade and Finance

## Foreign Trade

Crude oil, refined products and natural gas liquids accounted for the bulk of Saudi exports. Nevertheless, the percentage of crude oil and petroleum product exports fell slightly during the 1980s as a result of the growth in petrochemical and other chemical exports. These products have come mainly from Sabic's companies. After declining to their lowest levels in the 1970s and 1980s, following the oil price crash of 1986, exports had steadily recovered by 1992, both as a result of improved oil prices and Saudi Arabia's international market share of world oil supplies. Moreover, as Sabic created a new petrochemical capacity, nonoil exports rose as well. The direction of exports has been influenced by Saudi Arabia's oil customers. During the early 1980s, Asia and Western Europe were the major purchasers of Saudi oil. By the end of the decade, Europe had ceded its share to Asia and North America (see table 10, Appendix).

Saudi import levels have closely followed overseas oil earnings and government expenditures. SAMA, which published data on imports, did not include military imports in merchandise import figures. Some military imports were included in the current account under government service imports (see Current Account, this ch.). Falling from a peak in the mid-1980s of US$40 billion to US$50 billion per annum, imports maintained levels of around US$20 billion during the late 1980s before starting to climb again in 1990 to 1992. Machinery, appliances, and electrical equipment constituted the largest import category, although in line with lower domestic investment these items fell in terms of total share. In 1984 this category accounted for 24 percent of imports but by 1990 it had declined to 16 percent. Foodstuffs have been the second largest category: in 1984 these items made up 16 percent and fell only slightly to 14 percent in 1990. The decline in food imports resulted mainly from domestic import substitution of vegetable products. During the 1980s, chemical products, jewelry and metals, and other transport items exhibited the largest growth in imports. Chemical products, the third largest import category in 1990, constituted around 12 percent of imports. The principal source of imports was Western Europe, which maintained its share at 44 percent for much of the 1980s. The United States supplied 17 percent of the kingdom's imports, whereas Japan's share was 15 percent, having decreased from around 20 percent in the mid-1980s. Saudi Arabia bought only 3 to 4 percent of imported goods from the rest of the Middle East.

## Current Account

During the first half of the 1980s, Saudi Arabia had substantial trade surpluses, but these were reduced in the period of low oil prices after 1986. After the Iraqi invasion of Kuwait and following the sharp increase in prices, the trade balance swelled to between US$23 billion and US$24 billion. In contrast, the services sector of the current account registered large deficits. Service receipts, consisting of freight and insurance connected with merchandise exports and investment income, fell in accordance with decreases in the volume of oil exports and the depletion of foreign assets. Service payments have been a major burden on the current account. Whereas freight, insurance, and tourism receipts remained stagnant or fell during the 1980s, government military equipment purchases and public and private transfers (both aid flows and workers' remittances) did not contract sufficiently to erase the services and transfers deficit. Between 1984 and 1988, oil revenue declines forced the authorities to restrict government purchases of military equipment, which helped cover the deficit on services. However, after 1989, particularly after Operation Desert Shield, this category, in addition to the outflow of workers' remittances, aggravated the services' deficit to levels not seen since the early 1980s. The services and transfers deficit rose from US$11.9 billion in 1988 to US$26.9 billion in 1990. As a result of these trade and services flows, the current account has remained persistently in deficit since 1986, although considerable progress was made up to 1988 in reducing the shortfall. Despite a sharply higher trade surplus in 1991, it was estimated that payments to foreign allies, greater arms purchases, and increases in remittances caused the current account deficit to balloon to US$24 billion in 1991. By 1992, with the normalization of the military situation, the current account deficit was estimated to return to levels more in line with the structural deficit of the economy.

## Capital Account

During the early 1980s, current account surpluses led to a sharp increase in foreign asset holdings (see table 11, Appendix). As a result, the capital account was dominated by outflows from both official institutions and the private sector. With the current account registering sizable deficits after 1983, the capital account has seen a reversal of these trends. A reduction of foreign assets was followed by a significant inflow of banking sector capital for the purchase of Saudi development bonds. The private sector only began repatriating capital after the Persian Gulf War ended. For much of the 1980s, private individuals and companies placed a substantial amount of funds overseas, a process that accelerated following the fall in oil prices in 1986 and as a result of the Iran-Iraq War. Increased confidence in the Saudi economy after the Persian Gulf War caused the return of these funds. The inflow of private capital in 1991 allowed SAMA to stabilize official foreign exchange holdings and spurred economic activity in the nonoil sector. Official asset flows constituted the bulk of current account financing, a process that became unsustainable following the massive depletions to pay for the Persian Gulf War costs. As a result, the government has engaged in significant commercial borrowing on the international markets and instructed some of its public enterprises (notably Saudi Aramco and Sabic) to do the same. With the expectation that Saudi Arabia will continue to run current account deficits during the foreseeable future, it is likely that the capital account will be dominated by debt flows and a good measure of private sector asset repatriation.

## Foreign Assets and Liabilities

Publicly available information on Saudi Arabia's foreign assets was scant. Newspaper accounts placed foreign assets held by SAMA overseas at around US$100 billion during the early 1980s. These assets have been substantially depleted to finance current account deficits. A sizable portion has become nonperforming as Saudi Arabia has been unable to recover loans to several countries, notably Iraq. By the end of 1991, foreign assets of the government were estimated at US$30 billion if nonperforming assets were excluded. This amount was only sufficient for purposes of currency cover, a statutory requirement of SAMA. Saudi commercial banks held an additional US$30 billion to US$35 billion in foreign assets, some of which was depleted in the late 1980s to finance government bond purchases and to cover domestic liquidity. Estimates of private sector assets were even more difficult to aggregate; however, based on Bank of International Settlements data and newspaper accounts, the figure could be as large as US$100 billion.

Until 1991 Saudi Arabia's foreign liabilities were restricted to foreign lines of credit necessary to conduct international trade and financing operations held by domestic commercial banks. The negative balance of payments caused the government to engage in a sizable borrowing program on international capital markets in 1991. The borrowing program included a loan from Morgan Bank of approximately US$4.5 billion. Saudi Aramco was reported to have borrowed US$2 billion to finance parts of its oil sector development program, and several Sabic corporations borrowed for new industrial investments. Further borrowings were likely. At the end of 1991, total medium-long-term debt, consisting largely of government debt, was estimated at US$9 billion and was expected to grow to US$12 billion by the end of 1992. Short-term, trade-related debt was estimated at US$11 billion at the end of 1991.

In summary, during the period of high oil prices beginning in the 1970s, the government transformed the kingdom into a modern economy with few vestiges of the pre-oil period remaining. Concurrently, the standard of living for the average Saudi grew markedly, thanks to such factors as government-provided social services and a plethora of subsidies. Despite these achievements, what struck most observers was the fragile base that supported this standard of living. Government oil revenues, supplemented by private reserves accumulated during the oil boom years, accounted for much of the gross domestic product. Whereas diversification of the economy has been an objective for most of the five-year development plans since the 1970s, oil still dominated and was likely to continue to do so. Oil's predominance was apparent in 1992 as the government was allocating large sums to expand crude oil production capacity to still higher levels in anticipation of growing international demand.

The large oil sector did not mean that the kingdom had not invested heavily in industrialization: in 1992 it ranked among the major industrial economies in the Middle East. But most Saudi industries were petroleum-based, in the public sector, and heavily dependent on subventions from the government budget. The private sector has been reluctant to establish domestic processing plants, and those created have been heavily subsidized. Similarly, modern, water-intensive, and import-dependent agriculture has come at a huge cost to the government.

Despite higher oil capacity and demand for Saudi Arabian crude oil and petroleum products, the kingdom will continue to face tight budgetary restrictions during the 1990s. The challenge facing the government in the aftermath of the Persian Gulf War, with all its costs, was maintaining the high Saudi standard of living while continuing to diversify the economy. With financial reserves at the bare minimum levels necessary to keep international confidence, this challenge became even more difficult.

\* \* \*

With the decline in oil prices in 1986, the number of books on Saudi Arabia and the Persian Gulf region markedly declined. There are, however, several excellent early monographs on the five-year plans and early development programs but few recent books that deal with the problems of deficits and stabilizing the economy. Two of the most up-to-date books on the Saudi economy are Robert E. Looney's *Economic Development in Saudi Arabia* and H. Askari's and B. Dastmaltschi's *Saudi Arabia's Economy: Oil and the Search for Economic Development.* The latter is highly recommended because of its detailed analysis of the development plans and real costs associated with them. Tim Niblock's *State, Society, and Economy in Saudi Arabia* provides an excellent background to the economic development effort and contains several insightful studies on the economic and social constraints facing the country. A particularly good book on the private sector is Michael Field's *The Merchants.* For ongoing coverage of the kingdom's economy, three sources are recommended: *Middle East Economic Digest, Middle East Economic Survey,* and *Financial Times.* A plethora of oil journals, especially *Petroleum Intelligence Weekly,* keep up with developments in the Saudi oil sector. The United States Embassy in Riyadh also produces a comprehensive annual summary of developments in the kingdom's oil sector. (For further information and complete citations, see Bibliography.)

# Chapter 4. Government and Politics

*The Kaaba in the Grand Mosque, Mecca*

ABD AR RAHMAN AL SAUD, who had begun conquering territory in the Arabian Peninsula in 1902, proclaimed the Kingdom of Saudi Arabia in 1932. It was then, and remained sixty years later, the only nation to have been named after its ruling family. Fahd ibn Abd al Aziz Al Saud, who in 1992 had been ruling for ten years, was the fourth son of Abd al Aziz to become king since his father's death in 1953. Although the Al Saud kings ruled as absolute monarchs, their power was tempered by Islamic law (sharia) and by the custom of reaching consensus on political issues among the scores of direct adult male descendants of Abd al Aziz.

Islam was a pervasive social and political force in Saudi Arabia. Because there was no separation of religion and state, the political role of religious scholars, or ulama, was second in importance to that of the ruling Al Saud family. The close association between the ulama, advocating the strict Islamic interpretations of Muhammad ibn Abd al Wahhab, and the Al Saud originated in the eighteenth century and provided the dynasty with its primary source of legitimacy. The ulama acted as a conservative force in maintaining the traditional social and political values that characterized Saudi Arabia in the early 1990s.

Although Saudi Arabia was established as a country based on a fundamentalist interpretation of Islam, the discovery of vast petroleum deposits led to significant changes in the role of religion. Since the 1950s, when oil revenues became abundant, Saudi rulers have sought to reap the economic benefits derived from oil resources while trying to minimize the political and social impact of change. Nevertheless, the transformation of Saudi Arabia from a relatively isolated, predominantly rural country into a wealthy, urbanized nation hosting millions of foreign workers inevitably produced tensions. From a political perspective, the most significant development was the emergence of a group of middle-class professionals. This important and highly educated group of Saudis generally resented the lack of opportunities for citizen participation in politics. Beginning in the 1960s, they tried to pressure the monarchy into creating an elective representative assembly. Saudi kings resisted demands for political liberalization by strengthening regime ties with the ulama, who tended to distrust the notion of popular government because of the implicit assumption that manmade legislation could be equal to sacred law.

Islam also was a significant factor in Saudi Arabia's foreign relations. The very close relationship that developed between the kingdom and the non-Muslim United States after 1945, for example, was partly a result of Saudi antipathy to the former Soviet Union's espousal of atheism. Beginning in the late 1950s, Riyadh and Washington shared similar misgivings about the ties that secular, republican regimes in the region established with Moscow. During the 1980s, the Saudis tried to counteract Soviet influence by providing military aid to Islamic groups that opposed secular governments in such countries as Afghanistan, Ethiopia, and the People's Democratic Republic of Yemen (South Yemen). In addition, the kingdom gave generous economic assistance to the predominantly Muslim states of Africa and Asia in the expectation that recipient countries would support its overall policy goals. Despite this largess, however, Jordan, Sudan, and the Republic of Yemen (a merger of the People's Democratic Republic of Yemen and the Yemen Arab Republic, North Yemen), three of the countries most dependent on Saudi foreign aid, failed to back the kingdom during its 1990–91 conflict with Iraq after the latter invaded Kuwait.

Saudi efforts to use Islam as a vehicle for rallying diplomatic support met with indifferent results because other Muslim countries generally did not base their foreign policies on religion. A notable exception was Iran, the kingdom's neighbor on the northern shore of the Persian Gulf. The shared Islamic heritage was not, however, a basis for Saudi-Iranian cooperation. On the contrary, the 1979 Iranian Islamic Revolution had brought to power Muslim clergy who espoused a version of Islam that Saudi ulama considered heretical. Moreover, Iranian officials throughout the 1980s denounced the Al Saud as corrupt and the institution of monarchy as un-Islamic. Consequently, the government of Saudi Arabia perceived Iran as a major threat to both domestic tranquility and regional security. Although Saudi Arabia remained officially neutral during the protracted Iran-Iraq War (1980–88), it supported the war aims of its former political rival, the secular government of Iraq, by providing Baghdad with loans and grants totaling several billion dollars.

Saudi financial assistance neither defeated Iran nor won Iraq's gratitude. In 1984 Iran initiated attacks on tankers carrying Saudi and Kuwaiti oil, justifying its actions on grounds that the monetary aid extended to Iraq had made both Saudi Arabia and Kuwait de facto Iraqi allies. As the war spread to the Persian Gulf, Riyadh began to perceive that the continuation of the conflict posed a major security threat. The government thus felt relieved in 1988 when both belligerents, weary of fighting, agreed to accept a United Nations-mediated cease-fire. However, the cessation of Iran-Iraq hostilities provided the Saudis only a brief respite from concerns about regional security. Iraq soon turned on Kuwait, Saudi Arabia's close ally and neighbor. After Kuwait had resisted Iraqi demands for more than a year, Baghdad retaliated in August 1990 by dispatching its army to occupy and annex the small, oil-rich state. King Fahd's government, shocked and frightened, called upon the United States for help. In an unprecedented development, thousands of United States troops, under authority of several United Nations resolutions, were deployed to the kingdom beginning in August 1990. The country's ulama tolerated their presence after receiving the king's assurances that the foreign military personnel, among whom were several thousand women, would have minimal contact with Saudi civilians and be required to obey Saudi laws such as the ban on consumption of alcohol.

By the beginning of 1991, it had become obvious that the massive United States military presence in Saudi Arabia would not persuade Iraq to withdraw from Kuwait. The Saudi government and its Arab allies consequently agreed to join the United States, which also had obtained support from its European allies, to force a withdrawal. Iraq's appeals for Arab and Islamic solidarity against the United States intervention failed to impress the Saudis, who noted that the sharing of similar religious traditions had not prevented Iraq from invading Kuwait nor threatening their country. During the forty-three-day Persian Gulf War, Iraqi missiles struck Riyadh and several other Saudi towns, and the Saudi armed forces participated with non-Muslims and non-Arabs in the fighting against Iraq. The war, which ended with Iraq's military defeat in February 1991, demonstrated to the Saudis the impracticality of trying to base foreign policy on their vision of Islam. Convinced that the kingdom's security interests required the long-term containment of Iraq and convinced that Iran had the same objective, Riyadh put aside its reservations about Iran's adherence to Shia (see Glossary) Islam and began the process of normalizing relations with Tehran.

## Structure of Government

Saudi Arabia was an absolute monarchy in 1992. The king was not constrained by a written constitution, a legislative assembly, or elections. Since 1962, Saudi kings periodically promised to establish a *majlis ash shura,* or consultative council, to advise them on governmental matters, but none of them undertook practical steps to establish such a body. In March 1992, King Fahd once again announced that a *majlis ash shura* would be appointed and specified its responsibilities. Fahd proposed a majlis of sixty-one members, all appointed by the king. The majlis would have limited authority to question ministers and propose legislation. The majlis would not have actual legislative powers but rather would serve as an advisory body that could make recommendations to the king.

As of the end of 1992, King Fahd had named only a single individual to the *majlis ash shura* that he had proposed ten months earlier. In appointing the speaker, the king made no promises as to when Saudi citizens could expect the convening of the full majlis. The International Committee for Human Rights in the Gulf and the Arabian Peninsula issued a public statement advising Saudis that the government had promised consistently for thirty years to establish a consultative council but never had fulfilled these promises.

Saudis considered the Quran, the holy book of Islam, their country's constitution. The Quran is the primary source of the sharia. Because the sharia does not specifically address the conduct of most governmental matters, Saudi rulers, beginning with Abd al Aziz, have promulgated numerous regulations pertaining to the functions of government. In early 1992, King Fahd became the first Saudi monarch to compile these regulations into a single document called the main code (*nizam*). Promulgated as a royal decree, this document codified bureaucratic procedures and prohibited government agencies from arbitrarily arresting citizens or violating their privacy. Although the main code was not a formal constitution, it fulfilled some of the same purposes of such a document. However, the main code lacked any explicit clause guaranteeing the basic rights of citizens to freedom of belief, expression, assembly, or political participation.

## The King

As one of world's last absolute monarchs, the Saudi Arabian king exercised very broad powers. He was both head of state and head of government. Ultimate authority in virtually every aspect of government rested with the king. All legislation was enacted either by royal decree or by ministerial decree, which had to be sanctioned by the king. In his capacity as prime minister, the king appointed all cabinet ministers, other senior government officials, and the governors of the provinces. In his capacity as commander in chief of the armed forces, the king appointed all military officers above the rank of lieutenant colonel. He also appointed all Saudi Arabia's ambassadors and other foreign envoys. All foreign diplomats in the country were accredited to the king. In addition, the king acted as the final court of appeal and had the power of pardon.

The legitimacy of the king's rule was based on the twin pillars of religion and the dynastic history of the Al Saud. The family's most important early ancestor, Muhammad ibn Saud (1710-65), had been a relatively minor local ruler in Najd before establishing a political and family alliance with the puritanical Muslim preacher and reformer Muhammad ibn Abd al Wahhab (1703-87) in 1744. Muhammad ibn Saud and his descendants—the Al Saud—ardently supported the preacher and his descendants—the Al ash Shaykh—and were determined to introduce a purified Islam, which opponents called Wahhabism (see Glossary), throughout Arabia. Religious fervor facilitated the conquest of Najd and at the height of their power in the early nineteenth century, the Al Saud had extended their control over most of the Arabian Peninsula (see The Al Saud and Wahhabi Islam, 1500-1818, ch. 1). Subsequent conflict with the Ottoman Empire and dynastic rivalries both diminished and enhanced the political fortunes of the Al Saud throughout the nineteenth century. Nevertheless, the Saudi alliance with the Al ash Shaykh endured.

The founder of the modern state of Saudi Arabia, Abd al Aziz ibn Abd ar Rahman Al Saud (1876-1953), was a grandson of the last effective nineteenth-century Saudi ruler, Faisal ibn Turki (1810-66). Abd al Aziz restored the family from virtual political extinction by reintroducing the crusading zeal of Wahhabi Islam (see The Rise of Abd al Aziz, 1890-1926, ch. 1). By 1924, when the Ikhwan, a select force of beduin religious fighters created by Abd al Aziz, conquered the Hijaz, almost all the territory of the present-day Saudi state was under Abd al Aziz's authority. In 1932 he proclaimed this territory the Kingdom of Saudi Arabia and himself its king.

Abd al Aziz ruled until his death in 1953. Although he had named his eldest son, Saud ibn Abd al Aziz Al Saud (1902-69), crown prince, he had not instituted an mechanism for orderly succession. Because Abd al Aziz was survived by more than thirty sons, the lack of a process for passing on the mantle of kingship constituted a source of potential political instability for the country. Problems emerged soon after King Saud began his reign. Like his father, Saud had more than thirty sons, and he was ambitious to place them in positions of power and influence. The new king's numerous brothers, who believed their nephews were too young and inexperienced to head ministries and major government departments, deeply resented their exclusion from power. The political and personal tensions among the Al Saud, combined with the extravagance and poor judgment of Saud, climaxed in a 1964 family coup. A number of brothers joined together to depose Saud and install as king the next eldest brother, Faisal ibn Abd al Aziz Al Saud (1904–75). The transfer of power was endorsed by Saudi Arabia's ulama, or religious authorities.

King Faisal strengthened the powers of the monarchy during his eleven-year reign. Although he had acted as prime minister during most of Saud's rule, he issued a royal decree stipulating that the king would serve both as head of state and as head of government. Faisal also increased central control over the provinces by making local officials responsible to the king, creating a Ministry of Justice to regulate the autonomous religious courts, and establishing a national development plan to coordinate construction projects and social services throughout the country. Faisal's concern for orderly government and durable institutions extended to the monarchy. In 1965 he persuaded his brothers to observe the principle of birth order among themselves to regulate the succession, although the next eldest brother, Muhammad (born 1910), voluntarily stepped down in favor of Khalid (1912–82).

Faisal's rule ended abruptly in 1975 when he was assassinated by one of his nephews. A meeting of senior Al Saud princes, the sons and surviving brothers of Abd al Aziz, acclaimed Crown Prince Khalid the new king. Because some of Khalid's brothers, who would have been next in line of succession according to age, renounced their right to the throne, the king and the princes designated a younger brother, Fahd (born 1921), crown prince. Fahd ascended to the throne in 1982 after Khalid suffered a fatal heart attack. In consultation with his brothers, Fahd named Abd Allah (born 1923) crown prince and Sultan (born 1927) third in line of succession. The relatively smooth transitions following the deaths of Faisal and Khalid thus seemed to have resolved the issue of succession among the sons of Abd al Aziz. In 1992, however, Fahd altered the procedure for designating future kings. In the same royal decree that announced the impending appointment of a majlis, Fahd declared that the king would henceforth name and could remove the crown prince. Furthermore, the crown prince would not automatically succeed on the death of the king, but serve as provisional ruler until he, or a descendant of Abd al Aziz deemed more suitable, was enthroned.

Fahd's decree on succession established two precedents: a royal prerogative to choose and to withdraw approval for the crown prince; and an acknowledgement that the more than sixty grandsons

*King Fahd ibn Abd al Aziz*
*Al Saud,*
*custodian of*
*the two holy mosques*
*Courtesy* Aramco World

*Crown Prince*
*Abd Allah ibn Abd al Aziz,*
*first deputy prime*
*minister and head of*
*the Saudi Arabian*
*National Guard*
*Courtesy* Aramco World

of Abd al Aziz were legitimate claimants to the throne. Previously, Saudi kings had not asserted the right to dismiss a designated crown prince. By proclaiming such a right, Fahd revived persistent rumors originating in the 1970s that he and his half brother Abd Allah disagreed on many political issues. To forestall speculation that his intent was to remove Abd Allah as crown prince and replace him with his full brother Sultan, Fahd reaffirmed Abd Allah's position. However, in declaring that successor kings would be chosen from the most suitable of Abd al Aziz's sons and grandsons, Fahd implied that Abd Allah or any future crown prince was not necessarily the presumed heir to the throne. The decision to include the grandsons in the selection process and as potential candidates for the throne symbolized the readiness of Fahd and his surviving brothers to pass substantive decision-making responsibilities to a younger generation of the Al Saud. However, this decision also introduced more uncertainty into the succession process. At least a dozen men of this Al Saud younger generation, including sons of Faisal, Fahd, Abd Allah, and Sultan, were actively involved in the Saudi government and presumably had a personal interest in the question of succession.

## The Royal Diwan

The primary executive office of the king is the Royal Diwan. The king's principal advisers for domestic politics, religious affairs, and international relations have offices in the Royal Diwan. The king's private office also is in the Royal Diwan. The king conducts most routine government affairs from this office, including the drafting of regulations and royal decrees. In addition, the heads of several government departments have their offices in the diwan. These include the chief of protocol; the Office of Beduin Affairs; the Department of Religious Research, Missionary Activities, and Guidance; and, as well, the *mutawwiin* or Committees for the Propagation of Virtue and Prevention of Vice (popularly known as the Committees for Public Morality). The Department of Religious Research, Missionary Activities, and Guidance is headed by the most senior of the country's ulama. In 1992 this person was the religious scholar Shaykh Abd al Aziz ibn Baz, who spent much of his time in Medina, where he was in charge of the Prophet's Mosque.

The king also held his regular majlis, or court, in the Royal Diwan. The purpose of the majlis was to provide Saudi citizens an opportunity to make personal appeals to the king for redress of grievances or assistance in private matters. Plaintiffs typically sought the king's intervention with the state's bureaucracy. During the reigns of King Khalid and King Fahd, it was customary for each person attending the majlis to explain his complaints and simultaneously present a written petition, which the monarch would later study and answer in a subsequent session.

## The Council of Ministers

The Council of Ministers, created in 1953 by King Abd al Aziz shortly before his death, was the principal executive organ of the government. The Council of Ministers had authority to issue ministerial decrees, but it had no power separate from the king, who approved all its decisions. The office of prime minister had been abolished by royal decree in 1964, but the king, in his capacity as president of the Council of Ministers, served as the de facto prime minister. The crown prince was designated the first deputy prime minister, and the next prince in the line of succession was the second deputy prime minister. In 1992 the Council of Ministers consisted of the king, the crown prince, three royal advisers who held official positions as ministers of state without portfolio, five other ministers of state, and the heads of the twenty ministries, including Minister of Defense and Aviation Amir Sultan, who also served as second deputy prime minister. The ministries included agriculture and water; commerce; communications; defense and aviation; education; finance and national economy; foreign affairs; health; higher education; industry and electricity; information; interior; justice; labor and social affairs; municipal and rural affairs; petroleum and mineral resources; pilgrimage affairs and religious trusts; planning; post, telephone, and telegraph; and public works and housing. In addition to these ministries, the Saudi Arabian National Guard, which was headed by Crown Prince Abd Allah, was similar in status to a ministry. The governors of Medina, Mecca, Riyadh, and the Eastern Province, as well as the governor of the Saudi Arabian Monetary Agency (SAMA) and the head of the General Petroleum and Mineral Organization (Petromin) also held ministerial rank (see fig. 8).

The Ministry of Interior, which was responsible for domestic security, was second in overall political influence to the Ministry of Defense and Aviation. Since 1975 Amir Nayif ibn Abd al Aziz Al Saud (born 1933), who was a full brother of King Fahd, has been minister of interior. In 1992 Nayif ranked as the fourth most powerful person in the country after Fahd, Abd Allah, and Sultan. Nayif supervised the expansion of the ministry into an organization that exercised considerable influence over the daily lives of Saudi citizens.

As crown prince under King Khalid and as king in his own right since 1982, Fahd brought into the government many talented men

199

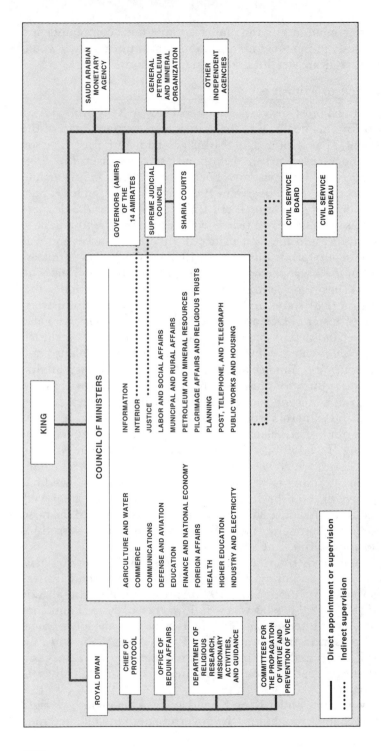

*Figure 8. Government Organization, 1992*

from families other than the ruling Al Saud. In 1992 about 75 percent of the Council of Ministers were of commoner backgrounds. Nevertheless, the key ministries of defense, foreign affairs, interior, and public works continued to be headed by Saudi princes. In addition, several of the king's younger brothers and nephews were deputy ministers in these same ministries, in effect acquiring on-the-job training to help ensure Al Saud control for another generation.

## The Civil Service and Independent Agencies

The nine-member Civil Service Board, responsible to the Council of Ministers, exercised formal authority over the employees of all ministries, government organizations, and autonomous agencies. It presided over the Civil Service Bureau, which implemented the decisions and directives of the Civil Service Board that pertained to grade classification, pay rates, recruitment and personnel needs, and personnel evaluation. Beginning in the early 1970s, the number of civil service employees in Saudi Arabia increased dramatically as the government expanded its social services. By 1992 an estimated 400,000 persons were government employees, including about 100,000 foreign nationals.

During the 1970s, the number of autonomous agencies also expanded. Although most of these agencies were under the administrative auspices of a particular ministry, each agency had its own budget and operated with considerable independence. Several agencies, including the General Audit Bureau, the Grievances Board, the Investigation and Control Board, and the Organization for Public Services and Discipline, were not attached to any particular ministry. The latter three agencies were responsible, respectively, for hearing complaints of misconduct by civil service employees, investigating complaints against government officials, and dispensing disciplinary action against civil servants judged guilty of malfeasance in office.

Civil servants were classified either as government officials (professionals who comprised three-quarters of total government employees in 1992) and lower-paid employees. All civil servants were ranked according to grade, and advancement depended on merit and seniority. Training was provided within each ministry and at the Institute of Public Administration, an autonomous government agency with its main training center in Riyadh, and at branches in Jiddah and Ad Dammam.

## The Legal System

The Saudi Arabian legal system in 1992 was based on the sharia, or Islamic law. The sharia was applied throughout the kingdom in strict accordance with the interpretation of the Hanbali school of Sunni (see Glossary) Islam. Because pious Muslims believed that the sharia was sacred law, they accepted as judges, or qadis, only men who had spent a number of years studying the accepted sources of the sharia: the Quran and the authenticated traditions (hadith) of the Prophet Muhammad's rulings and practices. Historically, the decisions of qadis were subject to review by the ruler, whose primary role was to ensure that the Islamic community lived in conformity with the sharia. In effect, the judiciary was not an independent institution but an extension of the political authority. This traditional relationship between qadis and the king still prevailed in Saudi Arabia.

The Ministry of Justice, established by King Faisal in 1970, was responsible for administering the country's more than 300 sharia courts. The minister of justice, appointed by the king from among the country's most senior ulama, was the de facto chief justice. He was assisted by the Supreme Judicial Council, a body of eleven members chosen from the leading ulama. The Supreme Judicial Council supervised the work of the courts, reviewed all legal decisions referred to it by the minister of justice, expressed legal opinions on judicial questions, and approved all sentences of death, amputation (of fingers and hands as punishment for theft), and stoning (for adultery). Since 1983, the minister of justice has also served as chief of the Supreme Judicial Council, a position that further enhanced his status as chief justice.

Sharia courts included courts of first instance and appeals courts. Minor civil and criminal cases were adjudicated in the summary courts of first instance. One kind of summary court dealt exclusively with beduin affairs. A single qadi presided over all summary court hearings. The general courts of first instance handled all cases beyond the jurisdiction of the summary courts. One judge usually presided over cases in the general courts, but three qadis sat in judgment for serious crimes such as murder, major theft, or sexual misconduct.

Decisions of the summary and general courts could be appealed to the sharia appeals court. The appeals court, or court of cassation, had three departments: penal suits, personal status suits, and all other types of suits. The appeals had two seats, one in Riyadh and one in Mecca. The chief justice and a panel of several qadis presided over all cases. The king was at the pinnacle of the judicial system, functioning as a final court of appeal and as a source of pardon.

Saudi Arabia's judicial code stipulated that specialized courts may be established by royal decree to deal with infractions of government regulations not covered by the sharia. Since the reign of Abd al Aziz, kings have created various secular tribunals outside of the sharia court system to deal with violations of administrative rules. The Grievances Board, for example, operated under the authority of the Bureau of the Presidency of the Council of Ministers. It reviewed complaints of improper behavior brought against both government officials and qadis. The Ministry of Interior was in charge of the special police who enforced motor vehicle regulations. The Ministry of Commerce supervised arbitration and appeals boards established to settle commercial disputes, especially those involving foreign businesses. Decrees pertaining to labor were enforced by special committees within the Ministry of Labor and Social Affairs.

## Local Government

Saudi Arabia consisted of fourteen provinces, or amirates (see fig. 1), each governed by an amir (governor) appointed by the king. In 1992 these amirates included Al Banah, Al Hudud ash Shamaliyah, Al Jawf, Al Madinah, Al Qasim, Al Qurayyat, Ar Riyadh, Ash Sharqiyah, Asir, Hail, Jizan, Makkah, Najran, and Tabuk. The larger, more populous amirates were subdivided into districts and subdistricts.

In theory, the governors were responsible to the minister of interior. In practice, however, the governors usually reported directly to the king. In 1992 all amirate governors and most of their deputies were members of the Al Saud. King Fahd's brothers, sons, and nephews ruled the most politically important amirates; other kin ruled the smaller amirates. The governors maintained administrative offices in the principal cities of their respective amirates, although none of these cities was designated a capital. The governors' principal responsibility was to oversee the work of both central government and municipal officials within the amirates. The governors also served as commanders of the local police and Saudi Arabian National Guard units and supervised the recruitment of local men for these security forces (see Saudi Arabian National Guard, ch. 5). In addition, each governor followed the example of the king and held a public majlis, often on a daily basis, at which he heard petitions from local residents. Typically, the petitions pertained to local disputes, which the governor either arbitrated or referred to an appropriate court. Some governors considered the majlis an important link between the people and government and employed several special assistants who investigated local disputes and grievances.

The governors were assisted by one, or sometimes two, deputies and, in some amirates, by one or more deputy assistant governors. In amirates that were subdivided into districts, the district officials were subordinate to the amirate governors. The mayors of each city, town, and village within an amirate were formally responsible to the Ministry of Municipal and Rural Affairs, although in practice they also were subordinate to the governor. Since the 1960s, the Al Saud princes have discussed the merits of creating amirate councils, elected or appointed bodies of local men to advise and assist the governors. In early 1992, King Fahd announced that he would appoint councils in each amirate; these councils would assume limited local authority over some central government functions.

## Political Dynamics

### The Royal Family

Although the Saudi king in 1992 was an absolute monarch in the sense that there were no formal, institutionalized checks on his authority, in practice his ability to rule effectively depended on his astuteness in creating and maintaining consensus within his very large, extended family. The king was the patriarch of the Al Saud, which, including all its collateral branches, numbered about 20,000 people. These persons traced their patrilineal descent to Muhammad ibn Saud, the eighteenth-century founder of the dynasty. The most important branch of the Al Saud family was known as Al Faisal. The Al Faisal branch consisted of the patrilineal descendants of Abd al Aziz's grandfather, Faisal ibn Turki. Only males of the Al Faisal branch of the family, estimated at more than 4,000 in 1992, were considered royalty and were accorded the title of *amir* (prince).

Even within the Al Faisal branch of the Al Saud family, the princes did not enjoy the same degree of influence. The several lineages within the Al Faisal branch derived from the numerous sons and grandsons of Faisal ibn Turki. His most important grandson, Abd al Aziz, married several women, each of whom bore the king one or more sons. The sons of Abd al Aziz by the same mother (full brothers) inevitably felt more affinity for one another than for their half brothers, and thus political influence within this patrilineal family actually tended to be wielded on the basis of matrilineal descent. Since Fahd's ascent to the throne in 1982, the most influential clan of the Al Faisal branch of the Al Saud family has been the Al Sudairi, known by the patronymic of Fahd's mother. Fahd had seven full brothers, including Minister of Defense Sultan, who

*Old amirate building, Najran*
*Courtesy Saudi Arabian Information Office*

was second in the line of succession, Minister of Interior Nayif, and Governor of Riyadh Salman. Sultan and Salman were considered to be Fahd's closest political advisers. In 1983 Fahd appointed one of Sultan's sons, Bandar, to be the Saudi ambassador to the United States. Another of Sultan's sons, Khalid, was the de facto commander of Saudi armed forces during the Persian Gulf War. At least once a week, the king and his full brothers met for a family dinner at which they shared perspectives about national and international politics. In addition to his full brothers, seven of Fahd's half brothers were sons of other Al Sudairi women whom his father had married. As the sons of Fahd and his brothers matured and assumed government responsibilities during the 1980s, some Saudis began to refer to the clan as Al Fahd instead of Al Sudairi.

The Al Thunayyan clan was closely allied to the Al Sudairi. King Faisal's favorite wife had been from the Al Thunayyan, a collateral branch of the Al Saud family that had intermarried with the Al ash Shaykh ulama family. During the Al Saud crisis that culminated in the 1964 deposition of King Saud, the Al Sudairi consistently supported Faisal. Because Faisal had no full brothers, he tended to favor those of his half brothers who had backed him during the prolonged political struggle with Saud. For example, Fahd, Sultan, and Nayif all received important ministerial positions from

205

Faisal when he was crown prince (1953–64) and for much of that period Saud's prime minister. Following Faisal's assassination in 1975, Fahd, the eldest of the Al Sudairi brothers, was named second in the line of succession. Before becoming king in 1982, Fahd served as King Khalid's de facto prime minister and used his influence to obtain ministerial-level appointments for Faisal's sons. One son, Saud ibn Faisal, was named minister of foreign affairs in 1975.

The Al Jiluwi was a third influential clan of the Al Saud family. The Al Jiluwi were descended from a brother of Faisal ibn Turki, the grandfather of Abd al Aziz. The mother of the late King Khalid and his only full brother, Muhammad (born 1910), had been an Al Jiluwi. In the early 1960s, Khalid and Muhammad had shared the critical views of their half brothers Faisal and Fahd with respect to Saud's style of rule, and they were among the select group of princes and ulama who joined to depose Saud in 1964. The following year Muhammad, who was older than Khalid and thus next in line of succession, renounced his right to the throne in favor of his brother. After Faisal's assassination, Muhammad was instrumental in persuading two younger brothers, whose birth order preceded that of Fahd, to defer and accept Fahd as crown prince. After Khalid's death in 1982, Muhammad remained one of the senior Saudi princes whom Fahd routinely consulted before making major political decisions. The sons of Khalid and Muhammad, however, have not demonstrated much interest in or aptitude for politics, and none of them held an important government position in 1992.

Unlike the Al Sudairi, Al Thunayyan, and Al Jiluwi, the fourth influential Al Saud clan, the Al Kabir, was not patrilineally descended from Abd al Aziz but from his first cousin, Saud al Kabir. Thus, the Al Kabir princes were not in the line of succession. Their influence actually derived from their matrilineal descent: they were the sons and grandsons of Saud al Kabir's wife Nura, the favorite sister of Abd al Aziz. The patriarch of the Al Kabir clan, Muhammad ibn Saud (born 1909, not to be confused with Muhammad ibn Abd al Aziz Al Saud), was considered one of the senior Al Saud princes and was widely respected for his intimate knowledge of tribal genealogies and oral histories. Muhammad ibn Saud's eleven adult sons were active in business and politics.

In addition to the clans, the Al Saud had numerous political factions. The factions tended to be centered on a brother or coalition of brothers. For example, Fahd and his six full brothers have been known as the ''Sudairi Seven'' since the late 1970s. When Fahd became king in 1982, the Sudairi Seven emerged as the most powerful of the family factions. Five of Fahd's brothers held important government positions in 1992. Outside the royal family, the Sudairi Seven were regarded as the faction most favorably inclined toward economic development, political and social liberalization, and a close relationship with the United States.

In 1992 the second most important family faction centered on Crown Prince Abd Allah, who headed the national guard. Abd Allah had no full brothers, but he cultivated close relationships with half brothers and nephews who also lacked family allies because they either had no full brothers or were isolated for some other reason. For example, in 1984 Abd Allah had appointed one of the sons of deposed King Saud as commander of the national guard in the Eastern Province. Prior to the 1991 Persian Gulf War, the Abd Allah faction had a reputation as traditionalists who opposed many of the domestic and foreign polices favored by the Al Sudairi. In particular, the Abd Allah faction criticized the kingdom's military dependence on the United States. The Abd Allah faction also was a proponent of closer relations with Iran and Syria. During the Persian Gulf War, however, Abd Allah supported the decision to permit stationing of United States troops in the country. Since then, foreign policy has receded as a divisive issue within the House of Saud.

The more than sixty grandsons of Abd al Aziz constituted a third discernible faction within the Al Saud. Among this generation, the sons of King Faisal and King Fahd have assumed the most important positions. The principal characteristic of the junior princes was their high level of education, often including graduate studies in the United States or Europe. In fact, during the 1980s, education, rather than seniority based on age, appeared to be the major source of influence for members of this generation. Fahd appointed many of them to responsible posts as ambassadors, provincial governors, and deputy ministers. Nevertheless, in terms of family politics, it was not clear whether the junior princes constituted a unified group, and if so, whether they were more favorably inclined toward the Al Sudairi faction or the Abd Allah faction.

King Fahd usually consulted with several dozen senior princes of the four principal Al Saud clans before making major decisions. These influential princes, together with a score of leading ulama, comprised a group known as the *ahl al hall wa al aqd* (literally, "those who loose and bind"). The *ahl al hall wa al aqd* numbered 100 to 150 men, but it was not a formal institution. The most important function of the group seemed to be to provide a broad elite consensus for government policy initiatives. Nevertheless, few analysts understood the precise nature of the relationship between the monarchy and the *ahl al hall wa al aqd.* In the past, the group had deposed one king (Saud in 1964) and had provided the public acclamation necessary to ensure the smooth accession to the throne of Faisal, Khalid, and Fahd.

## The Ulama

The ulama, or Islamic religious leaders, served a unique role by providing religious legitimacy for Saudi rule. Except for Iran, where the ulama participated directly in government, Saudi Arabia was the only Muslim country in which the ulama constituted such an influential political force. The kingdom's ulama included religious scholars, qadis (judges), lawyers, seminary teachers, and the prayer leaders (imams) of the mosques. As a group, the ulama and their families included an estimated 7,000 to 10,000 persons. However, only the thirty to forty most senior scholars among them exercised substantive political influence. These prominent clergy constituted the members of the Council of Senior Ulama, an official body created by Faisal in 1971 to serve as a forum for regular consultation between the monarch and the religious establishment. Fahd continued the precedent set by Faisal and Khalid of meeting weekly with Council of Senior Ulama members who resided in Riyadh.

The Council of Senior Ulama had a symbiotic relationship with the Saudi government. In return for official recognition of their special religious authority, the leading ulama provided tacit approval and, when requested, public sanction for potentially controversial policies. Because Saudi kings esteemed their Islamic credentials as custodians of the holy cities of Mecca and Medina, they considered ulama support critical. For example, in 1979 members of the Council of Senior Ulama signed the religious edict (*fatwa*) that sanctioned the use of force to subdue armed dissidents who had occupied the Grand Mosque in Mecca, Islam's holiest shrine. In 1990 the decision to invite thousands of United States military personnel to set up bases in the northeastern part of the country alarmed some devout Muslims who believed that the presence of so many non-Muslims on Saudi soil violated the sanctity of the holy land. Fahd defused such concerns by obtaining ulama approval for the United States military presence.

Historically, the royal family maintained close ties with the ulama, especially with members of the Al ash Shaykh. The Al ash Shaykh included the several hundred direct male descendants of the eighteenth-century religious reformer Abd al Wahhab. The Al Saud dynastic founder, Muhammad ibn Saud, had married a daughter of Abd al Wahhab, and subsequent intermarriage between the two families reinforced their political alliance. The mother of King Faisal, for example, was the daughter of an Al ash Shaykh qadi who was a direct descendant of Muhammad ibn Abd al Wahhab. The preeminence of the Al ash Shaykh thus derived not only from its reputation for religious erudition but also from its position as part of the country's ruling elite. In 1992 most of the Al ash Shaykh men were not members of the clergy but held key positions in government, education, the security services, the armed forces, and private business. Nevertheless, the Al ash Shaykh ulama dominated the kingdom's influential clerical institutions such as the Council of Senior Ulama, the Higher Council of Qadis, and the Administration of Scientific Study, Legal Opinions, Islamic Propagation, and Guidance. In addition, the most senior religious office, the grand mufti (chief judge), was traditionally filled by a member of Al ash Shaykh.

Not all of the kingdom's ulama belonged to the Al ash Shaykh. Ulama from less prominent families tended to criticize, usually privately, the senior clergy, especially after 1975. The increase in numbers of students in seminaries led to a larger number of clergy willing to challenge the senior ulama's role and to criticize their support of government policies. In December 1992, a group of ulama associated with the conservative Salafi religious trend signed a public letter criticizing King Fahd personally for failing to understand that the clergy had a religious duty to advise all believers—including the royal family—of their obligation to abide by God's principles. This unprecedented action caused a major stir in Saudi Arabia. The king rebuked the ulama establishment and dismissed several senior clergy from their official positions.

## Other Groups

The hereditary leaders of important beduin tribes and several merchant families have wielded political influence in the kingdom since its establishment. The principal tribes were the Anayzah, Bani Khalid, Harb, Al Murrah, Mutayr, Qahtan, Shammar, and Utaiba. In addition, there were at least fifteen minor tribes, including the predominantly urban Quraysh, the ancient Hijaz tribe to which the Prophet Muhammad belonged. The national guard, which has been headed by Crown Prince Abd Allah since 1963, recruited its personnel mostly from among the beduin tribes and its units were organized by tribal affiliation. Abd Allah's family ties to the tribes were also strong because his mother was the daughter of a shaykh of the Shammar, a Najdi tribe with clans in Iraq and Syria. Although the king and senior Al Saud princes did not usually consult with the tribal shaykhs before making decisions affecting national policy, the royal family routinely sought their advice on provincial matters. Consequently, tribal leaders still exercised significant influence in local politics.

The traditional merchant families, whose wealth rivaled that of the Al Saud, included the Alireza, Ba Khashab, Bin Ladin, Al Qusaibi, Jamjum, Juffali, Kaki, Nasif, Olayan, Al Rajhi, and Sulayman. During the long reign of Abd al Aziz, the royal family depended on these commercial families for financial support. After oil revenues became a steady source of government income, the relationship between the Al Saud and the merchant families began to change. Significantly, the monarchy no longer needed monetary favors from the merchants. Nevertheless, the families that had complied with Abd al Aziz's repeated requests for loans were rewarded with preferential development contracts. In addition, the post-1973 development boom led to the emergence of new entrepreneurial families such as Kamil, Khashoggi, Ojjeh, and Pharaon. The sons of Abd al Aziz continued to consult regularly with business leaders and appointed members of their families to government positions, including the Council of Ministers and the diplomatic corps.

The social changes resulting from government-sponsored development projects helped to create a new class of Saudi professionals and technocrats. These men comprised an urban-based, Western-educated elite that emerged from both the traditional merchant class and low-status families. The technocrats have had responsibility for implementing the country's economic development programs. Since the mid-1970s, a majority of the cabinet appointees to the Council of Ministers have been members of this group. Saudi kings recruited technocrats to high government positions on the basis of their demonstrated competency and loyalty to Al Saud dynastic rule. However, involvement with the extensive Al Saud carried political risks because implementation of economic policies inevitably interfered with the privileges or business interests of one or more princes. For example, Fahd summarily dismissed three of the country's most respected technocrats, former Minister of Health Ghazi al Qusaibi, former Minister of Oil Ahmad Zaki Yamani, and former Saudi Arabian Monetary Agency head Abd al Aziz Qurayshi after their advocacy of specific policies had alienated several Saudi princes.

Other than the Council of Ministers, the new class of technocrats had no institutional base from which to express its views. Even within the Council of Ministers, the influence of this new class was circumscribed; they provided advice when the king solicited it, but ultimate decision-making authority remained within the royal family. Because political parties and similar associations were not permitted, there were no legal means by which like-minded persons might organize. Nevertheless, evidence suggested that the Saudi professionals and technocrats were dissatisfied both with their exclusion from the political process and their expected conformity to rigid standards of social behavior. Periodically, individuals of this class petitioned the king, asking him to permit broader political participation. On the most recent occasion, at the end of 1990, several technocrats signed a petition asking for the creation of an elected majlis, a judiciary independent of the ulama, and a review of the restrictive codes that applied to women (see Cultural Homogeneity and Values, ch. 2). One of the boldest public protests was staged by more than forty educated women who drove their cars through the streets of Riyadh in the fall of 1990 in violation of an unofficial but strictly enforced ban on women driving automobiles.

The ulama, tribal leaders, wealthy merchants, and technocrats constituted the four major groups that enjoyed varying degrees of access to political influence. The major group excluded was the Shia minority concentrated in and near the towns of Al Hufuf and Al Qatif in the Eastern Province (see Shia, ch. 2). Most of Saudi Arabia's estimated 200,000 to 400,000 Shia believed that the government, and especially the Sunni ulama, discriminated against them. Shia resentment exploded in a series of violent demonstrations in 1979 and 1980; at least twenty people were killed in these incidents. Since 1980 the government has tried to reconcile the disaffected population through development projects in Shia communities. However, in 1992 the Shia minority still had no means of participating in the political process, and most held low-status jobs. Saudi Shia, in fact, comprised virtually the only indigenous members of the country's working class. Foreign laborers, who had obtained temporary permits to reside in the kingdom, performed almost all manual labor (see Saudis and Non-Saudis, ch. 2).

## Media

In 1992 a total of ten daily newspapers, all privately owned, were published in Saudi Arabia. Seven were printed in Arabic and three in English. The most widely read Arabic dailies were *Ar Riyadh* (circulation estimated at 140,000), published in Riyadh, and *Al Jazirah* (circulation 90,000), published in Jiddah. Smaller-circulation papers were published in both cities. The cities of Ad Dammam, Mecca, and Medina also had daily newspapers. All three English-language dailies were published in Jiddah. The largest of these was

*Arab News* with an estimated circulation of 110,000. The smaller *Saudi Gazette* (circulation 17,400) and *Saudi News* (circulation 5,000) were specialized publications that emphasized economic news and press releases from the state-owned Saudi Press Agency. In addition to the daily papers, there were fourteen weekly magazines, of which eight were published in Arabic and six in English, and twelve periodicals.

Although there was no prepublication censorship of Saudi newspapers, editors understood that articles expressing opposition to the government or its policies were unacceptable, and they thus exercised self-censorship. The Ministry of Information effectively supervised all periodicals through the Press Law of 1964. This law required the formation of a fifteen-member committee to assume financial and editorial responsibility for each privately owned newspaper. The members of these committees had to be approved by the Ministry of Information. In contrast to the local press, the foreign press was heavily censored before being permitted into the kingdom. The objective of the censors was not only to remove politically sensitive materials but also to excise advertisements deemed offensive to public morality.

Since 1990 several editors, reporters, and photojournalists have been suspended, dismissed, fired outright, or detained by Saudi security authorities for violating the unwritten press censorship code. In February 1992, the respected editor in chief of the English-language daily, *Arab News,* Khaled al Maeena, was fired for reproducing an Associated Press wire service report that featured an interview with the Egyptian cleric Shaykh Umar Abd ar Rahman, then residing in exile in New Jersey. In December 1992, the editor in chief of the Arabic-language daily *An Nadwah* also was fired summarily after his paper featured an article about Islamic groups in the kingdom.

As of 1991, the most recent year for which statistics were available, there were an estimated 4.5 million television sets in Saudi Arabia and an estimated 5 million radio receivers. One hundred twelve television stations throughout the country broadcast both Arabic and English programs. There were forty-three AM radio stations and twenty-three FM stations. The Saudi Arabian Broadcasting Service transmitted programs overseas in Arabic, Farsi, French, Indonesian, Somali, Swahili, and Urdu.

## Foreign Policy

Since at least the late 1950s, three consistent themes have dominated Saudi foreign policy: regional security, Arab nationalism, and Islam. These themes inevitably became closely intertwined during the formulation of actual policies. For example, the preoccupation with regional security issues, including concern for both regime stability and the safety of petroleum exports, resulted in the kingdom's establishing a close strategic alliance with the United States. Yet this relationship, which remained strong in 1992, often had complicated Saudi efforts to maintain solidarity with other Arab countries, primarily because many Arabs, especially during the 1960s and 1970s, believed United States support for Israel was detrimental to their national interests. The close ties with the non-Muslim United States also contrasted with the strained relations that existed between Saudi Arabia and certain predominantly Muslim countries that challenged the kingdom's efforts to portray itself as the principal champion of Islamic causes.

## Regional Security

Saudi leaders historically regarded both aggression and externally supported subversion as potential threats to their country's national security. Thus, their primary foreign policy objective was to maintain political stability in the broader Middle East area that surrounds the Arabian Peninsula. Their principal concerns tended to focus on their two more populous and more powerful neighbors, Iraq to the north and Iran across the Persian Gulf. Since 1970, Saudi Arabia has perceived each of these countries alternately as friend and foe, and the nature of its relations with Iran and Iraq at any given time has influenced the pattern of Saudi relations with other states.

### *Relations with Iraq*

Saudi relations with Iraq have been the most problematic, vacillating from tension to de facto alliance to war. Throughout the 1960s and into the early 1970s, Riyadh had suspected Baghdad of supporting political movements hostile to Saudi interests, not only in the Arabian Peninsula but also in other Middle Eastern countries. Saudi-Iraqi ties consequently were strained; the kingdom tried to contain the spread of Iraqi radicalism by strengthening its relations with states such as Iran, Kuwait, Syria, and the United States, all of which shared its distrust of Baghdad. Beginning about 1975, however, Iraq began to moderate its foreign policies, a change that significantly lessened tensions between Riyadh and Baghdad. Saudi Arabia's diplomatic relations with Iraq were relatively cordial by the time the Iranian Islamic Revolution erupted in 1979.

The Saudis and Iraqis both felt threatened by the Iranian advocacy of exporting Islamic revolution, and this shared fear fostered an unprecedented degree of cooperation between them. Although

213

Riyadh declared its neutrality at the outset of the Iran-Iraq War in 1980, it helped Baghdad in nonmilitary ways. For example, during the conflict's eight years, Saudi Arabia provided Iraq with an estimated US$25 billion in low-interest loans and grants, reserved for Iraqi customers part of its production from oil fields in the Iraq-Saudi Arabian Neutral Zone, and assisted with the construction of an oil pipeline to transport Iraqi oil across its territory (see External Boundaries, ch. 2).

Despite its considerable financial investment in creating a political alliance with Iraq, Saudi Arabia failed to acquire a long-term friend. On the contrary, in August 1990, only two years after Baghdad and Tehran had agreed to cease hostilities, Iraqi forces unexpectedly invaded and occupied Kuwait. From a Saudi perspective, Iraq's action posed a more direct and serious threat to its immediate security than the possibility of Iranian-supported subversion. The Saudis were genuinely frightened and requested the United States to bring troops into the kingdom to help confront the menace.

Riyadh's fears concerning Baghdad's ultimate intentions prompted Saudi Arabia to become involved directly in the war against Iraq during January and February 1991. Although the United States was the principal military power in the coalition of forces that opposed Iraq, the kingdom's air bases served as main staging areas for aerial strikes against Iraqi targets, and personnel of the Saudi armed forces participated in both the bombing assaults and the ground offensive (see Persian Gulf War, 1991, ch. 5). Iraq responded by firing several Scud-B missiles at Riyadh and other Saudi towns. This conflict marked the first time since its invasion of Yemen in 1934 that Saudi Arabia had fought against another Arab state. Saudi leaders were relieved when Iraq was defeated, but they also recognized that relations with Baghdad had been damaged as severely as Iraqi military equipment had been in the deserts of Kuwait and southern Iraq. Consequently, postwar Saudi policy focused on ways to contain potential Iraqi threats to the kingdom and the region. One element of Riyadh's containment policy included support for Iraqi opposition forces that advocated the overthrow of Saddam Husayn's government. In the past, backing for such groups had been discreet, but in early 1992 the Saudis invited several Iraqi opposition leaders to Riyadh to attend a well-publicized conference. To further demonstrate Saudi dissatisfaction with the regime in Baghdad, Crown Prince Abd Allah permitted the media to videotape his meeting with some of the opponents of Saddam Husayn.

*View of Jiddah, formerly Saudi Arabia's diplomatic capital*
*Courtesy Saudi Arabian Information Office*
*A building flanking the central plaza of the Riyadh*
*Diplomatic Quarter*
*Courtesy* Aramco World

## Relations with Iran

Saudi Arabia's postwar concerns about Iraq led to a rapprochement with Iran during 1991. Historically, relations with non-Arab Iran had been correct, although the Saudis tended to distrust Iranian intentions and to resent the perceived arrogance of the shah. Nevertheless, the two countries had cooperated on regional security issues despite their differences over specific policies such as oil production quotas. The Iranian Islamic Revolution of 1979 disrupted this shared interest in regional political stability. From a Saudi perspective, the rhetoric of some Iranian revolutionary leaders, who called for the overthrow of all monarchies as being un-Islamic, presented a serious subversive threat to the regimes in the area. Political disturbances in the kingdom during 1979 and 1980, including the violent occupation of the Grand Mosque in Mecca by Sunni religious extremists and riots among Saudi Shia in the Eastern Province, reinforced the perception that Iran was exploiting, even inciting, discontent as part of a concerted policy to export its revolution. The Saudi government consequently was not displeased when Iraq invaded Iran in September 1980. Nevertheless, Saudi Arabia remained officially neutral throughout the Iran-Iraq War, even though in practice its policies made it an effective Iraqi ally.

The thorniest issue in Saudi-Iranian relations during the 1980s was not Riyadh's discreet support of Baghdad but the annual hajj, or pilgrimage to Mecca, that took place in the twelfth month of the Muslim lunar calendar (see Tenets of Sunni Islam; Pilgrimage, ch. 2). Contention over the participation in hajj rituals of Iranian pilgrims, who numbered about 150,000 in this period and comprised the largest single national group among the approximately 2 million Muslims who attended the yearly hajj rites, symbolized the increasing animosity between Saudi Arabia and Iran. Tehran insisted that its pilgrims had a religious right and obligation to engage in political demonstrations during the hajj. Riyadh, however, believed that the behavior of the Iranian pilgrims violated the spiritual significance of the hajj and sought to confine demonstrators to isolated areas where their chanting would cause the least interference with other pilgrims. Because the Saudis esteemed their role as protectors of the Muslim holy sites in the Hijaz, the Iranian conduct presented a major dilemma: to permit unhindered demonstrations would detract from the essential religious nature of the hajj; to prevent the demonstrations by force would sully the government's international reputation as guardian of Islam's most sacred shrines. Tensions increased yearly without a satisfactory resolution until the summer of 1987, when efforts by Saudi security forces to suppress an unauthorized demonstration in front of Mecca's Grand Mosque led to the deaths of more than 400 pilgrims, at least two-thirds of whom were Iranians. This tragedy stunned the Saudis and galvanized their resolve to ban all activities not directly associated with the hajj rituals. In Tehran, angry mobs retaliated by ransacking the Saudi embassy; they detained and beat several diplomats, including one Saudi official who subsequently died from his injuries. These incidents severed the frayed threads that still connected Saudi Arabia and Iran; in early 1988, Riyadh cut its diplomatic relations with Tehran, in effect closing the primary channel by which Iranian pilgrims obtained Saudi visas required for the hajj.

Although Iran began to indicate its interest in normalizing relations with Saudi Arabia as early as 1989, officials in the kingdom remained suspicious of Tehran's motives and did not reciprocate its overtures for almost two years. The Persian Gulf War, however, significantly altered Saudi perceptions of Iran. The unexpected emergence of Iraq as a mortal enemy refocused Saudi security concerns and paved the way for a less hostile attitude toward Iran. For example, Riyadh welcomed Tehran's consistent demands for an Iraqi withdrawal from Kuwait and interpreted Iran's strict adherence to neutrality during the conflict as a positive development. Despite their lingering doubts about Tehran's aims vis-à-vis the Shia population of southern Iraq, the Saudis recognized after the war that they and the Iranians shared an interest in containing Iraq and agreed to discuss the prospects of restoring diplomatic relations. The issue that had proved so vexatious throughout the 1980s, the hajj, was resolved through a compromise that enabled Iranians to participate in the 1991 pilgrimage, the first appearance in four years of a hajj contingent sponsored by Tehran. In effect, once Saudi Arabia and Iran decided that cooperation served their regional interests, the hajj lost its symbolic significance as a focus of contention between two countries that defined themselves as Islamic. The reopening of embassies in Riyadh and Tehran accompanied the resolution of the hajj and other outstanding issues.

### Relations with the GCC Countries

In contrast to its relations with Iran or Iraq, Saudi Arabia's ties with the small Arab oil-producing states along its eastern flank have been historically close. In 1992 the kingdom was allied with its fellow monarchies and shaykhdoms of Bahrain, Kuwait, Oman, Qatar, and the United Arab Emirates (UAE) in the Gulf Cooperation Council (GCC), a regional collective security and economic organization. Saudi Arabia had taken the lead in forming the GCC. The outbreak of the Iran-Iraq War in September 1980 had provided the impetus Riyadh needed to convince its neighbors to join in a defensive pact. During the initial phase of that conflict, Iraqi forces achieved major victories inside Iran. Despite their distrust of the revolutionary regime in Tehran, Iraq's early successes alarmed the Saudis because they feared a defeat of Iran would embolden Baghdad to adopt an aggressive posture against other countries, especially in the Arabian Peninsula. Riyadh did not need to persuade the Kuwaiti and other gulf rulers about the security implications of a victorious Iraq; they all shared similar views of Iraqi ambitions, and they recognized the vulnerability of their small states. Representatives from Saudi Arabia and the five other countries began meeting in January 1981 to work out the details of an alliance, and the GCC was officially inaugurated four months later.

Although the Iran-Iraq War continued to preoccupy the GCC until the belligerents agreed to a cease-fire in 1988, the focus of security concerns had shifted from Baghdad to Tehran by late 1981, when it became obvious that Iraq would not be able to defeat Iran. Even before the Iran-Iraq War had begun, the Saudis and their allies believed Iranian agents fomented demonstrations and riots among the Shia population living in the countries on the Arab side of the Persian Gulf. Renewed alarm about Iran was aroused in December 1981, when Bahraini police announced the arrest of a clandestine group of Arab men associated with the illegal Islamic Front for the Liberation of Bahrain, based in Tehran. The Saudis and most other GCC rulers believed that the group, which had a large cache of arms allegedly provided by the Iranian embassy in Manama, planned to assassinate Bahraini officials and seize public buildings as part of a plot to overthrow the regime. This incident convinced Saudi Arabia that Iran sponsored terrorist groups and inclined the kingdom to support the Iraqi war effort more openly.

GCC concerns about Iranian involvement with regional terrorism remained high for almost three years following the Bahrain incident. Between 1982 and 1985, a series of assassinations, detonations of explosives-laden automobiles, and airplane hijackings throughout the Middle East, as well as the outbreak of the tanker war in the Persian Gulf, all contributed to reinforcing the strong suspicions about Iran. From a GCC perspective, the most unsettling example of terrorism was the 1983 truck bombing of several sites in Kuwait, including the United States embassy. The Saudis and their allies generally disbelieved Iranian denials of complicity. Nevertheless, GCC security forces failed to obtain conclusive

*Headquarters of the Gulf Cooperation Council, Riyadh*
*Courtesy* Aramco World

evidence directly linking Iran to the various Arab Shia groups that carried out violent acts. The lack of tangible proof prompted Oman and the UAE to improve their bilateral relations with Iran and to mediate between Riyadh and Tehran. These efforts actually led to a limited rapprochement between Saudi Arabia and Iran. For about a year, from 1985 to 1986, the two countries cooperated on several issues including oil policy.

During 1986 the intensification of the tanker-war phase of the Iran-Iraq conflict and the revelations of covert United States arms shipments to Tehran combined to refocus GCC concerns on conventional security matters. Saudi Arabia differed with Kuwait regarding the most effective means of dealing with the new threat. In particular, the Saudis rejected the Kuwaiti view that the presence of foreign warships in the Persian Gulf would intimidate Iran into ceasing retaliatory attacks on GCC shipping. The Saudis believed that the presence of foreign naval vessels would merely provoke Iran into widening the conflict, and the ultimate consequences would be adverse for all the GCC states. Riyadh therefore supported the renewal of United Nations (UN) efforts to negotiate a cease-fire between Iran and Iraq. After the UN Security Council passed Resolution 598 (1988) calling for a cease-fire and mediated peace talks between the warring countries, Saudi Arabia joined its

GCC allies in support of all diplomatic moves to bring sanctions against Iran if it refused to accept the resolution. All GCC countries were relieved when Iran agreed in 1988 to abide by the terms of Resolution 598.

The cessation of fighting between Iran and Iraq led to the realization of the GCC's deepest fears: that a militarily strong Iraq would try to intimidate its neighbors. By the end of 1988, Iraq had begun to pressure Kuwait for the rights to use Kuwaiti islands that controlled access to Iraqi ports. Tension between Iraq and Kuwait escalated, culminating in August 1990 with Iraq's invasion, occupation, and annexation of the small country. The aggression revealed to a stunned GCC that the alliance had insufficient power to deter or repel an attack on one of its members. Saudi Arabia thus requested United States assistance, as well as assistance from its Arab allies. All other GCC members provided military contingents for the coalition that was formed to confront Iraq. Following the liberation of Kuwait, the GCC decided that it would be necessary to maintain security alliances with countries from outside the Persian Gulf region. As of 1992, however, the GCC had not negotiated any arrangements for itself, although individual members had concluded bilateral defense pacts with other countries.

### Relations with Yemen

Yemen was the only country in the Arabian Peninsula that was not a member of the GCC. Saudi Arabia had excluded Yemen (actually two separate countries, the Yemen Arab Republic, YAR, or North Yemen and the People's Democratic Republic of Yemen, PDRY, or South Yemen from 1962 until unification in 1990) from GCC membership because of its republican form of government. Historically, Saudi relations with Yemen had been problematic. In 1934 Abd al Aziz had sent his army into Yemen in an unsuccessful effort to conquer the country. Although the hereditary Shia ruling family of Yemen, concentrated in the north, never lost its distrust of the Al Saud, it accepted military assistance from Riyadh after it was deposed in a republican coup in 1962. For the next five years, the Saudis supported the Yemeni royalists in their unsuccessful struggle to regain control from the republican regime backed by Egypt. In November 1962, Cairo tried to intimidate Riyadh into withdrawing its support by sending Egyptian aircraft over southern Saudi Arabia to bomb several towns, including Abha where a hospital was hit and thirty-six patients were killed (see The Reigns of Saud and Faisal, 1953–75, ch. 1). Following the June 1967 Arab-Israeli War, Saudi Arabia and Egypt resolved their differences over the YAR; in practice this meant that Riyadh

accepted the republican government in Sanaa. Relations gradually normalized; by the late 1970s, Saudi Arabia was providing
economic and military aid to the YAR. Nevertheless, the Saudis
remained suspicious of their republican neighbor, and major outstanding issues such as the demarcation of borders were not addressed.

Saudi Arabia's attitude toward the PDRY influenced its overall
Yemen policy. After Britain granted independence to its former
colony of Aden and the adjoining protectorate of South Arabia in
late 1967, a self-proclaimed Marxist government gained control
of the entire area. Riyadh became preoccupied with containing the
spread of Aden's Marxist ideas to the rest of the Arabian Peninsula, especially in Oman, where a PDRY-backed insurgency movement fought against the Al Bu Said Omani dynastic government
during the late 1960s and early 1970s. Until 1976, when diplomatic
relations with the PDRY were finally established, Saudi Arabia
actively supported efforts to overthrow the regime in Aden; Saudi
hostility did not abate after 1976 but assumed more discreet forms,
including covert aid to dissident factions within the ruling Yemeni
Socialist Party (YSP). Opposition to the unification of the YAR
and the PDRY also became a Saudi foreign policy objective, primarily because Riyadh feared the much disliked YSP would dominate
a unified Yemen and thus acquire an even larger base from which
to disseminate its radical ideas. When unification occurred in early
1990, the Saudis increased clandestine funding to various Yemeni
groups opposed to the YSP.

Saudi Arabia's displeasure with Yemen's unification was mild
compared with its reaction to Yemen's position in the Persian Gulf
War. Yemen adopted a neutral stance, condemning the Iraqi invasion and annexation of Kuwait but refusing to support UN sanctions or the use of force. Yemen's policy incensed the Saudis, who
terminated their economic assistance to the republic. In addition,
Riyadh expelled about 1 million Yemeni workers who were residing in the kingdom in 1990. Relations between Saudi Arabia and
Yemen remained strained in 1992.

### Relations with Jordan

The final country with which Saudi Arabia shared a land border was Jordan, in the extreme northwest. Although the Hashimite dynasty that ruled Jordan also had ruled the Hijaz before being
driven out by Abd al Aziz in 1924, past rivalries were buried after
World War II, and relations between the two monarchies were relatively cordial, especially between 1955 and 1990. After the 1958
overthrow of the Hashimite dynasty in Iraq, the Saudis assumed

a protective attitude toward Jordan. Riyadh provided economic assistance for development projects, and, following the June 1967 War, direct financial subventions for the budget. Saudi Arabia also mediated between Jordan and its various Arab adversaries, including the Palestine Liberation Organization (PLO) in 1970–71 and Syria in 1980.

Jordan's refusal to support Saudi Arabia during its confrontation with Iraq in 1990 shocked and angered Riyadh. Many Saudis viewed Jordan's action as that of stabbing a friend in the back. The Saudi government reacted severely: all grants to Jordan were terminated; low-priced oil sales were cut off; and Jordanian imports were restricted. After Iraq had been defeated, Riyadh spurned Jordan's initiatives to reconcile differences. In 1992 relations between the two former friends remained deeply strained.

## Relations with the United States

Although Saudi Arabia and the United States obviously did not share any borders, the kingdom's relationship with Washington was the cornerstone of its foreign policy as well as its regional security policy. The special relationship with the United States actually dated to World War II. By the early 1940s, the extent of Saudi oil resources had become known, and the United States petroleum companies that held the concession to develop the oil fields were urging Washington to assume more responsibility for security and political stability in the region. Consequently, in 1943 the administration of Franklin D. Roosevelt declared that the defense of Saudi Arabia was a vital interest to the United States and dispatched the first United States military mission to the kingdom. In addition to providing training for the Saudi army, the United States Army Corps of Engineers constructed the airfield at Dhahran and other facilities. In early 1945, Abd al Aziz and Roosevelt cemented the nascent alliance in a meeting aboard a United States warship in the Suez Canal. Subsequently, Saud, Faisal, Khalid, and Fahd continued their father's precedent of meeting with United States presidents.

The United States-Saudi security relationship steadily expanded during the Cold War. This process was facilitated by the shared suspicions of Riyadh and Washington regarding the nature of the Soviet threat to the region and the necessity of containing Soviet influence. As early as 1947, the administration of Harry S. Truman formally assured Abd al Aziz that support for Saudi Arabia's territorial integrity and political independence was a primary objective of the United States. This commitment became the basis for the 1951 mutual defense assistance agreement. Under this agreement, the United States provided military equipment and training for the Saudi armed forces. An important provision of the bilateral pact authorized the United States to establish a permanent United States Military Training Mission in the kingdom. This mission still operated in Saudi Arabia in 1992.

The United States-Saudi relationship endured despite strains caused by differences over Israel. Saudi Arabia had not become reconciled to the 1948 establishment of Israel in the former Arab-dominated territory of Palestine and refused to extend Israel diplomatic recognition or to engage in any form of relations with Israel (see Cooperation with the United States, ch. 5). Despite this position, Riyadh acknowledged that its closest ally, the United States, had a special relationship with Israel. After the June 1967 War, however, Saudi Arabia became convinced that Israel opposed Riyadh's strong ties with Washington and wanted to weaken them. During the 1970s and 1980s, periodic controversies over United States arms sales to the kingdom tended to reinforce Saudi concerns about the extent of political influence that supporters of Israel wielded in Washington. In several instances congressional leaders opposed United States weapons sales on the grounds that the Saudis might use them against Israel. Despite assurances from Saudi officials that the weapons were necessary for their country's defense, Congress reduced or canceled many proposed arms sales. Although the debates over Saudi weapons purchases were between the United States legislature and the executive branch, these political contests embittered Saudis and had an adverse impact on overall relations. From a Saudi perspective, the public policy disputes among United States leaders seemed to symbolize a weakening of the United States commitment to defend the kingdom's security.

Saudi uneasiness about United States resolve was assuaged by the United States response to the crisis unleashed by Iraq's invasion and occupation of Kuwait. In this ultimate test of the United States-Saudi security relationship, Washington dispatched more than 400,000 troops to the kingdom to ward off potential aggression. This was not the first time that United States forces had been stationed on Saudi soil. The huge Dhahran Air Base had been used by the United States Air Force from 1946 to 1962. In 1963, President John F. Kennedy had ordered a squadron of fighters to Saudi Arabia to protect the kingdom from Egyptian air assaults. In 1980 President Jimmy Carter loaned four sophisticated airborne warning and control system (AWACS) aircraft and their crews to Saudi Arabia to monitor developments in the Iran-Iraq War. However, the presence of United States and other foreign forces prior to and during the Persian Gulf War was of an unprecedented magnitude.

Despite the size of the United States and allied contingents, the military operations ran relatively smoothly. The absence of major logistical problems was due in part to the vast sums that Saudi Arabia had invested over the years to acquire weapons and equipment, construct modern military facilities, and train personnel.

After the war, Saudi Arabia again faced the prospect of congressional opposition to its requests for weapons. Riyadh believed that it cooperation in the war against Iraq demonstrated the legitimacy of its defense requirements. Nevertheless, the United States informed Saudi officials that Saudi Arabia's request to purchase US$20 billion of United States military equipment probably would not win the required approval of Congress. Riyadh reluctantly agreed to an administration proposal to revise its request into two or three separate packages, which would be submitted in consecutive years. This process tended to erode the positive feelings created during the war and revive Saudi resentments about being treated as a less than equal ally.

## Arab Nationalism

The politics of Arab nationalism have been as important a factor in Saudi foreign policy as have issues of regional security. The kingdom's relations with other Arab states in the Middle East and North Africa have been directly influenced by Arab nationalist concerns. Since the early 1950s, three persistent themes have dominated Arab nationalism: Arab unity, the unresolved grievances of the Palestinians, and the conflict with Israel. Although Saudi Arabia had its unique perspectives on these themes, it strove to remain within a broad inter-Arab consensus. At various times, however, Saudi views differed sharply from one or more of the powerful Arab states, and the kingdom consequently became enmeshed in the area's political tensions.

### Arab Unity

The concept of a single Arab state stretching from the Atlantic Ocean to the Persian Gulf never had much appeal within Saudi Arabia. Most Saudis interpreted Arab unity to mean that the seventeen principal Arab governments should strive for solidarity on major regional and international issues; respect the individual political and social differences of each Arab country; and refrain from interference in one another's internal affairs. This view of Arab unity was conservative in comparison with the ideas advocated by Arab intellectuals and political leaders in Egypt, Iraq, Libya, and Syria, as well as within the Palestinian movement. The differing perspectives engendered frequent ideological contests, especially with Egypt, the most populous Arab country, which was located across the Gulf of Aqaba and the Red Sea from Saudi Arabia. The most severe strain in Saudi-Egyptian relations occurred between 1957 and 1967 when Gamal Abdul Nasser was president of Egypt. Nasser was a charismatic leader whose Arab nationalist rhetoric included widely publicized denunciations of the Al Saud as corrupt rulers and subservient puppets of the United States. His government supported numerous revolutionary groups opposed to the Saudi regime and its regional allies. In addition, Riyadh believed that Nasser was involved in major political upheavals such as the military overthrow of monarchies in Iraq (1958), Yemen (1962), and Libya (1969).

The June 1967 War represented a defeat for radical Arab nationalists and contributed directly to a rapprochement between Saudi Arabia and Egypt. Initially, the normalization of relations proceeded gradually. After Anwar as Sadat became president of Egypt in 1970, however, close economic and political ties between the two countries developed rapidly. At Saudi urging, Sadat expelled Soviet military advisers from Egypt, halted Cairo's assistance to revolutionary groups operating in the Arabian Peninsula, and patched up strained relations with Syria. During the October 1973 War, Saudi Arabia supported Egypt by taking the unprecedented step of initiating an embargo on oil shipments to the United States and European countries that backed Israel. Subsequently, Riyadh encouraged Egyptian participation in United States-mediated negotiations aimed at obtaining phased Israeli withdrawals from Egyptian and Syrian territory occupied in 1967.

Although the Saudis valued the close relations they had achieved with Egypt by 1978, they were not prepared for a separate Egyptian peace treaty with Israel. The Saudis genuinely believed that resolving the grievances of the Palestinians was an essential requirement of a durable peace. Thus, they reacted negatively to news that Egypt and Israel, while attending a summit meeting at the United States presidential retreat of Camp David, Maryland, had reached agreement on terms for a comprehensive peace. Riyadh refused to support the Egyptian decision and joined with the other Arab states in condemning the initiative. After the Camp David Accords were signed in March 1979, Saudi Arabia broke diplomatic relations with Egypt and cut off economic aid. Sadat responded by broadcasting anti-Saudi speeches as vitriolic as any uttered by Nasser in the 1960s.

The cumulative impact of major developments such as the Soviet invasion of Afghanistan in 1979, the outbreak of the Iran-Iraq War in 1980, Sadat's assassination in 1981, the regional consequences of Israel's 1982 invasion of Lebanon, and persistent tensions with Libyan leader Muammar al Qadhafi encouraged Saudi leaders to reevaluate their policy of isolating Egypt. However, Riyadh was reluctant to undertake any bold initiatives toward normalizing relations with Cairo. Instead, it provided tacit approval for efforts by Iraq, Jordan, and Sudan to rehabilitate Egypt. Once an inter-Arab consensus had been achieved, including a decision to readmit Egypt to the League of Arab States, the Saudis felt comfortable that they could improve their ties to Egypt without encountering charges that they were betraying Arab nationalism. Saudi Arabia finally restored diplomatic relations with Egypt in November 1987. The cementing of the renewed ties took place during the Persian Gulf War, when Egypt sent a contingent of armed forces to Saudi Arabia to help defend the kingdom against an Iraqi attack.

Algeria, Iraq, Libya, Syria, and the PDRY were the other countries that the Saudis believed espoused a radical form of nationalism. These five states consistently criticized Saudi Arabia's ties to the United States during the 1970s and 1980s. Of all these countries, relations with Libya were the most strained. Libyan leader Qadhafi frequently denounced the Al Saud dynasty as corrupt and illegitimate and openly called for its overthrow. The Saudis were convinced that Qadhafi supported terrorist attacks on their diplomats and other Arab envoys and financed antigovernment groups in Egypt, Jordan, Sudan, and Tunisia. As part of the kingdom's propaganda campaign designed to counter Qadhafi's verbal assaults, in the mid-1980s King Fahd persuaded the Saudi ulama to declare Qadhafi a heretic.

### The Palestinians

The Saudis believed that the failure to resolve the grievances of the Palestinians was the primary reason for political instability and conflict in the Middle East. The Saudi position in 1992 was generally the same as the one set out by Fahd in an eight-point peace plan he proposed in August 1981. The key points called for an Israeli withdrawal from the West Bank and the Gaza Strip, Jordanian and Egyptian territories where the majority of the inhabitants were Palestinian that Israel occupied as a consequence of the June 1967 War; the dismantling of exclusive Jewish settlements created by Israel in these territories since 1967; the eventual establishment of an independent Palestinian state consisting of the West Bank and Gaza Strip, with East Jerusalem—part of the West Bank from 1948 to 1967—as its capital; and just compensation for Palestinians dispossessed of their lands and homes during the establishment of Israel in 1948. Fahd's proposals represented the mainstream consensus that had evolved among most Arabs and Palestinians by the early 1980s. The Saudis were convinced that the Fahd Plan was a workable solution; they felt extremely disappointed that neither Israel nor the United States gave the plan serious consideration.

During the 1980s, Saudi Arabia was the principal financial backer of the PLO. For Riyadh, this support was both a moral and a pragmatic imperative. Saudis sincerely believed that the Palestinians had suffered a grave injustice and that all Arabs had an obligation to provide assistance. On a more practical level, the Saudis acknowledged that conditions in the refugee camps helped to breed Palestinian radicalism; they thus perceived monetary aid to Palestinian leaders as a means of maintaining a moderate influence within the Palestinian movement. The PLO's public support for Saddam Husayn during the Persian Gulf War shocked the Saudis. The government retaliated by cutting off its aid to the PLO. As of early 1992, the Saudis remained bitter about the failure of the Palestinians to support them during the war, and relations with the PLO had not been normalized.

### The Arab-Israeli Conflict

The conflict between Israel and the Arab states is intimately connected with the Palestinians, although it has acquired distinct characteristics. Saudi Arabia, like all other Arab states except Egypt, has never recognized Israel. For Riyadh, such a step was unthinkable as long as the Palestinians continued to be denied their rights of national sovereignty. Nevertheless, Saudi Arabia accepted the reality of Israel's existence. In his 1981 peace plan, Fahd had called for the right of every state in the Middle East to live in peace. This was widely interpreted to mean that Saudi Arabia was ready to recognize Israel when all the points of the Fahd Plan pertaining to the Palestinians had been implemented. When the United States organized a conference to initiate Arab-Israeli peace talks in the fall of 1991, Saudi Arabia declined to participate, but it did encourage Syria to take part.

### Islam

Islam was a third factor that influenced Saudi foreign policy. Solidarity with Muslim countries in Asia and Africa was an important objective. Since the 1970s, countries such as Bangladesh, Pakistan, and Somalia have received special consideration in terms of foreign aid because of religious affinity. Many Pakistani military personnel were on secondment to the Saudi armed forces during the 1980s.

Islam was the principal motivation for Saudi Arabia's staunch anticommunist position throughout the Cold War era. Riyadh opposed the atheism that was the official policy of all communist regimes. For example, it closed the Saudi legation in Moscow in 1938 and declined to resume diplomatic ties with the Soviet Union. Following the dissolution of the Soviet Union at the end of 1991, however, Riyadh established relations with most of the fifteen separate republics. As an ally of the United States, Saudi Arabia was a de facto political foe of the Soviet Union and expended large sums over the years in an effort to counteract Soviet influence in the Middle East. In one instance, Afghanistan, Saudi Arabia actually became involved in a proxy war with the Soviets. Throughout the 1980s, the Saudis supported the Pakistan-based Afghan resistance groups whose guerrillas routinely crossed into Afghanistan to fight against Soviet forces occupying parts of the country from December 1979 until February 1989 in an effort to protect the Marxist government in Kabul.

From an Islamic perspective, it was permissible to maintain diplomatic relations with non-Muslim states that were not hostile to Islam. Saudi relations with non-Arab and non-Muslim countries consisted primarily of commercial ties to the countries of Western Europe, Japan, and South Asia. All these countries were important customers for Saudi oil. In addition, Saudi Arabia imported a wide range of consumer goods from Japan, Germany, Britain, Italy, and France. Countries such as India, the Philippines, Sri Lanka, and the Republic of Korea (South Korea) also supplied thousands of foreign laborers for the kingdom.

\*　　\*　　\*

Despite Saudi Arabia's significant strategic importance, few scholars have had an opportunity to undertake research in the country. Nevertheless, there are several studies that provide valuable insights into the kingdom's political processes. Robert Lacey's *The Kingdom: Arabia and the House of Saud* is essential reading for an understanding of how the extensive Al Saud operates as a political institution. Sandra Mackey's *The Saudis: Inside the Desert Kingdom,* although written in a less scholarly style, presents useful information about Saudi politics. *La péninsule arabique d'aujourd'hui* edited by Paul Bonnenfant contains several valuable articles dealing with aspects of Saudi society. Summer Scott Huyette's *Political Adaptation in Saudi Arabia: A Study of the Council of Ministers* is an informative study of the development of government institutions. (For further information and complete citations see Bibliography.)

# Chapter 5. National Security

*Beduin warrior*

DURING ITS INFANCY in the 1930s, the Kingdom of Saudi Arabia needed little as far as national security was concerned. Security forces focused on protection of the king and the royal family, safety of the holy places, and nominal defense of its territory, much of which needed no protection other than that provided by its natural desolation. Sixty years later, however, as producer and largest exporter of oil and owner of about one-fourth of all proven reserves, the land of the Al Saud (the House of Saud) was in the world limelight. Its security was of major international concern, not only because the economies of many industrialized countries depended on Saudi oil, but also because of the kingdom's contribution to stability and political moderation in the Middle East.

King Abd al Aziz ibn Abd ar Rahman Al Saud, restorer of the Al Saud and founder of the kingdom in 1932, had many sons, four of whom (all born to different mothers) have succeeded him to the throne. The defense and security organizations introduced under Abd al Aziz, and particularly promoted by King Faisal ibn Abd al Aziz Al Saud during his reign (ruled 1964–75), have grown and developed into three independent entities: the armed forces, the paramilitary forces of the national guard, and the police and security forces of the Ministry of Interior. In 1992 King Fahd ibn Abd al Aziz Al Saud, who had been on the throne for a decade, was at the apex of the security system, which was headed by three amirs (princes) of the royal family—all sons of Abd al Aziz. The regular armed forces—army, navy, air force, and air defense force—were under the Ministry of Defense and Aviation, headed by Amir Sultan ibn Abd al Aziz Al Saud. The internal security functions, the police functions, and the paramilitary frontier guard elements were under Amir Nayif ibn Abd al Aziz Al Saud, the minister of interior. The Saudi Arabian National Guard, charged with the protection of vital installations, maintaining internal security, and supporting the Ministry of Defense as required, was headed by Amir Abd Allah ibn Abd al Aziz Al Saud, who was also crown prince.

The manpower of the regular armed forces was estimated by the London-based International Institute for Strategic Studies to be 106,000 in 1992. The army was reported to have 73,000 personnel; the navy, 11,000; the air force, 18,000; and the air defense forces, 4,000. The active-duty strength of the national guard was believed to be about 55,000; part-time tribal levies accounted for 20,000 more personnel.

Despite the tens of billions of dollars spent on modernizing its armed forces, the kingdom remained vulnerable. Although the communist threat in the region had dissipated, the country's oil wealth made it a potential target for radical states with more powerful military establishments. The nation's defense presented complex problems. Its territory was as large as the United States east of the Mississippi River, and the limited Saudi forces had to be concentrated in widely scattered areas of greatest strategic sensitivity. Its stronger neighbors had greater experience in warfare and had larger numbers under arms. Although the country had never faced a direct threat of invasion, its situation changed dramatically in August 1990 when Iraq occupied Kuwait and massed its troops on Saudi Arabia's northern border. The national guard was rushed to the border, but it was clear that Saudi forces alone would be unable to prevent Iraq from seizing the Saudi and Persian Gulf states' oil assets. King Fahd accordingly turned to the United States and others for help.

A Saudi general, the son of the minister of defense and aviation, was named co-commander of Operation Desert Storm, the allied campaign that drove the Iraqi forces out of Kuwait in February 1991. The Saudi army had its first taste of combat operations, when it joined with United States forces and forces from a number of Western and other Arab states to liberate the city of Kuwait. The kingdom pledged more than US$16.8 billion to support the United States costs of deploying its forces and to provide financial assistance to other countries that had contributed forces to Desert Storm or were disadvantaged by compliance with sanctions imposed against Iraq. The war exposed the country's need for improved deterrence, and King Fahd announced that a major expansion of the armed forces would be carried out during the remainder of the 1990s. His goals included a doubling of the army's size, the creation of a new reserve system, and the purchase of additional combat aircraft for the air force and warships for the navy.

The army was the senior and largest of the services as well as the most influential in the military hierarchy and the government. The chief of staff of the armed forces has invariably been an army general. The air force was second in seniority, enjoying considerable popularity among the younger members of the royal family and other elites who joined to train as pilots and held many of the commands. The air force was the first line of defense against surprise attack aimed at Persian Gulf oil installations. Its skilled pilots flew thousands of sorties in the Persian Gulf War and repelled Iranian intrusions during the 1980–88 Iran-Iraq War. In the judgment of the United States Department of Defense, the air force and the national guard, the two branches with the closest affiliation with the United States, were the most combat-ready and reliable of the Saudi armed services during the Persian Gulf crisis.

The air defense force, separated from the army in the mid-1980s, operated fixed and mobile antiaircraft missile systems that guarded cities, oil facilities, and other strategic sites, chiefly along the Persian Gulf. These missile systems, along with the combat aircraft and ground radar stations, were linked to the Peace Shield air defense network, which depended heavily on surveillance by aircraft of the Saudi-operated and United States-supported airborne warning and control system (AWACS).

The Saudi navy remained a coastal force operating from bases along the Red Sea and the Persian Gulf. Its potential had grown with the delivery of four French guided-missile frigates in the mid-1980s; three more such frigates were scheduled to be commissioned in the mid-1990s. The navy assisted in escort and minesweeping operations in the Persian Gulf during the tense ''tanker war'' period of the 1980s.

A problem shared by all four armed services was the constant need for personnel qualified to operate and maintain a mixed inventory of advanced equipment and weapons. Because the pool of military recruits was limited, Saudi Arabia was forced to rely heavily on high technology. The country's policy of purchasing its weapons from diverse military suppliers contributed to the problem and introduced a hybrid character to the services that hampered their overall efficiency.

The special military relationship between the United States and Saudi Arabia since the mid-1940s has been built around United States policy to promote stability and peace in the Persian Gulf region. Although the two countries had no agreement on bases or facilities, Saudi Arabia has sought United States deployments of ships and fighter and surveillance aircraft in emergency situations. The huge scale of the Saudi base complexes and the interoperability of Saudi equipment have facilitated such deployments.

Initially, United States assistance consisted of weapons and equipment and of advisers to develop the organization and to help train Saudi forces. Since the mid-1960s, and the rise in oil revenues, the Saudis have been able to pay for the needed arms, equipment, and instructors, as well as for the services of the United States Army Corps of Engineers, which was responsible for the construction of bases, military housing, and other facilities. Until 1990, less than 20 percent of approximately US\$60 billion in military sales was used for weapons; most expenditures were for infrastructure, maintenance, spare parts, and training. The need for new weapons and replenishment of stocks used during the Persian Gulf War triggered a surge of new military orders that were pending as of 1992. Faced with political obstacles in obtaining United States arms, the Saudis have maintained supply relationships with other countries, notably Britain and France, which have had training missions in the kingdom for many years. The number of Western military personnel stationed in Saudi Arabia has deliberately been kept to a minimum, but large numbers of civilians—under contract to corporations—have worked in the kingdom in training, maintenance, and logistics functions.

# Historical Role of the Armed Forces
## Armed Struggle of the House of Saud

The kingdom was founded in 1932, about thirty years after Abd al Aziz had begun the reconquest of the Arabian Peninsula for the House of Saud. During the eighteenth century, the Al Saud established hegemony over many of the tribes of the peninsula but lost it during the nineteenth century. The Islam of the forces led by Abd al Aziz was based on Wahhabism (see Glossary), the creed of the Al Saud since the eighteenth century. Inspired by the stern reformer, Muhammad ibn Abd al Wahhab, the armies of the Al Saud gradually forced the other tribes of Najd to accept their dominance and slowly extended their rule to the shores of the Persian Gulf. In the first decade of the nineteenth century, they seized Mecca and Medina, destroying shrines and images they considered sacrilegious. Learning the fate of the two holy cities and of the Wahhabi practice of turning back Islamic pilgrims as idolaters, the Ottoman sultan-caliph in Constantinople sent his viceroy in Egypt, Muhammad Ali, to mount a campaign to destroy the Al Saud. In 1816 Mecca and Medina were recaptured and, after a bloody campaign, the Ottoman army conducted a savage invasion of the Al Saud homeland in Najd (see The Al Saud and Wahhabi Islam, 1500–1818, ch. 1).

During the course of the nineteenth century, the Al Saud gradually resumed their dominance of the central Najd region only to be superseded in the 1890s by the Al Rashid, who originated in Hail, northwest of Riyadh. After the dramatic capture of Riyadh in a dawn raid in 1902, Abd al Aziz and his allies defeated the Rashidi forces in a series of battles, gradually winning control of the remaining settled areas of Najd. Although Ottoman forces equipped with artillery combined with the Rashidi armies, they could not prevent Abd al Aziz from consolidating his mastery over all central Arabia in the middle of the first decade of the twentieth century.

Taking advantage of the crumbling of the Ottoman Empire and the weakening of Turkish garrisons on the peninsula, Abd al Aziz invaded the Eastern Province (also seen as Al Ahsa) in 1913 and then the entire gulf coast between Kuwait and Qatar after overcoming the Turkish garrison at Al Hufuf. Although it had remained part of the Ottoman Empire, most of the peninsula had been almost a world unto itself until the tribes were drawn into larger outside conflicts during World War I. Relying on the Ottomans to maintain stability in the Middle East before the war, Britain had earlier disdained a pact with Abd al Aziz, but after Britain's declaration of war against the Ottoman Empire in October 1914, the British sought an alliance with the House of Saud. By a treaty signed in December 1914, the British recognized Saudi independence from the Ottoman Empire and provided Abd al Aziz with financial subsidies and small arms. As his part of the agreement, Abd al Aziz promised to keep 4,000 men in the field against the House of Rashid, which was associated with the Ottomans. Bolstered by Ikhwan (brotherhood—see Glossary) forces, Saudi control was extended to the outskirts of Hail, the Rashidi capital, by 1917.

## The Ikhwan Movement

Seeking to win over beduin tribal leaders and obtain their loyalty to him and his cause, Abd al Aziz established Ikhwan communities in which the beduin tribesmen could settle and adopt a sedentary way of life. The Ikhwan were supported by Abd al Aziz with land, seed, tools, and money, as well as arms and ammunition. A mosque was built in each community, and these mosques also served as military garrisons. By 1915 there were more than 200 settlements and in excess of 60,000 men in readiness to heed Abd al Aziz's call for warriors in his continuing battles to unite the peninsula.

The Ikhwan became dedicated, even fanatical followers of the young Al Saud leader. Acquiescence to discipline was not an Ikhwan virtue, but Abd al Aziz was an uncommon leader able to use the power of the brotherhood and its prowess in battle to his advantage. The greatest of the Ikhwan successes was the conquest of the Hijaz after World War I, but the bold exploits of the Ikhwan also marked the beginning of their end. When Sharif Hussein, the Hashimite ruler of the Hijaz, entered into military negotiations with the Al Rashid, Abd al Aziz's reaction was swift and harsh. He sent the Ikhwan against the Al Rashid stronghold at Hail, which was captured with little difficulty in 1921. Emboldened by their success, the warriors disregarded orders and crossed the border into Transjordan. The raiding and plundering of their Hashimite ally aroused the British, who counterattacked with devastating effect, using armored cars and aircraft.

Other Ikhwan expeditions succeeded in overpowering Asir, an independent enclave in the southwest. In defiance of Abd al Aziz's authority, however, they continued to raid the British protectorates. Recognizing that the wild forays of the Ikhwan could only be a constant irritant and source of danger to his leadership, Abd al Aziz began to form a more conventional and more disciplined army. He entered Mecca and laid siege to Jiddah and Medina, which were occupied by the end of 1924. These successes led to the capitulation of the Hashimite kingdom of the Hijaz, leaving the Al Saud in control of the entire peninsula, except for Yemen in the southwest and the British gulf protectorates.

Having acquired such a tremendous area, Abd al Aziz then faced the daunting task of governing it. First, however, he had to deal with the rebellious Ikhwan. The zealots of the brotherhood regarded the Western-influenced modernization pursued by Abd al Aziz as a betrayal of the fundamentals of Islam that had been their raison d'être since the beginning of their association with the House of Saud. Renewed Ikhwan raids against defenseless groups in Iraq incensed the British, who were trying to stabilize the region, and finally compelled Abd al Aziz to force the submission of the Ikhwan. When the Ikhwan leadership revolted against Abd al Aziz, he took to the field to lead his army, which was now supported by four British aircraft (flown by British pilots) and a fleet of 200 military vehicles that symbolized the modernization that the Ikhwan abhorred. After being crushed at the Battle of Sabalah, the Ikhwan were eliminated as an organized military force in early 1930.

The suppression of the Ikhwan brought to an end the chronic warfare in the Arabian Peninsula except for a series of incidents between 1931 and 1934 along the poorly defined border with Yemen. Abd al Aziz placed his eldest son, Saud, at the head of an army that succeeded in occupying much Yemeni territory but could not defeat the Yemeni warriors so adept at defending their mountain passes. Pressure by European powers determined to maintain the status quo on the Arabian Peninsula finally brought peace, and much of the occupied territory was restored to Yemen.

During the 1930s, Abd al Aziz, who had made himself king, allowed the remnants of the Ikhwan to regroup as a beduin militia. They became known as the White Army because they wore traditional white robes rather than military uniforms. For Abd al Aziz, the White Army served as a counterbalance to the small regular army, thereby helping to ensure his control over internal security. In addition to the two armies, there was the Royal Guard, a lightly armed body of absolutely loyal officers and troops, whose mission consisted entirely of protecting the monarch and the growing royal family.

## World War II and Its Aftermath

Prior to the outbreak of World War II, Saudi Arabia was on good terms with the Axis powers, concluding an arms agreement with Nazi Germany on the eve of the war. Abd al Aziz maintained formal neutrality during most of the war, gradually leaning toward the Allied side. In early 1945, he abandoned his neutral posture and made a nominal declaration of war against Germany. The outbreak of the war and attendant shipping dangers had brought Saudi Arabian oil sales to a halt. As Allied needs for oil rose, the safeguarding of the Saudi oil reserves began to be regarded as of great strategic importance. In 1943 President Franklin D. Roosevelt declared that the defense of Saudi Arabia was of vital interest to the United States, thus making the kingdom eligible for Lend-Lease assistance. By the end of World War II, British power and influence in Arab affairs had begun to wane, and during the late 1940s and early 1950s the United States emerged as the dominant Western power on the Arabian Peninsula.

Abd al Aziz was instrumental in forming the League of Arab States (Arab League) in 1945, and in 1948 he sent a token battalion of noncombatant troops to participate in the first Arab-Israeli war. Gamal Abdul Nasser of Egypt, after leading the coup that deposed King Faruk in 1952, had become a spokesman for republicanism among the Arabs, vying for power and influence with the Arab monarchs. Nasser's broadcasts against the royal regimes and his calls for nationalist revolutions grew more inflammatory after Egypt's war over the Suez Canal with Israel, France, and Britain in 1956. Saud ibn Abd al Aziz Al Saud, who became king after Abd al Aziz's death in 1953, was associated with a clumsy plot to assassinate Nasser. This embarrassing episode, plus Saud's extravagance and lack of leadership qualities, compelled him to turn over executive power to his brother, Faisal, in 1958 (see The Reigns of Saud and Faisal, 1953–75, ch. 1). Faisal, who would become king six years later, dedicated himself to the development of a modern military force to protect the monarchy.

Egyptian intervention in the civil war of neighboring Yemen in 1962 provided ample proof of the need for reliable Saudi armed forces. An army coup against Imam Muhammad al Badr in Yemen triggered a civil war that was not resolved until 1967. The insurgents were supported by Nasser, who committed a large expeditionary force of Egyptian troops to the conflict. Imam Badr fled north, rallying loyal tribes and seeking support from Saudi Arabia. Within a short time, the royalist supporters of Imam Badr were engaged in combat against the insurgents, who established the Yemen Arab Republic (YAR—North Yemen). Saudi troops were deployed to the border, and the royalist guerrillas were given supplies and safe havens.

In November 1963, Egyptian aircraft overflew Saudi territory, dropping bombs on border villages. At the request of Saudi Arabia, the United States dispatched a squadron of F–100 jet fighters to the kingdom. Faced with this show of force and unity, the Egyptians backed off. Nevertheless, the presence of Egyptian military on the peninsula convinced Faisal of the need to upgrade the Saudi armed forces still further with United States and British assistance.

During the June 1967 War against Israel, Faisal sent a Saudi brigade to Jordan to bolster King Hussein's war effort. The brigade was still in Jordan at the time of the October 1973 War launched by Egypt and Syria against Israel. When war broke out, Faisal dispatched another brigade to Syria to lend support to the Syrian army. Neither of the Saudi brigades was involved in combat.

## Naval Warfare in the Persian Gulf, 1987

The Iran-Iraq War of 1980–88 brought enormous cost in lives and destruction to the two combatants. For a time, however, the war involved only the two belligerents and did not present a direct military threat to Saudi Arabia. The triumph of the radical Shia (see Glossary) movement in Iran and the Iranian Islamic Revolution under Ayatollah Sayyid Ruhollah Musavi Khomeini had raised alarm throughout the Arabian Peninsula, and the Persian Gulf states led by Saudi Arabia supported the Iraqi war effort with money and supplies. By 1986 the focus of the war had shifted to the waters of the gulf, where Iran's naval superiority enabled it to block shipping intended for Iraq and the export of Iraqi oil. Iran's naval attacks against tankers and its minelaying reached a peak in 1987. Forty attacks were mounted against shipping to and from Saudi Arabia, although oil movements were not seriously affected. The four minesweepers of the Saudi navy contributed to the international effort to locate and clear Iranian mines from the gulf. In cooperation with the United States, the fleet of five Saudi AWACS aircraft carried out surveillance of air traffic over the gulf. Two Iranian aircraft were shot down for violating Saudi air space. In October 1987, a fleet of missile-armed Iranian speedboats was observed moving toward As Saffaniyah, a major Saudi oil field, which had a processing complex at Ras al Khafji near the border with Kuwait. When Saudi ships and aircraft as well as ships of the United

States Navy moved quickly to intercept the force, the Iranian ships turned away.

## Persian Gulf War, 1991

At the conclusion of its bloody eight-year war with Iran, Iraq was able to maintain a huge, battle-tested army and vast stockpiles of modern weapons. To intimidate Kuwait over the issue of access to the gulf and Kuwait's unwillingness to limit its oil production, President Saddam Husayn massed Iraqi troops on Kuwait's border. On August 2, 1990, to the surprise of the world, Iraq invaded and occupied Kuwait, and Husayn announced Kuwait's annexation as Iraq's nineteenth province. Iraqi combat forces continued to move southward to the Saudi border, and enormous amounts of supplies were transported to the frontline troops. Intelligence sources indicated that Husayn planned to seize the nearby Saudi oil fields and processing installations. The Saudi Arabian National Guard was mobilized and deployed along the border, with army units to follow. Convinced that an Iraqi attack on Saudi territory was imminent and recognizing that available Saudi forces were no match for the divisions Husayn had moved into Kuwait, King Fahd authorized the deployment of United States forces to defend his northern border against Iraqi aggression.

In the ensuing months, an allied force of more than 600,000 ground, sea, and air force personnel was assembled to defend Saudi Arabia and to drive the Iraqis out of Kuwait. Command of the allied forces was divided. The head of the United States Central Command, General H. Norman Schwarzkopf, was in charge of United States, British, and French units; his Saudi counterpart, Lieutenant General Khalid ibn Sultan Al Saud, son of the minister of defense and aviation and nephew of the king, was in charge of units from twenty-four non-Western countries, including troops from Saudi Arabia, Egypt, Syria, Kuwait, and other states of the Persian Gulf. Saudi ground forces deployed for the allied undertaking (called Operation Desert Shield and renamed Operation Desert Storm when the war began in January 1991), consisted of one armored brigade, three mechanized brigades, and two national guard mechanized brigades.

Saudi military resources were strained by the need to manage the allied military buildup and to ensure that the nations contributing forces to the coalition were supplied with fuel, housing, power, and food. The Saudi air force flew 3,000 sorties, losing only one Tornado and two F–5E fighter aircraft to Iraqi fire. In one of the few engagements by any of the allied powers with the Iraqi air force, two Iraqi Mirage F-1 aircraft trying to attack allied shipping were shot down by a Saudi pilot. Saudi fighter units were frustrated by the absence of Iraqi air targets; Iraqi aircraft either were destroyed on the ground or shifted away from the fighting.

In their only ground attack on Saudi territory, the Iraqis captured the evacuated border town of Ras al Khafji on January 30, 1991. After two days of heavy fighting, three Saudi mechanized battalions, one tank battalion, and two national guard battalions, joined by a battalion from Qatar and supported by United States Marines and attack helicopters, succeeded in driving the Iraqis out of the town on February 2. Eleven Iraqi tanks and fifty-one other armored vehicles were destroyed. The Saudis reported casualties of eighteen dead, thirty-two wounded, and eleven missing in what was described as the greatest land battle in which the country's forces had ever been engaged. Some allied observers said that the national guard units acted more decisively and were more aggressive in using firepower against entrenched Iraqi troops than were the regular Saudi forces.

When the massive ground assault against the Iraqi positions began on February 24, 1991, the Saudi troops formed part of two Arab armies. The first, Joint Forces Command North, which also included Egyptian, Syrian, and Kuwaiti troops, was deployed on Kuwait's western border. Joint Forces Command East was deployed along the gulf, immediately south of Kuwait, and consisted of about five brigades from Saudi Arabia, Kuwait, Oman, Qatar, the United Arab Emirates, Morocco, and Senegal. The Saudi national guard formed part of a mobile reserve.

The main attack was led by United States, British, and French forces in the west, directly facing Iraqi territory, and was aimed at cutting links between the Iraqi forces in Kuwait and their sources of supply in Iraq. The ground assault on Kuwait by the Arab forces of Joint Forces Command North was led by two Egyptian divisions on the left and on the right, and the ad hoc Khalid Division, consisting of Saudi and Kuwaiti troops, including the Saudi Twentieth Mechanized Brigade and the Fourth Armored Brigade. As the Khalid Division advanced eastward toward the city of Kuwait, passages through Iraqi minefields were cleared by allied bombing and engineer operations. On the third day, after light fighting and the surrender of thousands of Iraqi soldiers, the city of Kuwait was liberated. In the four days of fighting before the Iraqi army defending Kuwait was destroyed, Saudi casualties were minimal. The Saudi navy was also involved, receiving credit for sinking an Iraqi minelayer with a Harpoon antiship missile.

*Giant oil spill resulting from the Persian Gulf War, 1991*
*Courtesy* Aramco World

## Security Perceptions and Policies
### The Military Threat

Until Iraq concentrated its forces on Saudi Arabia's northeastern border after the occupation of Kuwait in 1990, the kingdom had been exposed to few direct threats to its territory. The only overtly hostile actions were from Yemeni-based Egyptian air and naval units in 1963, YAR forces that attacked Saudi border posts in 1969 and 1973, and Iranian attacks on shipping in the Persian Gulf in the 1980s. Nevertheless, the nation's wide geographic expanse and lengthy coastlines on both the Red Sea and Persian Gulf, combined with a small, scattered population, presented unusual problems of defense. With the world's largest reserves of oil and vulnerable oil processing facilities, the kingdom saw itself as a tempting target for aggressive forces. Moreover, it was militarily weak in a highly volatile region of the world, amid heavily armed and potentially hostile neighbors.

Until the late 1980s, Saudi security concerns focused on the communist influence in nearby countries, notably in Ethiopia and the People's Democratic Republic of Yemen (PDRY), which gave the Soviet Union access to naval facilities in the Red Sea and on the Gulf of Aden. Saudi Arabia interpreted the Soviet invasion of

Afghanistan in December 1979 as a means of establishing a staging area for future operations in the Persian Gulf. The revolution in Iran earlier that year produced a radical Shia-dominated regime in Tehran and introduced a far more immediate threat to gulf stability. Iranian belligerence led Saudi Arabia to support Iraq during the Iran-Iraq War. The heating up of the tanker war in 1987 escalated tensions. The Saudis, concerned about domestic attitudes and the reaction of Arab states, discouraged deeper United States involvement in the crisis. In April 1987, the United States agreed to Kuwait's request that Kuwaiti tankers sail under the United States flag with naval escorts. Saudi Arabia cooperated with this operation by assisting in mine clearance and air surveillance.

The Saudi leadership considered Iran's condemnation of the Iraqi invasion of Kuwait in 1990 and its adherence to United Nations (UN) sanctions during the Persian Gulf War to be welcome signs of moderation. The overthrow of the Marxist regime in Addis Ababa in 1991 and the collapse of Soviet influence in the Middle East further reduced the threat of radical influences near the kingdom's borders.

The Persian Gulf War of 1991 battered the offensive capability of Iraq's formidable military machine. An estimated forty divisions were lost or rendered ineffective. About two-thirds of Iraq's 4,500 tanks were destroyed as well as more than 2,000 artillery pieces. Nevertheless, the Iraqi army's active manpower strength was an estimated 380,000 at the war's end, including three divisions of the Republican Guards, the troops considered most loyal to President Saddam Husayn. Despite crippling blows to its fighting potential, Iraq remained a potential adversary and a long-term security threat to Saudi Arabia's limited forces.

Relations with Yemen have always been troubled in modern times. The border has been the scene of periodic tribal clashes and boundary disputes. The Riyadh government's bases in the southern desert enabled it to maintain ground and air units near the Yemeni frontier. Saudi Arabia had subsidized the YAR government and the northern Yemeni tribes and tried to isolate the Marxist government of the PDRY.

The union of the two Yemens in May 1990 left Saudi Arabia uneasy that secular leftist elements of a more populous combined Yemen might prevail over the Islamic conservatism of the former YAR. Relations worsened when Yemen came out in support of Iraq, after the latter's invasion of Kuwait. Saudi Arabia retaliated by deporting about 1 million Yemeni workers whose repatriated earnings had formed a major part of Yemen's economy.

Long stretches of uninhabited desert, known as the Empty Quarter, or Rub al Khali, formed disputed territory between Yemen and Saudi Arabia. To counter Yemeni smuggling and to maintain better surveillance of the border area, Saudi Arabia announced in 1991 that it was seeking bids on an electronic security system to detect illegal crossings. In 1992 Saudi Arabia demanded that foreign oil companies discontinue test drilling in parts of the undefined territory that had long been under Yemeni control. The kingdom was thought to fear that a surge of oil revenues could be used to modernize the Yemeni armed forces. Saudi border patrols were increased and, according to the Yemenis, Saudi agents were active among residents of the disputed area for the purpose of undermining Yemen's authority.

The Saudis linked the influence of revolutionary Arab regimes to the continuation of the Arab-Israeli confrontation and the Israeli occupation of Arab territory on the West Bank and the Gaza Strip. Saudi Arabia viewed with concern the possibility of renewed Arab-Israeli hostilities, and the strong Israeli military establishment was seen as a potential threat to its security. Accordingly, Saudi Arabia considered a comprehensive settlement of the Palestinian question a primary objective of its policies. Saudi Arabia did not see war with Israel as an imminent threat, but it feared Israel's ability to mount strategic air strikes against sensitive Saudi targets at the outset of any future Arab-Israeli conflict. The possibility of such preemptive strikes by Israel had impelled Saudi Arabia to commit a major part of its modern air defense to its northern border zones. The most likely Israeli targets in the kingdom would be the complex of military bases around Tabuk in the northwest or the pipeline terminal and other oil facilities at Yanbu al Bahr on the Red Sea. More distant Saudi targets could be reached with aerial refueling.

In spite of past differences and their considerable military strengths, the neighboring Islamic countries of Egypt and Syria were not regarded in 1992 as potential adversaries. In certain respects, Saudi Arabia's geographic position on the peninsula was a favorable one. The harshness of its interior desert practically limited overland attack to the northwest corner facing Jordan and Israel and to the northeast corridor parallel to the Persian Gulf. Harassing attacks by air or sea could be very damaging, however, disrupting oil production and tanker traffic.

Countries surrounding the Arabian Peninsula—although heavily armed—were poorly equipped to mount and sustain a full-scale invasion by sea or air. Saudi Arabia would be less prepared to deal with intervention by a neighboring power in one of the smaller states of the peninsula, using local disturbances or turmoil as a pretext and then expanding its position. The politically vulnerable gulf oil states had been subject to outside intervention in the past; for this reason, Saudi Arabia and the smaller states had joined to form a system for collective security.

## Collective Security under the Gulf Cooperation Council

The Gulf Cooperation Council (GCC) was formed in 1981 by the six Persian Gulf states of the Arabian Peninsula—Bahrain, Kuwait, Oman, Qatar, Saudi Arabia, and the United Arab Emirates—to confront their security challenges collectively. The immediate objective was to protect themselves from the threat posed by the Iran-Iraq War and Iranian-inspired activist Islamism (also seen as fundamentalism). In a series of meetings, chiefs of staff and defense ministers of the gulf states developed plans for mutual defense and launched efforts to form a joint command and a joint defense network.

Ground and air units of the six member states carried out several multilateral exercises between 1983 and 1987 under the code name of Peninsula Shield. Military assistance, funded mainly by Saudi Arabia and Kuwait, was extended to Bahrain for up-to-date fighter aircraft and a modern air base, and to Oman to improve its defensive capability at the Strait of Hormuz. The GCC planned to integrate naval and ground radar systems and to create a combined air control and warning system based on Saudi AWACS aircraft. Problems of compatibility with different communication and electronic systems, however, delayed the introduction of these programs. In 1984 the GCC defense ministers agreed on the creation of a two-brigade (10,000-man) Peninsula Shield Force. This joint intervention force was based in Saudi Arabia near King Khalid Military City at Hafar al Batin under the command of a Saudi officer (see fig. 9). In addition to a headquarters staff, the force consisted of one infantry brigade of about 5,000 men with elements from all GCC states in 1992, according to *The Military Balance.* Its mission, however, had not been publicly defined. It was not clear, for example, whether the joint force would have authority to intervene in a domestic emergency. The force could be enlarged at a time of threat; it was apparently reinforced prior to the Persian Gulf War in 1991 but did not take part in the war as a distinct unit.

In March 1991, after the conclusion of the Persian Gulf War, the six members of the GCC, together with Egypt and Syria, declared their intention to establish a deterrent force to protect Kuwait, with Egypt and Syria to provide the bulk of the troops and the GCC states to provide the financing. The plan subsequently encountered a series of setbacks. At year's end, there appeared little chance that the Arab deterrent force would be installed. In the

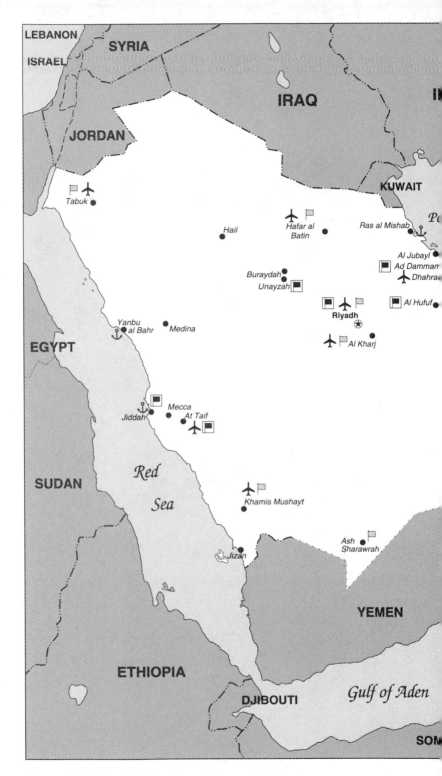

*Figure 9. Major Military Installations, 1992*

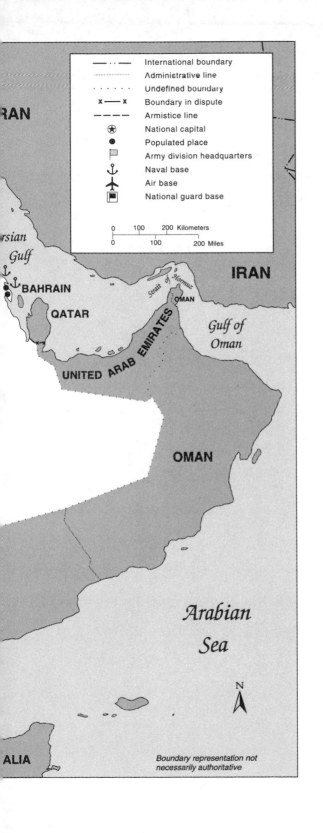

International boundary
Administrative line
Undefined boundary
x —— x Boundary in dispute
Armistice line
National capital
Populated place
Army division headquarters
Naval base
Air base
National guard base

0    100    200 Kilometers
0    100    200 Miles

RAN

Persian
Gulf

BAHRAIN
QATAR
UNITED ARAB EMIRATES

IRAN

Strait of Hormuz

OMAN

Gulf of
Oman

OMAN

Arabian
Sea

N

ALIA

Boundary representation not
necessarily authoritative

meantime, Kuwait had succeeded in obtaining security commitments from the United States and Britain and arranged for the prepositioning of United States military equipment.

## Threats to Internal Security

Despite the political and military upheavals in surrounding countries, Saudi Arabia's internal situation appeared to be under control in 1992. Most Saudis seemed to accept the authority of the Al Saud and strict observance of Islamic law to ensure domestic stability. However, the kingdom's sudden exposure to international scrutiny after Iraq's invasion of Kuwait in 1990 brought into sharp relief the polarization between the two competing forces of society— the powerful religious establishment and the liberal reformist elements. The modern sector pressed for greater popular participation in decision making and for greater accountability by the government (see Other Groups, ch. 4). Criticism and anger over corruption by members of the royal family and other members of the elite were more openly expressed than previously. King Fahd promised that he would create a *majlis ash shura* (consultative council) to respond to political grievances. Such promises had been made in the past, however, with little result.

Some potential for social instability arose from the modernists' belief that the ruling family remained too deferential to traditional Muslim interests. These liberal elements desired the opportunity for involvement in the political process and a share of political power. In May 1991, it was reported that even the conservative religious establishment had petitioned the government for a consultative assembly. This action was accompanied by demonstrations in several cities. Extremists accused the religious establishment of hypocrisy in adhering to Islamic practices and of the maldistribution of wealth, fueling resentments within broad segments of Saudi society.

Marginal political groups of the left and right were considered illegal and their members were subject to arrest and detention by government security organs. These groups included the Organization of Islamic Revolution in the Arabian Peninsula, the Arab Socialist Action Party, and the Party of God in the Hijaz. The sizable alien population, estimated at 4.6 million in 1992 and representing more than half the labor force, was feared as a possible source of divisiveness as well as a disruptive influence on the thinking and attitudes of the indigenous population. It was assumed that clandestine organs of external political movements such as the Palestine Liberation Organization (PLO) were represented in the labor force. Among the most numerous of the foreign workers were

Yemenis, who always tended to be regarded with suspicion. Because many of these workers were employed in strategic economic sectors and in the oil industry, strikes and sabotage were constant dangers. In 1990 the Saudi authorities took measures to identify illegal residents and to regularize their status or deport them. These efforts intensified after the Persian Gulf crisis began, and about 1 million Yemenis as well as Sudanese, Iraqis, and Palestinians were compelled to leave.

In the oil-rich Eastern Province (Al Ahsa) lived between 200,000 and 400,000 Shia. They had endured two centuries of Wahhabi subjugation and remained disaffected elements in Saudi society. Riots in late 1979 and early 1980 among the Shia were believed to have been inspired by taped messages of the Ayatollah Khomeini. Because Shia comprised possibly half of the labor force of the Arabian American Oil Company (Aramco), which from 1988 was called the Saudi Arabian Oil Company (Saudi Aramco), the government treated their presence as a security problem. During the 1980s, the government bolstered its security forces in the area, while at the same time attempting to allay Shia resentment by responding to their social and religious grievances. Among other groups with a distinct identity within the kingdom were the Hijazis, who lived along the mountainous western coast extending to the holy cities of Mecca and Medina, and the tribes of Asir Province just north of Yemen. Although both groups benefited from the rising wealth of the country, they lacked sympathy for the traditional royalist regime and for the strict religious leadership. Accordingly, questions of their fundamental loyalty to the Al Saud persisted.

The likelihood of schisms within the royal family arising from policy differences or personal rivalries seemed remote but could not be completely discounted. Factional disputes could arise over such issues as the closeness of ties with the United States or curbing the power of the religious establishment. For the most part, the informal assembly of princes has succeeded in keeping rivalries within bounds and has prevented internal differences from becoming public issues.

In view of elaborate security measures, such as the division of armed power between the regular military and the national guard, and the substantial benefits enjoyed by both officers and enlisted personnel, the possibility of an insurrection emerging from the armed forces was regarded as highly unlikely. Nevertheless, in 1991 leaflets critical of royal princes were reportedly distributed in garrisons. The influence of radical Islamists among soldiers and lower ranking officers was said to be growing.

The military leadership has been free from serious conspiracies against the regime except for an abortive coup by air force officers in 1969. About 300 air force personnel were arrested even before the plot was set in motion. The dissidents were tried and sentenced to prison, but by the mid-1970s all had been released. High wages and privileges tended to keep discontent among the officer corps to a minimum. The appointment of many members of the royal family to military positions also provided a measure of protection against intrigue. The separate national guard, with its tribal roots, provided an additional safeguard against any threat from the military.

The prestige of the House of Saud was closely associated with the protection of the holy places. When, in 1979, an armed group of about 500 religious extremists occupied the Grand Mosque of Mecca, the standing of the royal family was seriously affected. The insurgent leader condemned the Al Saud for corruption, declaring that the kingdom's rulers had forsaken the primary tenets of Islam. Security forces did not immediately respond to the occupation because of the Quran's strictures against shedding blood in the holy place. Partly as a result of lack of coordination and poor discipline, it took troops, national guard, and security forces fourteen days of heavy fighting to oust the insurgents. Many people were killed. The occupation of the Grand Mosque was followed by riots and demonstrations by Shia dissidents, which were answered by the liberal use of firearms and the sealing off of major trouble spots by the national guard (see The Reign of Khalid, 1975–82).

Followers of Ayatollah Khomeini tried to stir up trouble by disrupting the annual hajj, or pilgrimage to Mecca, on several occasions during the 1980s, but heavy security controls usually succeeded in preventing major incidents (see Pilgrimage, ch. 2). In July 1987, however, more than 400 people died as a result of a serious riot instigated by thousands of Iranian pilgrims. Khomeini called for the overthrow of the Saudi royal family to avenge the pilgrims' deaths. Saudi Arabia, in turn, accused Iran of staging the riots to support its demands that Mecca and Medina be internationalized as pan-Islamic cities. Several Saudi Shia were tried and executed for exploding bombs at Saudi oil facilities in 1988, probably as retaliation by Iran and its sympathizers against restrictions on Iranian attendance at the annual pilgrimage after the 1987 riots. A number of bomb attacks were made on Saudi agencies abroad—primarily offices of the national carrier, Saudi Arabian Airlines. Saudi diplomats were assassinated by groups calling themselves the Party of God in the Hijaz, Soldiers of the Right, and Arab Fury. Both types of attack were thought to be the work of Saudi Shia instigated by elements of the Iranian government. Saudi Arabia accused Iran in connection with two bomb incidents during the 1989 hajj in apparent retaliation for Saudi restrictions against Iranian pilgrims. Sixteen Kuwaiti Shia were executed for these attacks (see Regional Security, ch. 4).

Some easing of relations with Iran occurred after Khomeini's death in 1989. During the 1990 pilgrimage, more than 1,400 pilgrims were trampled to death or suffocated after they were stampeded in an underground tunnel. The incident, however, was not linked to Iran. Disputes over the size of the Iranian contingent and rules governing their conduct prevented Iranians from participating in the hajj for three years. In 1991 the Saudis accepted a quota of 115,000 Iranian pilgrims and allowed political demonstrations in Mecca. Although peaceful, the demonstrations included strident attacks on the United States and Israel.

The Persian Gulf War placed new strains on the government's efforts to maintain the allegiances of both the modern, secular segments of Saudi society and the traditional, religious elements. Although it offered some conciliatory gestures to the modernists, the government appeared adamant and ready to respond forcefully to any dissent against the authority of the Al Saud.

The existence of a large and diffuse royal family, the vast territorial extent of the kingdom, and its widely scattered population centers reduced the likelihood that an attempt to overthrow Saudi rule could succeed. Still, the government continued to exercise control over the information media and strictly supervised or prohibited independent interest groups such as political parties or labor unions.

Islamic radicals were few in number but had undeniable influence, projecting their messages from the public mosques and university classrooms. Their criticism that the government under King Fahd had weakened in its devotion to Islamic principles was difficult to silence because it was offered in an Islamic context. Islamist pressure for greater Islamization in education, the press, and foreign policy appeared to strengthen after the Persian Gulf War.

## The Armed Forces

Under the king, who was president of the Council of Ministers (effectively prime minister) and commander in chief of the armed forces, the minister of defense and aviation exercised operational control and supervision of the Royal Saudi Land Forces (army), the Royal Saudi Naval Forces, the Royal Saudi Air Force, and the Royal Saudi Air Defense Forces (see fig. 10). The total personnel strength of the four services was estimated at 76,500 in 1991, rising to 106,000 in 1992.

A National Security Council (also known as the High Defense Council) had formal responsibility for setting defense policy. Its members included, in addition to the king and the minister of defense and aviation, the ministers of interior, foreign affairs, and finance and national economy, and the chief of staff of the armed forces. Ultimate decisions about security, however, rested solely with the king, assisted by such advisers as he chose to consult.

Senior personnel, frequently princes of the royal family, usually retained their positions for long periods in the Saudi system. The minister of defense and aviation, Amir Sultan, a full brother of the king, had been appointed to his position in 1962. Crown Prince Abd Allah, a half brother of the king, had been commander of the national guard for the same length of time. The chief of the general staff, with operational responsibility for the four services, held the rank of general; the chiefs of the individual services usually held the rank of lieutenant general.

Similar to the organization of military staffs in the United States, the Saudi armed forces had four major sections: personnel (G–1), intelligence (G–2), operations and training (G–3), and logistics (G–4). The chiefs of the four sections were the principal advisers to the chief of staff, who invariably has been an army officer. The armed forces were further distributed among nine area commands. Their mission was to defend the integrity of the country's borders and to protect the country against foreign encroachments or invasion. During episodes of severe internal disorder, the armed forces had the additional mission of assisting the security forces in restoring public order.

The national guard was under the personal control of the king acting through its commander, Amir Abd Allah, the heir apparent and first deputy prime minister. The national guard's command structure was entirely separate from that of the regular armed services. Its mission was primarily internal security, including protection of the major oil facilities in the Eastern Province and assistance to the regular forces of public order against civil disturbances. The service was also expected to assist the regular armed forces in repelling threats to the security of the kingdom's borders, as was the case when the national guard participated in the Persian Gulf War alongside regular army units.

## Royal Saudi Land Forces

The army's strength of approximately 73,000 in 1992 was greater than the other three services combined and somewhat in excess of

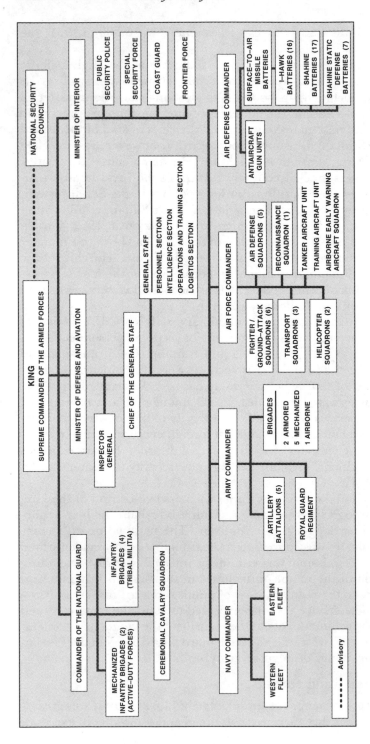

*Figure 10. Organization of National Security, 1992*

the national guard's active complement. The principal combat units were eight brigades: two armored, five mechanized, and one airborne. There were five artillery battalions. A separate Royal Guard Regiment consisted of three light infantry battalions. According to Norman Friedman's *Desert Victory: The War for Kuwait,* the Saudi land forces had deployed two armored brigades and two mechanized brigades on the Kuwaiti border in December 1990 prior to Operation Desert Storm. The disposition of the remaining ground units included a mechanized brigade on the western Iraqi border, a mechanized brigade on the Yemeni border, the Royal Guard Regiment in Riyadh, and the airborne brigade in reserve. The location of one mechanized brigade was not given.

Despite the addition of a number of units and increased mobility achieved during the 1970s and 1980s, the army's personnel complement has expanded only moderately since a major buildup was launched in the late 1960s. The army has been chronically understrength, in the case of some units by an estimated 30 to 50 percent. These shortages have been aggravated by a relaxed policy that permitted considerable absenteeism and by a serious problem of retaining experienced technicians and noncommissioned officers (NCOs). The continued existence of a separate national guard also limited the pool of potential army recruits. Two months after the Persian Gulf War, in April 1991, the government announced that a decision had been taken to expand the ground forces sufficiently to provide a more convincing deterrent against threats to the kingdom's borders. Possibly 90,000 or more troops would be recruited during the 1990s and organized into seven or eight divisions. With the expected organization of a reserve force, the total number that could be called upon in an emergency might reach 200,000. Foreign observers, however, aware of past failures to meet personnel goals, doubted that the limited manpower pool would permit a doubling of the size of the army.

Smaller and less important than the national guard until the 1960s, the army began to modernize after Egyptian incursions onto Saudi territory during the Yemeni civil war (1962–65). Radical Arab nationalism and the emergence of Marxist movements in nearby countries, as well as Israel's crushing defeat of Arab armies in the June 1967 War, also spurred efforts to build a credible ground force. The surplus of revenues from oil exports provided the means to spend lavishly on army facilities and advanced equipment. The first Saudi armored brigade, designated the Fourth Armored Brigade, was structured and trained along French lines. It was equipped with 300 AMX–30 main battle tanks and 500 AMX–10P armored infantry fighting vehicles, both French-made (see table 12, Appendix).

The other armored brigade, designated the Eighth Armored Brigade, was formed under United States guidance soon afterward in the late 1970s. To equip this brigade, Saudi Arabia purchased M–60A3 main battle tanks and M–113 armored personnel carriers (APCs) from the United States. In 1990 Saudi Arabia placed an order for 315 M1A2 Abrams, the most advanced United States tank; delivery was scheduled for 1993. Each brigade consisted of three tank battalions, a mechanized infantry battalion, and a support battalion. The French-equipped armored brigade was stationed at Tabuk in the northwest and the United States-equipped brigade at Khamis Mushayt in the southwest.

The army's four mechanized brigades had been converted from infantry brigades between the late 1970s and the mid-1980s and were equipped with a variety of United States and French armored fighting vehicles. Each brigade consisted of one tank battalion, three mechanized infantry battalions, an artillery battalion, and a support battalion. The infantry brigade consisted of three motorized battalions, an artillery battalion, and a support battalion. The airborne brigade consisted of two paratroop battalions and three special forces companies. Field artillery battalions were equipped with United States and French 155mm self-propelled howitzers and 105mm and 155mm towed guns. The principal antitank weapons, many of them mounted on armored vehicles, were the United States TOW, the British Dragon, and the French HOT. Tactical air defense weapons included self-propelled guns, the French Crotale surface-to-air missile (SAM), and Stinger and Redeye shoulder-fired missiles. The army used transport and medical evacuation helicopters but had no assault helicopters.

The most visible unit of the army, because of its deployment around Riyadh and wherever the king traveled in the country, was the Royal Guard Regiment. The Royal Guard had been autonomous until it was incorporated into the army in 1964; nevertheless, it remained directly subordinate to the king and maintained its own communications network. The mission of the regiment was protection of the House of Saud. Detachments accompanied the king as well as several other members of the Al Saud at all times. Mainly recruited from the tribes of Najd, guardsmen were selected on the basis of their loyalty to the king and the Al Saud. The regiment's equipment included light weapons and armored vehicles.

The army's strength was normally concentrated at four large military cities, built at great expense in the 1970s and 1980s with the assistance of the United States Army Corps of Engineers. The

*AMX-30 main battle tank used by the Royal Saudi Land Forces*
*Courtesy Armed Forces Office, Royal Saudi Arabian Embassy, Washington*

first of these cities was at Khamis Mushayt in the mountains of the southwest, about 100 kilometers from the Yemeni border. The second was at Tabuk, protecting the northwestern routes leading from Jordan, Israel, and Syria. A third site, Assad Military City, was at Al Kharj, about 100 kilometers southeast of Riyadh, where the national armaments industry was also located.

The largest of the military cities, King Khalid, began functioning in 1985 although construction continued throughout the 1980s. Located near Hafar al Batin close to the border area facing Kuwait and Iraq, King Khalid Military City was sited near the strategic Trans-Arabian Pipeline (Tapline) road connecting Ad Dammam with Jordan. It was a self-contained city of 65,000, both military and civilian, built with a perimeter in the form of a huge octagon within which were a series of concentric smaller octagons. Houses and apartments for 6,500 families were provided, as well as numerous schools and mosques, power plants, shopping arcades, theaters, and clubs. Water was supplied by seventeen deep wells. Adjacent to the main installation were a hospital, race course, maintenance and supply areas, underground command bunkers, and antiaircraft missile sites. The logistic and other base resources at King Khalid Military City were indispensable to the allied buildup before the sweep into Iraq during the 1991 Persian Gulf War. It was reported that construction would begin in 1992 on a fifth military city in the Empty Quarter, 550 kilometers south of Riyadh. The new base would have a residential area to accommodate 20,000 people and a large air base with hardened aircraft shelters. The existing army base at Ash Sharawrah in the Empty Quarter was remote but important because of its proximity to the Yemeni border.

The equipment of the land forces came from a variety of sources but primarily from Western countries. However, in 1989 it was revealed that Saudi Arabia had purchased the intermediate range (2,600-kilometer) CSS–2 surface-to-surface missile (SSM) from China. According to *The Military Balance, 1992–1993* published by the International Institute for Strategic Studies, as of 1992 Saudi Arabia had a stock of thirty launchers and fifty missiles. Of limited accuracy and reliability and with a payload of only 750 kilograms, the value of the SSMs was largely symbolic. Nevertheless, disclosure of the secret transaction—Saudi Arabia's first major acquisition of hardware from a communist country and a system that could strike anywhere in the Middle East and beyond—created an uproar in the United States. To placate Washington, King Fahd provided written assurances that the missiles would not be armed with chemical weapons, and Saudi Arabia later signed the Nuclear Nonproliferation Treaty to demonstrate that it had no intention of acquiring nuclear warheads.

## Royal Saudi Air Force

As of 1992, the first line combat air strength of the Royal Saudi Air Force (RSAF) consisted of some 200 aircraft, organized into six fighter/ground-attack squadrons and five fighter-air defense squadrons. The personnel strength of the air force was estimated to be about 18,000. Although modest in comparison to the air power of neighboring countries, the RSAF was considered to be the most modern and effective of the Saudi services. Its mission was to defend the economic installations and the widely scattered population centers of Saudi Arabia against attack and, particularly, to repel air attacks or amphibious assaults against the country's highly vulnerable oil pumping stations, processing and loading facilities, and oil platforms in the Persian Gulf.

The first-line combat fighters were deployed at four key airfields: Dhahran, to defend the main oil facilities of the Persian Gulf; At Taif, covering the ports and holy cities of the lower Red Sea; Khamis Mushayt, defending the Yemeni border zone; and Tabuk, to defend the key ports of the upper Red Sea area and Saudi air space adjacent to Jordan and Israel. These four bases and the air base at Riyadh were protected from air attack by Improved Hawk

*Alpha jet of the Royal Saudi Air Force*
*Courtesy Armed Forces Office, Royal Saudi Arabian Embassy, Washington*

(I-Hawk) SAMs, hardened aircraft shelters, and underground command posts.

The RSAF was established in 1950 during the reign of Abd al Aziz. Its early air operations had been under control of the army. In its initial years, the air force was influenced chiefly by the British, who provided aircraft and advisers and helped train Saudi pilots and maintenance personnel in the kingdom and in Britain. United States influence, emanating from the air base at Dhahran that was leased by the United States from 1952 to 1962, was also pivotal to the early development of the Saudi air force. Some United States aircraft were transferred to the RSAF from units operating at Dhahran and the United States Military Training Mission at Dhahran trained Saudi pilots and maintenance personnel.

In 1972 the first of 114 Northrop F–5s were delivered to the RSAF, and, as of 1992, the air force still used three squadrons of later versions of the F–5 in the fighter-ground attack role, one squadron for reconnaissance, and a number of aircraft as advanced jet trainers. In 1984 first deliveries were taken of the more advanced F–15s. By 1992 the SAF had seventy-eight F–15s, including fighter conversion trainers (see Cooperation with the United States, this ch.).

After the United States refused a Saudi arms request, Saudi Arabia turned to Britain to meet its requirements. In mid-1988, it was announced that as part of a huge transaction, Saudi Arabia would acquire Tornado fighters from Britain in their strike and air defense configurations, plus Hawk jet trainers and Pilatus PC–9 trainers built in Switzerland and outfitted in Britain. As of early 1992, three of the RSAF fighter-ground attack squadrons were equipped with Tornadoes and three squadrons were equipped with F–5Es. Two air defense squadrons were equipped with Tornadoes and three squadrons were equipped with F–15Cs. The three transport squadrons were equipped with C–130s in various versions and CASA C–212s, a medium transport of Spanish design. The two helicopter squadrons employed a variety of smaller rotary-wing aircraft (see table 13, Appendix). Undaunted by its previous failure to establish an assured supply of combat aircraft from the United States, Saudi Arabia announced in late 1991 that it had placed an order with McDonnell Douglas for an additional seventy-two F–15s. It appeared doubtful whether the sale would be approved by the United States administration and the Congress.

Because ground-based radar could not provide adequate advanced warning of attacks on sensitive targets along the Persian Gulf, particularly from nearby Iranian air bases, Saudi Arabia ordered five E–3A AWACS aircraft in 1981. To allay Israel's concerns, the aircraft were equipped specifically for the defensive needs of the Persian Gulf and Red Sea areas only. The first aircraft reached operational status in 1987 in time to assist United States naval operations in the tanker war in the Persian Gulf. Training and support services were provided by the Boeing Corporation and a United States Air Force team. Congress required that the United States have substantial control over the use of the airplanes and a sharing of the AWACS data.

In 1985 Saudi Arabia also contracted with a consortium headed by Boeing for the Peace Shield command, control, communications, and intelligence ($C^3I$) system. Its purpose was to link information collected by AWACS and ground-based surveillance radar with fighters and ground air defense, including the I-Hawk SAMs, to provide integrated air defense against attacks across the gulf and Red Sea and from the direction of Yemen. In 1991 it was announced that the Hughes Aircraft Corporation had assumed management of the project, which had been subject to delays in its completion.

## Royal Saudi Air Defense Forces

Saudi air defense units were separated from the army in the mid-1980s to form a fourth service branch responsible for territorial air defense. The new fourth command was initially entrusted to

Amir Khalid ibn Sultan Al Saud, son of the minister of defense and aviation.

The air defense forces, with an estimated 4,000 personnel in 1992, had as their primary responsibility the operation of thirty-three SAM batteries. Of these, sixteen batteries were equipped with 128 I-Hawk SAMs with a forty-kilometer range, which were emplaced around Riyadh, Ras Tanura, Dhahran, Jiddah, and key air bases at Khamis Mushayt, Hafar al Batin, and Tabuk, as well as the approaches to strategic oil facilities of the Eastern Province. The remaining seventeen batteries, forming a second line of air defense, were equipped with sixty-eight Shahine SAM fire units with a range of sixteen kilometers. These SAMs were a version of the French Crotale missile system mounted on AMX–30SA chassis. This mobile missile defense guarded the Saudi oil fields and other vital installations. An additional seventy-three Shahine fire units were employed as static defense. Both the I-Hawk and Shahine systems were linked to AWACS and to the Peace Shield command and control system. In addition to the missile defense, the air defense forces were equipped with Vulcan 20mm self-propelled guns and 30mm guns mounted on AMX–30SA chassis (see table 14, Appendix).

## Royal Saudi Naval Forces

The development of the navy as a guardian force in the Persian Gulf and Red Sea dates from 1974 when the Saudi Naval Expansion Program (SNEP) was initiated with the assistance of the United States. Previously, the navy had only a few obsolete patrol boats, landing craft, and utility boats. As of 1992, the main combat vessels were four guided-missile frigates and four corvettes, nine missile-armed fast attack craft, and four minesweepers.

Between 1980 and 1983, the United States supplied four PCG–1 corvettes (870 tons), each with eight Harpoon antiship missiles in addition to six torpedo tubes. Nine fast attack craft, also delivered in the early 1980s, were similarly equipped with Harpoon missiles. The principal combat ships of the navy were four French F–2000 frigates (2,870 tons) commissioned in 1985 and 1986, each armed with a Dauphin helicopter, eight Otomat antiship missiles having a range of 160 kilometers, torpedo tubes, and a 100mm gun. In the same contract with France were two logistic support ships, twenty-four Dauphin helicopters, most armed with AS–15 antiship missiles, and support programs for training and maintenance. Saudi Arabia had contracted to purchase three Lafayette-type frigates (3,700 tons) from the French, armed with Exocet antiship missiles, and a 100mm gun. The Lafayettes were scheduled to enter into service after 1995. Discussions had been held with

France and other countries for the supply of up to eight submarines. The large arms agreement with Britain in 1988 resulted in a contract for three Sandown-class minesweepers to be delivered between 1991 and 1993 (see table 15, Appendix).

Naval personnel strength, which was less than 1,000 in 1974, had reached 9,500 by 1991, including 1,500 marines. The marines were organized as an infantry regiment and were equipped with 140 armored vehicles of Spanish manufacture. It was reported in 1991 that an expansion of the marine corps was contemplated and new inventory requirements were being prepared.

The main naval headquarters were located at Riyadh. The navy was organized into the Western Fleet, with headquarters at Jiddah on the Red Sea, and the Eastern Fleet, with headquarters at Al Jubayl on the Persian Gulf. All four frigates were based in the Red Sea and the four corvettes in the Persian Gulf. Other naval facilities were located at Yanbu, Ad Dammam, and Ras al Mishab. The port of Ad Dammam had a large military sea terminal that proved fully adequate to handle United States and other cargoes during the buildup preceding the Persian Gulf War. The two main bases at Jiddah and Al Jubayl were constructed under SNEP. They were similar to the military cities of the army, with hardened command centers, family housing, schools, mosques, shopping centers, and recreational facilities for naval personnel and their families, in addition to maintenance, logistics, and training facilities.

## Saudi Arabian National Guard

Although not subordinate to the minister of defense and aviation and frequently referred to as a paramilitary or an internal security force, the national guard came to be regarded as a integral part of the Saudi military establishment with the modernization of its active units and its role in the Persian Gulf War. The force was a direct descendant of the Ikhwan, the tribal army that served Abd al Aziz so well during his long effort to retake the Arabian Peninsula for the House of Saud. After having to curb the independent military operations and excesses of the Ikhwan, Abd al Aziz permitted it to reappear as the so-called White Army (the name stemmed from the traditional Arab dress rather than uniforms worn by the members), which later became the national guard. It was not a reserve component similar to the national guard of the United States; at least part of it was an active-duty armed force existing parallel to, but separate from, the regular military service branches. The strength of the guard in 1992 was estimated at 75,000, but 20,000 of that total served in a militia status, on call for mobilization rather than on daily active duty.

*Trailer-mounted Hawk missile launcher*
*Courtesy Armed Forces Office, Royal Saudi Arabian Embassy, Washington*
*Truck carrying Shahine surface-to-air missiles*
*Courtesy Armed Forces Office, Royal Saudi Arabian Embassy, Washington*

The head of the national guard for three decades since 1962 was King Fahd's half brother and designated successor, Amir Abd Allah. Three of Abd Allah's sons also held positions in the guard organization. The guard chain of command was completely separate from regular military channels, as was its communication system. Commanders of major units reported directly to Abd Allah, and he reported to the king. In the post-World War II era, as Arab monarchs in other countries fell to coups and revolutions, the Saudi royal family evidently decided that a parallel army such as the national guard would be a form of insurance against coups. Its continued existence was, however, also a matter of tribal and family politics. Abd Allah was considered the leader of the Shammar branch of the Al Saud, a rival source of power to the Sudairi branch that dominated the regular armed forces (see The Royal Family, ch. 4).

Training of the national guard became the responsibility of the Vinnell Corporation of the United States in 1975. About 1,000 United States Vietnam veterans were initially recruited to serve in the long-term training program designed to convert the guard into a mobile and hard-hitting counterinsurgency force that could also reinforce the regular army if necessary. These contractors were supervised by a United States military group with the designation Office of the Program Manager—Saudi Arabian National Guard (OPM–SANG).

Extensive military infrastructure facilities have been built to ensure the comfort and well-being of national guard units. Their major cantonments were in Al Ahsa Oasis near Al Hufuf and the major oil installations of the Eastern Province and at Al Qasim in Najd Province in an area where many of the tribal elements were recruited and most training was conducted. A large new housing project for guard personnel, with associated schools, shops, and mosques, has been constructed near Riyadh, also the site of the guard's military academy, the King Khalid Military College. Other national guard military cities were located at At Taif, Ad Dammam, and Jiddah. A new headquarters complex was built in Riyadh in the early 1980s.

During the 1950s and early 1960s, the regular army and the national guard were both small and of roughly equal strength. The guard suffered when the army's expansion was given priority, but in the 1970s the decline was reversed when the guard was converted to a light mechanized force with the help of United States advisers. Initially consisting of four combined arms battalions, the active-duty component had by 1992 been enlarged to two mechanized brigades, each with four infantry battalions, an artillery battalion,

*F-2000 class frigate of the Royal Saudi Naval Forces*
*Courtesy Armed Forces Office, Royal Saudi Arabian Embassy, Washington*

and engineering and signals companies. The guard's mobility over desert terrain was assured by 1,100 V–150 Commando wheeled APCs. Firepower came from 105mm and 155mm towed howitzers, 106mm recoilless rifles, and TOW antitank missiles mounted on APCs (see table 16, Appendix).

The second component of the national guard, made up of tribal battalions under the command of local shaykhs, was organized into four infantry brigades. These men, often the sons of local chiefs or of veterans of the original Ikhwan forces, reported for duty about once a month for the purpose of receiving stipends. They were provided with obsolete rifles, although many had individually acquired Soviet AK–47 assault rifles. Although neither particularly well trained nor well equipped, they could be counted on to be loyal to the House of Saud if called for service. Their enrollment in the guard was largely a means to bolster the subsidies paid to local shaykhs and to retain the support of their tribes.

The national guard was swiftly deployed to the border area after Iraq's invasion of Kuwait in 1990 and was actively engaged in the war, notably in the fighting to retake the town of Ras al Khafji (see Persian Gulf War, 1991, this ch.). After the war ended, it was reported that an enlargement of the national guard to eleven or twelve active brigades was contemplated. In addition, the Commando APCs were to be replaced by more than 1,000 eight-wheeled light armored vehicles (LAVs) manufactured by General Motors in Canada. The LAVs were to be mounted with a variety of armaments, such as 25mm guns, kinetic energy guns, and TOW missile launchers.

## Training

Any Saudi male citizen—including citizens who had been naturalized for at least five years—could apply for training as an officer if he met the physical and mental standards. Most officer candidates attended military preparatory schools in Riyadh and other cities, where they received free tuition if they committed themselves to attend a military college upon graduation. The King Abd al Aziz Military Academy was the principal source of second lieutenants for the army. Designed for a capacity of 1,500 cadets, this modern facility was a self-contained small city about forty kilometers from Riyadh. The curriculum required three years of study, with successful completion leading to a bachelor of military science degree and a commission. After graduation the new second lieutenants attended a branch school for specialization in infantry, artillery, armor, ordnance, airborne units, the engineers, communications, military police, or administration. Officers in mid-career competed for places at the Command and Staff College at Riyadh to earn a master of military science degree, a required step toward promotion to the senior ranks. Selected officers also attended higher military colleges in the United States and other countries.

A network of army schools trained NCOs in branch and specialized services. Basic training of enlisted personnel was conducted by Saudi NCOs, but most subsequent training was carried out with the assistance of foreign military personnel or specialists under contract.

Science graduates of technical institutions and universities could obtain direct commissions as second lieutenants. In September 1990, the king issued a directive opening military training programs to all male university graduates without distinction as to geographical and tribal balance, which had been factors in the past.

Air force flight training took place at the King Faisal Air Academy at Al Kharj. The flight training consisted of a twenty-seven-month course that began with intensive instruction in the English language. British instructors under contract to British Aerospace (BAe—formerly the British Aircraft Corporation) held most of the faculty positions at the air academy as well as at the Technical Studies Institute at Dhahran, where Saudi aircraft technicians were trained.

After successful completion of primary training, cadets were assigned for several months of advanced training on British Strikemasters and Hawks, which had sufficient avionics and weapons for alternate use as light daytime interceptors. Prospective transport pilots and F–15 pilots were sent to the United States for advanced training.

A number of naval technical and training facilities were built with United States guidance. Much of the United States Navy's training in connection with its equipment deliveries, including that for enlisted men, was conducted at San Diego and at other United States training installations. In the 1980s, training and advisory responsibilities increasingly shifted to France, linked to the delivery of major ship units.

The Marine Training Institute at Jiddah, founded in 1982, had a capacity of 500 officers and NCO students. Officers could earn specialized degrees in mechanical, electrical, or electronic engineering, general science, or military science. The general course for NCOs was of twenty-six months' duration.

## Personnel and Conditions of Service

Saudi Arabia, a large country with a small population, has felt the strains of modernization, particularly since the mid-1960s. The military, because of the increasing complexity of its arms and equipment, has faced an ever-expanding requirement for technical skills within its ranks. As in many other countries—developing or developed—competition for technicians has been very high among all sectors of the rapidly modernizing economy, and, for the military, retaining trained specialists has been difficult.

Since the establishment of the kingdom, the Saudis have relied on volunteers to fill the ranks of the services. On several occasions, Saudi officials have indicated that a system of conscription would be introduced. A military draft has, however, never been instituted, presumably because it would be bitterly unpopular, difficult to enforce, and liable to introduce unreliable elements into the military. The intended radical increases in the size of the army and the national guard would seem to necessitate some form of compulsory service. Nevertheless, in June 1991, the minister of defense and aviation declared that no conscription was needed because the rush of volunteers sometimes exceeded the capacity of training centers to absorb them.

The government conducted regular advertising campaigns to inform young Saudi males of the benefits available to them in the armed forces. Recruiting stations existed throughout the country; the government tried to strike a geographic balance by attracting a representative cross section of the population to the enlisted ranks. The officer corps was still predominantly composed of members of the Najd aristocracy. The national guard continued to rely on an old system of tribal levies to fill its ranks, yielding a composition much less representative of the nation as a whole. Guardsmen were recruited mainly from a few of the important camel-rearing tribes of Najd, reputedly the most trustworthy in the kingdom.

The kingdom's population was 16.9 million, according to the 1992 census; of this number, 12.3 million were Saudi nationals. This population level would be sufficient to maintain the desired strength levels of the regular armed services, assuming the needed education and skill levels were available. (Population statistics for Saudi Arabia, however, were regarded by some Western sources as unreliable.) According to the United States Government, an estimated 159,000 males reached the military age of eighteen each year. The United States Arms Control and Disarmament Agency (ACDA) reported that Saudi Arabia had 5.4 persons in the armed forces per 1,000 of population. This figure was far lower than the average for the Middle East as a whole (18.3 per 1,000 of population).

The conservative Muslim attitude that strongly discouraged Saudi women from seeking jobs outside the home has eased only slightly. Some women worked in human services and medical occupations, but generally social and religious barriers precluded women from working in positions that would place them in public contact with men. Thus, the military services remained closed to female applicants.

The military enlistment period was three years; cash and other rewards were offered as inducements to reenlist. Pay scales were set at levels higher than that for other government service, and the military have been spared salary cuts that applied to civil servants. Allowances and fringe benefits were generous. The government spent huge sums of money to improve the amenities and comfort for personnel in order to increase the attractiveness of military careers. The military cities included excellent family housing for married officers and NCOs, as well as modern barracks for unmarried personnel. The military cities also offered excellent schools and hospitals as well as convenient shopping centers and recreational facilities.

To attract applicants to the military profession, the Ministry of Defense and Aviation founded its own technical high schools and colleges, which offered subsidized education and granted degrees. Anyone seeking a commission by attending a military academy had to be eighteen years old and a citizen by birth or a naturalized citizen for at least five years. The candidate also had to be of good reputation, having neither been subjected to a sharia penalty nor imprisoned for a felony within five years of the date of his application.

*Saudi princes perform a traditional sword dance at the Janadriyah festival in 1985, sponsored by the Saudi Arabian National Guard.*
*Courtesy* Aramco World

Officers were not free to resign. However, they enjoyed extensive benefits, including hardship pay for service in remote areas such as Ash Sharawrah in the southwestern desert. They were entitled to buy land and housing for themselves or as an income-producing investment with generously subsidized loans. Although officers were promoted on a regular basis, they were often frustrated by the lack of opportunity to assume increasing responsibility because of the small size of the services.

As a result of the advanced technology inherent in the military modernization programs, large numbers of foreign military and civilian personnel have been needed to service and maintain weapons systems and to train Saudi personnel in their use. Although precise data were not available, it was estimated that in the late 1980s about 5,000 United States civilians and 500 military technicians and trainers and perhaps 5,000 British, French, and other Europeans provided this support. In addition, a considerable number of officers from Muslim areas—including Pakistanis, Jordanians, Syrians, Palestinians, and Egyptians—were contracted on an individual basis, mostly in training and logistics assignments. As many as 11,000 to 15,000 Pakistani troops and advisers had been recruited to bring the two armored brigades to full strength,

267

as well as to serve in engineering units and the air force. The 10,000 troops in the armored service left the country beginning in late 1987, reportedly because Pakistan was unwilling to screen the Shia element from the force at a time when conflict with Iran seemed a possibility.

## Uniforms, Ranks, and Insignia

Uniforms worn by personnel of Saudi Arabia's armed services, including the national guard, were closely patterned on the British and United States models that influenced those forces during their early development. The most common uniform colors were khaki or olive drab for the army and national guard, blue or white for the navy, and blue for the air force. Officers had semidress uniforms for various functions and dress uniforms for formal occasions. All personnel wore berets, and officers also had visored caps. Members of the Royal Guard Regiment often wore the flowing white *thaub* (robe) and white *kaffiyah* and *qutrah* (traditional Arab headgear of skullcap and scarf). Berets were usually of distinctive colors that designated branches, e.g., paratroops wore maroon, tank troops wore black, and the Royal Guardsmen—when in conventional uniforms—wore bright green berets. National guardsmen wore the traditional red-checkered Arab headdress, although some more modern units wore red berets. Tribal units often wore the *thaub* with crossed bandoliers. The brass badge worn by all ranks depicted the national symbol—a date palm with crossed sabers beneath a crown, all enclosed by a wreath.

There were ten grades of commissioned officers in the army, navy, air force, and air defense force, corresponding to the grades of second lieutenant (ensign) to general (admiral) in the United States forces. The Saudi ranks in all services were known by the same designations; for example, *mulazim thani* corresponded to second lieutenant in the army, air defense force, and air force and to ensign in the navy (see fig. 11).

Enlisted rank structure was the same in all services, and ranks were known by the same terms. There were seven enlisted ratings plus the entry level of recruit. Chevrons to denote rank were worn on both sleeves; the recruit had no chevron. The NCO grades did not correspond exactly to those of the United States forces, and the Saudi army or air force warrant officer (the navy had none) corresponded more closely to master sergeant or sergeant major than to any of the four grades of warrant officer in the United States forces (see fig. 12).

## Military Justice

The administration of justice in the armed forces was regulated by the Code of Military Justice, decreed and published by the minister of defense in 1947. It was applicable to all members of the armed forces, all retired personnel, and civilians working for the armed forces who committed crimes or offenses of a military nature or in violation of military regulations. Military trial courts operating under the authority of the Ministry of Defense and Aviation had jurisdiction over personnel subject to the code. Crimes in violation of the sharia, however, were under the jurisdiction of sharia courts.

A military trial court consisted of officers, who had to be senior to the defendant if an officer were to be tried. The court included a president and four other voting members, plus a legal adviser, an attorney representing the government, and an attorney representing the accused. Trial procedures were direct and uncomplicated, and trials were conducted in a manner intended to protect the rights of the accused. The burden of proof was on the government. A case was brought to trial only after a thorough and impartial investigation, after which a complete report of the alleged crime or incident was submitted to the military commander having jurisdiction, who then could recommend either trial or dismissal of charges. The court's decision could be invalidated or a sentence commuted by the minister of defense and aviation or the king for irregularities, omissions, evidence of prejudice, or evidence that pressure had been brought to bear. The king and the minister had sole power of review of sentences imposed by military trial courts, and, subject to their concurrence, the judgments of the courts were final.

Punishable offenses under the Code of Military Justice were classified as felonies, misdemeanors, or disobediences. Felonies and misdemeanors were subject to trial, and upon conviction a defendant could be sentenced to severe punishment or to disciplinary punishment as prescribed by the court. Disobediences were less serious offenses and were punishable administratively.

Felonies punishable under the military code included high treason against the kingdom and disloyalty to the king or to the armed forces. Severe punishments were prescribed for those found guilty of such crimes. Military misdemeanors meriting the imposition of disciplinary punishment included such acts as misbehavior that brought discredit on the armed forces, misuse of authority, misuse of military funds or equipment, agitation to leave the service, and violation of military regulations and directives. Disciplinary punishments ranged from forfeitures of pay and allowances for from one to three months to imprisonment for up to eighteen months. Disobedience and failure to obey orders were punished administratively. Punishments, which ranged from forfeiture of one day's

| | MULAZIM | MULAZIM AWWAL | NAQIB | RAID | MUQADDAM | AQID | AMID | LIWA | FARIQ | FARIQ AWWAL |
|---|---|---|---|---|---|---|---|---|---|---|
| SAUDI ARABIAN RANK (ARMY) | MULAZIM | MULAZIM AWWAL | NAQIB | RAID | MUQADDAM | AQID | AMID | LIWA | FARIQ | FARIQ AWWAL |
| U.S. RANK TITLE | 2D LIEUTENANT | 1ST LIEUTENANT | CAPTAIN | MAJOR | LIEUTENANT COLONEL | COLONEL | BRIGADIER GENERAL | MAJOR GENERAL | LIEUTENANT GENERAL | GENERAL |
| SAUDI ARABIAN RANK (AIR FORCE) | MULAZIM | MULAZIM AWWAL | NAQIB | RAID | MUQADDAM | AQID | AMID | LIWA | FARIQ | FARIQ AWWAL |
| U.S. RANK TITLE | 2D LIEUTENANT | 1ST LIEUTENANT | CAPTAIN | MAJOR | LIEUTENANT COLONEL | COLONEL | BRIGADIER GENERAL | MAJOR GENERAL | LIEUTENANT GENERAL | GENERAL |
| SAUDI ARABIAN RANK (NAVY) | MULAZIM | MULAZIM AWWAL | NAQIB | RAID | MUQADDAM | AQID | AMID | LIWA | FARIQ | FARIQ AWWAL |
| U.S. RANK TITLE | ENSIGN | LIEUTENANT JUNIOR GRADE | LIEUTENANT | LIEUTENANT COMMANDER | COMMANDER | CAPTAIN | REAR ADMIRAL LOWER HALF | REAR ADMIRAL UPPER HALF | VICE ADMIRAL | ADMIRAL |

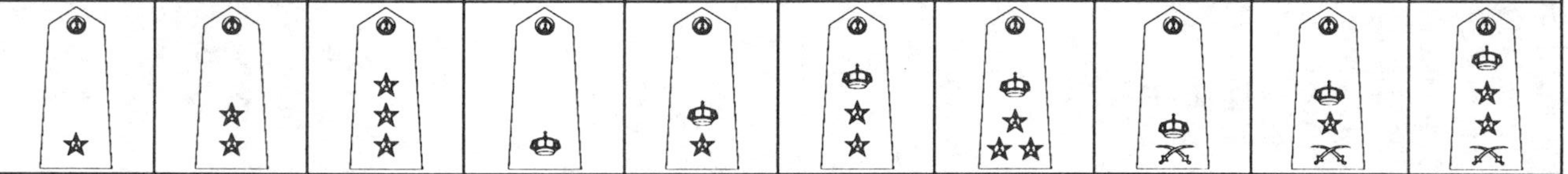

Figure 11. Officer Ranks and Insignia, 1992

| SAUDI ARABIAN RANK | NO RANK | JUNDI | JUNDI AWWAL | ARIF | WAKIL RAQIB | RAQIB | RAIS AWWAL | RAIS RUQUBA |
|---|---|---|---|---|---|---|---|---|
| ARMY AND AIR FORCE | NO INSIGNIA | NO INSIGNIA | (insignia) | (insignia) | (insignia) | (insignia) | (insignia) | (insignia)      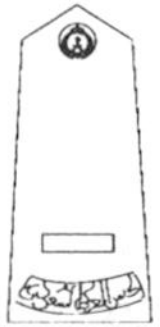 |
| U.S. ARMY RANK TITLE | BASIC PRIVATE | PRIVATE | PRIVATE 1ST CLASS | CORPORAL/SPECIALIST | SERGEANT / STAFF SERGEANT | SERGEANT 1ST CLASS | MASTER SERGEANT / FIRST SERGEANT | SERGEANT MAJOR / COMMAND SERGEANT MAJOR |
| U.S. AIR FORCE RANK TITLE | AIRMAN BASIC | AIRMAN | AIRMAN 1ST CLASS | SENIOR AIRMAN | STAFF SERGEANT / TECHNICAL SERGEANT | MASTER SERGEANT | SENIOR MASTER SERGEANT | CHIEF MASTER SERGEANT |
| SAUDI ARABIAN RANK | NO RANK | JUNDI | JUNDI AWWAL | ARIF | WAKIL RAQIB | RAQIB | RAIS AWWAL | RAIS RUQUBA |
| NAVY | NO INSIGNIA | NO INSIGNIA | (insignia) | (insignia) | (insignia) | (insignia) | (insignia) |      NO RANK |
| U.S. RANK TITLE | SEAMAN RECRUIT | SEAMAN APPRENTICE | SEAMAN | PETTY OFFICER 3D CLASS | PETTY OFFICER 2D CLASS / PETTY OFFICER 1ST CLASS | CHIEF PETTY OFFICER | SENIOR CHIEF PETTY OFFICER | MASTER CHIEF PETTY OFFICER |

*Figure 12. Enlisted Ranks and Insignia, 1992*

pay and imprisonment for twenty-four hours to imprisonment for forty-five days, were scaled according to the seriousness of the offense as prescribed in the Code of Military Justice.

## Defense Expenditures

During the 1980s, Saudi Arabia's outlays on national security were among the highest in the world in spite of its relatively small population. In 1989 its expenditures of US$14.7 billion ranked eleventh among the countries of the world. Nonetheless, this level of spending reflected a declining trend from a peak of US$24.8 billion reached in 1983. Budgeted defense expenditures maintained this gradual decline between 1988 and 1990. Actual defense expenditures rose dramatically in 1990, however, to almost US$31.9 billion to meet the costs of additional arms and the contributions to United States and British military expenditures necessitated by the Iraqi aggression against Kuwait. The defense budget of US$26.8 billion in 1991 included more than US$13.7 billion in contributions to the United States, French, and British war efforts, but did not include projected heavy additional arms purchases. Saudi Arabia also contributed to the costs of other non-Western members of the coalition forces facing Iraq.

In early 1991, Saudi officials estimated that during the first five months of the gulf crisis the country had earned roughly US$15 billion in windfall oil profits arising from increased production and higher market prices, while assuming an additional US$30 billion in commitments related to the crisis. The latter figure included US$13.6 billion in new arms and equipment, US$2.7 billion in extra mobilization and deployment costs and civil defense, with the remainder consisting of grants and loans to other governments to offset the economic effects of the crisis.

During 1983, when defense spending reached a peak, military expenditures per capita were at an annual level of nearly US$2,500. This amount was more than twice the per capita defense spending in the United States, and was not approached by any other country except Israel, Iraq, and the other oil-exporting states of the Persian Gulf. As a consequence of the reduced rate of defense spending after 1983, military expenditures per capita had declined to US$897 by 1989.

The share of gross national product (GNP—see Glossary) originally earmarked for defense in 1990 was 16.9 percent, materially below the peak of 22 percent reached in 1983 but still about twice as high as the Middle East as a whole. Defense outlays constituted 35.5 percent of central government expenditures in 1989; this percentage was also higher than the Middle East average of 32 percent.

The declining rate of defense spending between 1984 and 1990 resulted largely from reductions in oil revenues that produced a negative growth rate for the entire economy. A secondary factor may have been the completion of several large-scale infrastructure projects. Arms imports, which accounted for 16 percent of the defense budget in 1983, had risen to 25 percent by 1988. The major contracts for weaponry placed with Britain, the United States, and France since 1988; the extraordinary expenses of the Persian Gulf War; and plans for expansion of the armed forces during the 1990s seemed certain to impose pressure on the defense budget for years to come.

## Foreign Involvement and Influence

Until the 1930s, Abd al Aziz, concerned with conquest and the reestablishment of the House of Saud on the peninsula, showed little interest in developing armed forces for national defense, relying instead on British support and diplomacy. After the clash with Yemen in the early 1930s and the discovery of oil, the Saudi king recognized the need for a standing army and sought assistance from Britain, Egypt, and the United States. By the mid-1940s, the Saudis were relying more on the United States than on any other country, mostly because of the successful relations between Saudi officials and Aramco.

Only nominal sums were spent on defense until Saudi Arabia's involvement in the Yemeni civil war of the early 1960s. When the need for stronger national defense became apparent to the leadership, Saudi Arabia was obliged to turn to foreign sources for armaments, military training, and the construction of facilities. The long-standing military relationship between Saudi Arabia and the United States served as a foundation for the buildup of the defense forces and military infrastructure begun under Faisal.

### Cooperation with the United States

Between 1947 and 1991, Saudi Arabia's purchases under the Foreign Military Sales program of the United States Department of Defense totaled approximately US$60 billion. More than 80 percent of these purchases were for construction of infrastructure—bases and command and control facilities—together with maintenance, spare parts, and training. Fewer than 20 percent of the purchases were for weapons.

The first United States military mission of any consequence arrived in Saudi Arabia in 1943, but the first significant mutual defense agreement was not formalized until June 1951. As a result of that agreement, a United States Military Training Mission

(USMTM) arrived for duty in the kingdom in 1953 to supervise all military assistance and training activities. Until the late 1960s, this assistance was provided primarily on a grant basis. During the reign of Saud, the government was continually faced with large budget deficits despite increasing oil revenues. By 1964, after Saud had been deposed and Faisal had become king, the country was on a better economic footing and it was able to pay for the major purchases of arms, infrastructure, and training services that followed.

Initially, the primary purpose of the United States in establishing the special relationship with Saudi Arabia was to check the spread of Soviet influence in that area of the world and the consequent threat to Middle East oil. The Saudis were conscious of the Soviet danger, and the royal family was inherently anticommunist; nevertheless, because of proximity, Israel and Iran were perceived to be the most immediate threats to the security of the kingdom. Saudi Arabia did not want the Arabian Peninsula to become an arena of superpower contention and was opposed to the establishment of United States bases or to the stationing in the kingdom of large numbers of United States military personnel.

After the October 1973 Arab-Israeli war, which triggered a sharp increase in oil prices, Saudi Arabia was able to allocate large sums to the modernization and training of the armed forces. Until the late 1980s, the primary areas of activity by the United States were the wide range of construction activities by the Army Corps of Engineers, the Saudi Naval Expansion Program, and the Saudi Ordnance Corps Program to establish an integrated logistics, supply, and maintenance system. In 1988 the Corps of Engineers completed the program that had kept it engaged in the kingdom for twenty-three years.

President Jimmy Carter's proposal to sell advanced F–15 fighter aircraft to Saudi Arabia in 1978 and his proposal to loan and later to sell the kingdom AWACS aircraft after the outbreak of the Iran-Iraq War in 1980 touched off bitter disputes in Congress. The sale of the F–15s was approved under conditions that limited their range and offensive power because of fears that they could tip the regional balance against Israel. President Ronald Reagan decided the sale of the AWACS aircraft should proceed to help the Saudis guard against attacks on their oil installations. He urged that the transfer of five AWACS and seven aerial refueling tankers be approved. The package also included auxiliary fuel tanks for the F-15 fighters and more than 1,000 Sidewinder air-to-air missiles. For Saudi Arabia, the purchase request became a test of the firmness of the relationship, but for the United States it became a political nightmare because Israel and its supporters in the United States raised strenuous objections to the sale. After lengthy congressional hearings and investigations, the package was narrowly approved with special restrictions on the use of the AWACS aircraft.

In 1985 President Reagan sought authority to sell Saudi Arabia forty-two additional F-15s, antiaircraft missiles, Harpoon antiship missiles, and Blackhawk troop-carrying helicopters. Again, the proposal raised a storm of opposition in Congress and had to be withdrawn. In 1986 and 1988, scaled-down packages were introduced and eventually approved by Congress after Stinger antiaircraft and Maverick antitank missiles were deleted. Among the approved items were Bradley fighting vehicles, TOW II antitank missiles, electronic upgrades for the F-15s, and twelve additional F-15s to remain in the United States until needed as replacements.

United States arms transfer agreements with Saudi Arabia increased dramatically in 1990. Of a total of US$14.5 billion in contracts signed, US$6.1 billion preceded the Iraqi invasion of Kuwait. They included LAVs, TOW II launchers and missiles, and 155mm howitzers, all for the national guard; 315 M1A2 tanks; and thirty tank recovery vehicles. After the invasion, the United States hastily arranged a package that included F-15 aircraft; M1A2 and M-60A3 tanks and other armored vehicles; Stinger, TOW II, and Patriot missiles; Apache helicopters; and about 10,000 trucks.

A second phase of the arms package, worth an estimated US$14 billion, was postponed in early 1991 to reassess Saudi needs in the postwar atmosphere in the Persian Gulf. It was reported to include additional F-15s, M1A2 tanks, AWACS aircraft, and Bradley fighting vehicles. As of 1992, the United States faced the question of reconciling Saudi Arabia's desire for further large-scale arms purchases to build its deterrent strength with the United States desire to limit the export of advanced weaponry to the volatile Middle East region. The issue was linked to negotiations over the preliminary positioning of equipment for up to one army corps in depots on Saudi territory to permit the rapid deployment of United States ground forces in the event of renewed Middle East hostilities.

## Cooperation with Other Countries

Although the United States was the dominant foreign influence in the post-World War II development of the Saudi military establishment, the kingdom has regularly awarded contracts to other governments or to private corporations in other countries to avoid complete dependence on a single supplier. Britain and France have been the other two major recipients of Saudi contracts for weapons and equipment, maintenance, training, and construction of facilities.

According to ACDA statistics, Britain was actually the largest supplier of arms from 1985 to 1989, providing military goods and services totaling US$7.7 billion. France was second with $US7.0 billion, and the United States was third with US$5.0 billion. Imports from China were US$2.5 billion, arising principally from the sale of the CSS–2 missile system. Among the major French transactions, disclosed in 1984, was a US$4.5 billion contract for a Shahine mobile antiaircraft missile defense system to guard the Saudi oil fields and other sensitive targets. In addition to selling Saudi Arabia tanks and other armored equipment in the 1970s, France was a leading supplier of ships and helicopters.

During World War II, Britain, which had been the dominant foreign power in the Middle East for many years, and the United States coordinated their efforts to train and modernize Abd al Aziz's small armed forces. British training missions were active in the kingdom, and some Saudis were sent to Britain for military schooling. After the war, the United States took over most of the training and modernization of the Saudi military, but Britain continued to share in the contracts for arms, equipment, and services. For many years, a majority of Saudi combat aircraft were British Lightnings and Strikemasters manufactured by BAe, which had long-standing contracts to provide services and maintenance to the Royal Saudi Air Force. The company also operated the King Faisal Air Academy and the Technical Studies Institute.

In 1986, after being thwarted in its efforts to purchase additional F–15s from the United States, Saudi Arabia responded by announcing the purchase of Tornado fighter-bombers and interceptors built by a British-led consortium, as well as Hawk jet trainers and Pilatus training aircraft. The advanced Tornadoes were offered without the restrictions on basing and armaments that the United States had imposed on its sale of F–15s to reduce the risk of their being used against Israel. In July 1988, the Saudis announced an agreement in principle to purchase US$20 to US$30 billion worth of aircraft and other military equipment and construction services from Britain over a ten-year period. The 1986 and 1988 agreements were sometimes referred to by the code names, Al Yamamah I and Al Yamamah II. Under Al Yamamah II, Saudi Arabia signaled its intention to acquire additional Tornadoes, jet trainers, British versions of the Blackhawk helicopter, and minesweepers for the navy. The cost of the huge arms agreement was to be offset by proceeds from Saudi oil shipments and by British investments in military and civilian production plants in Saudi Arabia.

Under an agreement announced in 1983, Spain has supplied Saudi Arabia with CASA C–212 transport aircraft, built as a joint venture between Spain and Indonesia, as well as other equipment. In 1990 negotiations with West Germany over the sale of 300 Leopard II tanks reportedly failed when Germany decided not to proceed in light of its policy against arms sales to areas of tension and what it viewed as its moral obligation to the state of Israel.

## Western Cooperation in Domestic Arms Production

A small defense-manufacturing industry based on coproduction, offset, and licensing agreements with Western arms suppliers was still emerging in 1992. Saudi policy was to reduce its exposure to the political uncertainties of importing arms and to achieve a degree of self-sufficiency as a source of prestige in the Middle East. The chronic shortage of trained technicians and lack of skilled manpower, however, forced the industry to rely on foreign managers, technical assistance, and imported labor. Such joint ventures were entitled to industrial development loans, tax holidays, and other subsidies.

During the 1970s, Saudi Arabia had been involved with Egypt, Qatar, and the United Arab Emirates in establishing the Arab Organization for Industrialization (AOI). Its goal was to combine capital of the gulf oil states with Egyptian production capabilities to create an arms industry located mainly on Egyptian territory. Although Egypt carried out a number of coproduction schemes under the AOI designation, the plan foundered because of Arab anger over Egypt's 1979 peace treaty with Israel.

Saudi Arabia later established its own small arms industry at Al Kharj, producing United States and Federal Republic of Germany (West Germany) rifles, machine guns, and ammunition under license. In 1985 a royal decree by King Fahd led to the creation of the General Establishment of Military Industries to oversee and coordinate the kingdom's existing and proposed domestic defense projects. In the same year, a contract was concluded with a Boeing-led consortium committing the consortium to US$350 million worth of investments in Saudi Arabia as an offset to the cost of the Peace Shield air defense system. Under this arrangement, the Boeing group agreed to enter into a US$130 million joint project for an airframe maintenance facility and a US$117 million advanced jet maintenance and repair facility. A ten-year agreement was also concluded to develop a computer center and an aircraft hydraulics maintenance center, all to be built at King Khalid International Airport at Riyadh. The Boeing consortium also held a 50-percent interest in a local company to produce military tactical radios.

277

The Al Yamamah I arms agreement with Britain committed BAe to offset US$7.5 billion in Saudi arms purchases with US$1.5 billion of investments in Saudi Arabia. Three such projects were underway in 1991. They included a British-American joint venture to produce missiles for Tornado fighter aircraft, the local assembly of heavy-duty trucks, and a BAe investment in an aluminum smelter at Yanbu. A West German company had built a plant to produce mortar shells and as of 1990 was negotiating a contract to produce tank and howitzer ammunition.

## Public Order and the Justice System

The successful forging of the different tribes of the Arabian Peninsula into a coherent nation during the first half of the twentieth century must be credited to Abd al Aziz and the House of Saud. If there were one singular element in Saudi society that explained the relative stability during the first sixty years of the kingdom, it was the allegiance that had been exhibited by a preponderant segment of the population to the Al Saud. Internal order and the continued existence of the monarchy, however, did not come automatically to the country simply because of the leadership and charisma of Abd al Aziz. Of great significance during his reign was the establishment of the country's basic security forces and a code of behavior intended to instill fear and respect for the law and obedience to it.

With its tasks of preventing intertribal warfare and protecting the House of Saud from any possible threat, the national guard has been the primary agency for upholding the security of the government. The loyalty of the guard has, however, been more than blind allegiance to the person of the king. In 1964, when the kingdom was in trouble under King Saud, the guard supported Faisal and the Al Saud in deposing the monarch, acting as an instrument in a controlled process of succession. Under its commander, Abd Allah, one of the powerful princes in the kingdom, the national guard remained an important factor in national stability in 1992. It was, however, increasingly being supplanted by more modern agencies of control under the Ministry of Interior that had the king's full brother, Amir Nayif, at its head and another full brother, Amir Ahmad ibn Abd al Aziz, as the deputy minister.

Traditionally, the allegiance of the people has been to the tribe and to the extended family (see Diversity and Social Stratification; Cultural Homogeneity and Values, ch. 2). One of Abd al Aziz's truly significant accomplishments was to implant the concept of allegiance to the House of Saud and by extension to the government and the judicial system. Also important was the recognition by the

Saudis of their ethnic identity as an Arab people and their religious identity with Wahhabi Islam. Each aspect of a person's day-to-day conduct could be categorized as being within the bounds of acceptable behavior or outside those bounds, with no distinction between the secular and the religious spheres. Few Saudis chose to live outside the law, and their basic attitudes supported an orderly society.

In theory, all persons, including the king and foreigners, were equal before the law and subject to both the sharia and law by decree. In practice, however, members of the royal family and other leaders have rarely been brought to public trial. Cases involving foreigners have often been handled outside the court system, frequently by deportation.

## Law Enforcement

In the limited public security structure inherited from the Ottoman Empire, police work was done informally and justice was administered by local or tribal authorities. Gradually, during the reign of Abd al Aziz, modern organs of government were introduced and became responsible for maintaining public order. By royal decree in 1950, Abd al Aziz created a general directorate to supervise all police functions in the kingdom, and a year later he established the Ministry of Interior, which has since been in charge of police matters. Subordinate to the Ministry of Interior, general directorates charged with maintaining internal security included Public Security, Investigation, Coast Guard, and Special Security. The offices of the deputy ministers for administration, national security affairs, and immigration and naturalization, and the Internal Security Forces College were all on the same organizational level as the four general directorates. Governors of the amirates reported directly to the minister of interior (see fig. 8).

In return for their loyalty and the maintenance of peace and order in the tribal areas, the king provided subsidies to the shaykhs and a minimum of government interference in tribal affairs. Under this system, offenses and breaches of the peace were punished by the responsible shaykh. The national guard acted as a support force to quell disturbances or restore order if tribal authority could not.

The public security forces, particularly the centralized Public Security Police, could also get emergency support from the national guard or, in extremis, from the regular armed forces. The Public Security Police, recruited from all areas of the country, maintained police directorates at provincial and local levels. The director general for public security retained responsibility for police units, but, in practice, provincial governors exercised considerable autonomy. Provincial governors were frequently senior amirs of the Al Saud.

Since the mid-1960s, a major effort has been made to modernize the police forces. During the 1970s, quantities of new vehicles and radio communications equipment enabled police directorates to operate sophisticated mobile units, especially in the principal cities. Helicopters were also acquired for use in urban areas. Police uniforms were similar to the khaki and olive drab worn by the army except for the distinctive red beret. Policemen usually wore sidearms while on duty.

Dealings with the security forces were often a source of difficulty for foreigners in the kingdom. Ordinary policemen could be impatient with those who did not speak Arabic and, often, were illiterate. Darker-skinned workers were said to be treated more roughly than Europeans or North Americans. Everyone connected with a serious crime or accident could be detained until the police had investigated matters.

The police security forces were divided into regular police and special investigative police of the General Directorate of Investigation (GDI), commonly called the *mubahith* (secret police). The GDI conducted criminal investigations in addition to performing the domestic security and counterintelligence functions of the Ministry of Interior. The Directorate of Intelligence, which reported directly to the king, was responsible for intelligence collection and analysis and the coordination of intelligence tasks and reporting by all intelligence agencies, including those of the Ministry of Defense and Aviation and the national guard.

An important feature of domestic security was the Ministry of Interior's centralized computer system at the National Information Center in Riyadh. The computer network, linking 1,100 terminals, maintained records on citizens' identity numbers and passports, foreigners' residence and work permits, hajj visas, vehicle registrations, and criminal records. Reports from agents and from the large number of informants employed by the security services were also entered. Officials of the Directorate of Intelligence had authority to carry out wiretaps and mail surveillance.

The Special Security Force was the Saudi equivalent of a special weapons assault team (SWAT), such as had been incorporated into police forces in various parts of the world. Reporting directly to the minister of interior, the force was organized after the poor performance of the national guard during the revolt at the Grand Mosque at Mecca in 1979. The force was equipped with UR-416 armored vehicles from West Germany and nonlethal chemical weapons. According to *The Military Balance, 1992–1993*, the force had a personnel strength of 500 in 1992, although estimates from other sources have ranged much higher. It was reported in 1990 that the antiterrorism unit of the Special Security Force was being disbanded and its German training staff repatriated.

The strength of the Coast Guard was 4,500 as of 1992 and of the Frontier Force 10,500, according to *The Military Balance, 1992–1993*. The Frontier Force patrolled land borders and carried out customs inspections. The Coast Guard deployed its units from ports along the Persian Gulf and the Red Sea with a primary mission to prevent smuggling. Among its varied inventory of craft, the largest were four 210-ton offshore patrol craft acquired from West Germany in 1989. Two were based at Jiddah and two at Ad Dammam. The Coast Guard also had about thirty large patrol craft, 135 inshore patrol craft, and sixteen British-built Hovercraft.

An unusual, if not unique, internal security force in Saudi Arabia was the autonomous and highly visible religious police, or *mutawwiin* (see Glossary). Organized under the authority of the king in conjunction with the ulama, the *mutawwiin* were charged with ensuring compliance with the puritanical precepts of Wahhabism. A nationwide organization known in English as the Committees for the Propagation of Virtue and Prevention of Vice (also seen as Committees for Public Morality), the *mutawwiin* had earned a reputation for fanaticism and brutality that had become an embarrassment. The Al Saud, however, has seemingly been reluctant to confront the ulama in a showdown. Primarily, the *mutawwiin* enforced public observance of such religious requirements as the five daily prayers, fasting during Ramadan, the modesty of women's dress, and the proscriptions against the use of alcohol (see Wahhabi Theology, ch. 2).

Once an important instrument of Abd al Aziz for upholding standards of public behavior, by the early 1990s the ultraconservatism of the *mutawwiin* had become an anachronism, contrasting with the modernization processes working in other sectors of society. The government has occasionally disciplined overzealous *mutawwiin,* following complaints from a foreign government over treatment of its nationals. After a series of raids on rich and influential Saudis in 1990, the government appointed a new and more compliant leader of the religious police.

The religious police had the legal right to detain suspects for twenty-four hours before turning them over to the regular police and were known to have flogged detainees to elicit confessions. They often used switch-like sticks to beat those perceived to be in violation of religious laws. Foreign workers, including some from the United States, have been targets of harassment and raids. According to one estimate, there were about 20,000 *mutawwiin* in 1990. Most *mutawwiin* wore the traditional white *thaub,* were salaried, and were regarded as government employees. Some incidents of harassment have been attributed to self-appointed vigilantes outside the regular religious police hierarchy.

## Criminal Justice System

The judicial system is founded upon the sharia, particularly the Hanbali school of Sunni Islam, in accordance with a ruling by King Abd al Aziz in 1926. The Hanbali system of jurisprudence, which rejected analogy as a source of law and gave prominence to the traditions and sayings of the Prophet Muhammad, was regarded as especially rigid by most Muslim jurists. If there were no guidance in Hanbali texts, however, Saudi jurists could refer to other schools or exercise their own reasoning.

Two categories of crime are delineated in the sharia: those that are carefully defined and those that are implicit in the requirements and prohibitions of the sharia. For the first category, there are specific penalties; for the second, punishment can be prescribed by a judge (qadi) of a sharia court. A third category of crime has developed through the years as a result of various governmental decrees that specified codes of behavior and regulations considered necessary to maintain public order and security. The first two categories are tried in sharia courts. The third, dealing with corporate law, taxation, oil and gas, and immigration, is handled administratively by government officials (see The Legal System, ch. 4).

The sharia carefully defines crimes—such as homicide, personal injury, adultery, fornication, theft, and highway robbery—and prescribes a penalty (*hadd*) for each. Various degrees of culpability for homicide and bodily injury are recognized depending on intent, the kind of weapon used, and the circumstances under which the crime occurred. Homicide is considered a crime against a person rather than a crime against society in which the state administers justice of its own volition. Under the sharia, the victim or the victim's family has the right to demand punishment, to grant clemency, or to demand blood money (*diya*)—a set payment as recompense for the crime.

An act of self-defense is recognized as a right nullifying criminality. Retaliation is permitted to the male next of kin of the victim by killing the criminal in the case of a homicide or exacting the same bodily injury that was inflicted on the victim. Acceptance of *diya* is, however, considered preferable under the sharia. In cases involving death or grievous injury, the accused is usually held incommunicado. Imprisonment before trial can last weeks or even several months. The right of bail or habeas corpus is not recognized, although persons accused of crimes are sometimes released on the recognizance of a patron or employer. The accused is normally held not more than three days before being formally charged, but it is common for detainees to be held for long periods if the investigation is incomplete.

At trials for minor offenses, qadis hear complaints and then cross-examine plaintiffs, defendants, and any witnesses. The judge assigns great significance to a defendant's sworn testimony, although the testimony of two women is required to equal that of one man. In the absence of two witnesses, oral confessions before a judge are almost always required for conviction. Trials are held without jurors and are generally closed. They are normally held without counsel, although lawyers can advise the accused before the trial. Attorneys may also be allowed to act as interpreters for those unfamiliar with Arabic. Consular access is not usually permitted during the trials of foreign nationals. After guilt or innocence is determined, a sentence, if appropriate, is imposed by the judge. In certain criminal cases, punishment can be referred to a local governor or shaykh for sentencing upon the advice of a local Muslim jurist or the ulama.

Appeals against judges' decisions are automatically reviewed by the Ministry of Justice or, in more serious cases, by a court of appeal. In the early 1990s, there were two sharia courts of appeal, one sitting in Riyadh and the other in Mecca. Appeals are heard by panels of three judges except for sentences of death or amputation, which can only be adjudicated by a panel of five judges. Decisions of the appellate courts are final except for sentences of death and amputation. Cases of capital punishment are automatically referred to the king for final review.

## Crime and Punishment

The incidence of crime was considered to be relatively low in Saudi Arabia, and violent street crime was particularly unusual. Crime rates had, however, risen with the presence of foreign workers. An increase noted in the level of petty crime in 1989 was linked to unemployed Saudis and to Yemeni residents of the kingdom. The severity of penalties and the rigid system of enforcement were credited by both officials and ordinary citizens with contributing to the high standards of public safety. Supporters of severe punishment believed that, although carried out infrequently, a beheading or stoning reminded the people that such penalties remained in force. Some observers disagreed, citing cultural traits and the social forces bearing on Arabs of the peninsula as the main inhibiting factors. According to the *Statistical Yearbook* published by the Ministry of Finance and National Economy, the most common crimes in 1988 were theft (7,553 cases), the production, sale, and consumption of alcohol (5,085 cases), altercations and quarreling (3,651 cases), and moral offenses (2,576 cases). There were fifty-six murders and 340 cases of attempted and threatened murder. There were twenty-nine cases of arson and 574 cases involving forgery or fraud.

Crimes subject to the death sentence included murder, apostasy from Islam, adultery, drug smuggling, and sabotage. Under certain conditions, rape and armed robbery could also lead to execution. Executions could be carried out by beheading, firing squad, or stoning of the convicted person in a drugged state. All seventeen executions carried out in 1990 were by beheading.

The sharia sets forth rigorous requirements for proof of adultery or fornication. For the crime of adultery, four witnesses to the act must swear to having witnessed the crime, and if such an accusation does not hold up in court, the witnesses are then liable to punishment. No one was executed for adultery in 1990, although during 1989 there were reliable reports of nonjudicial public stonings for adultery.

Under the sharia, repeated theft is punishable by amputation of the right hand, administered under anesthetic. Because of its severity, a number of qualifications have been introduced to mitigate the punishment. If the thief repents and makes restitution before the case is brought before a judge, the punishment can be reduced; furthermore, the victim can demand recompense rather than punishment or can grant a pardon. Highway crime was considered a crime against public safety and thus subject to more severe punishment. Aggravated theft can be punished by cross-amputation of a hand and a foot. Such cases have been unusual, but Amnesty International reported four of them in 1986. In 1990 fewer than ten hand amputations took place, at least five of which were administered to foreigners.

Flogging with a cane was often imposed for offenses against religion and public morality, such as drunkenness and gambling and the neglect of prayer requirements and fasting. Although the flogging was painful, the skin was not broken. The purpose was to degrade rather than cripple the offender and serve as a deterrent to others. United States citizens have been flogged for alcohol-related offenses, usually receiving from thirty to 120 strokes. A Kuwaiti sentenced to prison in connection with terrorist bombings in Mecca was condemned to receive a total of 1,500 lashes over the course of his twenty-year sentence.

In 1987, based on a ruling by the ulama, drug smugglers and those who received and distributed drugs from abroad were made subject to the death sentence for bringing "corruption" into the country. First-time offenders faced prison terms, floggings, and fines, or a combination of all three punishments. Those convicted for a second time faced execution. By the end of 1987, at least nine persons had been executed for offenses that involved drug smuggling, most of them non-Saudis. According to the police, the antidrug campaign and the death penalty had by 1989 reduced addiction by 60 percent and drug use by 26 percent. By late 1991, more than 110 drug sellers had been arrested since the law was put into effect. Saudi officials claimed that the kingdom had the lowest rate of drug addiction in the world, which they attributed to the harsh punishments and the pious convictions of ordinary Saudis. Drug use was said to persist, however, among wealthy younger Saudis who acquired the habit abroad. Drug users allegedly included some members of the royal family, who took advantage of their privileged status to import narcotics.

## Prison Conditions

The administration of the kingdom's prisons was under the supervision of the director general of public security. Unsanitary and overcrowded prison conditions prior to King Faisal's reign were supposedly corrected after reforms adopted since the late 1960s. Nevertheless, it was clear from various published reports during the 1980s that conditions for most prisoners were very unpleasant. According to *Saudi Arabia: A MEED Practical Guide* published in 1983 by the Middle East Economic Digest, up to 200 prisoners might share a single room. Basic food was provided, usually eaten by hand from the floor, although prisoners' families often supplemented their diets. Inmates slept on a bare floor; in some cases, they were provided with a pad, but no mattress. They had to supply their own blankets. There was little ventilation, and a hole in the floor served as a toilet. Saudi prisons were not dangerous or violent, and treatment for ordinary inmates was not cruel. Little attention was given to rehabilitation or training for a trade after confinement, however. Boredom was a particular problem. According to the MEED guide, there was no provision for parole, but most prisoners were released for good behavior after serving three-quarters of their sentences. The *Country Reports on Human Rights Practices for 1988,* published by the United States Department of State, also described conditions as severe in some institutions, although not intentionally degrading. Prisoners were liable to suffer heat stroke and sometimes complained of difficulty in obtaining adequate medical treatment. The Department of State said that the Saudi government was making efforts to expand and improve prisons, but substandard conditions persisted, especially in deportation centers where large numbers of foreigners were held prior to deportation.

## Human Rights

Saudi Arabia has been cited by several international human rights monitoring groups for its alleged failure to respect a number of basic rights. London-based Amnesty International reported receiving credible testimony from political prisoners who alleged they were arbitrarily arrested, held in prolonged detention without trial, and routinely tortured during interrogations. Torture methods in the Mubahathat (office of secret police) prisons included months in solitary confinement, sleep deprivation, beatings to the soles of the feet, suspension by the wrists from ceilings or high windows, and the application of electric shocks to all parts of the body. Amnesty International cited reports that sixty-six persons had been detained without charge or trial for radical Shia activity, although forty-one of these, as well as other political opponents of the government, were released in 1990 on the occasion of a royal pardon for more than 7,000 common criminals.

The human rights organization Middle East Watch, the Minnesota Lawyers International Human Rights Committee, and the International Committee for Human Rights in the Gulf and the Arabian Peninsula issued reports in 1991 and 1992 that detailed extensive use of torture in Saudi prisons as a means to extract confessions from detainees. Prisoners reportedly signed confessions to crimes they had not committed in order to escape physical and psychological torture. As of October 1992, human rights organizations had identified forty-three political prisoners who had been detained for more than one year without formal charges. Several prisoners are alleged to have died while in police custody.

The Department of State reported in early 1991 that there was no automatic procedure for informing a detainee's family or employer of his arrest. Embassies usually heard of the arrest of their nationals informally within a few days; official notification took several months. A policy requiring Ministry of Foreign Affairs approval of consular access to prisoners has caused delays in consular visits.

In spite of calls after the Persian Gulf War for modernization of laws and relief from the influence of strict Islamism in the imposition of punishment, the royal family showed little disposition to liberalize the criminal justice system. As of early 1992, the conservative religious establishment seemed to have solidified its ability to block reforms of the codes of law and judicial procedures that were the sources of increasing domestic and international criticism.

\* \* \*

Among various works analyzing Saudi Arabia's defense posture, *The Gulf and the West: Strategic Relations and Military Realities* by Anthony H. Cordesman covers a range of topics, including development of the armed forces, modernization of the air force, various United States arms packages, and the naval confrontation in the Persian Gulf. Additional details on Saudi defense allocations and the arms buildup through the early 1980s are presented in Nadav Safran's *Saudi Arabia: The Ceaseless Quest for Security. The Middle East,* published by the Congressional Quarterly in 1991, includes a concise discussion of military sales from the United States political perspective and a summary of events in the Persian Gulf crisis.

Limited treatment of the role played by Saudi Arabia in the gulf war can be found in the work on Operation Desert Storm by Norman Friedman, *Desert Victory,* and in James Blackwell's, *Thunder in the Desert,* and in an article by David A. Fulghum in *Aviation Week and Space Technology.*

The aggression of Iraq against Kuwait and the decline of the Soviet threat in the Middle East have reduced the relevance of most earlier analyses of the strategic situation in the region. Several studies are still pertinent to Saudi Arabia, however. In *Arms and Oil: U.S. Military Strategy and the Persian Gulf,* Thomas L. McNaugher considers how Saudi Arabia deals with both external and domestic security threats as part of a broader review of United States military interests in the region. *Saudi Arabia and the United States,* a report prepared in 1981 by the Congressional Research Service of the Library of Congress, is still a useful appraisal of Saudi external and domestic security concerns and the strategic interests shared by the two countries. In *Saudi Arabia: The West and the Security of the Gulf,* Mazher A. Hameed examines the geopolitical environment in the gulf and the range of threats to the United States and the West.

A readable account of earlier Saudi military history can be found in *The Kingdom: Arabia and the House of Saud* by Robert Lacey. Several aspects concerning the armed forces, military production, and the administration of justice are treated in *Saudi Arabia Unveiled* by Douglas F. Graham. The operation of the judicial system and the Saudi record on human rights are briefly examined in the annual

*Country Reports on Human Rights Practices* of the Department of State and annual reports by Amnesty International.

Much of the data in the foregoing chapter concerning the size, organization, and equipment of the Saudi armed forces are based on *The Military Balance,* published annually by the International Institute for Strategic Studies, and on *Jane's Fighting Ships.* (For further information and complete citations, see Bibliography.)

# Appendix

## Table 1. *Metric Conversion Coefficients and Factors*

| When you know | Multiply by | To find |
|---|---|---|
| Millimeters | 0.04 | inches |
| Centimeters | 0.39 | inches |
| Meters | 3.3 | feet |
| Kilometers | 0.62 | miles |
| Hectares (10,000 m²) | 2.47 | acres |
| Square kilometers | 0.39 | square miles |
| Cubic meters | 35.3 | cubic feet |
| Liters | 0.26 | gallons |
| Kilograms | 2.2 | pounds |
| Metric tons | 0.98 | long tons |
| | 1.1 | short tons |
| | 2,204 | pounds |
| Degrees Celsius (Centigrade) | 1.8 and add 32 | degrees Fahrenheit |

*Table 2. Students, Teachers, and Institutions by*
*Level of Education, 1990–91* [1]

| Level of Education | Males | Females | Total |
|---|---|---|---|
| Students [2] | | | |
| Primary ........................... | 919,949 | 768,934 | 1,688,883 |
| Intermediate ........................ | 279,770 | 216,594 | 496,364 |
| Secondary ........................... | 127,042 | 114,231 | 241,273 |
| Higher | | | |
| University colleges [3] ................. | 73,166 | 37,562 | 110,728 |
| Girls' colleges ..................... | 0 | 19,570 | 19,570 |
| Total higher ..................... | 73,166 | 57,132 | 130,298 |
| Total students .................. 1,399,927 | | 1,156,891 | 2,556,818 |
| | | | |
| Teachers | | | |
| Primary ........................... | 55,381 | 45,321 | 100,702 |
| Intermediate ........................ | 20,559 | 15,159 | 35,718 |
| Secondary .......................... | 8,195 | 8,058 | 16,253 |
| Higher | | | |
| University colleges [3] ................. | 7,251 | 1,407 | 8,658 |
| Girls' colleges ..................... | 135 | 979 | 1,114 |
| Total higher ..................... | 7,386 | 2,386 | 9,772 |
| Total teachers .................. | 91,521 | 70,924 | 162,445 |
| | | | |
| Institutions | | | |
| Primary ........................... | 4,806 | 3,574 | 8,380 |
| Intermediate ........................ | 1,766 | 1,057 | 2,823 |
| Secondary .......................... | 581 | 486 | 1,067 |
| Higher | | | |
| University colleges [3] ................. | 67 | 0 | 67 |
| Girls' colleges ..................... | 0 | 11 | 11 |
| Total higher ..................... | 67 | 11 | 78 |
| Total institutions ............... | 7,220 | 5,128 | 12,348 |

[1] Table includes only institutions under the Ministry of Education, the Ministry of Higher Education, and the Directorate General of Girls' Education.
[2] Female students are under the supervision of the Directorate General of Girls' Education except those female students at university colleges.
[3] Includes girls' sections.

Source: Based on information from Saudi Arabian Monetary Agency, *Annual Report,*
*1410–1411* [1990], Riyadh, 1991, 119, 121.

### Table 3. Health Facilities and Medical Personnel, 1987–88 Through 1990–91 *

|  | 1987–88 | 1988–89 | 1989–90 | 1990–91 |
|---|---|---|---|---|
| Hospitals ................ | 157 | 162 | 162 | 163 |
| Beds ..................... | 25,902 | 26,315 | 25,918 | 25,835 |
| Primary health-care centers ... | 1,438 | 1,477 | 1,639 | 1,668 |
| Physicians ............... | 11,326 | 11,940 | 12,617 | 12,959 |
| Nurses .................. | 25,986 | 27,169 | 28,266 | 29,124 |
| Pharmacists and technicians ... | 12,793 | 14,013 | 15,125 | 15,329 |

* Includes Ministry of Health facilities only. In 1990–91 other ministries and government bodies had thirty-one additional hospitals with 3,785 beds. In addition, sixty-four private hospitals had 6,479 hospital beds.

Source: Based on information from Saudi Arabian Monetary Agency, *Annual Report, 1410-1411* [1990], Riyadh, 1991, 125-26.

### Table 4. Government Budget, 1986–91 [1] (in millions of riyals) [2]

|  | 1986 | 1987 | 1988 | 1989 | 1990 | 1991 |
|---|---|---|---|---|---|---|
| **Revenues** |  |  |  |  |  |  |
| Oil ............... | 164,500 | 154,250 | 74,183 | 73,525 | n.a. | 85,910 |
| Other ............. | 49,600 | 45,750 | 32,743 | 31,775 | n.a. | 32,090 |
| Total revenues ..... | 214,100 | 200,000 | 106,926 | 105,300 | n.a. | 118,000 |
| **Expenditures** |  |  |  |  |  |  |
| Human resources development ....... | 30,413 | 24,533 | 23,689 | 23,388 | 24,004 | 25,869 |
| Transportation and communications .... | 22,173 | 14,497 | 10,904 | 9,493 | 8,516 | 8,006 |
| Economic resources development ....... | 12,533 | 9,081 | 6,615 | 5,888 | 5,039 | 4,719 |
| Health and social development ....... | 16,134 | 12,892 | 11,094 | 10,806 | 10,634 | 11,239 |
| Infrastructure development ....... | 9,833 | 6,924 | 4,299 | 3,555 | 2,807 | 2,586 |
| Municipal services .... | 17,063 | 11,890 | 8,110 | 7,017 | 5,430 | 5,520 |
| Defense and security .. | 79,892 | 63,956 | 54,226 | 50,080 | 47,812 | 48,689 |
| Public administration .. | 43,928 | 38,584 | 30,974 | 25,058 | 31,345 | 29,188 |
| Government lending institutions ........ | 17,500 | 9,300 | 3,590 | 590 | n.a. | n.a. |
| Local subsidies ....... | 10,529 | 8,343 | 6,145 | 5,325 | 4,873 | 7,184 |
| Total expenditures .. | 259,998 | 200,000 | 159,646 | 141,200 | 140,460 | 143,000 |
| BALANCE ........... | −45,898 | 0 | −52,720 | −35,900 | n.a. | −25,000 |

n.a.—not available.

[1] As of 1986, Saudi Arabia changed from a fiscal year based on the Islamic lunar calendar to a fiscal year beginning December 31 and ending December 30.

[2] For value of the riyal—see Glossary.

Source: Based on information from Saudi Arabian Monetary Agency, Research and Statistics Department, *Statistical Summary, 1410-1411* [1990], Riyadh, 1991, 123.

### Table 5. Gross Domestic Product by Sector, 1985–89
#### (in millions of constant 1970 riyals) *

| Sector | 1985 | 1986 | 1987 | 1988 | 1989 |
|---|---|---|---|---|---|
| Agriculture, forestry, and fishing ................. | 3,193 | 3,673 | 4,275 | 4,736 | 5,068 |
| Crude petroleum and natural gas .................... | 7,402 | 11,160 | 9,578 | 11,672 | 11,581 |
| Other mining and quarrying ... | 182 | 177 | 173 | 175 | 181 |
| Petroleum refining ........... | 2,383 | 2,481 | 3,191 | 3,673 | 3,369 |
| Other manufacturing ......... | 3,071 | 2,985 | 2,975 | 3,064 | 3,186 |
| Electricity, gas, and water ..... | 979 | 1,033 | 1,093 | 1,159 | 1,218 |
| Construction ............... | 4,259 | 3,732 | 3,627 | 3,446 | 3,428 |
| Wholesale and retail trade ..... | 8,417 | 8,097 | 7,956 | 7,877 | 7,798 |
| Transportation and communications ........... | 4,522 | 4,398 | 4,293 | 4,336 | 4,358 |
| Finance, real estate, and business services ........... | 4,833 | 4,084 | 3,995 | 4,066 | 4,115 |
| Community, social, and personal services ........... | 864 | 829 | 819 | 845 | 858 |
| Producers of government services ................. | 5,185 | 5,199 | 5,175 | 5,191 | 5,329 |
| Import duties .............. | 369 | 312 | 337 | 810 | 658 |
| Imputed bank service charges .. | -355 | -337 | -323 | -317 | -322 |
| TOTAL .................. | 45,304 | 47,823 | 47,164 | 50,733 | 50,825 |

* For value of the riyal—see Glossary.

Source: Based on information from Saudi Arabian Monetary Agency, Research and Statistics Department, *Statistical Summary, 1410-1411* [1990], Riyadh, 1991, 132-35.

### Table 6. Oil and Gas Reserves, Discoveries, and Production, 1986–90 [1]

| | 1986 | 1987 | 1988 | 1989 | 1990 |
|---|---|---|---|---|---|
| Oil [2] | | | | | |
| Reserves | | | | | |
| Saudi Arabia ............... | 167 | 167 | 252 | 258 | 259 |
| Divided Zone ............... | 3 | 3 | 3 | 3 | 2 |
| Total reserves ............. | 170 | 170 | 255 [3] | 261 [3] | 261 |
| Cumulative discoveries .......... | 223 | 225 | 226 | 233 | 235 |
| Gas [4] | | | | | |
| Reserves | | | | | |
| Saudi Arabia ............... | 142 | 177 | 180 | 181 | n.a. |
| Divided Zone ............... | 6 | 6 | 6 | 6 | n.a. |
| Total reserves ............. | 148 | 183 | 186 | 187 | n.a. |
| Discoveries ................. | 13.1 | 7.4 | 0.0 | 4.5 | 2.0 |

n.a.—not available.
[1] As published.
[2] In billions of barrels.
[3] Based on reestimation.
[4] In trillions of cubic feet.

Source: Based on Organization of the Petroleum Exporting Countries, *Annual Statistical Bulletin, 1991,* Vienna, 1991, 11.

### Table 7. Petroleum Exports, 1986-91
### (in millions of barrels per day)

|  | 1986 | 1987 | 1988 | 1989 | 1990 | 1991 |
|---|---|---|---|---|---|---|
| Crude oil .............. | 3.270 | 2.420 | 3.030 | 3.340 | 4.820 | 6.740 |
| Refined products |  |  |  |  |  |  |
| Base oils ........... | 0.028 | 0.015 | 0.038 | 0.011 | n.a. | n.a. |
| Gasoline ............ | 0.142 | 0.220 | 0.252 | 0.263 | n.a. | n.a. |
| Kerosene and jet fuel .... | 0.041 | 0.091 | 0.100 | 0.155 | n.a. | n.a. |
| Diesel oil ............ | 0.183 | 0.260 | 0.225 | 0.119 | n.a. | n.a. |
| Fuel oil ............. | 0.062 | 0.136 | 0.203 | 0.209 | n.a. | n.a. |
| Other ............... | 0.002 | 0.000 | 0.001 | 0.001 | n.a. | n.a. |
| Total refined products .. | 0.458 | 0.722 | 0.819 | 0.758 | 0.734 | 0.612 |
| Liquid petroleum gas ...... | 0.298 | 0.334 | 0.402 | 0.417 | 0.530 | 0.615 |
| TOTAL .............. | 4.026 | 3.476 | 4.251 | 4.515 | 6.084 | 7.967 |

n.a.—not available.

Source: Based on information from United States, Embassy in Riyadh, *1991 Oil Survey: Saudi Arabia,* July 1991, n.p.

### Table 8. Direction of Oil Exports by Region, 1986-90
### (in percentages)

| Region | 1986 | 1987 | 1988 | 1989 | 1990 |
|---|---|---|---|---|---|
| Asia ............... | 40.5 | 50.1 | 43.3 | 43.7 | 46.7 |
| Western Europe ...... | 34.6 | 22.3 | 24.1 | 21.8 | 18.4 |
| North America ....... | 18.6 | 21.6 | 26.0 | 29.9 | 27.2 |
| Latin America ........ | 5.7 | 4.4 | 4.6 | 2.7 | 3.7 |
| Africa ............. | 0.6 | 1.6 | 2.0 | 1.9 | 4.0 |
| TOTAL ........... | 100.0 | 100.0 | 100.0 | 100.0 | 100.0 |

Source: Based on information from International Monetary Fund, *Saudi Arabia: Recent Economic Developments,* Washington, 1990, Table 25, 74.

### Table 9. Production of Major Crops, 1985-86 Through 1989-90
### (in thousands of tons)

| Crop | 1985–86 | 1986–87 | 1987–88 | 1988–89 | 1989–90 |
|---|---|---|---|---|---|
| Barley .................. | 120 | 154 | 285 | 331 | 362 |
| Citrus fruits .............. | 11 | 27 | 27 | 35 | 35 |
| Dates .................. | 457 | 503 | 514 | 518 | 520 |
| Eggplant ................ | 39 | 37 | 65 | 83 | 83 |
| Grapes ................. | 83 | 86 | 93 | 96 | 100 |
| Sorghum ................ | 43 | 117 | 126 | 163 | 200 |
| Tomatoes ............... | 327 | 427 | 401 | 437 | 463 |
| Watermelons ............. | 364 | 420 | 428 | 455 | 461 |
| Wheat ................. | 2,290 | 2,649 | 3,267 | 3,285 | 3,464 |

Source: Based on information from Saudi Arabian Monetary Agency, Research and Statistics Department, *Statistical Summary, 1410-1411* [1990], Riyadh, 1991, 121; and Ministry of Finance and National Economy, Central Department of Statistics, *Statistical Yearbook, 1408* [1988], Riyadh, n.d., 591.

Table 10. *Direction of Trade with Industrialized and Developing Countries, 1987–91*
(in millions of United States dollars)

|  | 1987 | 1988 | 1989 | 1990 | 1991 |
|---|---|---|---|---|---|
| **Exports** | | | | | |
| Industrialized countries | | | | | |
| Japan | 5,128 | 4,106 | 4,943 | 8,427 | 9,174 |
| United States | 4,477 | 5,265 | 7,284 | 10,652 | 11,049 |
| West Germany | 307 | 556 | 283 | 263 | 1,137 |
| Other | 4,985 | 5,459 | 6,163 | 8,754 | 12,971 |
| Total industrialized countries | 14,897 | 15,386 | 18,673 | 28,096 | 34,331 |
| | | | | | |
| Developing countries | | | | | |
| Asia | 4,290 | 4,711 | 5,157 | 8,475 | 10,887 |
| Middle East | 1,948 | 1,996 | 2,498 | 4,089 | 3,008 |
| Latin America | 907 | 948 | 660 | 1,478 | 1,375 |
| Africa | 316 | 420 | 396 | 1,121 | 988 |
| Other | 194 | 201 | 305 | 1,092 | 1,072 |
| Total developing countries | 7,655 | 8,276 | 9,016 | 16,255 | 17,330 |
| | | | | | |
| Unallocated | 50 | 75 | 52 | 65 | 58 |
| | | | | | |
| Total exports | 22,602 | 23,737 | 27,741 | 44,416 | 51,719 |
| **Imports** | | | | | |
| Industrialized countries | | | | | |
| Japan | 3,470 | 3,483 | 3,014 | 3,689 | 4,292 |
| United States | 3,069 | 3,540 | 3,843 | 4,022 | 7,229 |
| West Germany | 1,556 | 1,575 | 1,324 | 1,774 | 2,656 |
| Other | 6,873 | 7,229 | 7,559 | 9,068 | 13,154 |
| Total industrialized countries | 14,968 | 15,827 | 15,740 | 18,553 | 27,331 |
| | | | | | |
| Developing countries | | | | | |
| Asia | 3,303 | 3,555 | 3,140 | 3,154 | 4,845 |
| Middle East | 710 | 889 | 964 | 915 | 831 |
| Latin America | 302 | 426 | 337 | 388 | 435 |
| Africa | 202 | 285 | 184 | 376 | 433 |
| Other | 501 | 645 | 634 | 523 | 549 |
| Total developing countries | 5,018 | 5,800 | 5,259 | 5,356 | 7,093 |
| | | | | | |
| Unallocated | 124 | 157 | 154 | 160 | 163 |
| | | | | | |
| Total imports | 20,110 | 21,784 | 21,153 | 24,069 | 34,587 |

Source: Based on information from International Monetary Fund, *Direction of Trade Statistics Yearbook, 1992,* Washington, 1992, 341–42.

*Table 11. Balance of Payments, 1986–90*
(in millions of United States dollars)

| | 1986 | 1987 | 1988 | 1989 | 1990 |
|---|---|---|---|---|---|
| Merchandise exports ..... | 20,125 | 23,138 | 24,315 | 28,299 | 44,283 |
| Merchandise imports ..... | 17,066 | 18,283 | 19,805 | 19,231 | 21,490 |
| Trade balance ........ | 3,059 | 4,855 | 4,510 | 9,068 | 22,793 |
| | | | | | |
| Service exports ......... | 13,944 | 13,114 | 12,809 | 13,012 | 12,502 |
| Service imports ......... | 20,995 | 19,506 | 15,651 | 20,766 | 23,365 |
| Service balance ....... | −7,051 | −6,392 | −2,842 | −7,754 | −10,863 |
| | | | | | |
| Official transfers, net .... | −3,000 | −3,300 | −2,499 | −2,200 | −4,401 |
| Private transfers, net ..... | −4,804 | −4,935 | −6,510 | −8,342 | −11,637 |
| | | | | | |
| Unrequited transfers, net .............. | −7,804 | −8,235 | −9,009 | −10,542 | −16,038 |
| | | | | | |
| Current account balance .. | −11,796 | −9,772 | −7,341 | −9,228 | −4,108 |
| | | | | | |
| Direct foreign investment .......... | 967 | −1,175 | −328 | −312 | n.a. |
| Portfolio foreign investment ........ | 3,451 | 6,150 | 3,057 | −1,786 | n.a. |
| Direct foreign investment, net .............. | 4,418 | 4,975 | 2,729 | −2,098 | n.a. |
| | | | | | |
| Bank deposits ......... | −4,561 | −1,423 | −2,216 | 473 | −2,417 |
| Other sectors .......... | 4,319 | 8,862 | 5,308 | 7,346 | 1,147 |
| Other capital, net ..... | −242 | 7,439 | 3,092 | 7,819 | −1,270 |
| | | | | | |
| Capital account balance .. | 4,176 | 12,414 | 5,821 | 5,721 | −1,270 |
| | | | | | |
| Change in reserves (minus sign means increase) ... | 7,620 | −2,642 | 1,520 | 3,507 | 5,378 |

n.a.—not available.

Source: Based on information from International Monetary Fund, *International Financial Statistics Yearbook, 1992,* Washington, 1992, 610–11; and Saudi Arabian Monetary Agency, Research and Statistics Department, *Statistical Summary, 1410–1411* [1990], Riyadh, 1991, 120.

## Table 12. *Major Equipment, Royal Saudi Land Forces, 1992*

| Type and Description | Country of Origin | Estimated in Inventory |
|---|---|---|
| **Tanks** | | |
| AMX–30 ........................... | France | 300 |
| M–60A3 ............................ | United States | 400 |
| | | |
| **Armored vehicles** | | |
| AML 60/90 armored cars ................ | France | 235 |
| AMX–10P infantry fighting vehicles ........ | –do– | 500 + |
| M–2 Bradley infantry fighting vehicles ....... | United States | 200 |
| M–113 personnel carriers ................. | –do– | 1,700 |
| EE–11 Urutu personnel carriers ............ | Brazil | 30 |
| Panhard M–3 personnel carriers ............ | France | 150 |
| | | |
| **Self-propelled artillery** | | |
| M–109A1B/A2 155mm howitzers ........... | United States | 100 |
| GCT 155mm howitzers .................. | France | 60 |
| | | |
| **Towed artillery** | | |
| M–56 pack 105mm ...................... | United States | 24 |
| M–101/102 105mm (in store) .............. | –do– | 40 |
| M–198 155mm ........................ | –do– | 90 |
| | | |
| **Multiple rocket launchers** | | |
| ASTROS II 180mm .................... | Brazil | 70 |
| | | |
| **Mortars** | | |
| 107mm, 120mm ........................ | various | 400 |
| | | |
| **Antitank guided weapons** | | |
| TOW, self-propelled .................... | United States | 200 |
| M–47 Dragon .......................... | Britain | n.a. |
| HOT, self-propelled .................... | France | 90 |
| | | |
| **Recoilless rifles** | | |
| 75mm, 84mm, 90mm, 106mm ............. | various | n.a. |
| | | |
| **Surface-to-surface missile launchers** | | |
| CSS–2 intermediate range ................ | China | 30 |
| | | |
| **Surface-to-air missiles** | | |
| Crotale .............................. | France | n.a. |
| Stinger .............................. | United States | n.a. |
| Redeye .............................. | –do– | 500 |
| | | |
| **Helicopters** | | |
| UH–60 Blackhawk (transport) ............. | –do– | 17 |
| SA–365N medical evacuation .............. | France | 6 |

n.a.—not available.

Source: Based on information from *The Military Balance, 1992–1993,* London, 1992, 120.

### Table 13. Major Equipment, Royal Saudi Air Force, 1992

| Type and Description | Country of Origin | Estimated in Inventory |
|---|---|---|
| Fighter-ground attack aircraft | | |
| F–5E Tiger II ..................... | United States | 52 |
| Tornado IDS ..................... | Britain | 45 |
| | | |
| Air defense aircraft | | |
| F–15C Eagle ..................... | United States | 78 |
| Tornado ADV ..................... | Britain | 24 |
| | | |
| Reconnaissance aircraft | | |
| RF–5E Tiger ..................... | United States | 10 |
| | | |
| Transport aircraft | | |
| C–130E/H Hercules ............... | –do– | 41 |
| L–100–30HS (hospital) ............. | –do– | 5 |
| CASA C–212 ..................... | Spain/Indonesia | 35 |
| | | |
| Airborne early warning | | |
| E–3A .......................... | United States | 5 |
| | | |
| Jet fighter conversion trainer | | |
| F–5B/F ......................... | –do– | 35 |
| F–15D .......................... | –do– | 20 |
| | | |
| Training | | |
| BAC–167 Strikemaster ............. | Britain | 32 |
| Hawk Mk 60 ..................... | –do– | 30 |
| Pilatus PC-9 ..................... | Britain/Switzerland | 30 |
| | | |
| Tankers | | |
| KE–3A ......................... | United States | 8 |
| KC–130H ....................... | –do– | 7 |
| | | |
| Helicopters | | |
| AB–205 Iroquois .................. | Italy | 8 |
| AB–206B Jet Ranger ............... | –do– | 13 |
| AB–212 Agusta ................... | –do– | 27 |
| KV–107 Kawasaki ................. | Japan | 7 |

Source: Based on information from *The Military Balance, 1992-193,* London, 1992, 121.

### Table 14. Major Weapons, Royal Saudi
### Air Defense Forces, 1992

| Type and Description | Country of Origin | Estimated in Inventory |
|---|---|---|
| Surface-to-air missile launchers | | |
| Improved Hawk ...................... | United States | 16 |
| Shahine (mounted on AMX–30SA) ......... | France | 17 |
| Shahine (static defense) ................ | –do– | 73 |
| | | |
| Antiaircraft guns | | |
| M–163 Vulcan 20mm, self-propelled ....... | United States | 92 |
| 30mm (mounted on AMX–30SA) .......... | France | 50 |
| Oerlikon-Buhrle, 35mm ................. | Switzerland | 128 |
| Bofors L–70 40mm (in store) ............. | Sweden | 150 |

Source: Based on information from *The Military Balance, 1992–1993,* London, 1992, 121.

*Table 15. Major Equipment, Royal Saudi Naval Forces, 1992*

| Type and Description | Origin | Number | Date Commissioned or Entered Service |
|---|---|---|---|
| **Frigates** | | | |
| Medina class (F-2000), 2,870 tons, Otomat missiles, 100mm gun ................. | France | 4 | 1985–86 |
| **Corvettes** | | | |
| Badr class (PCG-1), 870 tons, Harpoon missiles ........ | United States | 4 | 1980–83 |
| **Fast attack craft** | | | |
| As Siddiq (US 58-m), Harpoon missiles ............... | –do– | 9 | 1980–82 |
| Dammam (Jaguar) torpedo craft .................. | West Germany | 3 | 1969 |
| **Mine warfare** | | | |
| MSC-322 minesweepers ..... | United States | 4 | 1978–79 |
| Sandown class minesweepers .. | Britain | 3 * | 1991–93 |
| **Amphibious** | | | |
| Landing craft, utility (LCU) 610 type ................. | United States | 4 | n.a. |
| Landing craft, medium (LCM) | United States/ West Germany | 8 | n.a. |
| **Helicopters** | | | |
| AS-365N Dauphin (20 with antiship missiles, 4 search and air rescue) ............. | France | 24 | 1989–90 |
| AS-332 B/F Super Puma (6 with torpedoes, 6 with AM 39 Exocet missiles) ......... | –do– | 12 | n.a. |

*—being delivered.
n.a.—not available.

Source: Based on information from Jane's Information Group, *Jane's Fighting Ships, 1991-92*, Coulsdon, United Kingdom, 1991, 473-78; and *The Military Balance, 1992-1993*, London, 1992, 120-21.

### Table 16. Major Equipment, Saudi Arabian
### National Guard, 1992

| Type and Description | Country of Origin | Estimated in Inventory |
|---|---|---|
| Armored personnel carriers | | |
| V–150 Commando, wheeled .............. | United States | 1,100 |
| Towed artillery | | |
| M–102 105mm howitzers ................ | –do– | 30 |
| M–198 155mm howitzers ................ | –do– | 4 |
| Recoilless rifles | | |
| M40A1 106mm ...................... | –do– | n.a. |
| Antitank guided weapons | | |
| TOW missiles ........................ | –do– | n.a. |

n.a.—not available.
Source: Based on information from *The Military Balance, 1992–1993,* London, 1992, 121.

# Bibliography

## Chapter 1

Adams, Michael. *The Middle East.* New York: Facts on File, 1987.

"Ahmad b. Muhammad b. Hanbal." Pages 20-21 in H.A.R. Gibb and J.H. Kramers (eds.), *Shorter Encyclopaedia of Islam.* Ithaca: Cornell University Press, 1953.

Al-Farsy, Fouad. *Saudi Arabia: A Case Study in Development.* London: Kegan Paul International, 1982.

Almana, Mohammed. *Arabia Unified: A Portrait of Ibn Saud.* London: Hutchinson-Benham, 1980.

Al-Rashid, Ibrahim. *Documents on the History of Saudi Arabia.* (3 vols.) Salisbury, North Carolina: Documentary Publications, 1976.

Anthony, John Duke. "The Gulf Cooperation Council," *Journal of South Asian and Middle Eastern Studies,* 5, No. 4, Summer 1982, 3-18.

Arjomand, Said. *The Shadow of God and the Hidden Imam.* Chicago: University of Chicago Press, 1984.

Ayoob, Mohammed (ed.). *The Politics of Islamic Reassertion.* New York: St. Martin's Press, 1981.

Bartel, G. *Geschichte der Araber.* Berlin: Akademie, 1983.

Beaumont, Peter, G.H. Blake, and J.M. Wagstaff. *The Middle East: A Geographical Study.* New York: Wiley, 1976.

Beling, Willard A. (ed.). *King Faisal and the Modernisation of Saudi Arabia.* Boulder, Colorado: Westview Press, 1980.

Berque, Jacques. *The Arabs.* (Trans., Jean Stewart.) New York: Praeger, 1964.

Bidwell, Robin. *Travellers in Arabia.* London: Hamlyn, 1976.

Birks, J.S., and C.A. Sinclair. *Arab Manpower: The Crisis of Development.* New York: St. Martin's Press, 1980.

Bloomfield, Lincoln P., Jr. "Saudi Arabia Faces the 1980s: Saudi Security Problems and American Interests," *Fletcher Forum,* Summer 1981, 243-77.

Bosworth, C. Edmund. "The Nomenclature of the Persian Gulf." Pages xvii-xxxvi in Alvin J. Cottrell (ed.), *The Persian Gulf States: A General Survey.* Baltimore: Johns Hopkins University Press, 1980.

Brent, Peter. *Far Arabia: Explorers of the Myth.* London: Weidenfeld and Nicolson, 1977.

Brown, Edward Hoaglann. *The Saudi Arabia-Kuwait Neutral Zone.* Beirut: Middle East Research and Publishing Center, 1963.

Brown, L. Carl (ed.). *From Medina to Metropolis: Heritage and Change in the Near Eastern City.* Princeton: Darwin Press, 1973.

Buchan, James. *Jeddah Old and New.* London: Stacey, 1980.

Chapman, Richard A. "Administrative Reform in Saudi Arabia," *Journal of Administration Overseas* [London], 13, No. 2, April 1974, 332–47.

Cheneb, Mohammed ben. "Ibn Taimiya." Pages 151–52 in H.A.R. Gibb and J.H. Kramers (eds.), *Shorter Encyclopaedia of Islam.* Ithaca: Cornell Univesity Press, 1953.

Cole, Donald Powell. "The Enmeshment of Nomads in Saudi Arabian Society: The Case of Al Murrah." Pages 113–28 in Cynthia Nelson (ed.), *The Desert and the Sown: Nomads in the Wider Society.* (Research Series, No. 21.) Berkeley: Institute of International Studies, University of California, 1973.

_____. *Nomads of the Nomads: The Al Murrah Bedouin of the Empty Quarter.* Chicago: Aldine, 1975.

Cottrell, Alvin J. "Islam," *National Defense,* 68, No. 389, July–August, 1983, 36–39.

Cottrell, Alvin J. (ed.). *The Persian Gulf States: A General Survey.* Baltimore: Johns Hopkins University Press, 1980.

Crystal, Jill. *Oil and Politics in the Gulf: Rulers and Merchants in Kuwait and Qatar.* Cambridge: Cambridge University Press, 1990.

De Gaury, Gerald. *Faisal: King of Saudi Arabia.* New York: Praeger, 1966.

Dougherty, James E. "Religion and Law." Pages 281–313 in Alvin J. Cottrell (ed.), *The Persian Gulf States: A General Survey.* Baltimore: Johns Hopkins University Press, 1980.

Doughty, Charles Montague. *Travels in Arabia Deserta.* (2 vols.) New York: Dover, 1979.

Edens, David G. "The Anatomy of the Saudi Revolution," *International Journal of Middle East Studies,* 5, No. 1, January 1974, 50–64.

Eilts, Hermann F. "Social Revolution in Saudi Arabia," Pt. 1, *Parameters: The Journal of the Army War College,* 1, No. 1, Spring 1971, 4–18.

_____. "Social Revolution in Saudi Arabia," Pt. 2, *Parameters: The Journal of the Army War College,* 1, No. 2, Fall 1971, 22–33.

El Mallakh, Ragaei. *Saudi Arabia. Rush to Development: Profile of an Energy Economy and Development.* Baltimore: Johns Hopkins University Press, 1982.

Esposito, John L. *Islam: The Straight Path.* New York: Oxford University Press, 1991.

Fisher, Sidney Nettleton. *The Middle East.* New York: McGraw Hill, 1990.

Freedman, Robert O. *The Middle East after the Israeli Invasion of Lebanon.* Syracuse: Syracuse University Press, 1986.

Gibb, H.A.R. "''Arabiyya." Page 386 in H.A.R. Gibb et al. (eds.), *Encyclopaedia of Islam,* 1. (2d ed.) Leiden, Netherlands: Brill, 1960.

Gibb, H.A.R., et al. (eds.). *Encyclopaedia of Islam,* 1. (2d ed.) Leiden, Netherlands: Brill, 1960.

_____. *Encyclopaedia of Islam,* 2. (2d ed.), Leiden: E.J. Brill, 1965.

Goldberg, Jacob. *The Foreign Policy of Saudi Arabia.* Cambridge: Harvard University Press, 1986.

_____. "How Stable Is Saudi Arabia?" *Washington Quarterly,* 5, No. 2, Spring 1982, 157–63.

Habib, John S. *Ibn Sa'ud's Warriors of Islam: The Ikhwan of Najd and Their Role in the Creation of the Sa'udi Kingdom, 1910–1930.* Leiden, Netherlands: Brill, 1978.

Halliday, Fred. *Arabia Without Sultans: A Political Survey of Instability in the Arab World.* New York: Vintage Books, 1975.

Hawley, Donald. *The Trucial States.* New York: Twayne, 1970.

Haykal, Mohamed Hassanein. *The Life of Muhammad.* Indianapolis: American Trust, 1976.

Helms, Christine Moss. *The Cohesion of Saudi Arabia: Evolution of Political Identity.* Baltimore: Johns Hopkins University Press, 1981.

Hitti, Philip K. *History of the Arabs.* London: Macmillan, 1956.

Hodgson, Marshall. *The Venture of Islam.* (3 vols.) Chicago: University of Chicago Press, 1974.

Holden, David, and Richard Johns. *The House of Saud: The Rise and Rule of the Most Powerful Dynasty in the Arab World.* New York: Holt, Rinehart, and Winston, 1981.

Holt, P.M., Ann K.S. Lambton, and Bernard Lewis (eds.). *The Cambridge History of Islam, 1: The Central Islamic Lands.* Cambridge: Cambridge University Press, 1970.

*The Holy Qur'an.* (Trans., Abdallah Yusuf Ali.) Brentwood, Maryland: Amana, 1989.

Hopwood, Derek (ed.). *The Arabian Peninsula: Society and Politics.* Totowa, New Jersey: Rowman and Littlefield, 1972.

Hourani, Albert. *A History of the Arab Peoples.* Boston: Harvard University Press, 1991.

Howarth, David. *A Desert King: Ibn Saud and His Arabia.* New York: McGraw-Hill, 1964.

Humphreys, R. Stephen. "Islam and Political Values in Saudi Arabia, Egypt, and Syria," *Middle East Journal,* 33, No. 1, Winter 1979, 1–19.

Hurgronje, C. Snouck. *Mekka in the Latter Part of the 19th Century.* London: Luzac, 1931.

Kilidor, A.R. "The Arabian Peninsula in Arab and Power Politics." Pages 145–59 in Derek Hopwood (ed.), *The Arabian Peninsula: Society and Politics.* Totowa, New Jersey: Rowman and Littlefield, 1972.

Knauerhase, Ramon. "Saudi Arabia: Fifty Years of Economic Change," *Current History,* 82, No. 480, January 1983, 19–23.

Korany, Bahgat. *The Foreign Policies of Arab States.* Boulder, Colorado: Westview Press, 1984.

Koury, Envery M. *The Saudi Decision-Making Body: The House of al-Saud.* Hyattsville, Maryland: Institute of Middle Eastern and North African Affairs, 1978.

Kraft, Joseph. "Letter from Saudi Arabia," *New Yorker,* July 4, 1983, 41–59.

Lacey, Robert. "How Stable Are the Saudis?" *New York Times Magazine,* November 8, 1981, 35–40.

_____. *The Kingdom: Arabia and the House of Saud.* New York: Harcourt Brace Jovanovich, 1982.

Lancaster, William. *The Rwala Bedouin Today.* Cambridge: Cambridge University Press, 1981.

Lebkicker, Roy, George Rentz, and Max Steineke. *The Arabia of Ibn Saud.* New York: Moore, 1952.

Lees, Brian. *A Handbook of the Al Sa'ud Ruling Family of Saudi Arabia.* London: Royal Genealogies, 1980.

Lewis, Bernard. *The Arabs in History.* New York: Harper and Row, 1960.

_____. *Origins of Isma'ilism.* Cambridge: Heffer, 1940.

Lindsey, Gene. *Saudi Arabia.* New York: Hippocrene Books, 1991.

Lippman, Thomas W. *Islam: Politics and Religion in the Muslim World* (Headline Series, No. 258.) New York: Foreign Policy Association, 1982.

Looney, Robert E. *Saudi Arabia's Development Potential: Application of an Islamic Growth Model.* Lexington, Massachusetts: Lexington Books, 1982.

MacDonald, Charles G. *Iran, Saudi Arabia, and the Law of the Sea: Political Interaction and Legal Development in the Persian Gulf.* Westport, Connecticut: Greenwood Press, 1980.

MacIntyre, Ronald R. "Saudi Arabia." Pages 9–29 in Mohammed Ayoob (ed.), *The Politics of Islamic Reassertion.* New York: St. Martin's Press, 1981.

Magnus, Ralph H. "Societies and Social Change in the Persian Gulf." Pages 369–413 in Alvin J. Cottrell (ed.), *The Persian Gulf States: A General Survey.* Baltimore: Johns Hopkins University Press, 1980.

Makdisi, George. "Ibn Taimiya: A Sufi of the Qadariya Order," *American Journal of Arab Studies*, 1, 1973, 118–29.

Malone, Joseph J. "America and the Arabian Peninsula: The First Two Hundred Years," *Middle East Journal*, 30, No. 3, Summer 1976, 406–24.

_____. "Security: A Priority for Gulf Council," *Journal of Defense and Diplomacy*, 1, No. 6, September 1983, 15–17.

Memon, Muhammad. *Ibn Taimiya's Struggle Against Popular Religion.* The Hague: Mouton, 1976.

*The Middle East and North Africa, 1991.* London: Europa, 1990.

Miller, Aaron David. *Search for Security: Saudi Arabian Oil and American Foreign Policy, 1939–1949.* Chapel Hill: University of North Carolina Press, 1980.

Monroe, Elizabeth. "Faisal: The End of an Era," *Middle East International* [London], No. 47, May 1975, 11–13.

Mortimer, Edward. *Faith and Power: The Politics of Islam.* New York: Random House, 1981.

Niblock, Tim (ed.). *State, Society, and Economy in Saudi Arabia.* New York: St. Martin's Press, 1982.

Penrose, Edith. "Oil and State in Arabia." Pages 271–85 in Derek Hopwood (ed.), *The Arabian Peninsula: Society and Politics.* Totowa, New Jersey: Rowman and Littlefield, 1972.

Pesce, Angelo. *Makkah A Hundred Years Ago.* London: Immel, 1986.

Peters, F.E. *Allah's Commonwealth.* New York: Simon and Schuster, 1973.

Philby, H. St. John. *Forty Years in the Wilderness.* London: Hale, 1957.

_____. *Sa'udi Arabia.* London: Benn, 1955.

Powell, William. *Saudi Arabia and Its Royal Family.* Secaucus, New Jersey: Lyle Stuart, 1982.

Quandt, William B. "Saudi Arabia: Security and Foreign Policy in the 1980s," *Middle East Insight*, 2, No. 2, January–February 1982, 25–30.

Rentz, George. "Dir'iyya." Pages 320–22 in H.A.R Gibb et al. (eds.), *Encyclopaedia of Islam*, 2. (2d ed.) Leiden, Netherlands: Brill, 1965.

_____. "Djazirat al-'Arabiya." Pages 551–54 in H.A.R Gibb et al. (eds.), *Encylopaedia of Islam*, 1. (2d ed.) Leiden, Netherlands: Brill, 1960.

_____. "Saudi Arabia." Pages 115–25 in J.H. Thompson and R.C. Reischauer (eds.), *Modernization of the Arab World.* Princeton: Van Nostrand, 1966.

_____. "Saudi Arabia: The Islamic Island," *Journal of International Affairs*, 19, No. 1, 1965, 77–86.

_____. "Wahhabism and Saudi Arabia." Pages 54–66 in Derek Hopwood (ed.), *The Arabian Peninsula: Society and Politics.* Totowa, New Jersey: Rowman and Littlefield, 1972.

Rihani, Amin. *Around the Coasts of Arabia.* Delmar: Caravan Books, 1983.

Rizvi, Hasan Askari. "Gulf Cooperation Council," *Pakistan Horizon* [Karachi], 35, No. 2, 1982, 10–28.

Rugh, William A. "Emergence of a New Middle Class in Saudi Arabia," *Middle East Journal,* 27, No. 1, Winter 1973, 9–20.

Ruthven, Malise. *Islam in the World.* Oxford: Oxford University Press, 1984.

Sabini, John. *Armies in the Sand: The Struggle for Mecca and Medina.* London: Thames and Hudson, 1981.

Saudi Arabia. Central Planning Organization, *Development Plan, 1395–1400 (1975–1980).* Springfield, Virginia: National Technical Information Service, 1976.

Savory, Roger M. "A.D. 600–1800." Pages 14–40 in Alvin J. Cottrell (ed.), *The Persian Gulf States: A General Survey.* Baltimore: Johns Hopkins University Press, 1980.

_____. "The Ancient Period." Pages 3–13 in Alvin J. Cottrell (ed.), *The Persian Gulf States: A General Survey.* Baltimore: Johns Hopkins University Press, 1980.

Schacht, Joseph. *An Introduction to Islamic Law.* Oxford: Clarendon Press, 1964.

Shahid, Irfan. "Pre-Islamic Arabia." Pages 3–29 in P.M. Holt, Ann K.S. Lambton, and Bernard Lewis (eds.), *The Cambridge History of Islam, 1: The Central Islamic Lands.* London: Cambridge University Press, 1970.

Shaw, John A., and David E. Long. *Saudi Arabian Modernization: The Impact of Change on Stability,* 10. (Washington Papers, No. 89.) Washington: Praeger, with the Center for Strategic and International Studies, Georgetown University, 1982.

Tetreault, Mary Ann. *The Organization of Arab Petroleum Exporting Countries: History, Policies and Prospects.* Westport, Connecticut: Greenwood Press, 1981.

Thesiger, Wilfred. *Arabian Sands.* New York: Dutton, 1959.

Thompson, J.H., and R.C. Reischauer (eds.). *Modernization of the Arab World.* Princeton: Van Nostrand, 1966.

Troeller, Gary. *The Birth of Saudi Arabia: Britain and the Rise of the House of Sa'ud.* London: Cass, 1976.

Voll, John Obert. *Islam: Continuity and Change in the Modern World.* Boulder, Colorado: Westview Press, 1982.

Ward, Phillip. *Ha'il: Oasis City of Saudi Arabia.* New York: Oleander Press, 1983.

Watt, W. Montgomery. "Muhammad." Pages 30–56 in P.M. Holt, Ann K.S. Lambton, and Bernard Lewis (eds.), *The Cambridge History of Islam, 1: The Central Islamic Lands.* London: Cambridge University Press, 1970.

_____. *Muhammad: Prophet and Statesman.* London: Oxford University Press, 1961.

Winder, R. Bayly. *Saudi Arabia in the Nineteenth Century.* New York: St. Martin's Press, 1961.

Wright, Robin. *Sacred Rage: The Wrath of Militant Islam.* New York: Touchstone, 1986.

# Chapter 2

Abu-Lughod, Lila. *Veiled Sentiments: Honor and Poetry in a Bedouin.* Berkeley: University of California Press, 1988.

Al-Baadi, Hamad. "Social Change, Education, and the Roles of Women in Arabia." (Ph.D. dissertation.) Palo Alto: Stanford University, 1982.

Alireza, Marianne. *At the Drop of a Veil.* Boston: Houghton Mifflin, 1971.

Al-Khuli, Muhammad Ali. *The Light of Islam.* Riyadh: Al Farazdak Press, 1981.

Almana, Aisha Mohamed. "Economic Development and its Impact on the Status of Women in Saudi Arabia." (Ph.D. dissertation.) Boulder: University of Colorado, 1981.

Altorki, Soraya. "Family Organization and Women's Power in Urban Saudi Arabian Society," *Journal of Anthropological Research,* 33, Fall 1977, 277–87.

_____. *Women in Saudi Arabia: Ideology and Behavior among the Elite.* New York: Columbia University Press, 1986.

Altorki, Soraya, and Donald Powell Cole. *Arabian Oasis City: The Transformation of 'Unayzah.* Austin: University of Texas Press, 1989.

_____. "Expatriate Workers in Saudi Arabia: Cornerstone of Development or By-Product of a Boom?" (Paper presented at annual meeting of Middle East Studies Association, San Antonio, Texas, 1990.)

_____. "Was Arabia Tribal?" (Paper presented at annual meeting of Middle East Studies Association, San Antonio, Texas, 1990.)

Al-Umar, Abd ar Rahman ibn Hamad. *Islam, the Religion of Truth.* Riyadh: Al Farazdak Press, 1394 (1974).

Al-Yassini, Ayman. *Religion and State in the Kingdom of Saudi Arabia.* Boulder, Colorado: Westview Press, 1985.

Al-Zaid, Dr. Abdulla Mohamed. *Education in Saudi Arabia: A Model with a Difference.* (Trans., Omar Ali Afifi.) Jiddah: Tihama, 1981.

Amos, Deborah. *Lines in the Sand: Desert Storm and the Remaking of the Arab World.* New York: Simon and Shuster, 1992.

Anthony, John Duke. *Arab States of the Lower Gulf: People, Politics, Petroleum.* Washington: Middle East Institute, 1975.

Askari, Hossein. *Saudi Arabia's Economy: Oil and the Search for Economic Development.* (Contemporary Studies in Economic and Financial Analysis, No. 67.) Greenwich, Connecticut: Jai Press, 1990.

Attar, Ahmad Abd al-Ghafour. *Muhammad ibn Abd al-Wahhab.* (Trans., Rashid al Barrawi.) Mecca: Mecca Printing and Information, 1979.

Bahry, Louay. "The New Saudi Woman: Modernizing in an Islamic Framework," *Middle East Journal,* 36, No. 4, Autumn 1982, 502–15.

Beling, Willard A. (ed.). *King Faisal and the Modernisation of Saudi Arabia.* Boulder, Colorado: Westview Press, 1980.

Birks, J.S., and C.A. Sinclair. "International Migration in the Arab Region: Rapid Growth, Changing Patterns, and Broad Implications," *Population Bulletin of the UN Economic Commission for Western Asia,* No. 17, December 1979.

_____. *Saudi Arabia into the '90s.* Durham, United Kingdom: Mountjoy Research Center, University of Durham, 1988.

Brent, Jeremy. *Far Arabia: Explorers of the Myth.* London: Weidenfeld and Nicolson, 1977.

Cole, Donald Powell. "Bedouin Life and Social Change in Saudi Arabia." Pages 128–49 in John B. Galaty and Philip C. Salzman (eds.), *Change and Development in Nomadic and Pastoral Societies.* Leiden, Netherlands: Brill, 1981.

_____. "The Enmeshment of Nomads in Saudi Arabian Society: The Case of Al Murrah." Pages 113–27 in Cynthia Nelson (ed.), *The Desert and the Sown: Nomads in the Wider Society.* (Research Studies, No. 21.) Berkeley: Institute for International Studies, University of California, 1973.

_____. *Nomads of the Nomads: The Al Murrah Bedouin of the Empty Quarter.* Chicago: Aldine, 1975.

_____. "Pastoral Nomads in a Rapidly Changing Economy: The Case of Saudi Arabia." Pages 106–20 in Tim Niblock (ed.), *Social and Economic Development in the Arab Gulf.* New York: St. Martin's Press, 1980.

Crystal, Jill. *Oil and Politics in the Gulf: Rulers and Merchants in Kuwait and Qatar.* Cambridge: Cambridge University Press, 1990.

_____. "State and Society in the Gulf." (Paper presented at Council on Foreign Relations, New York, January 1992.)

Day, Alan J. (ed.). *Border and Territorial Disputes.* Detroit: Gale Research, 1982.

Dickson, H.R.P. *The Arab of the Desert: Bedouin Life in Kuwait and Saudi Arabia.* London: Allen and Unwin, 1949.

Doughty, Charles Montague. *Travels in Arabia Deserta.* (2 vols.) New York: Dover, 1979.

Doumato, Eleanor Abdella. "Arabian Women: Religion, Work, and Cultural Ideology in the Arabian Peninsula." (Ph.D. dissertation.) New York: Columbia University, 1989.

_____. "Gender, Monarchy and National Identity in Saudi Arabia," *British Journal of Middle Eastern Studies* [London], 19, No. 1, 1992.

_____. "Women and the Stability of Saudi Arabia," *Middle East Report,* No. 171, July–August 1991, 34–37.

Ebrahim, Mohammed Hossein Saleh. "Problems of Nomad Settlement in the Middle East with Special Reference to Saudi Arabia." (Ph.D. dissertation.) Ithaca, New York: Cornell University, 1981.

Esposito, John L. *Islam: The Straight Path.* New York: Oxford University Press, 1991.

_____. *The Islamic Threat: Myth or Reality.* New York: Oxford University Press, 1992.

Fabietti, Ugo. "Sedentarisation as a Means of Detribalisation: Some Policies of the Saudi Arabian Government Towards the Nomads." Pages 186–97 in Tim Niblock (ed.), *State, Society, and Economy in Saudi Arabia.* New York: St. Martin's Press, 1982.

Habib, John S. *Ibn Sa'ud's Warriors of Islam: The Ikhwan of Najd and Their Role in the Creation of the Sa'udi Kingdom, 1910–1930.* Leiden, Netherlands: Brill, 1978.

Helms, Christine Moss. *The Cohesion of Saudi Arabia: Evolution of Political Identity.* Baltimore: Johns Hopkins University Press, 1981.

Hopkins, Nicholas. "Class and State in Rural Arab Communities." Pages 239–59 in Adeed Dawisha and I. Zartman (eds.), *Beyond Coercion: The Durability of the Arab State.* London: Croom Helm, 1988.

Hopwood, Derek (ed.). *The Arabian Peninsula: Society and Politics.* Totowa, New Jersey: Rowman and Littlefield, 1972.

Horsman, Paul V. *The Environmental Legacy of the Gulf War.* London: Greenpeace Publications, 1992.

Katakura, Motoko. *Bedouin Village.* Tokyo: University of Tokyo Press, 1977.

Khuri, Fuad. *Tribe and State in Bahrain: The Transformation of Social and Political Authority in an Arab State.* Chicago: University of Chicago Press, 1980.

Kostiner, Joseph. "Kuwait and Bahrain." Pages 116–29 in Shireen Hunter (ed.), *The Politics of Islamic Revivalism: Diversity and Unity.* Bloomington: Indiana University Press, 1988.

_____. "Transforming Dualities: Tribe and State Formation in Saudi Arabia." Pages 226–51 in Philip Khoury and Joseph Kostiner (eds.), *Tribes and State Formation in the Middle East.* Berkeley: University of California Press, 1990.

Lancaster, William. *The Rwala Bedouin Today.* Cambridge: Cambridge University Press, 1981.

Lawson, Fred. "Opposition Movements in the Arab Gulf States." (Paper presented at Council on Foreign Relations, New York, January 1992.)

Looney, Robert E. *Economic Development in Saudi Arabia: Consequences of the Oil Price Decline.* Greenwich, Connecticut: Jai Press, 1990.

Mernissi, Fatima. *Beyond the Veil: Male-Female Dynamics in Modern Muslim Society.* (Rev. ed.) London: Al Saqi Books, 1985.

Moghadam, Valentine M. *Development and Patriarchy: The Middle East and North Africa in Economic and Demographic Transition.* (WIDER Working Papers.) Helsinki: World Institute for Development Economics Research, 1992.

Mortimer, Edward. *Faith and Power: The Politics of Islam.* New York: Random House, 1986.

Nakhleh, Emile. *Bahrain, Political Development in a Modernizing Society.* Lexington, Massachusetts: Lexington Books, 1976.

Niblock, Tim (ed.). *State, Society, and Economy in Saudi Arabia.* New York: St. Martin's Press, 1982.

Ochsenwald, William. *Religion, Society, and the State in Arabia: The Hijaz under Ottoman Control, 1840–1908.* Columbus: Ohio State University Press, 1984.

_____. "Saudi Arabia." Pages 103–15 in Shireen Hunter (ed.), *The Politics of Islamic Revivalism.* Indianapolis: Indiana University Press, 1988.

Osama, Abdul Rahman. *The Dilemma of Development in the Arabian Peninsula.* London: Croom Helm, 1986.

Parssinen, Catherine. "The Changing Role of Women." Pages 145–70 in Willard A. Beling (ed.), *King Faisal and the Modernisation of Saudi Arabia.* Boulder, Colorado: Westview Press, 1980.

Philby, H. St. John. *Arabian Days: An Autobiography.* London: Hale, 1948.

_____. *Arabia of the Wahhabis*. London: Cass, 1977.

Piscatori, James P. (ed.). *Islamic Fundamentalisms and the Gulf Crisis*. (Fundamentalism Project, American Academy of Arts and Sciences.) Chicago: 1991.

Quandt, William B. *Saudi Arabia in the 1980s: Foreign Policy, Security, and Oil*. Washington: Brookings Institution, 1981.

Rentz, George. "Wahhabism and Saudi Arabia." Pages 54–66 in Derek Hopwood (ed.), *The Arabian Peninsula: Society and Politics*. Totowa, New Jersey: Rowman and Littlefield, 1972.

Richards, Alan, and John Waterbury. *A Political Economy of the Middle East: State, Class, and Economic Development*. Boulder, Colorado: Westview Press, 1990.

Saudi Arabia. Higher Committee for Educational Policy. *The Educational Policy in the Kingdom of Saudi Arabia*. (2d ed.) Riyadh: 1974.

_____. Ministry of Finance and National Economy. Central Department of Statistics. *Statistical Yearbook, 1410–1411* [1990]. Riyadh: 1991.

_____. Ministry of Planning. *Fifth Development Plan, 1410–1415* [1990–1995]. Riyadh: 1990.

Saudi Arabian Monetary Agency. *Annual Report, 1408–1409* [1988]. Riyadh: 1989.

_____. *Annual Report, 1409–1410* [1989]. Riyadh: 1990.

_____. *Annual Report, 1410–1411* [1990]. Riyadh: 1991.

Sebai, Zohair A. *The Health of the Family in a Changing Arabia: A Case Study of Primary Health Care*. Jiddah: Tihama, 1981.

Shamekh, Ahmed A. "Spatial Patterns of Bedouin Settlement in Al-Qasim Region of Saudi Arabia." (Ph.D. dissertation.) Lexington: University of Kentucky, 1975.

United Nations. Economic and Social Commission for Western Asia. *National Manpower in the Cooperation Council for the Arab States of the Gulf*. Baghdad: 1985.

_____. *The Sex and Age Distribution of Population*. New York: 1990.

United States. Department of State. *Country Reports on Human Rights Practices for 1991*. (Report submitted to United States Congress, 102d, 2d Session, Senate, Committee on Foreign Relations, and House of Representatives, Committee on Foreign Affairs.) Washington: GPO, 1992.

World Bank. *World Development Report*. New York: Oxford University Press, 1987.

Yamani, May. "Women in Saudi Arabia: Traditional Roles and Modern Aspirations." (Paper presented at Council on Foreign Relations, New York, January 1992.)

(Various issues of the following publication were also used in the preparation of this chapter: Cooperation Council for the Arab States of the Gulf, Secretariat General, *Economic Bulletin* [Riyadh].)

# Chapter 3

Abdeen, Adnan M., and Dale N. Shook. *The Saudi Financial System in the Context of Western and Islamic Finance.* New York: Wiley, 1984.

Abir, Mordechai. *Saudi Arabia in the Oil Era: Regime and Elites, Conflict and Collaboration.* Boulder, Colorado: Westview Press, 1988.

Ahrari, Mohamed. *OPEC: The Failing Giant.* Lexington: University Press of Kentucky, 1986.

Al-Jarbous, A. "Basic Industries Development by SABIC: Eight Years Experience," *Forum,* 56, 193–200.

Al-Naqeeb, Khaldoon. *Society and State in the Gulf and Arab Peninsula.* London: Routledge, 1990.

Amuzegar, J. *Oil Exporters' Economic Development in an Interdependent World* (Occasional Paper No. 18.) Washington: International Monetary Fund, 1983.

Anderson, Lisa. "Absolutism and the Resilience of Monarchy in the Middle East," *Political Science Quarterly,* 106, Spring 1991, 1–15.

Askari, H., and B. Dastmaltschi. *Saudi Arabia's Economy: Oil and the Search for Economic Development.* Greenwich, Connecticut: Jai Press, 1990.

Belgrave, Charles D. *Personal Column.* London: Hutchinson, 1960.

Bligh, Alexander. "The Saudi Religious Elite (Ulama) as Participant in the Political System of the Kingdom," *International Journal of Middle East Studies,* 17, No. 1, February 1985, 37–50.

Carter, J.R.L. *Merchant Families of Saudi Arabia.* London: Scorpion Books, 1984.

Caesar, J. "Saudi Dissent: Rumblings under the Throne," *Nation,* No. 251, December 17, 1990, 762–64.

Chaudhry, Kiren Aziz. "The Price of Wealth: Business and State in Labor Remittance and Oil Economies," *International Organization,* 43, Winter 1989, 101–45.

Conant, M. *Oil Prices and the Saudi-United States Connection.* Washington: Conant, 1991.

Crane, R. *Planning the Future of Saudi Arabia.* New York: Praeger, 1978.

Duguid, S. "A Biographical Approach to the Study of Social Change in the Middle East: Abdullah Tariki as a New Man," *International Journal of Middle East Studies,* 1, No. 1, 1970, 195–220.

El-Kuwaiz, Abdullah. "OPEC and the International Oil Market: The Age of Realism," *OPEC Review* [Oxford], 10, No. 4, Winter 1986, 393–408.

Fesharaki, F., and D.T. Issac. *The New Saudi Export Refineries: The Role of Shipping Costs in Determination of Product Prices and Competitiveness.* (OPEC Downstream Project.) Hawaii: East-West Center, 1983.

Field, Michael. *The Merchants: The Big Business Families of Saudi Arabia and the Gulf States.* Woodstock, New York: Overlook Press, 1985.

Helms, Christine Moss. *The Cohesion of Saudi Arabia: Evolution of Political Identity.* Baltimore: Johns Hopkins University Press, 1981.

Ibrahim, I. *Arab Resources: The Transformation of a Society.* London: Croom Helm, 1981.

International Monetary Fund. *Direction of Trade Statistics Yearbook, 1992.* Washington: 1992.

_____. *International Financial Statistics Yearbook, 1992.* Washington: 1992.

_____. *Saudi Arabia: Recent Economic Developments.* Washington: 1990.

Johany, A.D., M. Berne, and Wilson J. Mixon, Jr. *The Saudi Arabian Economy.* Baltimore: Johns Hopkins University Press, 1986.

Kerr, M.H., and El Sayed Yassin (eds.). *Rich and Poor States in the Middle East.* Boulder, Colorado: Westview Press, 1982.

Lackner, Helen. *The House Built on Sand: A Political Economy of Saudi Arabia.* London: Ithaca Press, 1978.

Lenczowski, G. *Middle East Oil in the Revolutionary Age.* Washington: American Enterprise Institute, 1976.

_____. "Tradition and Reform in Saudi Arabia," *Current History,* 52, No. 306, February 1967, 98–104.

Looney, Robert E. *Economic Development in Saudi Arabia: Consequences of the Oil Price Decline.* Greenwich, Connecticut: Jai Press, 1990.

_____. "Saudi Arabia's Development Strategy: Comparative Advantage versus Sustainable Development," *Orient,* March 1989, 75–96.

_____. "Saudi Arabia's Islamic Growth Model," *Journal of Economic Issues,* 16, No. 2, June 1982, 453–60.

Mattione, R.P. *OPEC's Investments and the International Financial System.* Washington: Brookings Institution, 1985.

Meir, S. *Strategic Implications of the New Oil Reality.* Boulder, Colorado: Westview Press, 1986.

Niblock, Tim (ed.). *State, Society, and Economy in Saudi Arabia.* New York: St. Martin's Press, 1982.

Organization of the Petroleum Exporting Countries. *Annual Statistical Bulletin, 1991.* Vienna: 1991.

Pressely, J.R. *A Guide to the Saudi Arabian Economy.* London: Macmillan, 1989.

Quandt, William B. *Saudi Arabia's Oil Policy.* Washington: Brookings Institution, 1982.

Richards, Alan, and John Waterbury. *A Political Economy of the Middle East: State, Class, and Economic Development.* Boulder, Colorado: Westview Press, 1990.

Rugh, W. "Emergence of a Middle Class in Saudi Arabia," *Middle East Journal,* 27, No. 1, Winter 1973, 7–20.

Ryan, M. *Health Services in the Middle East.* (Special Report No. 184.) London: Economist Intelligence Unit, 1984.

Salameh, Ghassane. "Political Power and the Saudi State," *Middle East Report,* No. 160, October 1989, 5–22.

Saleh, N.A. *The Emergence of Saudi Arabian Administrative Areas: A Study in Political Geography.* (Ph.D. dissertation.) University of Durham, United Kingdom, 1975.

Sampson, A. *The Seven Sisters: The Great Oil Companies and the World They Made.* New York: Viking Press, 1975.

Sandwick, J.A. (ed.). *The Gulf Cooperation Council: Moderation and Stability in an Interdependent World.* Boulder, Colorado: Westview Press, 1987.

Saudi Arabia. Ministry of Agriculture and Water. *Annual Report* (1980 through 1990). Riyadh: 1981 through 1991.

_____. Ministry of Finance and National Economy. Central Department of Statistics. *Foreign Trade Statistics* (annuals 1973 through 1990). Riyadh: 1974 through 1991.

_____. Ministry of Finance and National Economy. Central Department of Statistics. *Statistical Yearbook* (annuals 1973 through 1990). Riyadh: 1974 through 1991.

_____. Ministry of Information. *A Decade of Progress.* Riyadh: 1984.

_____. Ministry of Planning. *Achievement of the Development Plans, 1390–1403* [1970–83]. Riyadh: 1984.

_____. Ministry of Planning. *Fourth Development Plan, 1405–1410.* Riyadh: 1985.

Saudi Arabian Monetary Agency. Research and Statistics Department. *Statistical Summary, 1410–1411* [1990]. Riyadh: 1991.

"Saudi Arabian Petrochemical Exports: The EEC Protectionist Measures and Sabic's Prospects," *Arab Gulf Journal* [Exeter, United Kingdom], 1, 1985, 9–20.

Sayigh, Yusif. *The Arab Economy: Past Performance and Future Prospects.* Oxford: Oxford University Press, 1982.

Seymour, Ian. *OPEC: Instrument of Change.* New York: St. Martin's Press, 1981.

Shaw, John A., and David E. Long. *Saudi Arabian Modernization: The Impact of Change on Stability.* (Washington Papers, No. 89.) Washington: Praeger, with the Center for Strategic and International Studies, Georgetown University, 1982.

Troeller, Gary. *The Birth of Saudi Arabia: Britain and the Rise of the House of Sa'ud.* London: Cass, 1976.

Turner, L. *Middle East Industrialization: A Study of Saudi and Iranian Downstream Investments.* New York: Praeger, 1979.

Turner, Louis, and James Bedore. "Saudi and Iranian Petrochemicals and Oil Refining: Trade Warfare in the 1980s," *International Affairs* [London], 53, October 1977, 572–86.

_____. "Saudi Arabia: The Power of the Purse Strings," *International Affairs* [London], 54, July 1978, 405–20.

Turner, Louis, and V. Yorke. *European Interests and Gulf Oil.* Brookfield, Vermont: Gower, 1986.

United States. Department of Commerce. *Foreign Economic Trends Report: Saudi Arabia.* Washington: 1992.

_____. Embassy in Riyadh. *1991 Oil Survey: Saudi Arabia.* Riyadh: 1991.

Wells, D. *Saudi Arabian Development Strategy.* Washington: American Enterprise Institute for Public Policy, 1976.

Wenner, Manfred W. "Saudi Arabia: Survival of Traditional Elites." Pages 157–92 in Frank Tachau (ed.), *Political Elites and Political Development in the Middle East.* Cambridge: Schenkman, 1975.

(Various issues of the following publications were also used in the preparation of this chapter: *Aviation Week and Space Technology;* Bank for International Settlements, *International Banking and Financial Market Developments, Maturity and Sectoral Distribution of International Bank Lending* [Basel, Switzerland]; *Economist* [London]; *Energy Compass* [London]; *Euromoney* [London]; *Financial Times* [London]; Institute of International Finance, *Saudi Arabia Update and Report: Institutional Investor;* International Monetary Fund, *Balance of Payments Statistics, Direction of Trade Statistics,* and *International Financial Statistics; Middle East* [London]; *Middle East Economic Digest* [London]; *Middle East Economic Survey* [Nicosia, Cyprus]; Organisation for Economic Co-operation and Development, *Financing and External Debt of Developing Countries* and *Statistics on External Indebtness* [Paris]; *Petroleum Argus* [London]; *Petroleum Economist* [London]; *Petroleum Intelligence Weekly; Petroleum Quarterly and Update; Platts Oilgram Price Report;* Saudi Arabian Monetary Agency, *Quarterly Bulletin* [Riyadh]; and Wharton Econometric Forecasting, *Middle East Quarterly.*)

# Chapter 4

Abdeen, Adnan M., and Dale N. Shook. *The Saudi Financial System in the Context of Western and Islamic Finance.* New York: Wiley, 1984.

Abir, Mordechai. *Saudi Arabia in the Oil Era: Regime and Elites, Conflict and Collaboration.* Boulder, Colorado: Westview Press, 1988.

Abu-Dawood, Abdul-Razzak S., and P.P. Karan. *International Boundaries of Saudi Arabia.* New Delhi: Galaxy, 1990.

Al-Farsy, Fouad. *Modernity and Tradition: The Saudi Equation.* London: Kegan Paul, 1990.

_____. *Saudi Arabia: A Case Study in Development.* London: Kegan Paul, 1982.

Altorki, Soraya. *Women in Saudi Arabia: Ideology and Behavior among the Elite.* New York: Columbia University Press, 1986.

Altorki, Soraya, and Donald Powell Cole. *Arabian Oasis City: The Transformation of 'Unayzah.* Austin: University of Texas Press, 1989.

Al-Yassini, Ayman. *Religion and State in the Kingdom of Saudi Arabia.* Boulder, Colorado: Westview Press, 1985.

*Amnesty International Report, 1990.* New York: Amnesty International, 1990.

Aruri, Naseer H. "Disaster Area: Human Rights in the Arab World," *Middle East Report,* No. 149, November–December 1987, 7–15.

Bligh, Alexander. "The Saudi Religious Elite (Ulama) as Participant in the Political System of the Kingdom," *International Journal of Middle East Studies,* 17, No. 1, February 1985, 37–50.

Bonnenfant, Paul (ed.). *La péninsule arabique d'aujourd'hui.* Paris: Centre nationale de la recherche scientifique, 1982.

Burrowes, Robert. "Oil Strike and Leadership Struggle in South Yemen: 1986 and Beyond," *Middle East Journal,* 43, No. 3, Summer 1989, 437–54.

Carapico, Sheila. "Yemen: Unification and the Gulf War," *Middle East Report,* No. 170, May–June 1991, 26.

Dahlan, Ahmed Hassan (ed.). *Politics, Administration, and Development in Saudi Arabia.* Brentwood, Maryland: Amana, 1990.

Dawisha, Abdeed I. "Saudi Arabia's Search for Security," *Adelphi Papers.* (No. 158.) London: International Institute for Strategic Studies, 1979.

Doumato, Eleanor Abdella. "Women and the Stability of Saudi Arabia," *Middle East Report,* No. 171, July–August 1991, 34–37.

Field, Michael. *The Merchants: The Big Business Families of Saudi Arabia and the Gulf States.* Woodstock, New York: Overlook Press, 1985.

Halliday, Fred. *Arabia Without Sultans: A Political Survey of Instability in the Arab World.* New York: Vintage Books, 1975.

Heller, Mark, and Nadav Safran. *The New Middle Class and Regime Stability in Saudi Arabia.* (Harvard Middle East Papers, No. 3.) Cambridge: Harvard University Press, 1985.

Hooglund, Eric. "The Other Face of War," *Middle East Report,* No. 171, July–August 1991, 3–7, 10–12.

––––––. "The Persian Gulf." Pages 414–24 in Peter Schraeder (ed.), *Intervention into the 1990s: U.S. Foreign Policy in the Third World.* Boulder, Colorado: Rienner, 1992.

Hunter, Shireen T. "The Gulf Cooperation Council: Security in the Era Following the Iran-Contra Affair." Pages 145–66 in Robert O. Freedman (ed.), *The Middle East from the Iran-Contra Affair to the Intifada.* Syracuse: Syracuse University Press, 1990.

Huyette, Summer Scott. *Political Adaptation in Saudi Arabia: A Study of the Council of Ministers.* Boulder, Colorado: Westview Press, 1985.

Ingham, Bruce. *Bedouin of Northern Arabia: Traditions of the Al-Dhafir.* New York: Kegan Paul, 1986.

Johany, Ali D., Michel Berne, and J. Wilson Maxon. *The Saudi Arabian Economy.* Baltimore: Johns Hopkins University Press, 1986.

Kechichian, Joseph. "The Role of the Ulama in the Politics of an Islamic State: The Case of Saudi Arabia," *International Journal of Middle East Studies,* 18, No. 1, February 1986, 57–66.

Korany, Bahgat. "Defending the Faith Amid Change: The Foreign Policy of Saudi Arabia." Pages 310–53 in Bahgat Korany and Ali E. Hillal Dessouki (eds.), *The Foreign Policies of Arab States: The Challenge of Change.* (2d ed.) Boulder, Colorado: Westview Press, 1991.

Lacey, Robert. *The Kingdom: Arabia and the House of Saud.* New York: Harcourt Brace Jovanovich, 1982.

Lackner, Helen. *A House Built on Sand: A Political Economy of Saudi Arabia.* London: Ithaca Press, 1978.

Lawson, Fred. *Bahrain: The Modernization of Autocracy.* Boulder, Colorado: Westview Press, 1989.

Long, David E. *The United States and Saudi Arabia: Ambivalent Allies.* Boulder, Colorado: Westview Press, 1985.

Mackey, Sandra. *The Saudis: Inside the Desert Kingdom.* New York: Signet, 1990.

Middle East Watch. *Empty Reforms: Saudi Arabia's New Basic Laws.* New York: 1992.

Moon, Chung In. "Korean Contractors in Saudi Arabia: Their Rise and Fall," *Middle East Journal,* 40, No. 4, Autumn 1986, 614–33.

Nonneman, Gerd. *Iraq, the Gulf States, and the War: A Changing Relationship, 1980-1986 and Beyond.* Atlantic Highlands, New Jersey: Ithaca Press, 1986.

Norton, Augustus Richard. "Breaking Through the Wall of Fear in the Arab World," *Current History,* January 1992, 91, No. 561, 37-41.

Paul, Jim. "Insurrection at Mecca," *MERIP Reports,* No. 91, October 1980, 3-4.

Peterson, Erik. *The Gulf Cooperation Council: Search for Unity in a Dynamic Region.* Boulder, Colorado: Westview Press, 1988.

Quandt, William B. *Saudi Arabia in the 1980s: Foreign Policy, Security, and Oil.* Washington: Brookings Institution, 1981.

Ramazani, R.K. *Revolutionary Iran: Challenge and Response in the Middle East.* Baltimore: Johns Hopkins University Press, 1986.

Safran, Nadav. *Saudi Arabia: The Ceaseless Quest for Security.* Cambridge, Massachusetts: Belknap, 1985.

"Saudi Arabia." Pages 761-65 in *The Middle East and North Africa, 1991.* (37th ed.) London: Europa, 1990.

*Statesman's Year-Book, 1991-1992.* (Ed., Brian Hunter.) New York: St. Martin's Press, 1991.

Watkins, Eric. "Yemen: Oil Calms Troubled Waters," *Middle East* [London], No. 206, December 1991, 37-38.

Woodward, Peter. *Oil and Labor in the Middle East: Saudi Arabia and the Oil Boom.* New York: Praeger, 1988.

(Various issues of the following publications were also used in the preparation of this chapter: *Arabia Monitor; Arab News* [Jiddah]; Foreign Broadcast Information Service, *Daily Report: Middle East and South Asia; New York Times;* and *Washington Post.*)

## Chapter 5

Abir, Mordechai. *Saudi Arabia in the Oil Era: Regime and Elites, Conflict and Collaboration.* Boulder, Colorado: Westview Press, 1988.

———. "Saudi Security and Military Endeavor," *Jerusalem Quarterly* [Jerusalem], No. 33, Fall 1984, 79-94.

Amin, S.H. *Middle East Legal Systems.* Glasgow: Royston, 1985.

*Amnesty International Report, 1991.* New York: Amnesty International, 1991.

Apple, R.W., Jr. "For Saudis, a Ground War Will Be a Test of Will," *New York Times,* Febuary 17, 1991, I18.

Blackwell, James. *Thunder in the Desert: The Strategy and Tactics of the Persian Gulf War.* New York: Bantam, 1991.

Bloomfield, Lincoln P., Jr. "Commentary: Saudi Arabia's Security Problems in the 1980s." Pages 95–111 in Stephanie G. Neuman (ed.), *Defense Planning in Less-Industrialized States: The Middle East and South Asia.* Lexington, Massachusetts: Heath, 1984.

Cordesman, Anthony H. "Defense Planning in Saudi Arabia." Pages 67–93 in Stephanie G. Neuman (ed.), *Defense Planning in Less-Industrialized States: The Middle East and South Asia.* Lexington, Massachusetts: Heath, 1984.

_____. *The Gulf and the West: Strategic Relations and Military Realities.* Boulder, Colorado: Westview Press, 1988.

David, Peter. *Triumph in the Desert.* New York: Random House, 1991.

*Defense and Foreign Affairs Handbook, 1990–1991.* (Ed., Gregory R. Copley.) Alexandria, Virginia: International Media, 1990.

Defense Marketing Services. *DMS Market Intelligence Reports: Foreign Military Markets—Near East and Africa, 1989.* Alexandria, Virginia: Jane's Information Group, 1989.

Dyer, Gwynne, and John Keegan. "Saudi Arabia." Pages 502–13 in John Keegan (ed.), *World Armies.* Detroit: Gale Research, 1983.

Economist Intelligence Unit. *Country Profile: Saudi Arabia, 1991–92.* London: 1991.

_____. *Country Profile: Saudi Arabia, 1992–93.* London: 1992.

Friedman, Norman. *Desert Victory: The War for Kuwait.* Annapolis: Naval Institute Press, 1991.

Fulghum, David A. "Allied Air Power: Forward Controllers Back Arabs to Make Their Drive Succeed," *Aviation Week and Space Technology,* 134, No. 16, April 22, 1991, 71–73.

Graham, Douglas F. *Saudi Arabia Unveiled.* Dubuque, Iowa: Kendall/Hunt, 1991.

Grimmett, Richard F. *Conventional Arms Transfers to the Third World, 1983–1990.* Washington: Congressional Research Service, Library of Congress, 1991.

Hameed, Mazher A. *Arabia Imperilled: The Security Imperatives of the Arab Gulf States.* Washington: Middle East Assessments Group, 1986.

_____. *Saudi Arabia: The West and the Security of the Gulf.* Wolfeboro, New Hampshire: Croom Helm, 1986.

*Jane's Fighting Ships, 1991–92.* (Ed., Richard Sharpe.) Coulsdon, United Kingdom: Jane's Information Group, 1991.

Keegan, John (ed.). *World Armies.* Detroit: Gale Research, 1983.

Lacey, Robert. *The Kingdom: Arabia and the House of Saud.* New York: Harcourt Brace Jovanovich, 1982.

Long, David E. *The United States and Saudi Arabia: Ambivalent Allies.* Boulder, Colorado: Westview Press, 1985.

McNaugher, Thomas L. *Arms and Oil: United States Military Strategy and the Persian Gulf.* Washington: Brookings Institution, 1985.

Mansfield, Peter. *A History of the Middle East.* New York: Viking, 1991.

*The Middle East.* (7th ed.) (Ed., Daniel C. Diller.) Washington: Congressional Quarterly, 1991.

*Middle East Contemporary Survey, 1989.* (Ed., Ami Ayalon.) Boulder, Colorado: Westview Press, 1991.

*The Middle East Military Balance, 1988-1989.* (Eds., Shlomo Gazit and Zeev Eytan.) Boulder, Colorado: Westview Press for the Jaffee Center for Strategic Studies, 1989.

Middle East Watch. *Empty Reforms: Saudi Arabia's New Basic Law.* New York: Human Rights Watch, 1992.

*The Military Balance, 1990-1991.* London: International Institute for Strategic Studies, 1990.

*The Military Balance, 1991-1992.* London: International Institute for Strategic Studies, 1991.

*The Military Balance, 1992-1993.* London: International Institute for Strategic Studies, 1992.

Miller, Judith. "The Struggle Within," *New York Times Magazine,* March 10, 1991, 27-39, 46.

Minnesota Lawyers International Human Rights Committee. *Shame in the House of Saud: Contempt for Human Rights in the Kingdom of Saudi Arabia.* Minneapolis: 1992.

Morton, John F. "Saudi Arms Deal: Down, Not Out," *Defense and Diplomacy,* 9, Nos. 3-4, March-April 1991, 12-13.

Mostyn, Trevor (ed.). *Saudi Arabia: A MEED Practical Guide.* London: Middle East Economic Digest, 1983.

Neuman, Stephanie G. (ed.). *Defense Planning in Less-Industrialized States: The Middle East and South Asia.* Lexington, Massachusetts: Heath, 1984.

Ottaway, David B. "For Saudi Military: New Self-Confidence," *Washington Post,* April 20, 1991, A12-A14.

Peterson, Erik R. *The Gulf Cooperation Council: Search for Unity in a Dynamic Region.* Boulder, Colorado: Westview Press, 1988.

Peterson, J.E. *Defending Arabia.* New York: St. Martin's Press, 1986.

Quandt, William B. *Saudi Arabia in the 1980s: Foreign Policy, Security, and Oil.* Washington: Brookings Institution, 1981.

Ramazani, R.K. *The Gulf Cooperation Council: Record and Analysis.* Charlottesville: University Press of Virginia, 1988.

Safran, Nadav. *Saudi Arabia: The Ceaseless Quest for Security.* Ithaca: Cornell University Press, 1988.

*Saudi Arabia and the United States: The New Context in an Evolving "Special Relationship."* (Library of Congress, Congressional Research Service.) Washington: GPO, 1981.

Saudi Arabia. Ministry of Finance and National Economy. Central Department of Statistics. *Statistical Yearbook, 1408* [1988]. Riyadh: 1989.

Shaw, John A., and David E. Long. *Saudi Arabian Modernization: The Impact of Change on Stability.* (Washington Papers, No. 89.) Washington: Praeger, with the Center for Strategic and International Studies, Georgetown University, 1982.

Sinai, Joshua. "Arms Sales to the Middle East: Security or 'Pattern of Destructive Competition'?" *Armed Forces Journal International,* 129, No. 1, August 1991, 40–44.

United States. Arms Control and Disarmament Agency. *World Military Expenditures and Arms Transfers, 1989.* Washington: GPO, 1990.

———. Arms Control and Disarmament Agency. *World Military Expenditures and Arms Transfers, 1990.* Washington: GPO, 1991.

———. Department of State. *Background Notes: Saudi Arabia.* Washington: GPO, 1989.

———. Department of State. *Country Reports on Human Rights Practices for 1988.* (Report submitted to United States Congress, 101st, 1st Session, Senate, Committee on Foreign Relations, and House of Representatives, Committee on Foreign Affairs.) Washington: GPO, 1989.

———. Department of State. *Country Reports on Human Rights Practices for 1989.* (Report submitted to United States Congress, 101st, 2d Session, Senate, Committee on Foreign Relations, and House of Representatives, Committee on Foreign Affairs.) Washington: GPO, 1990.

———. Department of State. *Country Reports on Human Rights Practices for 1990.* (Report submitted to United States Congress, 102d, 1st Session, Senate, Committee on Foreign Relations, and House of Representatives, Committee on Foreign Affairs.) Washington: GPO, 1991.

———. Department of State. *Patterns of Global Terrorism: 1990.* Washington: 1991.

———. Department of State and Defense Security Assistance Agency. *Congressional Presentation for Security Assistance: Fiscal Year 1992.* Washington: 1991.

(Various issues of the following publications were also used in the preparation of this chapter: *Aviation Week and Space Technology; Economist* [London]; Economist Intelligence Unit, *Country Report:*

Saudi Arabia [London]; *Facts on File;* Foreign Broadcast Information tion Service, *Daily Report: Middle East and North Africa; Jane's Defence Weekly* [London]; Joint Publications Research Service, *Near East/South Asia Report; Keesing's Record of World Events* [London]; *Middle East International* [London]; *New York Times;* and *Washington Post.*)

# Glossary

Al—Uppercase connotes family or belonging to, as in Al Saud (*q.v.*), or Al Sudairi; lowercase represents the definite article *the,* as in Rub al Khali.

Al Saud—Literally, the House of Saud; the patrilineal descendants of Muhammad ibn Saud.

amir—Strictly speaking, commander. In Saudi Arabia, amir often means prince, but can mean governor of a province.

barrels per day (bpd)—Production of crude oil and petroleum products is frequently measured in barrels per day and often abbreviated as bpd. A barrel is a volume measure of forty-two United States gallons. Conversion of barrels to tons depends on the density of the specific product. About 17.3 barrels of average crude oil weigh one ton. Light products such as gasoline and kerosene would average close to eighteen barrels per ton.

Divided Zone—Originally a shared area between Saudi Arabia and Kuwait. Each country annexed its half of the zone in 1966 but continued to respect the other country's right to the national resources in the whole zone.

downstream—The oil industry views the production, processing, transportation, and sale of petroleum products as a flow process starting at the wellhead. Downstream includes any stage between the point of reference and the sale of products to the consumer. Upstream is the converse. Upstream of the wellhead includes exploration and drilling of wells.

*fatwa*—An authoritative legal interpretation by a mufti or religious jurist that can provide the basis for court decision or government action.

fiscal year (FY)—Initially based on Islamic lunar year (see Preface). Since December 1986 based on Gregorian calendar. Fiscal year begins December 31 and runs through following December 30.

GDP (gross domestic product)—A value measure of the flow of domestic goods and services produced by an economy over a period of time, such as a year. Only output values of goods for final consumption and investment are included because the values of primary and intermediate production are assumed to be included in final prices. GDP is sometimes aggregated and shown at market prices, meaning that indirect taxes and subsidies are included; when these have been eliminated, the result is GDP at factor cost. The word *gross* indicates that deductions for depreciation of physical assets have not been made. *See also* GNP.

GNP (gross national product)—The gross domestic product (*q.v.*) plus the net income or loss stemming from transactions with foreign countries. For Saudi Arabia, GNP in the 1970s and early 1980s was significantly larger than GDP because of surplus oil revenues. GNP is the broadest measurement of the output of goods and services by an economy. It can be calculated at market prices, which include indirect taxes and subsidies. Because indirect taxes and subsidies are only transfer payments, GNP is often calculated at factor cost by removing indirect taxes and subsidies.

hadith—Tradition based on the precedent of the Prophet Muhammad's words and deeds that serves as one of the sources of Islamic law.

*hijra*—Literally, to migrate, to sever relations, to leave one's tribe. Throughout the Muslim world, *hijra* refers to the migration to Medina of Muhammad and his early followers. In this sense, the word has come into European languages as hegira.

*hujar* (collective pl.)—Refers to the agricultural settlements of the Ikhwan (*q.v.*), which combined features of religious missions, farming communities, and army camps. Word from same root as *hijra;* has sense of separation from previous affiliation.

Ikhwan—The brotherhood of desert warriors, founded by Abd al Aziz, who were settled in the *hujar* (*q.v.*).

imam—A word used in several senses. In general use, it means the leader of congregational prayers; as such it implies no ordination or special spiritual powers beyond sufficient education to carry out this function. It is also used figuratively by many Sunni (*q.v.*) Muslims to mean the leader of the Islamic community. Among Shia (*q.v.*) the word takes on many complex meanings; in general, however, and particularly when capitalized, it indicates that particular descendant of the House of Ali who is believed to have been God's designated repository of the spiritual authority inherent in that line. The identity of this individual and the means of ascertaining his identity have been major issues causing divisions among Shia.

International Monetary Fund (IMF)—Established along with the World Bank (*q.v.*) in 1945, the IMF is a specialized agency affiliated with the United Nations and is responsible for stabilizing international exchange rates and payments. The main business of the IMF is the provision of loans to its members (including industrialized and developing countries) when they experience balance of payments difficulties. These loans frequently carry conditions that require substantial internal economic adjustments by the recipients, most of which are developing countries.

majlis—Tribal council; in some countries, the legislative assembly. Also the audience of the king, amir (*q.v.*), or shaykh (*q.v.*) open to all citizens.

*mutawwiin*—Literally, those who volunteer or obey; sometimes known by popular name of Committees for Public Morality, or more formally, as the Committees for the Propagation of Virtue and Prevention of Vice.

riyal (SR)—Saudi Arabia's currency unit. Riyal is pegged to the International Monetary Fund (*q.v.*) special drawing right (SDR—a unit consisting of a basket of international currencies) as SR4.28 = SDR1. In May 1993 the exchange rate was SR3.75 = US$1, a rate that had not changed since June 1, 1986.

sharia—Islamic law.

sharif (Arabic pl., *ashraf*)—Specifically, one who has descent from Muhammad through his daughter Fatima. Literally, noble, exalted, having descent from illustrious ancestors. Frequently used as an honorific.

shaykh—Leader or chief. Applied either to political leaders of tribes or towns or learned religious leaders. Also used as an honorific.

Shia (from Shiat Ali, the Party of Ali)—A member of the smaller of the two great divisions of Islam. The Shia supported the claims of Ali and his line to presumptive right to the caliphate and leadership of the Muslim community, and on this issue they divided from the Sunni (*q.v.*) in the major schism within Islam. Later schisms have produced further divisions among the Shia over the identity and number of imams (*q.v.*). Most Shia revere Twelve Imams, the last of whom is believed to be hidden from view.

spot oil—Oil sold on the open market without any precontractual arrangement.

Sunni—The larger of the two great divisions of Islam. The Sunni, who rejected the claims of Ali's line, believe that they are the true followers of the sunna, the guide to proper behavior set forth by Muhammad's personal deeds and utterances.

Wahhabi—Name used outside Saudi Arabia to designate adherents to Wahhabism (*q.v.*).

Wahhabism—Name used outside Saudi Arabia to designate official interpretation of Islam in Saudi Arabia. The faith is a puritanical concept of unitarianism (the call to the oneness or unity of God—*ad dawa lil tawhid*) that was preached by Muhammad ibn Abd al Wahhab, whence his Muslim opponents derived the name.

waqf—In Muslim law, a permanent endowment or trust, usually of real estate, in which the proceeds are spent for purposes designated by the benefactor. Usually devoted to charitable purposes.

World Bank—Informal name used to designate a group of four affiliated international institutions: the International Bank for Reconstruction and Development (IBRD), the International Development Association (IDA), the International Finance Corporation (IFC), and the Multilateral Investment Guarantee Agency (MIGA). The IBRD, established in 1945, has the primary purpose of providing loans to developing countries for productive projects. The IDA, a legally separate loan fund but administered by the staff of the IBRD, was set up in 1960 to furnish credits to the poorest developing countries on much easier terms than those of conventional IBRD loans. The IFC, founded in 1956, supplements the activities of the IBRD through loans and assistance specifically designed to encourage the growth of productive private enterprises in the less developed countries. The MIGA, founded in 1988, insures private foreign investment in developing countries against various noncommercial risks. The president and certain senior officers of the IBRD hold the same positions in the IFC. The four institutions are owned by the governments of the countries that subscribe their capital. To participate in the World Bank group, member states must first belong to the International Monetary Fund (IMF—*q.v.*).

# Index

Abbasids, 10

Abd al Aziz ibn Abd ar Rahman Al Saud, 3, 195; battles of, 234; British support for 21, 28; client-patron relations under, 70; death of, 28; descendants of, 191, 231; exiled to Kuwait, 20; expansion under, xxi, 15, 50, 84, 191, 234; goals of, 23; grandsons of, 107; Ikhwan under, 23–24, 25, 84, 118; as Khadim al Haramayn, 24; League of Arab States formed by, 237; meeting of, with Roosevelt, 222; modernization under, 26, 47–48; official recognition of, 21; oil concessions under, 134; oil revenues under, 113–14; problems of, 25; religion under, 87–88; rise of, 20–24; rule of (1926–53), 24–28; settlement of beduin by, 118; succession to, 28; support of Muslim community for, 25, 26; Wahhabism as cohesive device under, 83–84

Abd al Aziz Military Academy, 264

Abd Allah ibn Abd al Aziz Al Saud, 24, 214; as commander of national guard, xxv, 38, 209, 231, 251, 262, 278; as crown prince, 43, 196, 207, 231; diplomatic missions of, 42; as second deputy prime minister, xxii, 38

Abd Allah ibn Faisal, 19, 20

Abd Allah ibn Rashid, 17

Abd Allah ibn Saud ibn Abd al Aziz, 16; executed, 16

Abd Allah ibn Thunayyan, 20

Abd al Wahhab, Muhammad ibn, 21; alliance of, with Muhammad ibn Saud, xxi, 15, 80, 195; attack by, on Shia, 14, 80; background of, 14; condemnation of polytheism by, 81–82; death of, 16; ideas of, 14, 81, 234; search by, for political support, 14–15; significance of theology of, 14

Abd ar Rahman Al Saud, 20

Abqaiq oil field, 148; gas-oil separation plant in, 154; oil production in, 149

Abu Ali Island, 59

Abu Bakr: as caliph, 9, 12, 75; death of, 9

Abu Dhabi: border with, 38, 51

Abu Hadriyah oil field, 148; production, 149

Abu Hanifa, 79

Abu Safah oil field, 148

Abu Talib: death of, 8; protection of Muhammad by, 7–8

Ad Dahna, 52

Ad Dahna desert, 56

Ad Dammam: airport, 168; national guard in, 262; naval base, 260; port of, 167

*ad dawa lil tawhid. See* Islam, Wahhabi

Ad Dibdibah plain, 56

Ad Diriyah, 15; captured by Tursun, 16, 17, 81; as center for religious studies, 81; origins of Al Saud in, 13; recaptured by Turki, 17

Aden, 221

Administration of Scientific Research and Fatwa, xxvi

Administration of Scientific Study, Legal Opinions, Islamic Propagation, and Guidance, 209

adoption, 69

adultery, 285

Afghanistan: military aid to, xxvii, 192, 228; Soviet invasion of, 42, 225, 241–42

Africa: economic assistance to, xxvii, 192; sharia in, 79

Africans: in Eastern Province, 62; in Hijaz, 62; as slaves, 63

agricultural development: under Khalid, 39; in pre-Islamic period, 5

agricultural settlements (*see also hujar*), 21

agriculture, 171–77; constraints on, 171; environmental impact of, 171; expansion of, 129; export crops, 171; government modernization of, 174; growth rate, 130, 131–32, 133, 176, 177; inefficiency in, 124; labor force in, 133; modern, 174–77; oasis, 52, 117; private investment in, 132, 176; restructuring of, 171; subsidies for, 122, 124; traditional, 171–72; water consumed by, xxviii, 57, 160, 171, 176

*ahl al hall wa al aqd,* 207–8; function of, 207; number of, 207

*ahl at tawhid. See* Islam, Wahhabi

Ahmad ibn Abd al Aziz Al Saud, 41, 278

air defense force, 250, 258–59; batteries

Islamic Awakening, 89–90
Islamic calendar, 8, 75
Islamic Development Bank, 94
Islamic Front for the Liberation of Bahrain, 218
Islamic fundamentalists. *See* Islamists
Islamic law. *See* sharia
Islamic period, early (622–700), 6–10
Islamic summit conference: of 1965, 32; of 1969, 36; of 1981, 43
Islamic University of Medina, 96, 102, 104
Islamic values, 119; and cultural homogeneity, 64–68; and modernization, 47–48
Islamism, xxiv, 86–91; factors contributing to, 90; goals of, 86; popular reaction to, 90–91; of Qadhafi, 42; rise of, 86
Islamists: government suppression of, 89–90; Grand Mosque seized by, 39–40, 86; influence of, on military, 248; pressure by, on government, 250; punishment of, 40; as security threat, 244, 247
Ismailis, 12–13
Israel, 119; Arab conference judgment of, 36; invasion of Egypt by, 29, 237; invasion of Lebanon by, 226; opposition to, 223; proposed Arab recognition of, 43; as security threat, 243
Italy, 228

Jabal an Nur, 92
Jabal Shammar, 17, 20
Jabal Tuwayq, 51, 53, 56; water resources in, 57
Jamjum family, 210
Japan: imports from, 183, 228; oil exports to, 164–65
Jerusalem, 36
Jews: under Islamic rule, 9, 76, 77; in Medina, 76; as monarchs, 6; Muhammad's contact with, 8; in pre-Islamic Arabia, 6; role of, 6
Jiddah, 236; airport, 123, 168; foreign population in, 62; merchants in, 117; national guard in, 262; oil refinery, 154 port of, 167
jihad: by Al Saud, 18, 81; as Muslim duty, 79
Jizan, 203; climate in, 57; port of, 167

Joint Forces Commands, 240
joint ventures, xxviii, 125, 142, 155, 165, 277
Jordan, 226; assistance to, 222; border with, 4, 50; financial support for, 37; guestworkers from, xxvi, 60; military personnel from, 267; Palestine Liberation Organization recognized by, 37; relations of, with Israel, 36; relations of, with Syria, 42; relations with, xxvi, 29, 221–22; support by, for Iraq in Persian Gulf War, 192, 222
journalists, 212
judiciary, 31
judges, 64
Juffali family, 210
Juhaiman al Utaiba, 39, 86
June 1967 War, 36, 223, 225, 238

Kaaba, 40, 75; attack on, 13; pilgrimage to, 92–93
Kaki family, 210
Kamil family, 210
Karbala: sacked, 15
*kauf,* 58
Kennedy, John F., 31, 223
Khadim al Haramayn, xxi, 24, 94, 216
*khadira,* 63
Khalid Division, 240
Khalid ibn Abd al Aziz Al Saud, 205; agricultural development under, 39; as crown prince, xxii, 32, 196, 206; death of, xxiii, 43, 206; as deputy prime minister, 31; as king, 37–43, 196; leadership style, 37–38; preparation of, 37; succession of, xxii, 37; visit of, to United States, 222
Khalid ibn Saud Al Saud, 19
Khalid ibn Sultan Al Saud: as commander of air defense forces, 258–59; as commander of armed forces in Persian Gulf War, 205, 239
Khalid tribe, 209
Khalifa, Ali, 146
Khamis Mushayt Military City, 255; air base at, 256
Kharijite movement, 10–12; ideals of, 11
Khartoum Conference (1967), 36
Khashoggi family, 210
Khaybar: lava bed, 52; siege of, 9
Khomeini, Sayyid Ruhollah Musavi (ayatollah), 40, 41; export of revolutionary ideology of, 85–86, 238, 249

Khurays oil field: gas-oil separation plant in, 153
*khuwa,* 70
King Abd al Aziz International Airport, 168
King Abd al Aziz University: expansion of, 102; funding for, 32
Kingdom of Saudi Arabia: legitimacy of, 84; meaning of name of, xxi, 3–4; proclaimed, xxii, 3, 113, 191, 195, 234; stages of establishment of, 21
King Fahd International Airport, 168
King Fahd Medical City, 104
King Fahd University. *See* University of Petroleum and Minerals
King Faisal Air Academy, 264
King Faisal University, 101
King Khalid Eye Specialist Hospital, 105
King Khalid International Airport, 168, 277
King Khalid Military City, 255; population of, 255; resources of, 255
King Khalid Military College, 262
King Saud University (*see also* Riyadh University): colleges in, 101, 105
Korea, Republic of (South Korea): guestworkers from, 228; oil refining assets in, 115, 155
*kuttab,* 96
Kuwait, 36; Al Saud exiled to, 3, 20; border with, 50; guestworkers from, 60; in Gulf Cooperation Council, 42, 217, 244; Iraqi invasion of, xxvi, 116, 126, 144, 146, 193, 214, 220, 239; Iraqi threat to invade, 145–46, 239; military assistance from, 244; oil production levels, 145; ownership of, in Arabian Oil Company, 140–41; protection of, 244, 247; relations with, 213
Kuwait, city of: liberation of, 240

labor, 133–34; disturbances, 85; organization of, 74
labor force: changes in, 133; domestic, 133; foreign, 48, 60–61, 100, 122, 133; growth of, 133; in oil industry, 134; percentage of women in, 61, 108
Lakhmids, 77
land: arable, 49; area, 49; distribution, 118, 174
lava beds (*harrat*), 52
law enforcement, 279–82

League of Arab States (Arab League), 226; established, 237; peacekeeping force in Lebanon, 38
Lebanese National Assembly, xxiii, 43
Lebanon: civil war in, xxiii, 38, 42, 43; Israeli invasion of, 226
legal system, 201–3
Lend-Lease program, 237
Libya, 36, 42, 226; and Arab unity, 224; rejection by, of Fahd Plan, 43
literacy rate, 96
literature: conservative revival in, 87
livestock, 177
living standards: increase in, 114, 186; maintenance of, 117; plans to improve Shia, 41
loans: to farmers, 176
LPG. *See* gas, liquid petroleum
Luberef. *See* Petromin Lubricating Oil Refining Company

Madain Salin, 6
Madinat al Jubayl as Sinaiyah: effect of Persian Gulf War on, 59
Madinat an Nabi. *See* Medina
Maeena, Khaled al, 212
magazines, 212
Mahd adh Dhahab gold mine, 162
main code, xxiv, 194
majlis (court): purpose of, 198–99
*majlis ash shura. See* Consultative Council
Makkah Province, 203
Malik ibn Anas, 10, 79
Manifah oil field, 148; production, 149
manufacturing, 162–66; government involvement in, 162–64; growth rate, 130, 131, 133; private investment in, 132, 158, 162, 166; shift to, 162
Marine Training Institute, 265
maritime claims, 51
marriage: age at, 108; arranged, 66; and genealogy, 69; housing arrangements in, 66; interethnic, 63; polygynous, 66; political alliance by, 71; women in, 65–66
matériel: acquisition of, xxvii, 184; air force, 274–75; army, 254, 256; attempts to purchase from United States, 224; from Britain, xxvii, 234, 254, 272, 275, 276; from China, 276; domestic, 277–78; foreign, 273; from France, 233, 234, 254, 272, 275, 276; from

Palestine: Arabs in, 4; demands for liberation of, 29; guestworkers from, expelled, xxvi, 127; military personnel from, 267

Palestine Liberation Organization (PLO), 222, 247; acceptance by, of Fahd Plan, 43; and Arab unity, 224; financial support for, 227; recognized by Jordan, 37; support for Iraq in Persian Gulf War, 227

Palestinian problem, 39, 42, 243

Palestinians, 39, 226–27; Arab support for, 36; desire for state for, 43; expelled, 248; rejection by, of Fahd Plan, 43

Palmyra, Syria, 5

Party of God in the Hijaz, 247, 249

PDRY. *See* Yemen, People's Democratic Republic of

Peace Shield air defense network, 233, 258, 259, 277

Peninsula Shield, 244

Peninsula Shield Force, 244

Pension Fund, 182

Persian Gulf, 10; effect of, on temperature, 57; rights in, 33

Persian Gulf states: Khalid's visits to, 38

Persian Gulf War (1991), 193, 214, 239–40; air force in, 232, 239–40; allied forces in, 239; conservatism inspired by, 87; countries supporting Iraq in, 61, 192, 221, 227; damage to oil industry, 140, 152; defeat of Iraq in, 242; effect of, on economy, 116–17, 185; effect of, on environment, xxviii, 58–59; effect of, on foreign policy, xxvi, 217, 226; expense of, 272; impact of, xxviii–xxix, 49, 250; logistics of, 239–40, 255; national guard in, 251, 260, 263; oil as reason for, 114; oil consumption during, 162; Saudi armed forces in, 205, 233–34; as stimulus to economy, 127; trade during, 142

Persians, 6; expelled, 9

Petra, Jordan, 5

petrochemical industry, 164

Petroline pipeline, 156

Petrolube. *See* Petromin Lubricating Oil Company

Petromin. *See* General Petroleum and Mineral Organization

Petromin Lubricating Oil Company (Petrolube), 142

Petromin Lubricating Oil Refining Company (Luberef), 142

Pharaon family, 210

Philippines: guestworkers from, 60, 228

physicians, 104–5

PIF. *See* Public Investment Fund

pilgrimage, 10, 40, 91–94; accommodations for, 91; addressed by king, 94; duty of, 78, 79; government support for, 94; guild of special assistants for, 92; income from, 28; Iranians barred from, 250; performance of, 13; political demonstrations during, 216, 249; pre-Islamic, 6, 75; rituals of, 92–93; significance of, 93–94; special visas for, 92; suspended, 13; transportation for, 91

pilgrims: deaths of, 94, 250; demonstrations by, 94; experiences of, 91; number of, 91–92; ritual purification of, 92

Place of Abraham, 93

Plain of Arafat, 93

PLO. *See* Palestine Liberation Organization

Point Four economic aid mission: terminated, 29

political activity: in the Middle Ages, 10

political associations: prohibited, 247

political dissidence, xxix, 48–49; repression of, xxv

political dynamics, 204–11

political ideology: religious purpose in, 15, 80–81

political protest, 247; conservative revival in, 87; during pilgrimage, 216; by Shia, 122, 216; by women, 88

political representation: demands for, 49

population (*see also* census), 59–74, 266; death rate, 106; distribution of, 49, 62–64; diversity of, 62; estimates of, 59, 60; growth rate, 60; indigenous, 60; infant mortality rate, 106; official, 59–60; percentage of, in urban areas, 107; projected, 60; rural, 48; Shia community as percentage of, xxiii, 84, 85

ports, 157; construction of, 121, 122, 129

prayer, 78

pre-Islamic period, 5–6; religion in, 6

Press Law of 1964, 212

prisoners: political, 64, 86

prison system: conditions in, 285–86; torture in, 286

private sector: foreign assets of, 185; investment by, 158, 166; role in industrialization, 166

# Contributors

**Eleanor Abdella Doumato** is Lecturer in History at the University of Rhode Island and the author of numerous articles on the Middle East.

**Eric Hooglund** currently serves as Editor of the *Middle East Journal;* he has taught courses on the Middle East at several universities.

**Helen Chapin Metz** is Supervisor, Middle East/Africa/Latin America Unit, Federal Research Division, Library of Congress.

**Fareed Mohamedi** is Senior Economist, Petroleum Finance Company, and author of articles on the Middle East and international oil affairs.

**William Smyth** is an independent author who writes on the Middle East; he served as Visiting Assistant Professor at Emory University from 1989 through 1991.

**Jean R. Tartter** is a retired Foreign Service Officer, who has written extensively on the Middle East and Africa for Country Study volumes.

# Published Country Studies

## (Area Handbook Series)

| | | | | |
|---|---|---|---|---|
| 550-65 | Afghanistan | 550-87 | Greece |
| 550-98 | Albania | 550-78 | Guatemala |
| 550-44 | Algeria | 550-174 | Guinea |
| 550-59 | Angola | 550-82 | Guyana and Belize |
| 550-73 | Argentina | 550-151 | Honduras |
| | | | |
| 550-169 | Australia | 550-165 | Hungary |
| 550-176 | Austria | 550-21 | India |
| 550-175 | Bangladesh | 550-154 | Indian Ocean |
| 550-170 | Belgium | 550-39 | Indonesia |
| 550-66 | Bolivia | 550-68 | Iran |
| | | | |
| 550-20 | Brazil | 550-31 | Iraq |
| 550-168 | Bulgaria | 550-25 | Israel |
| 550-61 | Burma | 550-182 | Italy |
| 550-50 | Cambodia | 550-30 | Japan |
| 550-166 | Cameroon | 550-34 | Jordan |
| | | | |
| 550-159 | Chad | 550-56 | Kenya |
| 550-77 | Chile | 550-81 | Korea, North |
| 550-60 | China | 550-41 | Korea, South |
| 550-26 | Colombia | 550-58 | Laos |
| 550-33 | Commonwealth Caribbean, Islands of the | 550-24 | Lebanon |
| | | | |
| 550-91 | Congo | 550-38 | Liberia |
| 550-90 | Costa Rica | 550-85 | Libya |
| 550-69 | Côte d'Ivoire (Ivory Coast) | 550-172 | Malawi |
| 550-152 | Cuba | 550-45 | Malaysia |
| 550-22 | Cyprus | 550-161 | Mauritania |
| | | | |
| 550-158 | Czechoslovakia | 550-79 | Mexico |
| 550-36 | Dominican Republic and Haiti | 550-76 | Mongolia |
| 550-52 | Ecuador | 550-49 | Morocco |
| 550-43 | Egypt | 550-64 | Mozambique |
| 550-150 | El Salvador | 550-35 | Nepal and Bhutan |
| | | | |
| 550-28 | Ethiopia | 550-88 | Nicaragua |
| 550-167 | Finland | 550-157 | Nigeria |
| 550-155 | Germany, East | 550-94 | Oceania |
| 550-173 | Germany, Fed. Rep. of | 550-48 | Pakistan |
| 550-153 | Ghana | 550-46 | Panama |